Context

Nord

Context · Ausgabe Nord

Im Auftrag des Verlages herausgegeben von
Dr. Annette Leithner-Brauns, Dresden; Ingrid Becker-Ross, Krefeld; Prof. Hellmut Schwarz, Mannheim

Erarbeitet von
Irene Bartscherer, Bonn; Ingrid Becker-Ross, Krefeld; Friederike von Bremen, Hannover; Ulrike Elsäßer, Stuttgart; Gerit Fredrich, Grabfeld; Prof. Dr. Britta Freitag-Hild, Potsdam; Veronika Gastpar, Schweitenkirchen; Dr. Peter Hohwiller, Landau; Markus Hözel, Köln; Ulrich Imig, Wildeshausen; Elke Jentsch, Lengenfeld; Sylvia Loh, Ebersbach an der Fils; Dr. Paul Maloney, Hildesheim; Markus Marzinzik, Landau; Claudia Meixner, Kunreuth; Neil Porter, Tel Aviv; Birgit Rietgraf, Backnang; Angela Ringel-Eichinger, Bietigheim-Bissingen; Victoria Schoeneberg, Köln; Dr. Andreas Sedlatschek, Esslingen; Claudia Spieler, Gießen; Marcel Sprunkel, Köln; Michael Thürwächter, Heidelberg; Inga Wittbrodt, Sankt Augustin

unter beratender Mitwirkung von
Martina Baasner, Berlin; Dr. Sabine Buchholz, Hürth; Bernd Koch, Marburg; Jochen Lüders, München; Gunthild Porteous-Schwier, Moers; Sieglinde Spranger, Röhrsdorf

in Zusammenarbeit mit der Englischredaktion
Elke Lehmann *(Projektleitung)*; Dr. Marion Kiffe, Laura Morgenthal, Dr. Georg-Christian v. Raumer, Ingrid-Maria Sauer, Anna Schwarz, Hartmut Tschepe, Ralph Williams sowie Katrin Gütermann, Berlin, und Neil Porter, Tel Aviv

Layoutkonzept
zweiband.media, Berlin

Layout und technische Umsetzung
designcollective, Berlin

Umschlaggestaltung
axeptDESIGN, Berlin; Michaela Müller für agentur corngreen, Leipzig

---

Weitere Bestandteile des Lehrwerks
- E-Book zum Schülerbuch
- Workbook (978-3-06-031640-3)
- VOCABI (978-3-06-033490-2)
- Vokabeltrainer-App
- Audio-CDs (+ MP3) (978-3-06-033487-2)
- Video-DVD (978-3-06-033488-9)
- Lehrerfassung des Schülerbuchs (978-3-06-031481-2)
- Handreichungen für den Unterricht (978-3-06-031501-7)
- Digitaler Unterrichtsmanager
- Vorschläge zur Leistungsmessung (978-3-06-033590-9)
- More Speaking Practice (Rollen- und Bildkarten) (978-3-06-031504-8)

Website zum Lehrwerk: www.cornelsen.de/context

Die Links zu externen Webseiten Dritter, die in diesem Lehrwerk angegeben sind, wurden vor Drucklegung sorgfältig auf ihre Aktualität geprüft. Der Verlag übernimmt keine Gewähr für die Aktualität und den Inhalt dieser Seiten oder solcher, die mit ihnen verlinkt sind.

1. Auflage, 1. Druck 2015

Alle Drucke dieser Auflage sind inhaltlich unverändert und können im Unterricht nebeneinander verwendet werden.

© 2015 Cornelsen Schulverlage GmbH, Berlin

Das Werk und seine Teile sind urheberrechtlich geschützt. Jede Nutzung in anderen als den gesetzlich zugelassenen Fällen bedarf der vorherigen schriftlichen Einwilligung des Verlages.
Hinweis zu den §§ 46, 52a UrhG: Weder das Werk noch seine Teile dürfen ohne eine solche Einwilligung eingescannt und in ein Netzwerk eingestellt oder sonst öffentlich zugänglich gemacht werden.
Dies gilt auch für Intranets von Schulen und sonstigen Bildungseinrichtungen.

Druck: Mohn Media Mohndruck, Gütersloh

ISBN 978-3-06-031478-2 – broschiert
ISBN 978-3-06-031480-5 – gebunden

PEFC zertifiziert
Dieses Produkt stammt aus nachhaltig bewirtschafteten Wäldern und kontrollierten Quellen.
www.pefc.de

Contents

Page	Part of chapter	Title/Subject/Focus	Text type/Media	
Chapter 1		**Modern Media – Tools or Tyrants?**		
10	Lead-in			
12	Words in Context	Living interactive lives	Informative text	🎧
	Part A	Dis-connected		
14	A1	Lonely friends *Ms Moem*	Online poem	🎧
15	Culture Spot	New media art: Viewpoint of Billions with Google Glass (2013) *David Datuna*	Photo, film clip	▶️
16	A2	Online learning in 2044 *Ernest Cline*	Novel extract	
18	Focus on Skills	WRITING Writing an argumentative text		
20	A3	MEDIATION Digital media at school *Gerhard Witossek*	German online article	
	Part B	Being on display		
22	B1	Should classrooms have video cameras?	Online contributions to a debate	
23	Fact File	CCTV (Closed-Circuit Television)	Informative text	
24	B2	9/11 – a game changer *Barack Obama*	Speech	🎧
	Part C	Reality TV		
26	C1	Big Brother out of this world *Ellie Zolfagharifard*	Newspaper article	
27	C2	The ultimate reality TV show *DBC Pierre*	Novel extract	
29	Chapter Task	Discussing the pros an cons of modern media		

Page	Part of chapter	Title/Subject/Focus	Text type/Media	
Chapter 2		**Science – Enhancing Life?**		
30	Lead-in			
32	Words in Context	Science – motor of progress?	Informative text	🎧
	Part A	The genetic engineering debate		
34	A1	A saviour sibling *Laura Roberts*	Newspaper article	
36	Fact File	Ethics in science	Informative text	
36	A2	You are mine to kill *Nick Dear*	Drama extract	
38	A3	At the lab	Cartoon	
39	Culture Spot	The Long Awaited (2008) *Patricia Piccinini*	Sculpture	
40	A4	Animals with bonus features *Bob Holmes*	Magazine article	
41	Focus on Skills	READING Using reading strategies (scientific text)		
	Part B	Modifying mankind		
42	B1	A brain-enchancing pill	TV news report	▶️
43	B2	Gene doping *Tim Franks*	Online article	
45	B3	Transhumanism *Zoltan Istvan*	Online article	
	Part C	Quenching the thirst for energy		
47	C1	The global demand for energy	Graphs	
48	C2	MEDIATION The future of energy in Germany	Informative text	
49	Focus on Skills	MEDIATION Mediating written texts		
50	C3	A possible future	Interview	🎧
50	C4	Biofuels – the green alternative?	Film clips	▶️
51	Chapter Task	Doing a WebQuest		

3

Contents

Page	Part of chapter	Title/Subject/Focus	Text type/Media	
Chapter 3		**Living One's Life – Individuals in Society**		
52	**Lead-in**			
54	**Words in Context**	Young people in a multi-faceted society	Informative text	🎧
	Part A	**Future success**		
56	A1	What is a role model? *Marilyn Price-Mitchell*	Online article	
57	A2	Successful children *Amy Chua*	Non-fictional text	
60	A3	Childhood – the 21st century *Ernestine Northover*	Poem	
	Part B	**Them and us**		
61	B1	Stereotypes in Los Angeles *Paul Haggis*	Screenplay	
62	**Fact File**	Stereotypes	Informative text	
64	**Focus on Skills**	SPEAKING Resolving a heated argument		
65	**Culture Spot**	Graffiti	Photos	
	Part C	**Getting involved**		
66	C1	Volunteering in the wake of the Olympics	Film clip	🎬
66	C2	Volunteering in Germany *Sophia Seiderer*	German online article	
68	C3	The Hunger Games: an individual in a utopian society	Film trailer	🎬
69	**Fact File**	From Utopia to Dystopia	Informative text	
70	C4	Young people raising their voices	Photos, quotes	
71	**Chapter Task**	Getting your message across		

Page	Part of chapter	Title/Subject/Focus	Text type/Media	
Chapter 4		**The Power of Words – from Shakespeare to Today**		
72	**Lead-in**			
74	**Words in Context**	The power of the spoken word	Informative text	🎧
	Part A	**Shakespeare's power of language**		
76	**Fact File**	William Shakespeare	Informative text	
76	A1	Lady Macbeth persuades her husband (Macbeth *William Shakespeare*)	Drama extract	
78	**Focus on Skills**	READING Close reading (drama extract)		
79	A2	Richard courts his enemy (Richard III *William Shakespeare*)	Drama extract	
	Part B	**Shakespeare's words updated**		
82	B1	My future wife (The Taming of the Shrew *William Shakespeare*)	Drama extract	
84	**Focus on Skills**	VIEWING Evaluating a modern Shakespeare adaptation	Film extract	🎬
85	B2	Responding to a sonnet (Sonnet 116 *William Shakespeare*, Marital Sonnet 4 *James Simmons*)	Poems	
86	**Culture Spot**	Shakespeare for the masses	Photo	
	Part C	**The powerful words of today's poets**		
87	**Fact File**	Performance poetry	Informative text	
87	C1	Performance poetry (Dis Poetry *Benjamin Zephaniah*, Famous for what? *Hollie McNish*)	Film clips, poems, audio text	🎬 🎧
89	C2	The psychological power of words (The right word *Imtiaz Dharker*, You should've stopped there *William Marr*)	Poems, audio text	🎧
91	**Chapter Task**	Writing a review		

Contents

Page	Part of chapter	Title/Subject/Focus	Text type/Media	
Chapter 5		**The UK – a Kingdom United?**		
92	Lead-in			
94	Words in Context	Character of a country	Informative text	🎧
	Part A	A crowned nation		
96	A1	Dangerous books *Alan Bennett*	Novel extract	
98	Fact File	Parliamentary system	Informative text	
99	Focus on Skills	LISTENING Listening for gist and detail		🎧
100	A2	Does Britain still need the monarchy?	Podcast	🎧
	Part B	The multicultural face of the UK		
101	Fact File	From Empire to Commonwealth	Informative text	
101	B1	The British Empire report	Documentary	▶️
102	B2	Between two cultures *Mike Bartlett*	Drama extract	
105	B3	The British and their tea	Podcast	🎧
105	Culture spot	The Fourth Plinth	Photograph	
106	B4	Halal food festival	Press release	
107	B5	Eastern Europeans in the UK *Amelia Gentleman*	Newspaper article	
	Part C	Where do we go from here?		
108	C1	A referendum on the EU	Statistics, political speech	🎧
108	C2	MEDIATION Merkel's speech in London	German newspaper article	
110	C3	It's OK to like the Germans *Stewart Wood*	Newspaper article	
111	Chapter Task	A podcast on British culture		🎧

Page	Part of chapter	Title/Subject/Focus	Text type/Media	
Chapter 6		**India – a Kaleidoscope**		
112	Lead-in			
114	Words in Context	India then and now	Informative text	🎧
	Part A	India's past: echoes and reflections		
116	A1	India's UNESCO World Heritage sites	Photos	
117	A2	Colonizers and colonized	Speech	
117	A3	The British Empire from an Indian perspective *Gurcharan Das*	Non-fictional text	
119	A4	Gandhi remembered *Chetan Bhagat*	Newspaper article	
119	Fact File	Gandhi and India's struggle for independence	Informative text	
122	Focus on Skills	LISTENING Listening to a radio interview		🎧
	Part B	Tales from modern India		
123	B1	Urbanization in India: the big picture	Graph	
123	B2	Life in a megacity	Film poster	
124	Focus on Skills	VIEWING Watching a film trailer		▶️
125	B3	Celebrating Indian culture	Film extract, interview	▶️
126	Culture Spot	Indian truck art	Photographs	
	Part C	Indians abroad		
127	C1	The Indian diaspora		
127	C2	A taste of the Indian diaspora *Michelle Warwicker*	Online article	
128	C3	English lessons *Shauna Singh Baldwin*	Short story	
131	Chapter Task	Presenting India		

5

Contents

Page	Part of chapter	Title/Subject/Focus	Text type/Media	
Chapter 7		**The USA – Still the Promised Land?**		
132	**Lead-in**			
134	**Words in Context**	A country like no other	Informative text	🎧
	Part A	**The American dream**		
136	**A1**	Viva America! *Liz Balmaseda*	Online story	
137	**A2**	Reinventing the American dream *June Sochen*	Newspaper article	
140	**Culture Spot**	Flag (1954) *Jasper Johns*	Photo	🎧
	Part B	**Dealing with diversity**		
141	**Fact File**	Ethnic neighbourhoods	Informative text	
141	**B1**	The new neighbours *Bruce Norris*	Drama extract	🎧
144	**B2**	The changing face of America *William J. Clinton*	Speech	
146	**Focus on Skills**	SPEAKING Speaking in front of an audience		
	Part C	**Equality and inequality**		
148	**C1**	The danger to the dream *Barack Obama*	Speech	🎧
149	**C2**	How to become homeless	Film extract	▶️
149	**Fact File**	Home ownership	Informative text	
150	**C3**	A politics lesson *Todd Strasser*	Novel extract	
	Part D	**America's place in the world**		
152	**D1**	Facts and figures	Statistics	
152	**D2**	MEDIATION The German view *Michael Hochgeschwender*	German podcast	🎧
153	**D3**	Better than its reputation *Anne Applebaum*	Magazine article	
155	**Chapter Task**	Giving a speech on why you would like to visit the USA		
Chapter 8		**Beyond the Nation – Europe and a Globalized World**		
156	**Lead-in**			
158	**Words in Context**	Globalization: Europe, the world	Informative text	🎧
	Part A	**European integration as a model?**		
160	**A1**	A great achievement of the past *Herman Van Rompuy*	Speech	🎧
162	**A2**	Young, educated – and leaving the country *Liz Alderman*	Newspaper article	
164	**A3**	MEDIATION Hunting for personnel *Sascha Schmierer*	German newspaper article	
165	**Focus on Skills**	MEDIATION Mediating texts in oral communication		
	Part B	**Chances and risks of globalization**		
166	**B1**	How big is the impact?	Film clip	▶️
167	**B2**	The need for a new Label *Lucy Siegle*	Newspaper article	
168	**B3**	The Dutch footballer from Japan *Elko Born*	Newspaper article	
170	**Focus on Skills**	READING Using reading strategies (newspaper article)		
	Part C	**English as a global language**		
171	**C1**	Keeping the accent *Aoife Mannix*	Poem	
172	**C2**	English as a global language *David Crystal*	Interview	🎧
172	**C3**	Linguistic diplomacy: the Eurovision Song Contest *R. L. G.*	Newspaper article	
174	**Culture Spot**	Keeping our language clean?		🎧
175	**Chapter Task**	'Slavery? Not today, not in Germany!' An exhibition		

Contents

Page	Part of chapter	Title/Subject/Focus	Text type/Media	
Chapter 9		**Work and Business – Careers and Perspectives**		
176	**Lead-in**			
178	**Words in Context**	The world of work and business	Informative text	🎧
	Part A	**The right to a job – the right job**		
180	**A1**	The second Bill of Rights *Franklin D. Roosevelt*	Speech	
181	**A2**	Moving on after recession *Barack Obama*	Speech	
183	**A3**	Income inequality and guaranteed income *Felix Oberholzer-Gee*	Online article	
184	**Fact File**	Minimum wage and unconditional basic income	Informative text	
185	**A4**	Teenagers' career aspirations *Sean Coughlan*	Survey (table), online article	
186	**Focus on Skills**	SPEAKING From informal to formal dialogues		
188	**A5**	MEDIATION Do you love your job? *Uwe Jean Heuser*	German newspaper article	
189	**Culture Spot**	Corporate Head (1991) *Terry Allen, Philip Levine*	Sculpture, poem	
	Part B	**Stepping into the world of work**		
190	**B1**	Mitch's first glimpses of the world of work *Carl Deuker*	Novel extract	
192	**B2**	Ten things not to say in a job interview *Mark King*	Online article	
193	**B3**	The best job in the world is back! *Emanuel Wetterqvist*	Job advertisement	
195	**Focus on Skills**	WRITING Writing a letter of motivation		▶️
196	**B4**	Surviving a telephone interview	Audio text	🎧
196	**B5**	Look them in the eye – the job interview	Film clip	▶️
197	**Chapter Task**	Writing your personal statement		

198	**Context Task**

Support Pages

Page	Chapter	Page	Chapter	Page	Chapter
200	**Chapter 1**	206	**Chapter 4**	212	**Chapter 7**
202	**Chapter 2**	208	**Chapter 5**	214	**Chapter 8**
204	**Chapter 3**	210	**Chapter 6**	216	**Chapter 9**

Reference Section

Language Practice

Page		Focus on Grammar
218		**Focus on Grammar**
218	LP1	Simple and progressive verb forms
219	LP2	present or future tense?
220	LP3	Simple present and present perfect
221	LP4	Present perfect and simple past
222	LP5	Infinitive or gerund after certain verbs
223	LP6	Infinitive or gerund after certain nouns
224	LP7	The passive
225	LP8	Conditional sentences
226	LP9	Articles, quantifiers and countability
227	LP10	Using adjectives and adverbs

Page		Focus on Style	
228		**Focus on Style**	
228	LP11	Using the right register	
228	LP12	Avoiding German-sounding sentence patterns	
229	LP13	Placing emphasis on key points	🎧
231	LP14	Linking words and phrases	
233	LP15	Connecting your thoughts (sentence structure)	
234		**Focus on Vocabulary**	
234	LP16	Avoiding Germanisms	
235	LP17	Spelling	
235	LP18	Writing about texts	
236	LP19	Collocations	
238	LP20	Word formation	

7

Contents

Everyday English

240	EE 1	Eating in and out
240		Fact File: Eating out – American style
241	EE 2	Planning a trip using the internet
242	EE 3	Dealing with medical emergencies
242		Fact File: Getting medical assistance
243	EE 4	Making phone calls
244	EE 5	Watch your valuables!

Communicating across Cultures

245	CC 1	Cultural awareness
246	CC 2	The language of politeness
247	CC 3	Polite behaviour
247	CC 4	Meeting and greeting
248	CC 5	Making small talk
248	CC 6	Talking about sensitive issues
249		Fact File: Political correctness
249	CC 7	Making polite complaints

Skills File

250		**Language and study skills**
250	SF 1	Dealing with unknown words
251	SF 2	Learning new words
252	SF 3	Using a dictionary
253	SF 4	Using a grammar book
253	SF 5	Doing research
254	SF 6	Doing project work
255	SF 7	Making visual aids
256	SF 8	Structuring ideas
256	SF 9	Paraphrasing
257	SF 10	Working with closed test formats
258		**Text skills**
258	SF 11	Analysing pictures
259	SF 12	Analysing charts and graphs
261	SF 13	Analysing cartoons
263	SF 14	Reading strategies
264	SF 15	Marking up a text/Making and taking notes
265	SF 16	Identifying text types (non-fiction)
266	SF 17	Analysing stylistic devices
268	SF 18	Analysing non-fiction
269	SF 19	Analysing narrative prose
271	SF 20	Analysing drama
273	SF 21	Analysing poetry

275		**Listening and viewing skills**
275	SF 22	Listening
276	SF 23	Analysing a film
278		**Speaking skills (monologues and dialogues)**
278	SF 24	Giving a presentation
280	SF 25	Giving a speech
282	SF 26	Taking part in an interview
282	SF 27	Having a discussion
284	SF 28	Having a debate
286		**Writing skills**
286	SF 29	Writing a formal letter or email
287	SF 30	Writing an application
289	SF 31	Writing a summary
290	SF 32	Writing a review
293	SF 33	Writing a report
294	SF 34	Argumentative writing
296	SF 35	Writing a character profile
298	SF 36	Writing a text analysis
299	SF 37	Doing a creative writing task
300	SF 38	Writing a well-structured text
301	SF 39	Quoting a text
303	SF 40	Proofreading
304		**Mediation skills**
304	SF 41	Mediation of written and oral texts

Exam Practice

306	EP 1	How to do exams in general
307	EP 2	Working with texts
315	EP 3	Mediation
316	EP 4	Listening and viewing
318	EP 5	Speaking
322	EP 6	Closed test formats

323	**Glossary**
340	**Verbs for Tasks ('Operatoren')**
342	**Charts**
344	**Historical Documents**
349	Acknowledgments

Abbreviations and labels used in *Context*

adj	adjective	**CC**	Communicating across Cultures
adv	adverb	**EE**	Everyday English
AE/BE	American English / British English	**EP**	Exam Practice
ca. *(Latin)*	circa = about, approximately	**LP**	Language Practice
cf.	confer (compare), see	**SF**	Skills File
derog	derogatory (*abfällig, geringschätzig*)	**PREVIEW**	refers to the advance organizer (chapter preview) in the Lead-in of each chapter.
e.g. *(Latin)*	exempli gratia = for example	**LANGUAGE HELP**	will give you ideas, words and phrases to get started on tasks.
esp.	especially	**TROUBLE SPOT**	will point out language difficulties and common mistakes.
et al. *(Latin)*	et alii = and other people/things		
etc. *(Latin)*	et cetera = and so on	**CHALLENGE ▶**	marks a more difficult text or task.
ff.	and the following pages/lines	**SUPPORT ▶**	refers you to the Support Pages (pp. 200–217) where you can find more help to do the assignment.
fml/infml	formal/informal English		
i.e. *(Latin)*	id est = that is, in other words		
jdm./jdn.	jemandem/jemanden	**YOU CHOOSE ▶**	lets you decide which of the two given assignments you would like to do.
l./ll.	line/lines	**BASIC**	marks a task that tests language skills you should already be familiar with.
n	noun		
pt(s)	point(s)	*metaphor	indicates that a word or expression (here: *metaphor*) is explained in the Glossary (pp. 320–335).
p./pp.	page/pages		
pl	plural	▶ SF 21	directs you to the Skills File (here: Skill 21).
sb./sth.	somebody/something	▶ LP 7	directs you to the Language Practice section (here: Language task 7).
sing	singular		
sl	slang	🎧 CD 04	indicates that the sound file can be found on the accompanying audio CD (here: Track 4).
usu.	usually		
v	verb	DVD 07	indicates that the film or video clip can be found on the accompanying video DVD (here: Track 7).
vs. *(Latin)*	versus (*gegen, im Gegensatz zu*)	Webcode	can be entered at www.cornelsen.de/web-codes to connect you directly to a specific website or download (e.g. a worksheet).

About the photograph on the cover of this book
The cover photo, taken in April 2013 near the junction of St Mary Axe and Leadenhall Street in London, shows a number of well-known buildings in the City of London's 'Tower Cluster' zone:

1 *St Helen's*, 1 Undershaft, Gollins Melvin Ward Partnership 1969, 28 storeys

2 *The Leadenhall Building (the Cheesegrater)*, 122 Leadenhall Street, Rogers Steark Harbour + Partners 2013, 48 storeys

3 *Lloyd's building*, 1 Lime Street, Richard Rogers 1986, 14 storeys

4 *Willis Building*, 51 Lime Street, Foster + Partners 2007, 26 storeys

5 *St Andrew Undershaft*, 1532

6 *30 St Mary Axe (the Gherkin)*, Foster + Partners 2003, 41 storeys

1 Modern Media – Tools or Tyrants?

Download a chronological word list here:

 Webcode context-00

[1] **retard** ['riːtɑːd] (*taboo, *slang) stupid person

▶ SF 13: Analysing cartoons

BEiNG FiVE — A kid who blogs using voice recognition software — by GEORGE SFARNAS ©2014 beingfive.blogspot.com

I'M A DIGITAL NATIVE, WHICH MEANS I WAS BORN IN THE AGE OF TECHNOLOGY...SO IT COMES NATURAL TO ME!

MY PARENTS ARE DIGITAL IMMIGRANTS, WHICH MEANS THEY CAN LEARN TECHNOLOGY, BUT THEY HAVE TO WORK AT IT!

AND MY GRANDPARENTS ARE DIGITAL RETARDS,[1] WHICH MEANS THEY BARELY KNOW HOW TO USE A TOASTER!

1 Talking about a cartoon
   a THINK Make a few notes on the message of the cartoon above.
   b PAIR With a partner, collect examples to illustrate the degree of media literacy that is to be expected of each of the three groups referred to in the cartoon.
   c SHARE Present your findings in class. Focusing on your peer group, agree on the three types of media you use most.

Lead-in

I hate television. I hate it as much as peanuts. But I can't stop eating peanuts.
Orson Welles (1915–1985)

I fear the day technology will surpass[1] our human interaction. The world will have a generation of idiots.
Albert Einstein (1879–1955)

The concept of surveillance[2] is ingrained[3] in our beings. God was the original surveillance camera.
Hasan M. Elahi (born 1972)

We're still in the first minutes of the first day of the internet revolution.
Scott Cook (born 1952)

[1] **surpass sth.** [sə'pɑːs] (fml) be better or greater than sth. else
[2] **surveillance** [sə'veɪləns] the careful watching of a person or place
[3] **ingrained** firmly established and therefore difficult to change

2 MARKETPLACE (MILLING-AROUND ACTIVITY) **The digital age**
 a Walk around your classroom. As soon as your teacher tells you to stop, turn to the student nearest to you and discuss one of the four quotes above. Say how much you agree or disagree with the statements by Welles, Einstein, Elahi or Cook. Justify your opinion (and take notes).
 When your teacher gives a signal, swap partners. Repeat this activity until everyone has discussed all the four quotes.
 b Present and evaluate the results of your discussions in class.

PREVIEW

This chapter invites you to explore the impact of modern media on our lives now and in the future.
Main topics
- Pleasures and problems of interactive internet use .... p. 14
- Surveillance media – pros and cons .... p. 22
- Reality TV – where will it stop? .... p. 26

Focus on Skills: WRITING
- Writing an argumentative text .... p. 18

Chapter Task:
Discussing the impact of the media on our future lives .... p. 29

Modern Media – Tools or Tyrants? Chapter 1

11

1 Words in Context

CD1 02
Listen to an audio version of the text on the CD or download it here:
Webcode context-00
01

Living interactive lives

Connected

In recent years a great many social networks have been developed to cater for people of different age groups and interests. Not only do they offer an easy way of staying in touch with friends and acquaintances, they also provide a platform to 'meet' like-minded people, exchange ideas and material, seek advice and collaborate on a private and professional level. However, people's 'likes' and 'dislikes' are carefully stored, along with a great number of other details gathered about the users, to be exploited by businesses or political organizations. This pool of information allows for personalized ads as well as effective campaigning, but with it comes the danger of subtle manipulation. Despite warnings as to the potential abuse of data inadvertently revealed, social networks continue to grow in popularity, especially among younger people, who have embraced a virtual lifestyle from an early age on and are therefore used to sharing their everyday lives with an online community.

Digital media has also had a major impact on the educational system. Though banned or at least restricted at first, its potential for supporting self-initiated learning has by now been recognized, turning it into a valuable teaching tool for research, cooperative learning and self-study, to name but a few of its numerous uses. With the demand for media literacy increasing in every type of job and schools responding to the requirements of the 21st century, there has been a shift to a more media-based way of teaching, which is more able to integrate students with special needs.

Surveillance

Digital media gives users access to a huge amount of unfiltered information. However, it also reveals details about individual users, be it intentionally or by chance. Hence secret services have benefitted greatly from sophisticated surveillance technology. Moreover, CCTV is starting to be used in schools, both as a security measure and a means of quality control.

Reality TV

Even though most people show some degree of uneasiness when it comes to video or data surveillance, there seem to be fewer qualms about watching common people's lives exposed on TV for entertainment. The growing popularity of reality TV, which can turn anybody into a celebrity or failure depending on the audience's response, reflects the general trend of people's more interactive approach to the media.

5
10
15
20
25
30
35
40
45

■ **TROUBLE SPOT**
the media (l. 34) + singular verb or plural verb
Digital media gives/give …
The media has/have …

Living interactive lives

1

1 Words in use

Find the highlighted words or phrases in the text that match these definitions:
1 engage in a way of life that is centred on the internet
2 encourage independent studying
3 make something available
4 feeling uncomfortable with something
5 work and study together
6 friends or contacts you don't know very well
7 show something that is usually hidden
8 unintentionally

2 Improving your style

a Gather phrases from the text that express the idea of 'a lot of'. Go beyond the highlighted words.

b Collect linking words from the text. Classify them in three categories according to their meaning:

▶ LP 15: Linking words and phrases

Adding a similar aspect	Introducing a contrast	Drawing a conclusion

Fill in additional linking words that you know. Compare your results with those of your partner and present them in class.

3 Grammar and style: Participle constructions

▶ SF 4: Using a grammar book

a Rewrite the underlined clauses using participle constructions.
1 People who use smartphones sometimes seem to become addicted to them.
2 As they are afraid that they might miss out on something, they constantly check their digital device.
3 They often annoy their parents or even friends by the fact that they are glued to their screen while they are having a conversation.
4 Although they realize that they may get into trouble if they use their phone in class, some of them just can't stop playing with their mobile anyway.

b How is the following participle construction different from the others in the text? How would you translate *with* here?
With the demand for media literacy increasing in every type of job and schools responding to the requirements of the 21st century, there has been a shift to a more media-based way of teaching, which is more able to integrate students with special needs. (ll. 26–32)

Rewrite this sentence, using *with* followed by a participle construction.
As the rules at school strictly forbid the use of mobile phones in class, teachers are required to take action against mobile phone use in their classrooms.

4 Discussion

Has Facebook changed the concept of 'friendship'? Discuss this question with a partner, using as many of the highlighted words from the text as possible.

Modern Media – Tools or Tyrants?   Chapter 1

1 Part A

Ms Moem

 DVD

Find the print version of the poem here:

 Webcode context-00

Dis-connected

A1 Lonely friends *Ms Moem*

Ms Moem is a contemporary English poet, who writes *poems, *rhymes and *verses on all topics. She has her own *poetry *blog website.

- Watch and listen to Ms Moem's poem 'Connected' – a poem about Facebook, Twitter, YouTube and social media in general.

— COMPREHENSION ◄

1 First impressions
   a Make notes on the effect of listening to the poem and watching its words unfold in the video clip. Then compare your experiences in class and discuss your first understanding of the content of the poem.
   b Sum up the essence of this poem as a Twitter message of no more than 140 characters.

2 Understanding the speaker's attitude towards social media
   a List the aspects that are important for the *speaker with regard to social networks.
   b State how important the speaker considers her own role as a social media user. Give evidence from the text.

3 Mediation (English → German)
   Your friend is fascinated with social networks and has shared Ms Moem's video clip with you and other friends on Facebook. He recommended it because he feels it reflects his positive attitude towards social media. Explain to him in German why you think he may have misunderstood the purpose of the poem.

— ANALYSIS ◄

4 Poetic devices
   Examine which means the poet uses to draw our attention to the influence of social media on our lives. SUPPORT p. 200

5 The message
   Interpret what impact the internet has had on human relationships according to Ms Moem's poem.

— BEYOND THE TEXT ◄

6 Creating images
   In small groups, discuss how you could underline the message of the poem with video sequences or stills instead of showing the words in the video clip. You may also include ideas for background music. Present your ideas to each other.

7 Writing a comment
   'Oh why can't we turn the time back.
   It was simpler when we could just be friends, and that didn't depend on whether someone had accepted your friend request.'
   Write a short *comment in which you state why you do or do not agree with this statement from Ms Moem's poem. ► LANGUAGE HELP

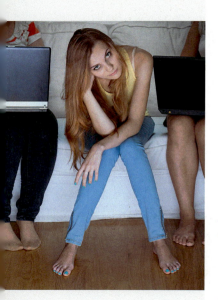

LANGUAGE HELP
- win a friend ↔ lose a friend
- make friends with sb. = forge/form/develop/build a friendship with sb.
- cultivate a friendship
- a close/special/intimate ['ɪntɪmət]/trusted/loyal/true/lifelong/long-time/long-lost/new-found friend
- a fair-weather friend (= sb. who will let you down when you are in need)
- a casual acquaintance [əˈkweɪntəns] (= a person you don't know very well)

Chapter 1   Modern Media – Tools or Tyrants?

Dis-connected   1

CULTURE SPOT

New media art:
Viewpoint of Billions with Google Glass *(2013)*

- American artist David Datuna was the first to incorporate internet-connected smartglasses ('wearable computing') into a piece of modern art.
- Four interactive cameras have been built into a 12-foot (3.67m) American flag. These will automatically connect with viewers wearing Google Glass.
- Photos, newspaper clippings and videos of famous moments in US history have been placed behind thousands of optical lenses. They will be projected to the wearer's 'third eye' when they look at the artwork.
- For up to three minutes viewers will have a unique experience, e.g. they can answer questions posed by Glass and have their responses and experiences recorded and uploaded onto the artist's website, YouTube and Tumblr.

Watch a video on David Datuna's interactive installation 'Viewpoint of Billions with Google Glass'. DVD

1. Describe David Datuna's art installation. How is art created with new media?
2. Explain the title of the installation. Work in pairs and exchange your opinions on this work of art.
3. Discuss in class whether or not you would like to contribute to Datuna's interactive installation.

Modern Media – Tools or Tyrants?   Chapter 1   15

Part A

A2 Online learning in 2044   Ernest Cline

The following text is an excerpt from a science-fiction *novel. It's the year 2044, and Wade Watts, the teenaged *protagonist, escapes his depressing reality by spending his waking hours immersed in the OASIS, a virtual utopia where you can be anything you want to be on any of ten thousand planets, if you can pay for it.

I'd attended school in the real world up until the sixth grade. It hadn't been a very pleasant experience. I was a painfully shy, awkward kid, with low self-esteem and almost no social skills – a side effect of spending most of my childhood inside the OASIS. Online, I didn't have a problem talking to people or making friends. But in the real world, interacting with other people – especially kids my own age – made me a nervous wreck. I never knew how to act or what to say, and when I did work up the courage to speak, I always seemed to say the wrong thing.

My appearance was part of the problem. I was overweight, and had been for as long as I could remember. My bankrupt diet of government-subsidized sugar and starch-laden food was a contributing factor, but I was also an OASIS addict, so the only exercise I usually got back then was running away from the bullies before and after school. To make matters worse, my limited wardrobe consisted entirely of ill-fitting clothes from thrift stores and donation bins – the social equivalent of having a bull's-eye painted on my forehead.

Even so, I tried my best to fit in. Year after year, my eyes would scan the lunchroom like a T-1000, searching for a clique that might accept me. But even the other outcasts wanted nothing to do with me. I was too weird, even for the weirdos. And girls? Talking to girls was out of the question. To me, they were like some exotic alien species, both beautiful and terrifying. Whenever I got near one of them I invariably broke out in a cold sweat and lost the ability to speak in complete sentences.

For me, school had been a Darwinian exercise. A daily gauntlet of ridicule, abuse, and isolation. By the time I entered sixth grade, I was beginning to wonder if I'd be able to maintain my sanity until graduation, still six long years away.

Then, one glorious day, our principal announced that any student with a passing grade-point average could apply for a transfer to the new OASIS public school system. The real public school system, the one run by the government, had been an underfunded, overcrowded train wreck for decades. And now the conditions at many schools had gotten so terrible that every kid with half a brain was being encouraged to stay at home and attend school online. I nearly broke my neck sprinting to the school office to submit my application. It was accepted, and I transferred to OASIS Public School #1873 the following semester.

TROUBLE SPOT

attend school (l. 1) = **go to school** = die Schule besuchen, in die Schule gehen
visit a school = einen Schulbesuch machen (z. B. als Schulaufsicht zur Kontrolle oder als Besucher am Tag der offenen Tür)

4 **oasis** [əʊˈeɪsɪs] a retreat, a pleasant place in the middle of something unpleasant
13 **thrift store** (AE) = charity shop (BE)
16 **T-1000** a fictional robot consisting of liquid metal and therefore capable of changing its shape, the evil terminator in Terminator 2
19 **invariably** [ɪnˈveərɪəbli] always
21 **(run a) gauntlet** [ˈɡɔːntlət] deal with a lot of people criticizing or attacking you
23 **sanity** [ˈsænəti] mental health
24 **a passing grade-point average** i.e. the average of the grades achieved in all of the classes throughout a school year is sufficient to proceed to the next year

16   Chapter 1   Modern Media – Tools or Tyrants?

Dis-connected

Prior to my transfer, my OASIS avatar had never left Incipio, the planet at the center of Sector One where avatars were spawned at the time of their creation. There wasn't much to do on Incipio except chat with other noobs or shop in one of the giant virtual malls that covered the planet. If you wanted to go somewhere more interesting, you had to pay a teleportation fare to get there, and that cost money, something I didn't have. So my avatar was stranded on Incipio. That is, until my new school e-mailed me a teleportation voucher to cover the cost of my avatar's transport to Ludus, the planet where all of the OASIS public schools were located.

There were hundreds of school campuses here on Ludus, spread out evenly across the planet's surface. The schools were all identical, because the same construction code was copied and pasted into a different location whenever a new school was needed. And since the buildings were just pieces of software, their design wasn't limited by monetary constraints, or even by the laws of physics. So every school was a grand palace of learning with polished marble hallways, cathedral-like classrooms, zero-g gymnasiums, and virtual libraries containing every (school board-approved) book ever written.

On my first day at OPS #1873, I thought I'd died and gone to heaven. Now, instead of running a gauntlet of bullies and drug addicts on my walk to school each morning, I went straight to my hideout and stayed there all day. Best of all, in the OASIS, no one could tell that I was fat, that I had acne, or that I wore the same shabby clothes every week. Bullies couldn't pelt me with spitballs, give me atomic wedgies, or pummel me by the bike rack after school. No one could even touch me. In here, I was safe.

From: Ernest Cline, *Ready Player One*, 2012

43 **incipio** *(Latin)* I am beginning, I begin
44 **spawn sth.** produce sth.
45 **noob** *(slang)* a person that has just started doing something and is very inexperienced in it
49 **ludus** *(Latin)* game, school
55 **monetary constraints** [BE: ˈmʌnɪtri, AE: -teri] financial restrictions
57 **school board-approved** [əˈpruːvd] the school board is an institution in charge of local public schools. One of its tasks is to determine which educational materials are suitable to be used at school. Only school board-approved books are available at school.
63 **pelt sb. with sth.** attack sb. by throwing things at them
give sb. atomic wedgies *(infml)* pull sb.'s underwear up forcefully as a kind of bullying, usually performed on male victims
64 **pummel sb.** [ˈpʌml] keep hitting sb.

COMPREHENSION

1 **Understanding the situation**
   a Name Wade's reasons for wanting to attend the new OASIS public school.
   b Describe the schools on Ludus.
   c Point out what makes OPS #1873 so much better in Wade's opinion.

ANALYSIS

2 **Telling names** ('Sprechende Namen')
   Refer to the annotations and analyse what the names reveal about the
   *character and the *setting. SUPPORT p. 200

LANGUAGE AWARENESS

3 **Telling images**
   a Study the following (parts of) sentences in their contexts and paraphrase their meaning.
      1 My bankrupt diet of government-subsidized sugar and starch-laden food was a contributing factor … (ll. 9–10)
      2 … the social equivalent of having a bull's-eye painted on my forehead. (ll. 13–14)
      3 For me, school had been a Darwinian exercise. A daily gauntlet of ridicule, abuse, and isolation. (ll. 21–22)
      4 The real public school system, the one run by the government, had been an underfunded, overcrowded train wreck for decades. (ll. 26–30)
   b The sentences in a all contain *images. Interpret what they tell you about the protagonist.
   c CHALLENGE Go over the text again, gather further examples of *imagery and interpret them within the context of the story.

1 Part A

- SF 8: Structuring ideas
- SF 34: Argumentative writing
- SF 38: Writing a well-structured text

WRITING FOCUS ON SKILLS

Writing an argumentative text

In argumentative writing, we present arguments for and against a topic in order to convince others of our point of view. Writing an argumentative text is often a requirement in both school-leaving and international language proficiency examinations. You usually have a time limit and must keep within a certain number of words.

A typical assignment could be:
'Will attending OASIS public school solve Wade's problems? Discuss. Write about 150–200 words.'

1 **Examining the task**
   Before gathering any arguments, make sure you are familiar with the meaning of the keywords of the task, i.e. *OASIS public school* and *Wade's problems*. (Refer to your work on Text **A2**, p. 17)

2 **Collecting arguments**
   Divide the class into two groups. One half of the class has to find at least three reasons why OASIS might be considered the perfect school for Wade, the other half has to collect at least three arguments supporting the idea that his problems will remain. Work on your own and make notes.

3 **Developing a thesis and an antithesis**
   Arrange a central meeting point in the classroom, the so-called database. As soon as you have finished collecting your arguments, go to the database and pair up with a student from the other group. Exchange your arguments. Discuss and reach an agreement on how to answer the topic question. The position you support is called the *thesis ['θiːsɪz], the one you reject is called the *antithesis [æn'tɪθəsɪs].

4 **Composing the argumentative text**
   1 **Introduction**
      Start your text with an interesting example, quote, definition or statistic related to your topic in order to grab your reader's attention. Then introduce the topic itself with a clear statement or *rhetorical question. Compare and evaluate the following three introductions:

A	B	C
Online schooling is a type of distance learning. You take courses without attending an actual school. Students and teachers interact via the internet, rather than meeting face-to-face. Wade sees this aspect as a big improvement on his old school. But will changing schools really solve his problems?	*'On my first day at OPS #1873, I thought I'd died and gone to heaven.' This is Wade's first impression of his new online school, after leaving the bullies of his old school behind. But will his opinion change as he gets to know his new school better?*	*Statistically, one in four students is regularly bullied at school in the USA. So there are lots of real-life Wades looking for a way out of their difficult situation. Wade chooses to attend an online school to escape his problems at school. But will online-education really turn out to be a positive alternative for Wade?*

Either choose one of these introductions for your argumentative text or create your own.

Chapter 1   Modern Media – Tools or Tyrants?

Dis-connected

2 Main part

On the basis of your notes from **3** on the opposite page, compose the main part of your argumentative text. Remember to start a new paragraph for every part of your text and avoid using contracted forms like *there's*, *she's*, *he'll*, etc.

Use some of the linking words from **Words in Context** to connect your ideas. Here are some additional phrases to help you structure your text:

▶ LP 15: Linking words and phrases
▶ LP 16: Connecting your thoughts (sentence structure)

Presenting various options	on the one hand – on the other hand not only – but also either – or
Giving reasons	because as since ('da', 'weil')
Giving examples	for example (e.g.) for instance such as

Complete the following sentences and add your own reasons and examples illustrating your arguments:

On the one hand, Wade's difficult situation may improve for a while because …
On the other hand, online education is unlikely to completely solve his problems as …

3 Conclusion

The purpose of the conclusion is to round off your argumentative text. For this reason you should not present any new arguments but rather draw a logical conclusion from your line of arguments in order to support your thesis, for example predict what will happen to Wade.

Summing up	In brief ('kurz gesagt'), … To sum up, … In conclusion, I would like to say that … In the final analysis ('letztendlich', 'alles in allem'), …

Complete the following conclusion by briefly stating your view and adding your own idea of how Wade might overcome his problem.

To sum up, in my opinion Wade's escape into the virtual world will only create more problems. Instead of trying to avoid all human interaction, he should rather …

Who wrote this essay, Perkins? You or Google?

Modern Media – Tools or Tyrants?   Chapter 1

Part A

A3 Digital media at school *Gerhard Witossek*

The following text is from the home page of a German educational institution. It includes information on the kinds of devices and services that are suitable for school, their benefits and potential drawbacks.

Digitale Medien im Lehr- und Lernprozess

Im Wandel

Ist von digitalen Medien im Unterricht die Rede, heißt das in vielen Schulen die Nutzung von Internet, Lernplattformen und Beamern. Diese sind in die Klassenräume eingezogen und sind weitgehend Bestandteil modernen Unterrichts.

In den letzten Jahren hat sich die Veränderungsdynamik deutlich beschleunigt: In der gegenwärtigen Diskussion geht es um die Nutzung von „interaktiven Whiteboards", „Clouds", „Tablet-PCs" und „Smartphones". Insbesondere die Tablet-PCs, großformatige Smartphones und die Arbeitsmöglichkeiten in der Cloud entwickeln sich rasant weiter.

Dabei stellt sich die Frage, wie diese Medien zielgerichtet im Unterricht eingesetzt werden können. Digitale Medien sollen nicht zum Selbstzweck werden, sondern den Lehr-Lern-Prozess fördern. Darüber hinaus soll den Schülerinnen und Schülern ein sinnvoller und reflektierter Umgang mit den neuen Technologien vermittelt werden. Es gilt also, mediendidaktische, medienerzieherische und mediengestalterische Kompetenzen zu entwickeln und miteinander in Einklang zu bringen.

Im Unterricht

Digitale Medien sicher zu beherrschen, die neuen Entwicklungen zu verfolgen und sinnvoll in den Lehr-Lern-Prozess zu implementieren, stellt für die einzelne Lehrkraft eine große Aufgabe dar. Neben anderen und bewährten Medien und Methoden sollen digitale Medien den Unterricht bereichern: Veranschaulichung, Handlungsorientierung oder die Förderung sozialer Kompetenzen sind nur einige Anforderungen an den Unterricht, die leichter mit digitalen Medien erfüllt werden können.

Die Arbeit mit digitalen Medien ermöglicht auch neue Unterrichtsstrukturen. Die üblichen 45-Minuten-Einheiten können besser verbunden werden. An Kreidetafeln lebte das erarbeitete Ergebnis bislang meist nur in den Heften der Schüler fort. Bedient man sich digitaler Tafeln oder Lernplattformen zur Sicherung der Ergebnisse, können diese wieder gezeigt, verändert und weiterentwickelt werden. Der „rote Faden" einer Unterrichtssequenz wird dadurch deutlicher und die Entwicklungsschritte im Unterricht greifbarer.

Digitale Medien können Schülerinnen und Schülern auch ein anderes Lernen außerhalb der Schule ermöglichen. Beispielsweise können Unterrichtsmaterialien in die Cloud gestellt, interaktive Übungen im Internet genutzt oder Apps sinnvoll eingesetzt werden. […]

False friends
Beamer = video projector
Handy = mobile phone / cellphone
(Lautsprecher-)Box = (loud)speaker

Dis-connected

Die Chancen

Der Einsatz digitaler Medien im Unterricht ist integraler Bestandteil zeitgemäßen pädagogischen Handelns. Schülerinnen und Schüler wachsen mit den neuen Technologien auf, sie gehören zu den Kulturtechniken unserer Gesellschaft. Deshalb liegt es auch in der Verantwortung der Schule, dazu beizutragen, dass Kinder und Jugendliche Medienkompetenz entwickeln können. Es darf auch nicht vergessen werden, dass Jugendliche bereits von sich aus digitale Medien für die Schule nutzen. Beispielsweise recherchieren sie mit Hilfe des mobilen Internets, tauschen sich per Facebook über Unterrichtsinhalte aus oder stellen sich in der Cloud gegenseitig Arbeitsmaterialien bereit. Diese generelle Bereitschaft zum Umgang mit digitalen Medien kann für den Unterricht produktiv genutzt werden.

Digitale Medien können auch die Lehrkraft entlasten. Im Internet finden sich Unterrichtsmaterialien, Freeware, Apps oder Lernplattformen, die schnell verfügbar und benutzerfreundlich sind. Zum Beispiel können der Tafelanschrieb am interaktiven Whiteboard abgespeichert, interaktive Übungen nach Hause mitgegeben oder Arbeitsblätter online zur Verfügung gestellt werden.

Die Nutzung neuer Medien im Unterricht bereitet Jugendliche auf ihr Arbeitsleben vor: In fast allen Berufen ist der Computer das Arbeitsmittel schlechthin. Die hohe Veränderungsdynamik sorgt auch hier für schnelle Entwicklungen, auf die Schülerinnen und Schüler vorbereitet werden müssen.

Die Risiken

Jugendliche werden häufig als „digital natives" bezeichnet, also als eine Generation, die mit neuen Medien aufwächst und in deren Alltag die Nutzung digitaler Medien ganz normal ist. Dies führt allerdings nicht automatisch zu einem reflektierten und bedachten Umgang mit den Möglichkeiten der digitalen Welt. Beschäftigt man sich im Unterricht näher mit dem Schutz persönlicher Daten in sozialen Netzwerken, so zeigt sich sehr schnell, dass längst nicht alle Schülerinnen und Schüler die Risiken überblicken.

From: *Münchner kommunaler Bildungsserver* (www.muc.kobis.de), October 2014

Mediation (German ➔ English)
Imagine you are spending a school year as an exchange student at a high school in Oregon, USA. Your exchange school is about to introduce a new media concept. In order to incorporate a wide range of ideas, all of its exchange students are asked to outline the role of digital media at school in their home countries. Use the German article as the basis for your English presentation to the school board.

▶ SF 41: Mediation of written and oral texts
▶ SF 24: Giving a presentation

Modern Media – Tools or Tyrants?   Chapter 1

21

1 Part B

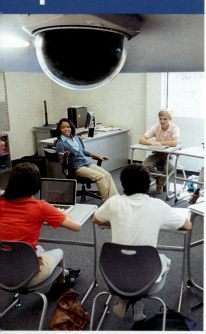

Being on display

B1 Should classrooms have video cameras?

- Work in pairs. Partner A deals with text **1** (T1), partner B with text **2** (T2). Read your text and make notes on the arguments you find.

T1 YES

Cameras will protect students and teachers
Video cameras need to be in the classroom in order to protect the safety of both students and teachers. In today's society we have video cameras in lots of public spaces such as libraries, school buses, parks, beaches, public streets, etc. A public school is a public place just like any other public place so people are not entitled to privacy rights.   5

1. A video recording could be the one thing that saves a teacher's job when there are false accusations.
2. Video recording could protect a student who wants protection from a teacher who is abusing them.   10
3. A video recording could ensure students are being protected from wrongdoing by other students.

For people who are worried about the security of it, the camera data and controls could be kept in the Principal's office. For people complaining about privacy rights and 'Big Brother': in public property the right to privacy does   15
not exist. If you don't like it, you can either homeschool or pay to go to a private school. Oh by the way, the only eyewitness of the Boston Marathon Bombers? A video camera.

T1
6 **be entitled to (do) sth.** have the right to (do) sth.
8 **false accusations** being charged with sth. one has not done

T2
3 **police sth.** monitor sth. closely, keep control over sth.
interfere with sth. disturb sth., prevent sth. from succeeding
4 **benefit sb.** ['benɪfɪt] be to sb.'s advantage
11 **dehumanize sb.** [ˌdiːˈhjuːmənaɪz] make sb. lose their human dignity
train sth. on sb. aim a camera, gun, etc. at sb.
16 **deter sth.** [dɪˈtɜː] prevent sth. from happening
19 **resemble sth.** be similar to sth.
20 **trapped** unable to move or escape

▶ LP 12: Using the right register

COMPREHENSION

1 Collecting arguments
Share your arguments with your partner and discuss which ones you consider most convincing.

LANGUAGE AWARENESS

2 Using more formal language
Texts T1 and T2 contain some elements of informal language. In an argumentative text, you should aim at using more formal language. Rewrite the underlined parts of these sentences using a more formal *register:
1 A public school <u>is a public place just like any other public place</u>. (T1, l. 5)
2 A video recording could be <u>the one thing that saves a teacher's job</u>. (T1, ll. 7–8)
3 You're treating them <u>like they are already criminals.</u> (T2, l. 12)
4 <u>Think about how you would feel</u> if you had a camera on you. (T2, ll. 20–21)

22 Chapter 1 Modern Media – Tools or Tyrants?

Being on display

■ FACT FILE

CCTV (closed-circuit television) is a system in which television signals are not publicly broadcast but are monitored only by those people who have access to the system's content (**'closed circuit'** [ˈsɜːkɪt]). The primary purpose of CCTV is to reduce crime and anti-social behaviour, especially in public places and shops. With around 4.2 million CCTV cameras (one for every 14 people), Britain has become the most watched country in the world, a **'surveillance society'**.

What would be your immediate reaction to CCTV cameras in your classroom? Make notes and discuss them with a partner.

NO 👎   **T2**

The possibility of abuse of power is too great.
I do not believe that cameras in the classroom would be / will be used to prevent bullying and abuse, rather to police and interfere with teaching. It would be too easy to manipulate and use the tapes in a way that benefits
5 the administration and not the teacher. Furthermore, students and teachers should never be observed without their knowing, and I can see that becoming a problem.
You may wonder why teachers have such a problem with the invasion of privacy. It's not about having something to hide, after all, they are
10 frequently observed and, after all, the classroom is full of students. It's dehumanizing to have cameras trained on teachers and students at all times. You're treating them like they are already criminals, and I think students especially have enough to deal with.
Claiming that this will prevent/end teacher or student abuse ignores the
15 real problem. If there is abuse going on, there needs to be actual action taken. It's not enough to think that cameras will deter certain actions, as most people will not think of their actions as bullying, and if they do, they might be talented in hiding it.
I think schools resemble prisons enough as it is. I do not think students
20 need further reason to feel trapped and exposed. Think about how you would feel if you had a camera on you while trying to learn.

From: the website of the online community *Debate.org*

■ TROUBLE SPOT

the possibility of (doing) sth. (l. 1)
the possibility that sth. may happen
Not: ~~the possibility to do sth.~~

■ TROUBLE SPOT

actual [ˈæktʃuəl] (l. 15) = *tatsächlich, wirklich, konkret*
But: *aktuell* = **topical, current**

▶ LP 18: Avoiding Germanisms

▶ BEYOND THE TEXT ◀

3 Discussing the pros and cons of surveillance at school
Get together in groups of four and do the following task:
As there have been some cases of bullying and vandalism at your school, the school board wants to introduce CCTV cameras inside and outside the school building (except for the private toilet cubicles) to monitor and protect the students.
As student representatives you are on a committee that will be heard before the school board's final decision.
  a Discuss the pros and cons of the proposed idea.
  b Develop a concept that you consider acceptable for your school.
  c Present your concept to the school board (i.e. the class).
    SUPPORT ▶ p. 200

▶ SF 27: Having a discussion

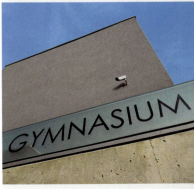

1 Part B

🎧 **CD1** 03

[1] **game changer** something that changes a situation completely

B2 9/11 – a game changer[1]   Barack Obama

The following extract is taken from remarks on US intelligence programmes by Barack Obama, American President 2009–2016, on 17 January 2014.

- Study the word cloud below, which contains the most frequently used words in Obama's remarks. The size of the letters indicates the frequency of the words. Work with a partner and speculate on the general content of Obama's remarks, using as many words from the cloud as possible.

1 **intelligence** [ɪnˈtelɪdʒəns] secret information about an enemy
2 **President Truman (Harry S. Truman)** 33rd US President (1945–1953)
4 **avert sth.** [ˈrevl] prevent sth.
6 **anchor sth.** [ˈæŋkə] fix sth. firmly
7 **checks and balances** mutual control

■ **TROUBLE SPOT**

ordinary [BE: ˈɔːdnri, AE: ˈɔːrdneri] (ll. 7–8) = gewöhnlich, durchschnittlich
But: *ordinär* = **vulgar** [ˈvʌlgə]

9 **informer** somebody who gives away secrets, usually for money
13 **revelation** [ˌrevəˈleɪʃn] the act of disclosing secrets
15 **twilight** (here) the final stage of something when it becomes weaker or less important than it used to be
18 **emerge** [iˈmɜːdʒ] appear, to become known
19 **proliferation** [prəˌlɪfəˈreɪʃn] rapid increase

Throughout American history, intelligence has helped secure our country and our freedoms. [...] (I)n the early days of the Cold War, President Truman created the National Security Agency, or NSA, to give us insights into the Soviet bloc, and provide our leaders with information they needed to confront aggression and avert catastrophe.

Throughout this evolution, we benefited from both our Constitution and our traditions of limited government. U.S. intelligence agencies were anchored in a system of checks and balances – with oversight from elected leaders, and protections for ordinary citizens. Meanwhile, totalitarian states like East Germany offered a cautionary tale of what could happen when vast, unchecked surveillance turned citizens into informers, and persecuted people for what they said in the privacy of their own homes.

In fact, even the United States proved not to be immune to the abuse of surveillance. And in the 1960s, government spied on civil rights leaders and critics of the Vietnam War. And partly in response to these revelations, additional laws were established in the 1970s to ensure that our intelligence capabilities could not be misused against our citizens. In the long, twilight struggle against Communism, we had been reminded that the very liberties that we sought to preserve could not be sacrificed at the altar of national security.

If the fall of the Soviet Union left America without a competing superpower, emerging threats from terrorist groups, and the proliferation of weapons of mass destruction placed new and in some ways more complicated demands on our intelligence agencies. Globalization and the Internet made these threats more acute, as technology erased borders and empowered individuals to project great violence, as well as great good. Moreover, these new threats raised new legal and new policy questions.

24   Chapter 1   Modern Media – Tools or Tyrants?

Being on display

For while few doubted the legitimacy of spying on hostile states, our framework of
25 laws was not fully adapted to prevent terrorist attacks by individuals acting on their
own, or acting in small, ideologically driven groups on behalf of a foreign power.

The horror of September 11th brought all these issues to the fore. Across the political spectrum, Americans recognized that we had to adapt to a world in which a bomb could be built in a basement, and our electric grid could be shut down by operators
30 an ocean away. We were shaken by the signs we had missed leading up to the attacks – how the hijackers had made phone calls to known extremists and traveled to suspicious places. So we demanded that our intelligence community improve its capabilities, and that law enforcement change practices to focus more on preventing attacks before they happen than prosecuting terrorists after an attack.

35 It is hard to overstate the transformation America's intelligence community had to go through after 9/11. Our agencies suddenly needed to do far more than the traditional mission of monitoring hostile powers and gathering information for policymakers. Instead, they were now asked to identify and target plotters in some of the most remote parts of the world, and to anticipate the actions of networks that, by their
40 very nature, cannot be easily penetrated with spies or informants. [...]

From: the official website of the *White House*, 17 January 2014

24 **hostile** [BE: ˈhɒstaɪl, AE: ˈhɑːstl] belonging to the enemy
26 **on behalf of** as a representative of
27 **bring sth. to the fore** gain public attention for sth.
38 **plotter** somebody making secret plans to harm others

> **FACT FILE**
> **9/11** refers to September 11th, 2001. On this date four planes were hijacked by terrorists in the USA. One plane crashed in Pennsylvania, one destroyed part of the Pentagon in Virginia, and two flew into the World Trade Center, New York City. About 3,000 people were killed in these attacks which were conducted by the extreme Islamic group Al Qaeda [ælˈkaɪdə].

▶ SF 38: Writing a well-structured text

COMPREHENSION

1 The structure of the text
  a Divide this extract into parts and give headings to each part.
  b Outline Obama's argumentation in your own words.

ANALYSIS

2 Understanding the title
Explain why 9/11 can be considered a 'game changer' with regard to US security policy.

3 Analysing stylistic devices
  a The phrases in the box on the right are quotes from the text. Explain their meaning.
  b Point out what *stylistic device is used in all of these phrases and analyse the effect achieved by employing it.
  c Go over the text again and find at least one example of an *antithesis. Describe its effect on the reader.

▶ SF 17: Analysing stylistic devices
▶ Glossary, p. 323

- 'U.S. intelligence agencies were anchored in a system of checks and balances' (ll. 6–7)
- 'states like East Germany offered a cautionary tale' (ll. 8–9)
- 'the very liberties that we sought to preserve could not be sacrificed at the altar of national security' (ll. 16–17)

BEYOND THE TEXT

▶ SF 13: Analysing cartoons

4 Evaluating a cartoon
  a Describe and analyse the cartoon on the right, keeping in mind some of the information presented in Obama's *speech.
  b **CHALLENGE** 'It is hard to overstate the transformation America's intelligence community had to go through after 9/11.' (ll. 35–36)
  Look for a cartoon on the internet that expresses the idea of the quote, print it and bring it along to class. Tape it to the wall of your classroom and analyse it orally with your classmates as they walk from cartoon to cartoon.
  After examining all the cartoons, stand next to the one you prefer in order to select the most popular cartoon. Be prepared to give reasons for your choice.

Modern Media – Tools or Tyrants?   Chapter 1

Part C

Reality TV

C1 Big Brother out of this world Ellie Zolfagharifard

Creators of a reality TV show plan to broadcast the selection and training of a group of candidates who will be sent on a one-way mission to Mars in 2025. Is Big Brother going to take on the red planet?

It takes a certain type of person to apply for a one-way ticket to Mars. Not only will they require mental and physical strength, but now, they will also need to have the makings of the next reality-TV star. Endemol, the production company behind Big Brother, has announced that it will document the progress of a group of hopefuls as they compete for a 2025 ticket to the red planet.

The reality series will follow the selection process of the privately-funded Mars One mission, which aims to launch 20 humans on Mars within the next decade. During the first selection round, more than 200,000 people signed up to be part of the first human colony on the red planet. The applicants have now been shortlisted to 705 candidates – 418 men and 287 women – who will undergo what is described as 'the world's toughest job interview'.

Darlow Smithson Productions (DSP), an Endemol company, will film the hopefuls as they are 'tested to the extreme as part of an elite training programme'. Candidates do not need to have any scientific qualifications and a Big Brother-style audience vote will be used to make the final choice. Any chosen Mars settlers will then be required to dedicate eight years of their lives preparing for the 300 million-mile pioneering mission. The ticket is one-way and Mars One plans to send additional crews every two years to expand the colony.

DSP said its production will be seen around the world, with the first series likely to be appearing in early 2015. The plan is for the cameras to also follow the first human settlers on the planet as they attempt to build a new society from scratch.

'Our team felt all along that we needed a partner whose strength lies in factual storytelling to an international audience,' Mars One co-founder Bas Lansdorp said in a statement. 'DSP will provide that to Mars One, while allowing our selection committee to maintain control of the applicant selection process.' [...]

The majority of applicants for the one-way trip to Mars came from the US, with India and China coming in second and third place. The second round will include an interview with Mars One committee members, and candidates advancing to the third round will compete against one another. The third round will include a series of challenges to prepare candidates for the potential mission and will be broadcast on television and online.

The group said it aims to have a human settlement on Mars within a decade. Journey time to Mars, which is approximately 40 million miles away depending on its position in orbit, would be around 200 days.

From: *Daily Mail*, 3 June 2014

FACT FILE

Reality TV shows feature ordinary people instead of professional *actors or *actresses. There are basically two types. In one, participants are exposed to TV audiences 24/7 and are required to share an artificial environment with complete strangers for a limited period of time. The second type of show depicts a mixture of carefully selected 'scenes' from participants' real lives and acted-out events in order to create an entertaining and attention-grabbing story for viewers.

2 **require sth.** [rɪˈkwaɪə] need sth.
have the makings of sth. have the necessary qualities for becoming a particular type of person
4 **hopeful** (n) sb who wants to succeed or is likely to win
7 **launch sb. on Mars** [lɔːnʃ] send sb. to Mars
decade [ˈdekeɪd, dɪˈkeɪd] a period of ten years
9 **be shortlisted** (BE) be selected from a longer list of applicants
10 **undergo sth.** experience sth. challenging or unpleasant
16 **dedicate sth.** [ˈdedɪkeɪt] give all of one's attention and effort to sth.
pioneering [ˌpaɪəˈnɪərɪŋ] (adj) first of its kind
18 **expand sth.** make sth. grow larger
21 **from scratch** from the very beginning, with very little preparation
22 **factual** [ˈfæktʃuəl] based on facts
25 **maintain sth.** [–'–] make sth. continue
38 **approximately** [əˈprɒksɪmətli] nearly; more or less

Bride-to-be Kellie Gerardi (25) says she will leave her fiancé on Earth if she is selected to live on the red planet forever as part of a reality TV show.

Reality TV

◀ **COMPREHENSION**

1 How the project works
  a Outline the basic idea of the project and the stages of the selection process.
  b Summarize the role reality TV plays in the project described in the text.

▶ SF 31: Writing a summary

◀ **ANALYSIS**

2 What makes the text engaging for readers?
Analyse the methods used to make the text engaging (e.g. heading, *register, *stylistic devices, quotes, objective/biased?). SUPPORT ▶ p. 201

◀ **LANGUAGE AWARENESS**

3 Word order
  a Look at the beginning of the 2nd sentence of the text again (ll. 1–2). Explain why the auxiliary *will* comes <u>before</u> *they* in the first half of the sentence (*will they require*) but <u>after</u> *they* in the second half (*they will … need*).
  b CHALLENGE ▶ Write two more sentences about the Mars mission that start with *Not only … (but …)*.

◀ **BEYOND THE TEXT**

4 Applying for the Mars One astronaut selection programme
  a Work out a list of criteria that you consider important when selecting a potential settler on Mars. Try to decide on the three most relevant criteria.
  b Write a formal *letter of application to the selection committee of Mars One trying to convince them to send you to Mars.

▶ SF 29: Writing a formal letter or email

5 ROLE-PLAY The world's toughest job interview
Act out an interview between the members of the selection committee and four applicants for the Mars One project. The rest of the class then vote on the two applicants to be accepted and give reasons for their choice.

C2 The ultimate reality TV show *DBC Pierre*

Vernon Little is a teenager who has been wrongly convicted of murdering classmates and is now on death row¹. In his cell he is watching an interview on TV in which Lally (the nickname of Eulalio Ledesma), a journalist, explains his idea of 'the ultimate reality TV show' to the reporter Bob.

'So you're effectively proposing to fund the State's penal system by selling broadcast rights to the prisoners' executions? I mean – isn't a prisoner's last hour a little *personal*?'

'Not at all – don't forget that all executions are witnessed, even today. We're simply
5 expanding the audience to include anyone with an interest in the proper function of law.' Lally puts a hand on his hip. 'Not so long ago, Bob, all executions were public – even held in the town square. Crime went down, public satisfaction went up. Throughout history it's been society's right to punish delinquents by its own hands. It makes plain sense to give that right back to society.'

10 'Hence the web-vote?'

'Exactly. And we're not just talking executions here – we're talking the ultimate reality TV, where the public can monitor, via cable or internet, prisoners' whole lives on death row. They can live amongst them, so to speak, and make up their own minds about a convict's worthiness for punishment. Then each week, viewers across the
15 globe can cast a vote to decide which prisoner is executed next. It's humanity in action – the next logical step toward true democracy.' 'But surely, due process dictates the fate of prisoners?'

¹ **be on death row** [rəʊ] be a prisoner sentenced to death, waiting for the death penalty to be carried out
1 **fund sth.** provide money for sth.
 penal ['piːnl] connected with lawful punishment
8 **delinquent** [dɪˈlɪŋkwənt] criminal
10 **hence** (*fml*) consequently
12 **monitor sth.** watch and check sth.
16 **due** (*adj*) right and proper

Part C

18 **tamper with sth.** interfere with sth. **appeals process** [BE: 'prəʊses, AE: 'prɑːses] taking a court case one has lost to a higher court 19 **recourse** [BE: rɪˈkɔːs, AE: ˈriːkɔːrs] (fml) being able to use something that may provide help in a difficult situation 20 **roster** list **hooshy laugh** (slang) laughter with loud breathing sounds ('hooshy' is a made-up word – similar to 'whoosh') 21 **momentous** [məˈmentəs] important 25 **breach sth.** violate sth. 26 **forfeit** [ˈfɔːfɪt] loss of something as a punishment **con** (infml) convict, prisoner 27 **languish** [ˈlæŋgwɪʃ] (fml) suffer something unpleasant for a long time 29 **expediency** [ɪkˈspiːdiənsi] being useful to achieve a purpose 33 **nod at sb.** move one's head in sb.'s direction **gear up for sth.** prepare for sth. 34 **a shot at sth.** (infml) an attempt at sth., an effort for sth.	'Absolutely, and we can't tamper with that. But the new fast-track appeals process means prisoners' last recourses at law are spent much sooner, after which I say the public should have a hand in the roster of final events.' Lally lets fly a hooshy laugh at the reporter, and spreads his hands wide. 'In the tradition of momentous progress, it's blindingly simple, Bob: criminals cost money. Popular TV makes money. Criminals are popular on TV. Put them together and, presto – problem solved.' The reporter pauses as a helicopter settles in the background. Then he asks, 'What do you say to those who claim prisoners' rights will be breached?' 'Oh *please* – prisoners, by definition, live in *forfeit* of their rights. Anyway, cons today can languish in institutions for years without knowing their fate – wouldn't you say *that* was cruel? We're finally giving them what the law has always promised but never delivered – expediency. Not only that, they'll have greater access to spiritual counsel, and musical choices to accompany their final event. We'll even craft a special segment around their final statement, with the background imagery of their choice. Believe me – prisoners will welcome these changes.' The reporter smiles and nods at Lally. 'And what of reports that you're gearing up for a shot at the senate?' I switch off the set. I ain't looking forward to cameras in here. We just have an open toilet, see? I guess that's where the money gets made. Internet viewers will be able to choose which cells to watch, and change camera angles and all. On regular TV there'll be edited highlights of the day's action. Then the general public will vote by phone or internet. They'll vote for who should die next. The cuter we act, the more we entertain, the longer we might live. I heard an old con say it'd be just like the life of a real actor. From: DBC Pierre, *Vernon God Little*, 2003

◀ **COMPREHENSION**

1 Lally's ultimate reality TV show
In pairs, briefly sum up the concept of Lally's ultimate reality TV show and exchange your opinions of it. Discuss whether you would have asked similar questions if you had been the reporter.

◀ **ANALYSIS**

2 Lally's mode of argumentation
a Explain Lally's line of argumentation to convince the reporter and the audience of his idea. **SUPPORT** ▶ p. 201
b Identify *stylistic devices that he uses to underline his point of view.

3 Vernon's reaction
Examine and evaluate Vernon's reaction to the interview.

◀ **BEYOND THE TEXT**

4 Interpreting a cartoon
Compare the cartoon on the left with the content of the *novel extract above.

▶ SF 17: Analysing stylistic devices

5 Responding to the interview
Imagine Lally/Eulalio Ledesma invited the viewers to send him some *comments on his project. Write him an email.

REALITY TV

6 Commenting
'Your remote control is the most powerful weapon you have to show the country what you want.' (taken from: *Hazard County* by Allison Moore)
a Discuss this statement with a partner and take notes.
b **CHALLENGE** ▶ Write a comment on the statement.

▶ SF 13: Analysing cartoons

Chapter Task 1

Discussing the pros and cons of modern media

Write a text on the following topic:

> *Will the media change our lives for better or worse over the next ten years? Discuss.*

Instructions

1. Create four posters to place along the walls of your classroom. Each poster will have one of the following headings: **the internet – TV – school/work – surveillance**. Divide the posters vertically into two parts for the positive and negative aspects of the headings.

The internet	TV	School/Work	Surveillance
positive	positive	positive	positive
negative	negative	negative	negative

2. Choose one expert per poster.
3. The rest of the class walk from poster to poster, suggesting their ideas for each of the topics to the experts, who are to write down the entries on the posters.
4. Stand next to the poster which you would like to use as the basis for your text.
5. Discuss with your classmates who have chosen the same poster as you, which aspects on the poster you consider most important.
6. Check *Focus on Skills* (pp. 18–19) and write an argumentative text, narrowing down the topic ('Will the media change our lives for better or worse over the next ten years?') to the heading of your chosen poster.
7. Having finished this task, exchange your composition with a classmate who has chosen the same topic. Your teacher will give you an assessment sheet to fill in. Evaluate each other's texts, keeping in mind what you have learnt in this chapter.

▶ SF 40: Proofreading

2 Science – Enhancing Life?

Transhumanism
human advancement through technology
Genetic engineering
manipulation or modification of organisms using biotechnology
Energy transition
the path to a sustainable economy, e.g. by using biofuels
Gene pharming
the use of genetically modified organisms to produce pharmaceutical products

Download a chronological word list here:
 Webcode context-00

1 Identifying current trends in science
  a Study the pictures, then match them to one of the topics in the box.
  b Pick the photo you find most interesting and speculate about which development in modern science it depicts.
  c Find a partner who chose the same photo. Exchange your ideas, and on the basis of your findings make a chart outlining chances and risks these developments might have for the future.
  d With your chart, move around the classroom. Find a couple who made a chart based on a different picture. Discuss your charts and decide together whether the developments you have discussed will have a positive or negative impact on the future.

Lead-in

2 A look into the future
Predicting the future is difficult if not impossible. Use your imagination and look into the future.

YOU CHOOSE ▸ **Examining new technology**

a Choose your own technology (such as google glass, 3D printers, driverless cars, etc.) and say why you think it has the capability to transform our society in the future. In small groups present and discuss your ideas.

OR

b Make a ranking of new technologies according to their importance to you. In small groups compare your lists and together choose the three technological inventions that have the biggest potential in the future.

PREVIEW

In this chapter you will learn about attempts to improve human life through genetic engineering and technological advancements. You will also examine the challenges of acquiring energy.

Main topics
- Genetic engineering .... p. 34
- Mind- and body-enhancing drugs .... p. 42
- Transhumanism .... p. 45
- Future energy policy .... p. 47

Focus on Skills: READING and MEDIATION
- Using reading strategies (scientific text) ...... p. 41
- Mediating written texts .... p. 49

Chapter Task: Doing a WebQuest on genetically modified food .... p. 51

Science – Enhancing Life?   Chapter 2

31

2 Words in Context

 CD1 04
Listen to an audio version of the text on the CD or download it here:
Webcode context-00

Science – motor of progress?

Feeding the world, healing deadly diseases and finding renewable sources of energy are some of the challenges we have to meet in the 21st century if we want to continue to live well. And it is probably in the realms of science and technology that we will be able to tackle these challenges.

Genetic Engineering
Scientists are now able to map the DNA sequence of the genes of many plants, animals and humans. They hope to use this information to improve the robustness or yield of crops and livestock and to cure human diseases. Genetic engineering (GE) is the process by which the sequence of an organism's DNA is altered by technological means, e.g. by inserting a foreign gene to produce a more desirable result.

In order to provide food for an ever-faster-growing world population the commercial use of GE in farming may help increase food production. The first genetically modified (GM) crop was introduced in 1995 – the slow-softening tomato. Others have been made more insect-resistant or disease-resistant. In 2013, GM crops, including maize, cotton and rice, were being grown on more than 175 million hectares in 29 countries.

In medicine, genetic engineering may one day be used to repair defect genes.

A new widely-debated approach is gene pharming. Pharma crops are genetically modified plants like maize that produce much-needed medicines. The genes for human proteins like insulin could be transferred to animals, which then produce the protein in their milk. However, there are ethical concerns about genetic engineering:

- **Risk and safety:** Transgenic plants or animals (i.e. containing one or more foreign genes) may in the end prove to be unhealthy or even dangerous.
- **Meddling with reproduction:** In-vitro-fertilization (IVF) offers the opportunity to preselect an embryo that is free from genetic disorders. Many fear this will lead to custom-made designer babies – children designed to have a particular eye colour or IQ.

These are reasons why GE requires public approval and careful regulation.

Quenching the thirst for energy
With the rise of emerging countries like Brazil and India the global thirst for energy is growing rapidly. Since the Fukushima nuclear disaster of 2011 many nations have agreed on a nuclear power phase-out. Even though renewable sources of energy like wind, solar and hydropower do not seem to be cost-efficient at the moment, experts are researching ways to switch from finite energy sources such as coal, gas and petroleum to sources that are sustainable and more environmentally-friendly. This is seen as an important step to reduce humanity's carbon footprint and to stop global warming.

Using plants like rapeseed or oil palm to produce biofuels is another way to avoid using fossil fuels. However, environmental concerns about such technologies are growing.

'They used to be called sheep, and they produced wool. Now they're some sort of bioengineered creatures, and they produce antibiotics.'

32   Chapter 2   Science – Enhancing Life?

Science – motor of progress?

1 Information Stock Exchange
a Choose two of the issues in the text that you feel well-informed about. Write them on green cards.
b Write two terms on red cards that you would like to find out more about.
c Walk around the classroom and find three people with green cards that match your red cards. Ask them to give you the information you want.
d Explain the terms on your green cards to three students.
e On the blackboard arrange your cards in three columns:
- Still lost: red cards with terms that still need clarifying
- Lost and found: green and red matches
- Information pool: green cards that were not talked about

2 Formal vs. informal language
Scientific reports strive for accuracy and precision, which is why they rarely use phrasal verbs. Try to substitute the phrasal verbs or informal expressions below with a formal verb from the text.

1 put sth. into sth.
2 move sth. from one place to another
3 make sth. different
4 make sth. less or smaller

3 Compound adjectives
Compound adjectives make texts more formal by condensing information. Find examples of compound adjectives such as *custom-made* (l. 33) in the text and categorize them according to their structure:
noun + adjective • noun + participle • adjective + adjective • adjective/adverb + participle • other

a Make these sentences shorter by forming compound adjectives.
1 Genetic engineering is a business that is growing fast.
2 GE companies hope to make progress at a speed that will break all records.
3 They hope to help farmers keep their fields free from pollution.
4 The development took ten years before GE crops could hit the market.

▶ LP 10: Using adjectives and verbs

■ TROUBLE SPOT
*hyphenated compound adjectives are only used **before** nouns.*
It was a well-written report.
↔ The report was well written.

4 Creative writing
Describe the picture and discuss it with reference to genetic engineering.

Science – Enhancing Life? Chapter 2

Part A

The genetic engineering debate

A1 A saviour sibling   *Laura Roberts*

Genetic screening is a new technology that has been helping families with genetically transmitted diseases.

Megan Matthews, nine, received tissue donated by her 18-month old brother Max who was created specifically so that he could aid her medical treatment. [...]

Megan, from King's Lynn, Norfolk, was born with a rare blood disorder which can cause bone marrow failure and a worldwide search for a suitable bone marrow donor failed. The condition, Fanconi Anaemia, meant she needed transfusions every few weeks and was unable to fight infections.

Her parents Katie and Andy Matthews wanted another child but natural conception would have provided only a one in four chance that the sibling would be a perfect tissue match. The new child could also have been born with the same life-threatening genetic disorder. To avoid this, Cambridge, Bristol and Nottingham medical teams were involved in a treatment which used donated cells from the specifically created baby and taken to treat Megan's disorder.

Two embryos were implanted into Mrs Matthews by CARE Fertility in Nottingham after they were checked for transplant suitability. Initially umbilical cord blood was saved and after Max was born an operation was carried out to take bone marrow. The tissue transplant took place in July this year at Bristol Royal Hospital for Sick Children. Compared to her frequent and invasive hospital visits, Megan now only requires a weekly check-up at Addenbrookes hospital in Cambridge.

Simon Fishel, managing director of Care Fertility, said that ethical concerns over creating children with specific genetic material were outweighed by the benefits. He said: 'The ethical issues are in favour of doing this work. We are trying to save the life of a child and achieve a family without the enormous burden of a child with this disorder who would die.' Mrs Matthews also said she had no ethical problems with the treatment her family had received. She said: 'Max is loved for being him and not for what he has done. He has completed our family and now I have a bubbly and healthy girl.'

The use of genetically engineered children for medical treatment has been widely criticised. Josephine Quintavalle, Director of Comment on Reproductive Ethics told the BBC: '[Max] owes his life to his capacity to be of therapeutic use to his sick sister, otherwise he would not have been chosen in the first place. This is the big ethical problem.' Sufferers of Fanconi Anaemia may suffer long-term health problems and Megan may require further treatment.

From: 'First complete "saviour sibling" transplant carried out in the UK', *Daily Telegraph*, 22 December 2010

Part A

2

────────────────────────────────── COMPREHENSION ◀

1 Understanding the concept of saviour siblings
Choose the statement which fits best and give the line that provides
evidence for your choice.
  a A saviour sibling is a brother or sister …
    1 who has been specifically created for the purpose of curing a sick
      brother or sister.
    2 whose life was saved by receiving a transplant from a brother or sister.
  b Without a transplant Megan would …
    1 have died within a short period of time.
    2 have had to go in and out of hospitals to receive transfusions.
  c The use of IVF was necessary to …
    1 produce a healthy embryo.
    2 make sure that the baby would not suffer from Frankoni anaemia.
  d The procedure has been widely criticized as …
    1 human beings seem to have been reduced to commodities.
    2 embryos are killed in the process.

2 Summarizing information
Use the drawing and the information from the text to explain how a saviour
sibling is produced.

▶ SF 31: Writing a summary

────────────────────────────────────── ANALYSIS ◀

3 Argumentative structure
  a Look at the last sentence of the article and decide whether the writer is
    in favour of the use of saviour siblings, whether he is against their use or
    whether he takes a neutral position.
  b Analyse the argumentative structure of the article, paying particular
    attention to the effect of the writer's use of direct and indirect speech.
    SUPPORT ▶ p. 202

──────────────────────────── LANGUAGE AWARENESS ◀

4 Using the passive
  a Scientific texts usually contain many passive constructions. Look at the use
    of the passive voice in ll. 2, 13, 15, 16, 17–18, 28, 34, 36, and analyse its
    effect. (Hint: it may help to transform one or two into the active voice to
    see the difference.)
  b In German, active sentences with 'man' are often used instead of a passive
    sentence. In which cases do you think 'man' might be better than the
    passive voice if you were to translate the sentences.

▶ LP 7: The passive

──────────────────────────────── BEYOND THE TEXT ◀

5 Case Studies
PLACEMAT ACTIVITY Choose one of the cases below and use a placemat to
note down the pros and cons for that case. Use the guidelines from the Fact
File on p. 36 to consider the ethical dimensions of the topic. Discuss the
issue with your group members and prepare a group statement in which you
state your position.
  1 Megan's case (cf. text).
  2 A pair of deaf parents wants to use genetic screening to ensure that their
    child is also deaf.
  3 Parents who want to use genetic screening to test their foetus for genes
    that indicate a high risk of their child developing particular conditions, so
    that they can abort the foetus if they so wish.

Science – Enhancing Life?   Chapter 2

2 Part A

FACT FILE

Ethics in science

Science is advancing at an ever-accelerating speed. New discoveries and new technologies are affecting all areas of our life. Many new inventions or discoveries have sparked public discussions on whether their use is desirable or should be avoided.

In order to find out which course of action is the moral one, people turn to ethics. Ethics is the branch of philosophy that studies the principles of what is morally right or wrong.

When it comes to ethical decision making, the following questions can help you. You can use them to test whether your decision is morally acceptable:

- Are the rights of everyone involved respected?
- Which solution would be the most just, fair or responsible?
- Which solution will probably have the best overall consequences, even if it means that some will not benefit from it?
- Which solution will be most sustainable and help everyone?
- Think of the wisest person you know. What would he or she do in this situation?

Read the Fact File and write down: 3 words or expressions that are new to you and worth adding to your word bank on genetic engineering. 2 ethical principles that are particularly important when it comes to ethical decision making. 1 reason why ethical decision making is important.

The National Theatre's production of Nick Dear's Frankenstein

A2 You are mine to kill *Nick Dear*

The excerpt below is from Nick Dear's 2011 stage adaptation of Mary Shelley's novel Frankenstein (1818). *Considered by many to be one of the first horror stories, Shelley's gothic novel poses many moral and ethical questions about the role of science in a society that was beginning to change due to scientific advances. Victor Frankenstein, a young scientist, has succeeded in creating life. From dead bodies and with the help of newly-discovered electricity he has brought a creature to life. Appalled by its ugliness, he sends it away. After he learns that the creature has killed his brother William, he searches for it in the Arctic ice, where the creature has fled.*

With a partner come up with a list of guidelines that a responsible scientist should follow, e.g. a scientist should make his findings publicly available.

There is a sound like a great exhalation of breath, as the glacier shudders and shifts. Through the snowstorm the Creature is suddenly visible, standing very still on the ice. He makes a great leap towards Victor.

VICTOR	My God! Muscular coordination – hand and eye – excellent tissue – perfect balance! And the sutures have held! I failed to make it handsome, but I gave it strength and grace.

Victor circles the Creature. The Creature swivels to keep an eye on him.

	What an achievement! Unsurpassed in scientific endeavour! God, the madness of that night – the heat, the sweat, the infusions, the moment when I saw it crawl towards me, and I – and I –
CREATURE	You ran away.
VICTOR	What?
CREATURE	You abandoned me.
VICTOR *(stunned)*	It speaks!
CREATURE	Yes, Frankenstein. It speaks.
VICTOR	You know my name?

The Creature hands Victor the tattered journal.

---

5 **suture** Naht
7 **swivel** turn round quickly
8 **unsurpassed** better or greater than any other
endeavour attempt to do sth. new and difficult
10 **crawl** walk on your hands and knees
13 **abandon sb.** leave sb. with no intention of seeing them again

The Genetic Engineering Debate 2

	CREATURE	My journal! Why did you abandon me?
20	VICTOR	I was terrified – what had I done?
	CREATURE	Built a man, and given him life –
	VICTOR	Well, now I have come to take it away –
	CREATURE *(laughs)*	Oh, have you?
	VICTOR	I have come to kill you!
25	CREATURE	To kill me? Why then did you create me?
	VICTOR	To prove that I could!
	CREATURE	So you make sport with my life?
	VICTOR	In the cause of science! You were my greatest experiment – but an experiment that has gone wrong. An experiment that must be curtailed!

30 curtail sth. *(here)* bring to an end
31 disarm sb. take weapon away from sb.

Victor runs at him and attacks him with his stick, but the Creature swiftly disarms him and throws him to the ground.

	CREATURE	Be still, genius! I have a request.
	VICTOR	Damn you, you can't have requests!
35	CREATURE	Oh, I can! Listen to me. It's your duty.
	VICTOR	I have no duty to a murderer.

From: Nick Dear, *Frankenstein*, 2001

COMPREHENSION ◀

1 Creature and creator
Describe the situation as presented in this scene.

ANALYSIS ◀

2 Responsible or irresponsible scientist?
Examine the attitude of Frankenstein to his creation. Use your list from above to judge whether his attitude shows him to be a responsible or an irresponsible scientist.

BEYOND THE TEXT ◀

3 `CHALLENGE` **The experiment**
Creature or human? Comment on this question taking ethical and legal aspects and the character of the Creature as depicted in the extract into consideration.

'We've created a teenager.'

4 Discussing statements
FOUR-CORNERS ACTIVITY Assign each of the four positions below to a corner in your classroom. Then stand next to the statement that comes closest to your own opinion. With the others in your corner discuss the reasons why you each chose that position.

▶ SF 27: Having a discussion

Scientists should have complete freedom in their research and not be controlled by the government.	'Science, in the very act of solving problems, creates more of them.' *Abraham Flexner*	'Whenever science makes a discovery, the devil grabs it while the angels are debating the best way to use it.' *Alan Valentine*	It is not for humans to create life forms and use them for their own purposes.

Science – Enhancing Life?   Chapter 2   37

2 Part A

A3 At the lab

► SF 13: Analysing cartoons

———————————————————— COMPREHENSION ◄

1 Describing a cartoon
Describe the cartoon and identify the topic the cartoon addresses.

———————————————————————— ANALYSIS ◄

2 Examining a cartoon
Analyse the means the cartoonist employs to criticize the 'designer babies' trend.

——————————————————— BEYOND THE CARTOON ◄

3 Comparing texts
Comment on how the creation of designer babies is similar or different to the dilemma dealt with in *Frankenstein*.

4 YOU CHOOSE **Practising speaking**

a Prepare a monologue on whether designer babies are desirable or not.

 OR

b Find a partner and discuss whether designer babies are desirable or not (in front of the class) with one of you taking the pro and one the con side.
Use the guidelines from the Fact File (cf. p. 36) to include the ethical dimension of the topic.
SUPPORT ► p. 202

► LANGUAGE HELP

■ **LANGUAGE HELP**
- The ethical / moral question raised by …. is …
- The most important / The profoundest argument is … / The least convincing argument
- A valid / sound / serious / plausible argument
- invalid / arbitrary / implausible argument
- As a consequence, …
- the result of which would be that …
- It seems important to me to emphasize / point out …

38 Chapter 2 Science – Enhancing Life?

The Genetic Engineering Debate

CULTURE SPOT

The hyperrealistic sculptures by Australian contemporary artist Patricia Piccinini address ethical issues of genetic engineering in an often disturbing or provocative way.

The Long Awaited (2008)

Silicone, fibreglass, human hair, plywood, leather, clothing. 152 x 80 x 92 cm high. Courtesy of the artist and Tolarno and Roslyn Oxley9 Galleries

Patricia Piccinini on *The Long Awaited*:

'Empathy is at the heart of my practice. I don't think that you really can – or indeed should – try to understand the ethics of something without emotions [...]. It is one thing to argue for or against cloning when it is just an intellectual issue. However, things change if you have a mother or son who might need it. I like to think that my work understands that the point at which "good" becomes "bad" does not stand still, which is why it is so difficult to find.'

1 Study the sculpture. Then discuss your reactions to it with a partner. Choose the adjectives from the list below to describe the sculpture and its effect on you.

aesthetic • calming • delightful • disturbing • embarrassing • harmonious • interesting • loving • obnoxious • quaint • shocking • supportive • tasteless • touching • tranquil • understanding • unsettling • warm

2 Analyse the relationship between the boy and the creature on the bench. Point out to what extent the sculpture illustrates Piccinini's comment.

3 Write a formal email to Patricia Piccinini in which you comment on *The Long Awaited* as a statement on genetic engineering.

Science – Enhancing Life? Chapter 2

39

Part A

A4 Animals with bonus features Bob Holmes

The text below examines the genetic engineering of animals so that they may benefit humans in more ways than they do today.

6 **tedious** ['tiːdiəs] taking a long time and requiring a lot of work
17 **jumping gene** gene that can insert copies of itself into other DNA sites in the same cell
24 **omega-3** type of fatty acid
31 **tack sth. on** add sth.
33 **antibodies** *Antikörper*
36 **anticoagulant** *Gerinnungshemmer*
41 **lymphoma** *Lymphdrüsenkrebs*

Unless you live in Europe, your last meal probably contained genetically modified ingredients – 80 per cent of soya grown worldwide is now genetically engineered, for instance. Yet while modified plants are rapidly taking over the planet's farms, the same cannot be said for GM animals. [...]

The main reason is that the genetic engineering of animals – with the exception of mice – has been a slow, tedious process needing a lot of money and not a little luck. Behind the scenes, though, a quiet revolution has been taking place. Thanks to a set of new tricks and tools, modifying animals is becoming a lot easier and more precise. That is not only going to transform research, it could also transform the meat and eggs you eat and the milk you drink. The first transgenic animals were produced by injecting DNA into eggs, implanting the eggs in animals and then waiting weeks or months to see if any offspring had incorporated the extra DNA. Often fewer than 1 in 100 had, making this a long, expensive process. [...]

In mice, geneticists found a way round this problem: producing cells with the desired modification first, before growing entire animals. [...] At the same time, biologists have developed more efficient ways of adding DNA to cells, by hijacking natural genetic engineers such as viruses, and jumping genes capable of 'copying and pasting' themselves. All these advances mean the effort and cost needed to produce GM animals has decreased a hundredfold. [...] The ability to easily and precisely modify animals will undoubtedly lead to huge pay-offs in research and medicine. [...]

Genetically modified farm animals could provide us with more nutritious meat, milk and eggs, while causing fewer pollution problems and perhaps suffering less too. Pigs whose muscles are enriched with omega-3s have already been created, and researchers are exploring similar options with milk. [...]

Genetic engineering is now a standard technique in the production of many protein-based drugs. Human insulin, for example, has long been produced by cultures of bacteria carrying the human insulin gene. Pharmaceutical companies are eager to turn animals into drug factories, too. That's because animal cells alter many of their proteins by tacking on sugars and other 'decorations', an extra step that bacteria cannot perform. As a result, many proteins – most importantly, antibodies – work much better if they are made in animal cells.

One such animal-produced protein has already been approved for clinical use by the US Food and Drug Administration. An anticoagulant called antithrombin III is purified from the milk of genetically engineered goats created by GTC Biotherapeutics, a biotech company in Framingham, Massachusetts. Many others are under development. [...] Open Monoclonal Technology of Palo Alto, California, has engineered rats to produce human antibodies. Its first product, an anti-cancer antibody for treating lymphoma, should be in clinical trials within two to three years.

From: 'Altered animals: creatures with bonus features', *The New Scientist*, 14 July 2010

The Genetic Engineering Debate

1 Animal rights

FOUR-CORNERS ACTIVITY Read the four statements displayed in four corners of your classroom, then stand next to the one you can identify with most. Discuss with the others in your corner why you chose it.

1 Through breeding and selection humans have always changed domestic animals. Gene pharming is basically no different.
2 The genetic engineering of animals should be forbidden as it violates animal rights and is potentially harmful to the animal.
3 Gene pharming is acceptable if it reduces severe human suffering.
4 Animals with human DNA should be entitled for special rights.

READING FOCUS ON SKILLS

Using reading strategies (scientific text)

Scientific texts are challenging both in terms of content and language. The tips below can help you to get a detailed and thorough understanding of such texts.

1 Understanding the gist

Skim the text quickly to get a basic understanding of what the text is about. The first sentence of a paragraph is usually the topic sentence that states the main idea of the paragraph. Summarize to a partner what you think the text is about.

2 Reducing the complexity of the text

Focus on the most relevant pieces of information only. Often it is not necessary to understand a sentence or paragraph word for word.
a Add headlines to the paragraphs to mark what they are about in general.
b The second and the third paragraphs deal with the advancements made in changing the genetic makeup of animals. In order to understand what these are, identify words that describe the development so that you will be able to explain it. (Hint: you can ignore technical details.)

3 Dealing with hard words

a Scientific texts are full of technical terms. Often they are of Latin or Greek origin and are similar to German words, e.g. precise (*präzise*) in l. 8. Find more examples in the text and explain their meaning.
b Scientific texts aim for accuracy. They use *formal instead of *informal style. Use the context to find the equivalent of these words in the text:

---
change · put sth. into sth. · include sth. · being able · go down · offer / make available · do · accept · make cleaner · create/design

---

c Often the meaning becomes clear when you look at the word family, e.g. *purify* (v) – *pure* (adj). Now use this strategy to find the meaning of *engineer* (l. 2), *nutritious* (l. 22) and *enrich* (l. 24).

4 Relating information

It is helpful to draw diagrams or flowcharts in order to understand processes. Try to draw a simple diagram or flowchart to illustrate the process of creating a transgenic animal as described in the second paragraph.

Science – Enhancing Life? Chapter 2

2 Part B

Modifying mankind

B1 A brain-enhancing pill

📀 DVD

Watch the short *news report on the use of Modafinil.

◂ COMPREHENSION

1 Understanding the effects of a neuro-enhancing drug
Describe the positive and negative effects of the neuro-enhancing pill as mentioned in the video. Explain why the drug is popular despite the risks that come with it.

2 Mediation (English ➔ German)
A fellow student of yours believes that it's possible to get such a drug without a prescription. Tell him or her (in German) what you have found out.

◂ ANALYSIS

3 Examining the tone
Choose adjectives from the list below to describe the *tone of the report. Provide evidence for your opinion from the news report.

objective • neutral • biased • sensational • critical • exaggerated

◂ BEYOND THE TEXT

4 What if there were 'smart pills'?
a SILENT WRITING DISCUSSION Get together in groups of four. Each of you write at the top of a piece of paper the question below and answer it. Then pass the paper on to the student to your right. Add your answer to the next question on the paper you receive. Continue until every student has the paper again that he or she started with.

Student A:	Student B:
Imagine there were pills that could really make people smarter. Should those pills be given to everyone for free?	Imagine there were pills that could really make people smarter. If people took such pills before an exam, would you consider it to be cheating?

Student C:	Student D:
Imagine there were pills that could really make people smarter. Should parents be allowed to give such pills to school-age children?	Imagine there were pills that could really make people smarter. Would taking such pills to enhance your brain power be any different from drinking coffee or energy drinks, taking vitamins or going for a run?

b Now read the responses and sum up the comments for your group members. Discuss the impact of neuroenhancers on society and recommend how society should deal with them.

Modifying Mankind 2

B2 Gene doping   *Tim Franks*

It seems the fight against doping in sport is an ever-losing battle. The text below points out how genetic engineering may make the fight for a clean sport even harder.
Before reading the text, speculate about the connection between genetic engineering and doping, then skim the article and check whether your guess was correct.

This could be a battle like no other in sport. The authorities are so concerned, they have been preparing for it for more than 10 years. But it is still unclear whether they have the tools to test for it – or whether anyone has done it successfully. It is gene doping. The idea is simple: to alter our genetic makeup, the very building blocks of
5 who we are, in order to make us stronger or faster. The practicalities are highly complex.

Gene therapists – for example those treating very sick children at London's Great Ormond Street hospital – add a synthetic gene to the patient's genome, and reintroduce it into the bone marrow via a disabled virus. The new gene is expressed by the
10 patient's cells and acts like a medicine, permanently incorporated in the bone marrow. [...]

Dr Philippe Moullier [...] had shown it was possible to produce artificially one particular gene – the erythropoietin gene – and introduce it into the body. And as anyone who had
15 a vague brush with professional cycling in the 90s knows, the hormone erythropoietin, or EPO – which controls the production of red blood cells – was the illicit dope of choice for competitors. It was the wonder drug Lance Armstrong kept in his fridge, to boost his oxygen-carrying red-blood-cell
20 count.

But while injected EPO has been detectable for years, introducing the EPO gene would result in the body producing its own EPO. Could this be an undetectable way of improving oxygen delivery? [...]

25 And while making a permanent change to the genome may be complex – using a disabled virus to carry the genetic medicine to the cells – Philippe Moullier says there is now a shortcut, which delivers temporary results: injecting the purified gene directly into your muscle. [...]

Even better for the would-be doper, says Moullier, this type of temporary boost may,
30 after a few days, be hard for the authorities to detect. So what is the World Anti-Doping Agency (Wada) doing about it?

Back in 2003, Wada banned gene doping. The agency argues that the practice would not just be unfair, it could be lethal – introducing an extra copy of the EPO gene into your body could lead to too many red blood cells being produced and your blood thick-
35 ening into sludge [...]

But there is a deeper question. Even if there were to be or already is a legally and biologically fireproof test for gene doping, what should happen if gene therapy were to become much more widespread, even routine? What if we were all able to buy, over the counter, genetic medicine to slow muscle deterioration? Should we – could we –
40 stop athletes from using the medicine, to prolong their careers or speed a return from injury?

From: 'Gene Doping: Sport's biggest battle', the website of the BBC, 12 January 2014

9 **express** cause (a gene) to manifest its effects in other cells
10 **bone marrow** *Knochenmark*
12 **Philippe Moullier** French doctor who first showed the possibilities of gene therapy
15 **brush** occasion when you have contact with or experience sth.
19 **boost sth.** make sth. more powerful
35 **sludge** thick, soft, wet substance
39 **deterioration** *Verschlechterung*
40 **prolong sth.** make sth. last longer

Science – Enhancing Life?   Chapter 2   43

2 Part B

The hormone erythropoietin became the illicit dope of choice for competitors in the Tour de France, bringing the competition into disrepute.

▶ SF 31: Writing a summary

COMPREHENSION

1 Getting the facts straight
Use the words below to summarize what the article is about. Include a definition of the term gene doping.

> authorities • synthetic gene • erythropoietin or EPO • red blood cells • cycling • undetectable • injection • purified gene • lethal • ethical issue • genetic medicine

ANALYSIS

2 Examining the tone
Identify how the writer's use of language reveals his attitude to the topic.
SUPPORT ▶ p. 203

LANGUAGE AWARENESS

3 Speculating about effects and consequences
Gene doping is a new technology that is not yet in use but that could become important quite soon. That is why the article contains many speculations about its possible consequences.
   a Conditional sentences type I or II are used to speculate about the future. Identify the conditional sentences in the text. Say why the writer uses this particular type here.
   b Collect examples of modal auxiliaries used in the text to express probability or possibility. Compare their use with the use of the conditional sentences.

▶ LP 8: Conditional sentences

BEYOND THE TEXT

4 Discussing doping in sports
   a Collect arguments in favour of or against allowing doping in professional sports.
   b **CHALLENGE** ▶ Debate the motion 'This house believes the ban on doping should be lifted'. Before debating, search the internet for arguments for your position in the debate. Then meet with your partners and work out a strategy how to convince the house to adopt your position. Make sure you anticipate your opponent's arguments and be prepared to counter them.

▶ SF 28: Having a debate

44   Chapter 2   Science – Enhancing Life?

Modifying Mankind

B3 Transhumanism *Zoltan Istvan*

The following text deals with the possibilties of transhumanist technology. Speculate what transhumanist technology means.

As long as they're earthbound, most people shrug off the idea of being anything other than a biological human. Some people are even repulsed or angered by the concept of scientifically tampering with the human body and brain too much. However, the time is coming when radical technology will allow us to expand and significantly
5 improve the abilities of our minds and the forms of our bodies. A transhumanist age is nearly upon the human race – an age where cyborgs, sentient robots, virtual lives based in computers and dramatically altered human beings may become commonplace.

Already, there are hundreds of universities, laboratories and companies around the
10 world where transhumanist projects are underway. A transhumanist is a person who aims to move beyond the human being via science and technology. Some of the most eye-opening projects are military-oriented, such as the 'Iron Man' armor suit being created for American soldiers. Trial runs of the suit are tentatively scheduled for this summer. Another well-known project
15 is at Chalmers University of Technology in Sweden where scientists are connecting robotic limbs to the human nervous system of amputees, essentially creating cyborg-like people. The first arm surgeries are scheduled to occur in less than 12 months. Of course, private companies like Google are also
20 very much involved in the broad field of transhumanism. They are spending many millions of dollars on creating artificial intelligence, which one day may have its own sentience and be thousands of times smarter than humans. [...]

Even though some of these technologies seem frightening
25 to the layperson, they should be here in a matter of years, not decades. One of the most exciting and controversial ideas of transhumanism is the complete integration of the human mind with a machine. Similar to the extraordinary technology featured in the movie *The Matrix*, humans may be able to download themselves into computers and live virtual existences.

From: 'Despite Skepticism, Many People May Embrace Radical Transhumanist Technology in the Future', *The Huffington Post*, 18 February 2014

1 **shrug sth. off** treat sth. as if it is not important
2 **repulse sb.** make sb. feel strong disgust
3 **tamper with sth.** make changes to sth. when one should not
6 **sentient** able to feel or see things through the senses
13 **trial run** a test of sth. to see how well it performs
    tentative not certain or definite
25 **layperson** person who is not an expert in a particular field

An army veteran gives a thumbs up with a prosthetic arm.

2 Part B

COMPREHENSION

1 **Transhumanism defined**
   a Define the term transhumanism.
   b List examples from the text of transhumanist technology that seeks to improve the human condition.
   c Match them to the categories given in the chart below. (Hint: there are more categories than examples.)

A augmenting	adding removable attachments that boosts capabilities
B boosting	enhancing capabilities and improving intelligence
C embellishing	changing an external part of a human for decorative purpose
D replacing	permanently replacing an organ or limb
E adding	integrating something additional into the human form
F altering	changing the actual biological structure of a human
G redefining	changing a human so much that the person is no longer recognisable as a human

   d **CHALLENGE** Match the examples below with the categories from **1c**.

   modified DNA • bionic legs • a piercing or tattoo • plastic surgery • consciousness upload • a brain chip • caffeine or steroids • google glasses

ANALYSIS

2 **YOU CHOOSE** New methods or new terms

   a Explain how the examples given in the text differ from popular enhancement techniques such as exercising or surgery.

   OR

   b Innovative new technologies require new words or new combinations of words to label them, e.g. the term *internet* first appeared in 1974. Such newly coined words are called neologisms. Collect examples of neologisms from the text and with the help of a dictionary check their origin.

BEYOND THE TEXT

3 **Using transhuman technologies**
   a List the transhuman technologies you would embrace, and the ones you would reject. Explain your reasons, and then discuss your views with a partner.
   b **CHALLENGE** Working out the ethics
   Use the guidelines from the Fact File (cf. p. 36) to formulate some ethical guidelines for using transhumanist technologies.

FACT FILE

Neologism
A word coined from the Greek terms:
neo = new
logos = speech, utterance

---

46 Chapter 2 Science – Enhancing Life?

Part C 2

Quenching the thirst for energy

C1 The global demand for energy

With an ever-increasing world population and the economic progress of emerging nations, the global demand for energy poses a challenge that includes environmental, political and technological aspects.

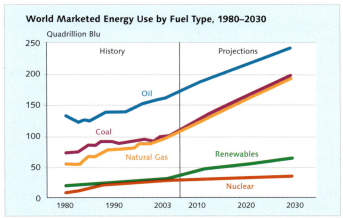

From: US Energy Information Administration, 2006

▶ SF 12: Analysing charts and graphs

──────────── COMPREHENSION ◀

1 Understanding graphs
Study the graphs and state what information they give about future trends of energy consumption. ▶ LANGUAGE HELP

──────────── BEYOND THE TEXT ◀

2 Thinking about future trends
  a In small groups discuss the positive or negative consequences these trends might have.
  b Suggest ways how to tackle the problematic aspects that these trends could cause.

LANGUAGE HELP
- The bar chart/line graph is about .../deals with ...
- The chart gives/compares/explains ...
- The size/the number of ...
- The number of ... has increased sharply/significantly
- Whereas in 2005 ...
- In comparison with .../Compared to ...

Science – Enhancing Life? Chapter 2 47

Part C

C2 The future of energy in Germany

You are taking part in an international youth conference about how different countries are reacting to environmental awareness. The conference intends to set up a website for young people dedicated to showing recent changes in global energy policies. You are to present the German 'Energiewende' in a text of about 200 words, explaining the German position and the aims of the 'Energiewende'. While searching for information you have come across the following text. Skim the text in order to get the gist of what it is about.

Die Energiewende ist der Kurzbegriff für eine fundamentale Wende in der Energieversorgung: Das bisherige Energiesystem, das auf Kernenergie, Kohle, Öl und Gas beruht, wird abgelöst von einer neuen Energieversorgung auf Basis Erneuerbarer Energie (EE) – Windkraft, Sonnenenergie, Wasserkraft, Biomasse und Erdwärme. Die wesentlichen Gründe für diese Wende in der Energieversorgung sind:

- Risikovorsorge: Die Risiken der Kernenergie sind prinzipiell nicht beherrschbar. Dies haben die Reaktorkatastrophen in Tschernobyl und Fukushima gezeigt. Zudem ist der hochradioaktive Abfall aus Kernkraftwerken für Hunderttausende von Jahren äußerst giftig, ohne dass bisher eine Lösung für die Endlagerung gefunden wäre.
- Klimaschutz: Bei der Verbrennung von Kohle, Öl und Gas entstehen klimaschädliche Treibhausgasemissionen, die die Hauptverursacher für den Klimawandel sind.
- Knappe Ressourcen: Kohle, Öl und Gas sind endlich. Je knapper sie werden, desto teurer wird ein auf fossile Energieträger basierendes Energiesystem.
- Wertschöpfung vor Ort: Während ein großer Teil der bisherigen Energieträger (insbesondere Öl, Gas, Uran und Steinkohle) importiert wird, sind die Erneuerbaren Energien heimische Energien, die somit die Wertschöpfung vor Ort erhöhen und die Importabhängigkeit reduzieren.

Die Frage der Energieversorgung war lange ein zentraler politischer Streitpunkt – insbesondere die Nutzung der Kernenergie war über Jahrzehnte Gegenstand heftiger Auseinandersetzungen. Seit den Beschlüssen des Bundestages vom Juni 2011 existiert in Deutschland jedoch ein parteiübergreifender Konsens, dass der Weg der Energiewende beschritten werden soll. So sind sowohl der Ausstieg aus der Kernenergie bis zum Jahr 2022 als auch konkrete Ziele für den Ausbau der Erneuerbaren Energien im Strombereich gesetzlich festgeschrieben. [...]

Was sind die zentralen Themen und Herausforderungen?

Stromerzeugung und -verbrauch haben eine besondere Bedeutung für die Energiewende, da die Erneuerbaren Energien hier die riskanten beziehungsweise CO_2-intensiven Energieträger Kernenergie, Braun- und Steinkohle ersetzen müssen. Zudem werden mittelfristig immer größere Anteile des Wärme- und Verkehrsbedarfs durch Strom bereitgestellt werden. Die Energiewende-Ziele im Stromsektor lauten:

- Erneuerbare Energien: mindestens 80 Prozent Anteil Erneuerbarer Energien an der Stromversorgung bis spätestens 2050 mit den Zwischenzielen von 40 Prozent bis 2025 und 55 bis 60 Prozent bis 2035.
- Energieeffizienz: Reduktion des Stromverbrauchs um 10 Prozent bis 2020 und 25 Prozent bis 2050 gegenüber dem Niveau von 2008.

From: the website of agora-energiewende, 2014

Quenching the Thirst for Energy

2

MEDIATION FOCUS ON SKILLS

Mediating written texts

When mediating a text from one language into another, you always have to take into consideration the following aspects.

1 Content: What information do you want to get across?
Remember that when you are mediating, the final text is always shorter than the original text, as you are only mediating the important or necessary information. Read the task again. What do you have to focus on? How do you find out what is important in the text? Look at the statements below. Which are correct and which are incorrect?

> a I have to summarize all the information in the text.
> b I need to include the dates by which time goals must be met.
> c I have to explain why the *Energiewende* took place.
> d I can show what the aims are by also explaining what Germany intends to stop doing.
> e I need to discuss why it will be a challenge to meet the aims.
> f I need to discuss the political background.
> g I need to point out the future goals of the German energy policy.

2 Recipient: Who are you mediating for?
Decide who you mediating for, and in which medium. Are you writing for people who speak English well? Are they experts on the matter?

3 Language: What style of language should you use?

▶ LP 11: Using the right register

After deciding who your audience is, consider how this may affect the style and structure of your text. Is the style of the original text formal or informal? Should it be retained in your text? What about the vocabulary?
In the text there are many words which you don't know in English. Try to translate or explain the following terms in English: *Erdwärme, Biomasse, Treibhausgas, Wasserkraft.* Check your results with a dictionary afterwards.
For your audience, how might it best to mediate theses terms?
Are there any structural features (e.g. bullet points, boxes, headlines) that you need in your text?

4 Intercultural aspects: Which aspects of the text might be hard to understand for people from a different culture?
Sometimes you have to explain things that are easy for you to understand but hard for other people, because they are specific to your culture. Think of the term *Energiewende*. How might you deal with a term like that if somebody has no idea what it is? Find other aspects in the text that would have to be adapted, stressed or explained, e.g. when mediating for a Japanese, African or Scottish person.

5 Write your text.

6 Peer Assessment
In groups of four evaluate your texts using the evaluation sheet your teacher will give you.

Science – Enhancing Life?   Chapter 2

2   Part C

▶ SF22: Listening

Raymond Kurzweiler

■ FACT FILE

Biofuels are a type of energy derived from renewable plant and animal materials. Approximately 100 billion litres of biofuel are produced each year. Biofuels provide about 3% of the world's fuels for road transport.

▶ DVD
▶ SF23: Analysing a film

▶ SF5: Doing research
▶ SF28: Having a debate

C3   A possible future

— COMPREHENSION ◀

1 Understanding an expert's perspective
Listen to the following interview with Raymond Kurzweiler, an expert on technology and say which of the following statements he said and which he did not.
1 Fossil fuels should be taxed to reflect the true cost they have on the environment.
2 Wind energy will be the most used renewable energy.
3 Within 14 years 100% of our energy needs will come from renewable sources.
4 Governments are unable to aid the change to renewable energies.

— BEYOND THE TEXT ◀

2 Examining predictions
a The interview was made in 2008. Discuss to what extent Kurzweiler's predictions have come true.
b Discuss how relevant his perspective is today.

C4   Biofuels – the green alternative?

The European Union has committed itself to producing 10% of its energy from renewable sources of energy by 2020. One way of achieving this goal is through the use of biofuels. This concept has been met with both approval and rejection.

— COMPREHENSION ◀

1 Arguments for and against
Watch the two video clips about biofuels and note down arguments for and against biofuels.

— ANALYSIS ◀

2 Comparing films
a Explain which one you found more convincing.
b Examine how the use of music, light, film techniques and the voiceover contributed to the ideas in the one you found most convincing.

— BEYOND THE TEXT ◀

3 Conducting a debate
In two groups find arguments in favour of and against biofuels. The motion could be as follows: 'Governments should subsidize biofuels'.
SUPPORT ▶ p. 203

'No you can't turn your vegetables into bio-fuel.'

50   Chapter 2   Science – Enhancing Life?

Chapter Task

Doing a WebQuest

Read the problem below and state spontaneously whether you would shop in that supermarket. Say why or why not. Do a quick opinion poll to find out what the class thinks about this issue. Repeat the poll after you have completed the chapter task.

The Problem
The supermarket in your hometown has announced that they are considering stocking genetically modified foods. The public is concerned about this decision and some people form a Committee of Concerned Citizens.

In order to decide how to react, the Committee of Concerned Citizens (CCC) decides to consult some experts. These experts are a scientist, a farmer, an environmentalist and a nutritionist.

Your task as a group is to become familiar with the issues surrounding genetically-modified foods. You will take on the roles of those experts and will make recommendations based upon your research. These recommendations must answer the following question:

The Big Question
Should your local supermarket stock products containing genetically-modified foods?

Steps
1. Your teacher will give you a handout. Do the WebQuest as shown in the handout.
2. Present your results to the Committee of Concerned Citizens.
3. Have a vote on the issue.
4. Evaluate the WebQuest with the assessment sheet your teacher will give you.

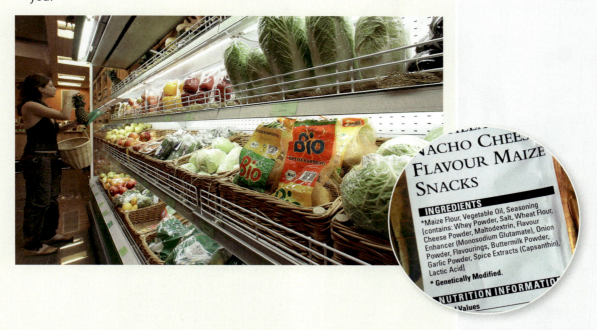

Science – Enhancing Life?   Chapter 2

3 Living One's Life – Individuals in Society

A

B

C

D

E

F

Chapter 3 Living One's Life – Individuals in Society

Lead-in

> It is only to the individual that a soul is given.
> **ALBERT EINSTEIN**

> Be the change you wish to see in the world.
> **MAHATMA GANDHI**

> Remember always that you not only have the right to be an individual, you have an obligation to be one.
> **ELEANOR ROOSEVELT**

> A hero is an ordinary individual who finds the strength to persevere and endure in spite of overwhelming obstacles.
> **CHRISTOPHER REEVE**

> Don't be afraid to fail. Be afraid not to try.
> **MICHAEL JORDAN**

> Ask not what your country can do for you – ask what you can do for your country.
> **JOHN F. KENNEDY**

> True individual freedom cannot exist without economic security and independence. People who are hungry and out of a job are the stuff of which dictatorships are made.
> **FRANKLIN D. ROOSEVELT**

> There is no such thing as society: there are individual men and women, and there are families.
> **MARGARET THATCHER**

> You grown ups say you love us, but I challenge you, please make your actions reflect your words.
> **SEVERN SUZUKI**

1 The Individual and Society
   a Describe one of the pictures and note down what words, phrases and concepts come to mind when you look at it. Make a list or mind map.
   b Now read the quotations. Comment on the one that speaks to you most.
   c Match one quotation and one illustration. Explain your decision.

2 Famous individuals
   a Work in groups of four. Each group picks one of the people who said the quotes. Do some research on their lives and find out what they did for society.
   b Present your findings to other groups.

Download a chronological word list here:
 Webcode context-00

▶ SF 11: Analysing pictures

▶ SF 5: Doing research

PREVIEW

In this chapter you will reflect on your own role in society, consider how people view each other, and discuss ideas for getting involved in society and making a difference.

Main topics
- Identity and goals .... p. 56
- Stereotypes and prejudice .... p. 61
- Getting involved and making a difference ... p. 66

Focus on Skills: SPEAKING
- Resolving a heated argument .... p. 64

Chapter Task: Making a vlog about your own aims and ambitions or about an issue that matters to you .... p. 71

Living One's Life – Individuals in Society   Chapter 3

3

Words in Context

CD1 06
Listen to an audio version of the text on the CD or download it here:
Webcode context-00

Young people in a multi-faceted society

A generation full of hope
Today's young generation has lots of ideas about how to improve our world. Young people are often full of hope and creativity and have an incredible energy. They are not afraid to try something new, to get involved in big issues and to fight for what they want or believe in. They take part in demonstrations against war and discrimination and for equality and education. They use the internet as a means of communication as well as for political purposes. Many young people commit themselves to improving their communities and to making a difference to our world. They volunteer or work for charities, often helping people on the fringes of society like the disabled and homeless or collecting money for victims of natural disasters throughout the world. Today's teens are able to stand up for their beliefs and basic rights, and are smart and strong enough to shape the future of society for the better.

The media and youngsters
Nevertheless, at the same time, the media often paint a grim picture of the younger generation, appealing to stereotypes of young anti-social trouble-makers. They are depicted as individuals who indulge in criminality, or who are obsessed by selfies and their self-image, or they may be depicted as alienated and socially impaired computer nerds with no time for real interaction with others. Age-based prejudice distorts the reality of the generation that will deal with the problems the older generation leaves behind.

Finding one's identity
Just like other generations, today's teens are not a uniform group. They do not all share a collective identity or share common experiences. Our individual character and our social background influence our identity. Family, education, culture and religion all have an influence on our moral values, attitudes and habits. Our sense of identity accounts for how we perceive ourselves and also how we are perceived and positioned by others. Our identities do not just determine our personal style but affect the opportunities we are given and the access we have to power, status, education and wealth. Like generations before them, young people must find out who they are and who they want to be in a diverse and ever-changing society. Unlike other generations, young people today have access to an immense variety of individual lifestyles. This opens up new possibilities for them to choose and construct their own identities, but it can also lead to conflicts and divided loyalties.

An unknown future
Living in a 'me-first' society and globalized world, young people are going to face big challenges in the future. Social inequality and unemployment, political instability and terrorism as well as environmental problems are just some of the pressing issues they will have to deal with. At the same time, the world is getting closer. With communication increasing, young people from different countries may be able to find creative solutions together to the most urgent problems.

54 Chapter 3 Living One's Life – Individuals in Society

Young people in a multi-faceted society

1 Definitions
Match the definitions below to highlighted words and phrases from the text.
1 engage in
2 way of interacting with other people
3 speak or act in support of
4 constantly changing or developing
5 thinking only of yourself
6 important topics requiring immediate attention or action.

2 Word formation and word families
Find the missing word. Use a dictionary if necessary.

verb	noun	adjective
improve		
volunteer		
	belief	
shape		
	stereotype	
		alienated
		moral
perceive		
	access	

▶ LP 24: Word formation

3 Words in use
a Complete each sentence with a verb from the grid.
1 Young people are often … as troublemakers.
2 Our identities are … by the people around us.
3 Young people are concerned about how society … and … them.
4 Many young people … family and friendship over having lots of money.

b **CHALLENGE** Activate your vocabulary
Translate the following sentences. Pay special attention to the underlined expressions, which are highlighted in the text.
1 Die großen Herausforderungen unserer vielschichtigen Welt erfordern kreative Lösungen und vor allem engagierte Individuen.
2 Viele junge Leute sind heute bereit, sich einzubringen und sich für die Verbesserung der Lebensbedingungen von Menschen in den unterschiedlichen Teilen der Erde einzusetzen.
3 Unsere Werte, Einstellungen und Gewohnheiten werden maßgeblich von unserer sozialen Herkunft geprägt.
4 Häufig wird die Wahrnehmung anderer Menschen beeinflusst durch Stereotypen Sichtweisen und Vorurteile, die das soziale Miteinander belasten.

▶ LP 18: Avoiding Germanisms
▶ LP 21: Choosing the right translation

4 Writing
Outline how you as a young person see your own generation and what you think are the greatest challenges your generation has to face. Write a short essay.

▶ SF 38: Writing a well-structured text

Part A

Future success

A1 What is a role model? Marilyn Price-Mitchell

The excerpt below is taken from a web article about a research study on how young people develop into engaged citizens. American teenagers were asked about their role models and the qualities role models have.

Before reading the excerpt, do a placemat activity based around the question: 'Who is your role model or – if you do not have one – who could be a role model to others, and why?'

Role models come into young people's lives in a variety of ways. They are educators, civic leaders, mothers, fathers, clergy, peers, and ordinary people encountered in everyday life. This study showed that being a role model is not constrained to those with fancy titles or personal wealth. [...]

Role models show passion for their work and have the capacity to infect others with their passion. [...] Role models live their values in the world. Children admire people who act in ways that support their beliefs. It helps them understand how their own values are part of who they are and how they might seek fulfilling roles as adults. [...] Role models are *other-focused* as opposed to *self-focused*. They are usually active in their communities, freely giving of their time and talents to benefit people.

Students admired people who served on local boards, reached out to neighbors in need, voted, and were active members of community organizations. Related to the idea that role models show a commitment to their communities, students also admired people for their selflessness and acceptance of others who were different from them. [...]

As Booker T. Washington [who was born into slavery and later became advisor of US presidents] once said, 'Success is to be measured not so much by the position that one has reached in life as by the obstacles which one has overcome.' Young people echoed this sentiment, showing how they developed the skills and abilities of initiative when they learned to overcome obstacles.

From: the website of Roots of Action, 2013

4 **fancy** that sounds good
16 **Booker T. Washington** (1856–1915) African-American campaigner
18 **obstacle** sth. that blocks sb.'s way
19 **echo sth.** *(here)* share sth.

→ COMPREHENSION ◀

1 Examining role models
  a Describe the qualities of role models that matter to American teens.
  b Compare these qualities with your own lists on the placemats and discuss with your group whether you agree with the American teens.

→ LANGUAGE AWARENESS ◀

2 The language of definition
  a Look at ll. 1–10 and examine what methods the writer uses to define the term 'role model'.
  b Write a similar definition of the word 'idol'. Check the difference between 'idol' and 'role model' in a dictionary first, and illustrate this in the way you use language to define it.

→ BEYOND THE TEXT ◀

3 People as models
  In groups of four, discuss the following statement by American linguist, philosopher and activist Noam Chomsky: 'I do not feel that we should set up people as "models"; rather actions, thoughts, principles.'

---

56   Chapter 3   Living One's Life – Individuals in Society

Future success

A2 Successful children *Amy Chua*

With a partner, discuss what your aims in life are, where these aims come from, who supports you on your way, and what helps you to achieve your aims.

Amy Chua, a professor of law at Yale University, is the child of Chinese immigrants and is herself the mother of two daughters. In her book *Battle Hymn of the Tiger Mother* she describes her strict parenting techniques, which she thinks make children successful.

A lot of people wonder how Chinese parents raise such stereotypically successful kids. They wonder what these parents do to produce so many math whizzes and music
5 prodigies, what it's like inside the family, and whether they could do it too. Well, I can tell them, because I've done it. Here are some things my daughters, Sophia and Louisa, were never allowed to do:

10 • attend a sleepover
• have a playdate
• be in a school play
• complain about not being in a school play
• watch TV or play Computer games
15 • choose their own extracurricular activities
• get any grade less than an A
• not be the #1 student in every subject except gym and drama
• play any instrument other than the piano
20   or violin
• not play the piano or violin.

Amy Chua and her daughters

I'm using the term 'Chinese mother' loosely. I recently met a supersuccessful white guy from South Dakota (you've seen him on television), and after comparing notes we decided that his working-class father had definitely been a Chinese mother. I know
25 some Korean, Indian, Jamaican, Irish, and Ghanaian parents who qualify too. Conversely, I know some mothers of Chinese heritage, almost always born in the West, who are not Chinese mothers, by choice or otherwise. [...]

What Chinese parents understand is that nothing is fun until you're good at it. To get good at anything you have to work, and children on their own never want to work,
30 which is why it is crucial to override their preferences. This often requires fortitude on the part of the parents because the child will resist; things are always hardest at the beginning, which is where Western parents tend to give up. But if done properly, the Chinese strategy produces a virtuous circle. Tenacious practice, practice, practice is crucial for excellence; rote repetition is underrated in America. Once a child starts to
35 excel at something – whether it's math, piano, pitching, or ballet – he or she gets praise, admiration, and satisfaction. This builds confidence and makes the once not-fun activity turn. This in turn makes it easier for the parent to get the child to work even more. [...]

I think there are three big differences between the Chinese and Western parental
40 mind-sets.

4 **whizz** *(infml)* person who is very good at sth.
30 **override sth.** reject; to cancel
fortitude strength of mind
33 **tenacious** not giving up; persistent
34 **rote repetition** learn sth. by repeating it continually
35 **pitching** *(in baseball)* throwing the ball at the batter

3 Part A

43 **notwithstanding** in spite of
44 **mediocre** [ˌmiːdiˈeʊkə] average
46 **fragility** weakness
56 **excoriate sb.** (fml) criticize sb. severely
65 **foist sth. on sb.** force sth. on sb.

First, I've noticed that Western parents are extremely anxious about their children's self-esteem. They worry about how their children will feel if they fail at something, and they constantly try to reassure their children about how good they are notwithstanding a mediocre performance on a test or at a recital. In other words, Western parents are concerned about their children's psyches. Chinese parents aren't. They 45 assume strength, not fragility, and as a result they behave very differently.

For example, if a child comes home with an A-minus on a test, a Western parent will most likely praise the child. The Chinese mother will gasp in horror and ask what went wrong. If the child comes home with a B on the test, some Western parents will still praise the child. [...] If a Chinese child gets a B – which would never happen – 50 there would first be a screaming, hair-tearing explosion. The devastated Chinese mother would then get dozens, maybe hundreds of practice tests and work through them with her child for as long as it takes to get the grade up to an A. Chinese parents demand perfect grades because they believe that their child can get them. If their child doesn't get them, the Chinese parent assumes it's because the child didn't work hard 55 enough. That's why the solution to substandard performance is always to excoriate, punish, and shame the child. The Chinese parent believes that their child will be strong enough to take the shaming and to improve from it. [...]

Second, Chinese parents believe that their kids owe them everything. [...] Anyway, the understanding is that Chinese children must spend their lives repaying their 60 parents by obeying them and making them proud. By contrast, I don't think most Westerners have the same view of children being permanently indebted to their parents. Jed [Amy Chua's husband] actually has the opposite view. 'Children don't choose their parents,' he once said to me. 'They don't even choose to be born. It's parents who foist life on their kids, so it's the parents' responsibility to provide for 65 them. Kids don't owe their parents anything. Their duty will be to their own kids.' This strikes me as a terrible deal for the Western parent.

Third, Chinese parents believe that they know what is best for their children and therefore override all of their children's own desires and preferences. That's why Chinese daughters can't have boyfriends in high school and why Chinese kids can't 70 go to sleepaway camp. It's also why no Chinese kid would ever dare say to their mother, 'I got a part in the school play! I'm Villager Number Six. I'll have to stay after school for rehearsal every day from 3:00 to 7:00, and I'll also need a ride on weekends.' God help any Chinese kid who tried that one.

Don't get me wrong: It's not that Chinese parents don't care about their children. 75 Just the opposite. They would give up anything for their children. It's just an entirely different parenting model I think of it as Chinese, but I know a lot of non-Chinese parents – usually from Korea, India, or Pakistan – who have a very similar mind-set, so it may be an immigrant thing. Or maybe it's the combination of being an immigrant and being from certain cultures. 80

From: Amy Chua, *Battle Hymn of the Tiger Mother*, 2011

COMPREHENSION ◀

1 Examining parental styles
Describe the two contrasting parenting styles Chua refers to.

ANALYSIS ◀

2 Examining a book title.
Analyse the title of Chua's book and explain what it tells us about her parenting philosophy.

Chapter 3   Living One's Life – Individuals in Society

Future success

LANGUAGE AWARENESS

3 What if …?
  a Read ll. 47 to 57 and say which type of conditional is being used.
    SUPPORT ▶ p. 206
  b Write 3 conditional sentences, one of each type, based around ideas in the text, for example:
    - *If Sophia and Louisa come across this text, they will probably understand their mother better.*
    - *If Sophia were like her younger sister, she would rebel against her mother.*
    - *If Amy's parents had not been so strict, she would not have become a successful professor.*
  c Find another example of a conditional sentence in the text. Explain what it reveals.

▶ LP 8: Conditional sentences

BEYOND THE TEXT

4 YOU CHOOSE Examining statements

  a Choose one or more of Amy Chua's statements and comment on them from your own point of view.

  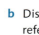

  b Discuss one of the following statements, referring to Chua:
    - Parents can never be friends with their children.
    - Strict parents create sneaky kids. (Banksy)
    - A child without discipline is, in a way, a lost child. (Ricardo Montalban)

▶ SF 34: Argumentative writing

5 Giving advice
  a Imagine that Chua's daughter, 17-year-old Louisa, is a friend of yours and rebels against her mother's strict parenting style. Discuss with a partner what advice you would give her. But try to see both sides.
  b Now write a longer email to Louisa, giving your advice. ▶ LANGUAGE HELP

6 A mother–daughter argument
  a Louisa refuses to obey her mother and they have an argument. Divide the class in two halves. One half prepares Louisa's arguments, the other half Amy's. You may take notes on little cue cards.
  b Pair up with another student from the other side and start your argument.
  c Tell the others in class about your argument. How did it come to an end? Could you solve the conflict? Why (not)?

> **LANGUAGE HELP**
> - If I were you, I'd …
> - The best thing to do is …
> - I don't think it's advisable to …
> - It might be better to …
> - You definitely should/ought to …
> - If you ask me, I would/wouldn't …

Part A

A3 Childhood – the 21st century Ernestine Northover

Before reading, name things that you remember about your childhood, and discuss whether they could have happened to children in earlier generations as well.

The following poem is by a British poet. In it she considers childhoods of the past and future.

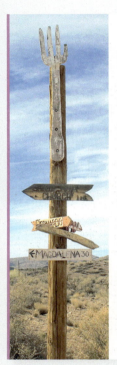

How advanced they are, these children of the future,
Like small adults, within their tiny frames,
They grow up in a fast 'speed driven' culture, 5
Where 'learning pressures' change their kind of games.
Where is their childhood, in all this hurly burly,
Where is their pure untainted view of things, 10
Why do they have to grow so old, so early,
And lose the joy that only childhood brings?

Our childhood was filled with thoughts of joy and gladness, 15
We lived our lives, oblivious to the world
And all the hardships, wars, the grief and sadness,
We stood, waiting for our lives to be unfurled. 20

We had time to grow, and gain an understanding,
Of each new phase, each change along the way,
As we grew slowly, our senses all expanding, 25
So with clarity, we slowly changed our play.

We had a framework on which to build and flourish,
Slow and steady, this was no rushed affair,
Taking each step, then step by step to nourish 30
Our childhood, so finally adulthood we would share.
What will become of these 'New Century' learners? 35
I doubt if they a dreamy childhood see.
Will they then tell to all those bright discerners
Of their own, how they remembered their childhood to be? 40

From: the website of poemhunter, 2005

▶ SF 21: Analysing poetry

=== COMPREHENSION ◀

1 The speaker
Describe the speaker's background.

2 Summarizing
Sum up the main idea expressed in the poem in one or two sentences.

=== ANALYSIS ◀

3 Formal elements
Analyse how the poem is structured (stanzas, rhyme scheme, rhythm) and what stylistic devices are used that contribute to the meaning.

4 Images
Examine the ideas used in the poem to refer to children now and in the speaker's past and explain their effect on you. SUPPORT ▶ p. 204

=== BEYOND THE TEXT ◀

5 YOU CHOOSE Another perspective

a Discuss to what extent you, having grown up in the 21st century, agree with the speaker's assessment. Include the results of your analysis of the speaker's own past in your discussion.

b Imagine you are Amy Chua (Text **A2**). Write a response to the poem as a comment you can upload on the internet site.

Chapter 3   Living One's Life – Individuals in Society

Part B 3

Them and us

B1 Stereotypes in Los Angeles *Paul Haggis*

The film *Crash* (2004) tells the interwoven stories of several individuals in Los Angeles and portrays the racial and social tensions between them.

Look at the film stills below and speculate about the characters, their personalities and the relationships between them. How might the lives of the two young men and the couple collide?

Scene 1: Ext.   Westwood – Night

Italian restaurant. Anthony flies out the door, Peter just one step behind him. They're in their early twenties, young, hip, well-dressed men, friends since third grade. They button their jackets as they head down the sidewalk.

5 ANTHONY   You see any white people in there waiting an hour and thirty-two minutes for a plate of spaghetti? Huh? And how many cups of coffee did we get?

   PETER   You don't drink coffee and I didn't want any.

   ANTHONY   That woman poured cup after cup to every single white person around
10 us. Did she even ask you if you wanted any?

   PETER   We didn't get any coffee that you didn't want and I didn't order, and this is evidence of racial discrimination? Did you happen to notice our waitress was black?

   ANTHONY   And black women don't think in stereotypes? When's the last time you
15 met one who didn't think she knew everything about your lazy ass before you even opened your mouth? That waitress sized us up in two seconds. We're black, and 'black people don't tip' so she wasn't gonna waste her time; someone like that, nothing you can do to change their mind.

20 PETER   So how much did you leave her?

   ANTHONY   You expect me to pay for that kinda service?

   Peter laughs; Anthony doesn't.

   ANTHONY   ... What? What?

   PETER   Nothing, nothing.

25 *Rick & Jean Cabot, white, early 40s, head for their car. Jean pulls her jacket closed as they walk.*

   RICK   You're seriously jealous of Karen??

1 **Ext.** exterior
   Westwood district of Los Angeles
16 **size sb. up** (infml) decide quickly what another person is like
21 **kinda** kind of

3 — Part B

FACT FILE

A **stereotype** is a fixed, over-generalized belief about a particular group of people. One advantage of a stereotype is that it enables us to respond quickly to situations because we may have had a similar experience before. One disadvantage is that it makes us ignore differences between individuals, so that we end up making simplistic generalizations about individuals or groups.

Prejudice is an unjustified or incorrect attitude that is usually negative towards an individual based solely on the individual's membership of a social group. For example, a person may hold prejudiced views towards a certain race or gender, etc.

Discrimination is negative behaviour or action towards an individual or group of people due to their sex/race/social class, etc.

Microaggressions are often unintended racist or sexist comments that make a person feel underestimated on the basis of their colour or gender.

38 **UCLA** (abbr) University of California, Los Angeles
43 **trigger-happy** who shoot people a lot
44 **LAPD** (abbr) Los Angeles Police Department
45 **Int.** interior
47 **locksmith** person who repairs locks (= Schlosser)
52 **pantry** small room next to a kitchen where food is stored
64 **patronize sb.** treat sb. like a child

JEAN	Hardly. I'd just like to see you get through a meal without calling her, or someone else at your office.	
RICK	See this? Off. No more calls tonight.	30

Jean notices Anthony and Peter and takes Rick's arm.

JEAN	Ten bucks says she calls on the car phone.	
ANTHONY	You see what that woman just did?	
PETER	She's cold.	
ANTHONY	She got colder as soon as she saw us.	35
PETER	Here it comes.	
ANTHONY	Look around! You couldn't find a whiter, safer or better-lit part of this city. But this white woman sees two black guys who look like UCLA students strolling down the sidewalk, and her reaction is blind fear. I mean, look at us. Are we dressed like gangbangers? Do we look threatening? No. Fact, if anybody should be scared around here, it's us: the only two black faces surrounded by a sea of over-caffeinated white people patrolled by the trigger-happy LAPD. So, why aren't *we* scared?	40

Scene 2: Int. Rick & Jean's Home – Night
45

Jean's feet descend the stairs to the expensive kitchen, where Daniel, the Hispanic locksmith, re-keys the door. He's twentyish, close-cropped hair, baggy pants, tattoos.

JEAN	How much longer are you going to be?	
DANIEL	This is the last door.	50
JEAN	Thanks.	

She exits, walking through the pantry into the dining room where several staff members work. She turns into the living room, where Rick and two aides work up strategy.

JEAN (interrupting)	I need to talk to you for a second.	55

She exits without waiting for a response. Rick turns to Karen, his top aide (young, black, brilliant).

RICK	Just find Flanagan.	

Karen dials as Rick exits to the [...] hall off the kitchen where Jean waits, arms crossed so tightly they're squeezing all the air out of her lungs.
60

JEAN	I want the locks changed again in the morning.	
RICK	Honey, why don't you go to bed? Did you check on James?	
JEAN	Of course I checked on James. I've checked on him every five minutes since we've been home, don't patronize me! I want the locks changed again in the morning!	65
RICK	Shhh, it's ok. You just need to lie down.	
JEAN	Didn't I just ask you no to treat me like a child? [...] I want the locks changed again in the morning. And you could mention that we'd appreciate it if next time they didn't send a gang member.	
RICK (lowering his voice)	You're talking about that kid in there?	70
JEAN	Shaved head, pants down around his ass, prison tattoos!	
RICK	Oh for Christ sakes, those aren't prison tattoos!	
JEAN	Right, and he isn't going to sell our key to one of his gang banger friends the moment he's out the door.	
RICK	Jean, it's been a tough night. Why don't you go upstairs and ...	75
JEAN	... wait for them to break in? *(in a rage)* I just had a gun pointed in my face.	
RICK	You lower your voice.	

62

Chapter 3   Living One's Life – Individuals in Society

Them and us   3

| JEAN | And it's my fault because I knew it was going to happen. But if a white person sees two black men walking towards them and turns and walks the other way, she's a racist, right? Well, I got scared, and I didn't say anything and ten seconds later I had a gun in my face. Now, I'm telling you that your amigo in there is going to sell our house key to one of his homies! And this time it would be really fucking nice if you acted like you actually cared!! |

Jean turns and storms into the kitchen. Rick stares at her as she makes a show of wiping down the counter.

From: *Crash Movie Script Screenplay*, 2005

82 **homie** member of the same gang

COMPREHENSION ◀

1 Knowing what happened
Something happened between these two scenes. What was it?
1 Rick and Jean's house was broken into, and most of the jewellery and computers were stolen.
2 Jean discovered that Rick is having an affair with Karen.
3 Daniel meets Anthony and Peter and discuss how to rob rich people's houses.
4 Rick and Jean were assaulted by Anthony and Peter, who stole their car, their money and their house keys.

2 Understanding disagreements
a Summarize Anthony and Peter's conversation
b Then write a summary of Jean and Rick's argument at home.

LANGUAGE AWARENESS ◀

3 Spoken language
Find words and phrases in the two scenes which show typical features of conversations. Discuss which of these words and phrases are acceptable in a written document, too, and which should be reformulated.

▶ SF 20: Analysing drama

ANALYSIS ◀

4 Examining the characters
a Describe the characters, their different views, their use of language and their behaviour.
b Now view the two film scenes. Analyse the characters' mimes, gestures and voices. How do these elements add to their characterization?
c Discuss your personal reaction to the characters with a partner and comment on the characters' views and behaviour.

DVD
▶ SF 23: Analysing a film

5 Examining stereotypes
a Explain what stereotypes are, and give examples from each scene. Use the Fact File for help.
b Analyse the role stereotypes and prejudice play in the dialogues in the text, reflecting on how the characters perceive each other and the influence this has on their relationships.

BEYOND THE TEXT ◀

6 YOU CHOOSE ▶ Stereotypes in everyday life

a Describe a situation in which you were or somebody else was confronted with stereotypes. Tell a partner about it and reflect about your experiences.

OR

b Discuss the function of stereotypes in everyday life: how they influence our perception of others and how we deal with them. SUPPORT ▶ p. 205

Living One's Life – Individuals in Society   Chapter 3   63

SPEAKING FOCUS ON SKILLS
Resolving a heated argument

When people have opposing points of view or interests, arguments may take place. Everybody – willingly or not – uses different strategies to heat up or cool down a conflict. Usually, people feel offended if somebody orders them around ('Stop this now.'), threatens them ('If you don't …, I will …'), blames them ('You are always …'), evaluates their behaviour ('You're always trying to …'), or shouts at them. A set of communicative strategies can be helpful to solve a conflict.

1 **Strategies to cool down a conflict**
   Choose five of the strategies below and rank them according to their importance. Exchange your ideas with a partner and try to agree on a list of the five most effective strategies. Present your results to the rest of the class.
   1 Respect the other.
   2 Try to find a win–win resolution.
   3 Relax. Take a deep breath. Speak slowly and softly.
   4 Listen closely to what the other is saying.
   5 Use 'I' messages. Such as: 'I feel bad when you do that.'
   6 Put what the other person said in your own words to make sure you understand. ('I understood … Is that what you meant?')
   7 Watch your language and use words like 'maybe' and 'perhaps'.
   8 Ask for a break if you need to collect your thoughts or release stress.

2 **Analysing and solving a conflict**
   a Go back to p. 62. Describe and analyse the conflict between Rick and Jean. Pay special attention to their language and behaviour.
   b Discuss what Rick and Jean might have done to achieve better communication. Which of the strategies could each of them use?
   c Rewrite parts of the dialogue between Rick and Jean to make it end in a positive way.

3 **Dealing with aggression**
   a List a few everyday conflicts between, for example parents and children, men and women, or friends, in which people become aggressive.
   b Together with a partner, role-play a few of these situations. One partner is verbally aggressive, while the other partner tries to calm the other by stating his or her observations, feelings, needs and requests. Here is how it might go:
      1 'I noticed you …' (observation).
      2 'When you did that, I felt …' (feeling).
      3 'I need …' (need)
      4 'therefore, I'm hoping you'll …' (request)
   c Change roles so that each of you can try out the observation-feeling-need-request method.
   d Report back to the group what you think about this way of reacting to aggression.

▶ LP 12: Using the right register

Them and us   3

CULTURE SPOT

Graffiti

'Imagine a city where graffiti wasn't illegal, a city where everybody could draw whatever they liked. Where every street was awash with a million colours and little phrases. Where standing at a bus stop was never boring. A city that felt like a party where everyone was invited, not just the estate agents and barons of big business. Imagine a city like that and stop leaning against the wall – it's wet.' Banksy

1. Look at the graffiti in the photos. Describe them and say why you think they were made.
2. State which ones you like, and why.
3. Discuss which ones should be saved.
4. Most art can be bought and sold at a price. Discuss who owns street art.
5. Comment on Banksy's statement.

Living One's Life – Individuals in Society   Chapter 3   65

3 Part C

DVD

SF 23: Analysing a film

Getting involved

C1 Volunteering in the wake of the Olympics

Pre-viewing
1 Discuss which of the photos in the Lead-in (p. 52) show people volunteering.
   SUPPORT ▶ p. 205
2 Discuss whether you have ever volunteered or been engaged in some form of social activism. If yes, tell the others about your experience. If not, explain why not.
3 Explain why people actually volunteer.

While-viewing
4 Watch the news report about volunteering in England after the Olympics and list reasons why young people volunteer.

Post-viewing
5 Explain your reaction to the various reasons given.

C2 Volunteering in Germany   *Sophia Seiderer*

A friend of yours from London is involved in 'Team London', a project to help people who want to volunteer. You have been discussing volunteering in England compared to Germany. You come across the following web article about volunteerism in Germany.

Männlich, zwischen 40 und 49 Jahre alt, gebildet, beruflich erfolgreich, Protestant, Familienvater, auf dem Land lebend, Vorstand des lokalen Fußballvereins. So würde er aussehen, der Prototyp eines bürgerschaftlich engagierten Menschen, wenn man den Statistiken folgt. [...]

   Mehr als jeder dritte Deutsche ab 14 Jahren ist über die Schule und den Beruf hinaus aktiv an Gruppen, Vereinen oder Organisationen beteiligt, besonders in   5

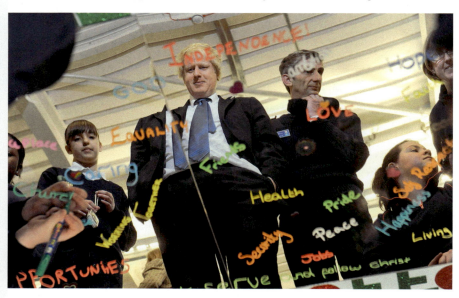

The mayor of London, Boris Johnson, at the launch of a Team London volunteer programme

66   Chapter 3   Living One's Life – Individuals in Society

Getting Involved

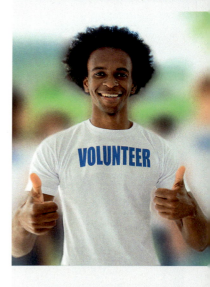

ländlichen Regionen. 36 Prozent haben darüber hinaus langfristig freiwillige und unentgeltliche Aufgaben übernommen. Zudem hat die Bereitschaft der Bürger dazu in den vergangenen zehn Jahren zugenommen. Von 26 Prozent im Jahr 1999 auf 37 Prozent 2009. Besonderes Potenzial liegt in der Altersgruppe der 14- bis 24-Jährigen: 35 Prozent von ihnen engagieren sich bereits, weitere 49 Prozent geben an, dass sie eine Tätigkeit übernehmen würden.

Doch all die Zahlen und Daten können eines nicht zeigen: Wer hinter diesem Engagement steht. Was ist das für ein Mann, der seit 30 Jahren täglich zu einer kleinen Kirche zwischen Müllberg und Autobahn fährt, um 'sein' Gotteshaus vor dem Abriss zu bewahren? Was bringt eine Bankerin dazu, jeden Samstag mit ihrem Hund in den Trümmern alter Fabrikhallen zu trainieren, damit sie und das Tier die Rettungshundeausbildung bestehen? Was treibt eine Doktorandin dazu, ihre Zeit in ein Projekt zu investieren, das jungen Studenten aus Nicht-Akademiker-Familien helfen soll, ihr Studium durchzuziehen? Sind das Menschen, die einfach 'sozialer' sind als andere? Die so erzogen sind? Die das tun, weil es sich so gehört? [...]

'Es handelt sich um Menschen, die über ein bestimmtes Leistungsethos verfügen, also beruflich recht erfolgreich sind. Dieses Ethos setzt sich oft auch außerhalb des Berufs fort', so Joachim Winkler [von der Hochschule Wißmar, der über das Ehrenamt promoviert]. Und: „Es muss immer aus ihrer eigenen Motivation herauskommen." Deswegen hält er auch nichts von dem Konzept, Arbeitslose für bürgerschaftliches Engagement zu gewinnen. „Arbeitslose denken an die fehlende Arbeit. Sie suchen Arbeit, haben also keine Motivation, zusätzliche unentgeltliche Arbeit anzunehmen."

Auch in der Politik erfährt das Thema Zivilgesellschaft und bürgerliches Engagement seit mehreren Jahren eine Konjunktur. Aktionen wie die „Initiative Zivilengagement" des Familienministeriums, der Deutsche Engagementpreis oder Internetforen wie Engagiert-in-deutschland.de, auf dem sich die Helfer vernetzen können, sollen die ehrenamtliche Tätigkeit fördern. Nicht zuletzt auch das „Europäische Jahr der Freiwilligentätigkeit", das die EU-Kommission für 2011 ausgerufen hat.

Mit der Förderung des Ehrenamts schwingt immer auch die Gefahr mit, dass der Staat sich aus seinen sozialen Aufgaben zurückzieht und diese immer mehr auf Ehrenamtliche abwälzt. [...] Matthias Freise von der Uni Münster sieht eine Verlockung für den Staat: „Er muss sparen, in teuren Bereichen kann er nicht ausbauen. Das Ehrenamt zu fördern, ist kein teures Politikfeld, einfach und sehr medienfreundlich – ein wunderbares Thema für die Politik."

From: 'Ehrenamtliches Engagement für die Gesellschaft', Die Welt, 24 March 2010

COMPREHENSION

1 Mediation (German → English)
Write an email to your friend, telling him or her the points made in the article. SUPPORT p. 205

▶ SF 41: Mediation of written and oral texts

BEYOND THE TEXT

2 To volunteer or not to volunteer
a With a partner, discuss the question whether the two of you should volunteer or not. One of you wants to, the other does not. You may take notes on little cue cards.
b Tell the class about your discussion and decision.

▶ SF 27: Having a discussion

Living One's Life – Individuals in Society   Chapter 3

3 Part C

DVD

C3 The Hunger Games: an individual in a utopian society

Taking a stand
You are going to watch the trailer for the blockbuster 2012 film The Hunger Games, *based on the novel by Suzanne Collins and starring Jennifer Lawrence.*

◂ COMPREHENSION

1 **Viewing for information**
Make notes on the characters, setting, plot and main themes of the film as can be derived from the trailer.

◂ ANALYSIS

2 **A volunteer**
   a The protagonist Katniss Everdeen offers herself as a volunteer. Explain what her volunteering means in the context of the film.
   b Explain how Katniss's volunteering relates to the concept of volunteering as you have learned about it in this chapter. **SUPPORT** ▸ p. 205

3 **Advertising**
Identify and analyse the means of advertising the trailer uses.

A dystopian society?
In this section you will watch an episode from the beginning of the film The Hunger Games.

DVD

◂ COMPREHENSION

1 **Layers of society**
In groups of three, outline how the different groups of society – the tributes, the audience and the game makers – are portrayed.

◂ ANALYSIS

2 **Examining the social structure**
   a Read the Fact File (cf. p. 69) and assess which elements of a dystopian society are visible in the film.
   b **CHALLENGE** ▸ Examine whether utopian elements are also visible in the society depicted in the film, and evaluate the relationship between the dystopian and utopian elements.

Chapter 3   Living One's Life – Individuals in Society

Getting Involved 3

FACT FILE

From Utopia to Dystopia

The term 'utopia' comes from Greek and means both 'no-place' and 'good place'. In 1516 the English lawyer, philosopher and adviser to the king, Thomas More, wrote a work of fiction called *Utopia*, describing a paradise-like place and society on an island of the same name. From then on, the term was used to refer to imaginary, paradise-like places, but also came to describe a particular kind of narrative, known as utopian literature.

In the course of the 20th century, former utopian ideals seemed absurd. Moreover, totalitarianism often led to the establishment of oppressive dictatorships instead of better societies. As a consequence, the belief in heaven on earth turned into a nightmarish vision: the term 'utopia' was replaced by 'dystopia', meaning 'bad' or 'hard' or – to put it simply – a utopia gone wrong. The main aim of a dystopia is to portray images of the future as realistic and threatening possibilities. In the 20th century, dystopia became the main form of visionary literature, mirroring society's failures and projecting today's divisive issues (such as capitalism, consumerism, self-indulgence, the power of science and technology and globalization) into the future. Often the true purpose of a dystopia is to make us aware of problems our society is facing.

The issues

Watch two further episodes. DVD

— COMPREHENSION ◀

1 A utopia gone wrong

Make notes on further elements of characterization, costume design and setting that are indicative of a dystopian society.

— ANALYSIS ◀

2 Violence

  a Evaluate the use of violence in the scenes you watched.
  b Assess which contemporary issues are dealt with in *The Hunger Games*.

— BEYOND THE TEXT ◀

3 YOU CHOOSE ▸ Watching the film

  a Some of you may not have seen the film. If you have not, get together with others who have not seen it and discuss whether or not you would like to watch the whole film. Keep notes of your discussion so that you can present your findings to the class.

  b If you have seen the film, discuss Katniss's role within her society.

Living One's Life – Individuals in Society   Chapter 3

3 Part C

C4 Young people raising their voices

1 Young people making a difference
a **EXPERT GROUPS** Get together in groups of three. Each of you in the group is responsible for researching one of the three young individuals featured below. Find information about them, their life, their stories and their achievements. Work on your individual by yourself.

Craig Kielburger

'Child labour is an issue of grave importance. It must become a top priority for all governments of the world. How can the world move into the twenty-first century with children still being exploited for their labour and denied their basic right to an education?'

Malala Yousafzai

'Let us pick up our books and our pens. They are our most powerful weapons. One child, one teacher, one book and one pen can change the world.'

Jack Andraka

'If a fifteen-year-old, who didn't even know he had a pancreas at the beginning of this project, could find a new way to detect pancreatic cancer, just imagine what you can do.'

b Meet with other experts on the same person from other groups and compare your findings. Then, for your presentation, make a mini-poster, designed as a one-page handout.
c Go back to your jigsaw group and present a report to the group.
d Listen carefully to the other members of your group.
e Discuss which of the three individuals and their work and vision you find most interesting, and why?

2 Hot seating
Find another who chose the same person as you. One of you acts as the person you chose while the rest ask questions about their life and work.

3 Raising your voice
Apart from children's rights, what do you think are pressing issues that should be discussed and that people should raise their voices for?

Chapter Task

Getting your message across

In this section you are going to create a vlog. A vlog is a video blog post or video podcast. Vloggers make videos of themselves or certain events and then upload them to the internet. Vloggers use video to express their thoughts, opinions and interests and to get their messages across. A vlog can be topical, instructional or entertaining.

1 **Examine a video campaign or vlog**
  Across the world, web video has become a medium to give people a voice concerning political and social issues. The United Nations, for example, created a YouTube channel called 'Raise your voice and change climate change!', where you can find a lot of videos made by people who wanted to speak their minds, among them Desmond Tutu, a South African social rights activist and first black Archbishop of Cape Town, and numerous young people from all over the world. Watch Tutu's video.
  a Describe your impressions of the video, and how Tutu tries to convey his message.
  b Find other videos from the campaign, and discuss whether such video campaigns can make a difference.

 DVD

▶ SF 23: Analysing a film

2 **YOU CHOOSE** **Choose a topic for your video**

Present yourself in a vlog. You may refer to some of the following aspects:	**OR**	Decide what issue matters to you the most. If you are uncertain, here are a few subjects you can choose from:
1 your aims and ambitions		1 environment
2 voluntary work you do		2 education
3 your philosophy of life		3 children's/women's/men's rights
4 a person that impresses you and could be a role model to others		4 freedom and human rights
5 a thing that is worth fighting for		5 homelessness

3 **Choose the class's favourite vlog**
  Get into groups of six and present your vlogs to each other. Choose one to be presented to the entire class. Be prepared to give reasons for your choice. In class, watch the videos you have chosen and discuss them. With the assessment sheet your teacher will give you, evaluate the vlogs and vote for the video you want to win the class contest.

With a video or cam and the Internet everyone can become a blogger.

Living One's Life – Individuals in Society

4 The Power of Words – from Shakespeare to Today

> Lackluster tennis tournament keeps fans away
>
> The suspect led the police on a wild goose chase
>
> Cruise ship returns to port a sorry sight
>
> Priest and pop star make strange bedfellows
>
> Referees urge fair play at World Cup
>
> 5 ways for shy people to break the ice

Download a chronological word list here:

 Webcode context-00

▶ LP 1: Simple and progressive verb forms

▶ SF 33: Writing a report

▶ Fact File, p. 76

1 **Examining powerful language**
   a Work with a partner. Translate the headlines which each contain a phrase that was first used or coined by Shakespeare. Use a dictionary if necessary.
   b Choose two of the phrases that you find particularly effective. Take turns explaining to each other what is so powerful about them that they are still being used in modern English.

2 **Writing a news report**
   Choose one of the headlines and write a short text about what you imagine is the story behind the headline. Write about 60 words.

3 **Who was William Shakespeare?**
   Brainstorm in class what you know about Shakespeare and the time he lived in. Speculate why phrases that he coined became well-known.

William Shakespeare, 'Cobbe Portrait'

Chapter 4   The Power of Words – from Shakespeare to Today

Lead-in

4 **Thinking about poetic word power**
   a Read the lines from poems that you will find in this chapter. With a partner decide on the two that appeal to you most.
   b With your partner, decide what it is about the phrases that suggest they come from a poem.
   c Share your ideas with other couples who have chosen different phrases. Compare the different ways in which poetic words appealed to you.

PREVIEW

In this chapter you will learn about the power of poetic language from Shakespeare to today.

Main topics
- Shakespeare: using word power to persuade .... p. 76
- Adapting Shakespeare's words to create new art .... p. 82
- Modern-day poets' use of words, sound and imagery .... p. 87

Focus on Skills: READING and VIEWING
- Close reading (drama extract) .... p. 78
- Evaluating a modern Shakespeare adaptation .... p. 84

Chapter Task:
Writing a review of a film or text you have seen or read .... p. 91

The Power of Words – from Shakespeare to Today   Chapter 4   73

4 Words in Context

🎧 CD1 09
Listen to an audio version of the text on the CD or download it here:
Webcode context-00

▶ SF 1: Dealing with unknown words

The power of the spoken word

The importance of the spoken word in Shakespeare's time
In Shakespeare's time people went to the theatre to 'hear' a play. The stage was equipped with only the most necessary props. The actors used body language and gestures, but the visual aspect was not so important for the overall dramatic impression. The most important element was the language, the words spoken by the actors. Sometimes we even speak of word-scenery, as the characters often describe the scenery for the audience.

Shakespeare included many scenes in his plays in which a character uses words to persuade other characters to do things they might not want to originally do. Quite a few plays rely on quick verbal exchange, in which characters reply to each other in witty comments. Sometimes the word-fights are playful, sometimes they contain an element of challenge and sometimes they are cynical or evil. All of them demonstrate Shakespeare's mastery of language, as well as his enjoyment at creating these scenes.

Shakespeare's themes and language in our time
Since Shakespeare's time, the English language has developed considerably, while the themes of his plays have remained relevant up to this day. That is why there is such a wealth of adaptations of the plays both in writing and in films. Sometimes, it is just the main theme that has been adapted, as in the musical *West Side Story* (1957), which is based on Shakespeare's play *Romeo and Juliet*. Here, the language has been changed to fit the setting of New York in the 1950s. Occasionally there are filmed versions of his plays that keep Shakespeare's language but are set in a different location. *William Shakespeare's Romeo and Juliet* (1996) is set in a fictitious modern American city called 'Verona Beach', complete with skyscrapers, large cars, and armed gangs – and yet the characters speak in Shakespeare's iambic pentameters. The film *Richard III* (1995), for example, is set in a 1930s dictatorship. The popularity of these films shows that Shakespeare's language is still understandable when accompanied by images that we can relate to.

Poetry as Drama
To this day, Shakespeare is not only remembered for his plays, but also for his poetry. His cycle of 154 sonnets deals in different ways with love, the passing of time, and death. While drama is no longer written in verse, poetry itself has remained popular. Poets of every age have found new ways of exploring the power of words to express feelings, attitudes and experiences in different types of verse. Sometimes they return to writing traditional formats such as sonnets, sometimes they write free verse that has no clear patterns either of rhyme or rhythm. One tendency in the 21st century is to perform poetry to an audience, thus lifting it off the page and making interaction between the poet and his or her listeners possible. Performance poetry can be said to create a link between Shakespeare's drama in verse and poetry of the 21st century.

The power of the spoken word   4

1 Performance words
List words from the text that you could use when talking about
a what you can see
b what you can hear
during the performance in a theatre. Add short definitions to each word.

2 Collocations
a Collocations are words that often 'go together'. Find as many collocations
as possible in the boxes below. In some cases you may have to add an
article, a pronoun or a preposition.

find	elements
contain	scenery
write	mastery
describe	verse
express	ways
perform	poetry
create	link
demonstrate	feelings

b Use at least four collocations to write a short text about a poem, play or
song that you like.

▶ SF 31: Writing a summary
▶ SF 32: Writing a review

3 Phrasal verbs
A phrasal verb consists of a verb and an adverb or preposition. Fill the gaps
with the correct phrasal verbs. Look at the text again for help.
1 While Shakespeare's theatres had little scenery, today's theatres are …
   up-to-date video and sound projectors.
2 Many of Shakespeare's plays have been … the big screen.
3 Shakespeare is best … his plays and sonnets.
4 The novel, which … a romance between an Englishman and a Lithuanian
   immigrant, is … a seaside town in England.
5 The reason why Shakespeare is still popular today is because people can
   still … his ideas and characters.
6 The play, which is … an old legend, has been updated to a modern
   setting.

4 Word families
a Find the corresponding nouns to these verbs and adjectives. Look at the
text for help or use a dictionary.

1 be set in	4 adapt sth.	7 interact with sb./sth.
2 express sth.	5 popular	8 persuade sb. to do sth.
3 perform sth.	6 relevant	9 equip sb./sth. with sth.

b Write a sentence with each of the nouns.

▶ SF 3: Using a dictionary

5 Writing
Write an email to a friend telling him or her why you are (not) looking
forward to seeing a Shakespeare play with your class. Include as many words
and phrases from the text as possible.

▶ SF 29: Writing a formal letter or
email

The Power of Words – from Shakespeare to Today   Chapter 4

4 Part A

Shakespeare's Power of Language

FACT FILE

William Shakespeare

Ordinary people did not leave behind much documentation in the 16th century, which is why we have few documents that mention Shakespeare. There is a lot of speculation about most of Shakespeare's life. We do know that he was born in Stratford-upon-Avon in 1564 and that he married Anne Hathaway in 1582, with whom he had three children. In 1592 he was working as actor and playwright in London with a company of actors. He also published popular books of poetry. In 1599 he and other members of his company opened The Globe, one of the largest and best theatres in London at that time. He wrote about 38 plays, 154 sonnets and two long poems, which together is often regarded as one of the greatest collections of literature created by one man. He moved back to Stratford shortly before his death in 1616.

In Parts A and B there are excerpts from three of Shakespeare's plays. In groups of three, each choose one of the following: Macbeth, Richard III or The Taming of the Shrew. Search the internet for information about your play. Give a *synopsis about it to the others who then formulate two questions about the play. Answer your classmates' questions. Then swap roles.

William Shakespeare, 'Chandos Portrait'

A1 Lady Macbeth persuades her husband

In Shakespeare's play Macbeth, Macbeth has told his wife about prophesies he heard promising him he will become king of Scotland. When the present king, Duncan, honours them with a visit, they plan to murder him so that Macbeth can become his successor. In a *soliloquy immediately before the passage printed below, Macbeth's conscience has warned him not to go ahead with the plan. His wife interrupts his thoughts at this point.

LADY MACBETH	He has almost supped: why have you left the chamber?	
MACBETH	Hath he asked for me?	
LADY MACBETH	Know you not he has?	
MACBETH	We will proceed no further in this business:	
	He hath honoured me of late; and I have bought	5
	Golden opinions from all sorts of people,	
	Which would be worn now in their newest gloss,	
	Not cast aside so soon.	
LADY MACBETH	Was the hope drunk	
	Wherein you dressed yourself? Hath it slept since?	10
	And wakes it now, to look so green and pale	
	At what it did so freely? From this time	
	Such I account thy love. Art thou afeard	
	To be the same in thine own act and valour	
	As thou art in desire? Wouldst thou have that	15
	Which thou esteem'st the ornament of life,	
	And live a coward in thine own esteem,	
	Letting 'I dare not' wait upon 'I would',	
	Like the poor cat i' the adage?	
MACBETH	Prithee, peace:	20
	I dare do all that may become a man;	
	Who dares do more is none.	

1 **supped** finished supper
5 **honoured me of late** showed respect lately
7 **would be worn** should be enjoyed
8 **cast aside** thrown away
13 **Such I account thy love** I consider your love to be like that
14 **to be the same … as thou art in desire** be as brave in what you do as in what you are wishing for
16 **esteem'st** (v) respect
17 **esteem** (n) great respect, admiration
18 **dare** be brave enough to do sth.
   wait upon be a servant to
19 **adage** proverb, saying; *here:* a cat likes to eat fish, but doesn't like to get its feet wet
20 **Prithee, peace** please be quiet

76   Chapter 4   The Power of Words – from Shakespeare to Today

Shakespeare's Power of Language

LADY MACBETH	What beast was't, then,
	That made you break this enterprise to me?
	When you durst do it, then you were a man;	25
	And, to be more than what you were, you would
	Be so much more the man. Nor time nor place
	Did then adhere, and yet you would make both:
	They have made themselves, and that their fitness now
	Does unmake you. I have given suck, and know	30
	How tender 'tis to love the babe that milks me:
	I would, while it was smiling in my face,
	Have plucked my nipple from his boneless gums,
	And dashed the brains out, had I so sworn as you
	Have done to this.	35
MACBETH	If we should fail?
LADY MACBETH	We fail!
	But screw your courage to the sticking-place,
	And we'll not fail. When Duncan is asleep -
	Whereto the rather shall his day's hard journey
	Soundly invite him – his two chamberlains	40
	Will I with wine and wassail so convince
	That memory, the warder of the brain,
	Shall be a fume, and the receipt of reason
	A limbeck only: when in swinish sleep	45
	Their drenched natures lie as in a death,
	What cannot you and I perform upon
	The unguarded Duncan? What not put upon
	His spongy officers, who shall bear the guilt
	Of our great quell?	50
MACBETH	Bring forth men-children only;
	For thy undaunted mettle should compose
	Nothing but males.

From: Macbeth, Act 1, Scene 7

---

25 durst *(past tense)* dared
27 Nor time … adhere did not know when and where it would happen
28 make both make sth. happen
29 have made themselves have offered themselves
fitness suitability, being right for sth.
30 give suck breastfeed a baby
33 plucked pulled away
boneless gums toothless mouth
38 screw your courage to the sticking-place *image taken from the tuning of a violin: the player tightens each string until it produces the right note and then fixes it* = get your courage up
40 Whereto … invite him to which his long travels will lead him soon
41 chamberlain *Kammerdiener*
42 wassail ale, spiced beer
43 warder guard
44 fume alcoholic steam
receipt of reason brain
45 limbeck *Destillierkolben*
46 drenched drunk
49 spongy like a sponge, soaked with liquid, *here:* drunk
bear take, stand
50 quell killing, murder
52 undaunted mettle fearless character

◼ FACT FILE

In **16th-century English** there were two forms of 'you': 'thou' (object form: 'thee'; possessive form: 'thy', 'thine' = your), which was used similarly to German *du*.
The other form was 'ye' or 'you'. This was used as a term of respect or as the plural form (like the old German use of *Ihr*).

Verbs following 'thou' ended in '-st', e.g. 'didst', 'camest', 'hast'. The second-person singular form of 'be' was 'art': thou art = you are.

In Shakespeare's time, the third-person singular verb often ended in '-th', e.g. 'doth' (does), 'hath' (has), 'seemeth' (seems).

▶ COMPREHENSION

1 Understanding the conflict
  a An argument is taking place between Macbeth and Lady Macbeth. Collect keywords that underline the position of each character.
  b Write a short summary of each of the speeches in modern English.
  c State what Lady Macbeth is trying to persuade her husband to do.

▶ LANGUAGE AWARENESS

2 Analysing ways of addressing
  a Study how Macbeth and Lady Macbeth address each other. Read the Fact File and explain what their ways of addressing mean.
  b In one part of the dialogue, Lady Macbeth changes the form of address. Identify the change and discuss what may have caused it.

3 Rewriting Shakespeare's questions
  Look at how Shakespeare formed questions. Instead of the modern use of the modal verb 'do' he used a different form of question. Identify those questions and rewrite them in modern English.

The Power of Words – from Shakespeare to Today   Chapter 4

4 Part A

- SF 14: Reading strategies
- SF 17: Analysing stylistic devices
- SF 20: Analysing drama
- Glossary, p. 324

READING FOCUS ON SKILLS

Close reading (drama extract)

Look at **A1** *again. Now you are going to analyse how the writer has made the content interesting by using the sound of the words, stylistic devices, metaphorical language and forms of characterization.*

1 **Reading aloud: The rhythm of the text**
   a Read the text aloud to get a feeling for its *metre.
   b Read the Fact File. Then count the syllables and the metric feet in ll. 1–22 of the extract from *Macbeth*.
   c Work with a partner. Read parts of the dialogue out loud again. Pay attention to the speakers completing the blank verse for each other.

> **FACT FILE**
> **Blank verse**
> The type of verse used most often by Shakespeare is called blank verse. It consists of iambic pentameters, which are five iambs. An iamb is an unstressed syllable followed by a stressed syllable, which sounds like 'Dah DUM'. Blank verse is considered particularly close to normal English speech rhythm, which was probably what made it so popular in Shakespeare's time.
> Note:
> Shakespeare's rhythm is varied, lively and never monotonous, because his characters are saying important things. That is why not all lines in the excerpt can be spoken in the 'dah DUM' rhythm.

2 **Understanding *stylistic devices**
   a Read Lady Macbeth's speeches and identify which form of punctuation appears a lot. Name the stylistic device and explain its purpose here.
   b Note down words that are repeated in the text and in which lines they occur. Describe the effect of their repetition.
   c Write a statement explaining what both stylistic devices tell you about the argumentation of both Macbeth and Lady Macbeth.

3 **Analysing *images**
   When reading, you should always try to visualize what the words are telling you and which mental images are created.
   a Read ll. 4–6 again. Macbeth speaks about 'buying golden opinions' that he wants to 'wear in their newest gloss': Apparently he sees 'opinions' as new clothes. Explain what that tells you about his character.
   b Lady Macbeth responds by using imagery herself. Read ll. 9–12 and explain how she takes up her husband's image and expands it.
   c In l. 23 Lady Macbeth mentions a 'beast'. Explain what she is referring to.

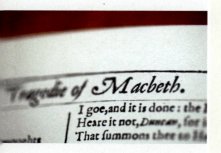

4 **Understanding *characterization**
   a Lady Macbeth's passage from ll. 30–35 gives us a good idea of the kind of woman she is. Read the passage out loud. Explain the image she uses and what it tells you about her character.
   b Read the extract either aloud or in silence slowly and purposefully. Compare lengths, content and messages of the speakers' passages. Draw conclusions about the characters.
   c FREEZE-FRAME Work with a partner. Imagine how the actor and actress would perform the dialogue and create a freeze-frame. Get together with another pair. Present your freeze-frame and let them guess which moment you have chosen.
   d Write an analysis about the couple Macbeth and Lady Macbeth on the basis of the complete passage. Write at least 150 words.

- SF 35: Writing a character profile

4 Shakespeare's Power of Language

A2 Richard courts his enemy

In *Richard III* Richard, Duke of Gloucester, killed his enemies King Henry VI and his son Edward Plantagenet. He wants to become king himself, and decides to marry Edward's widow Anne to strengthen his position. In this scene Richard approaches Anne as she accompanies the body of her father-in-law, Henry VI, to his burial place. Read the extract to see how Richard tries to persuade Lady Anne that he is courting her out of love. Try to visualize the scene, imagining how the two characters interact with each other.

> ■ **TROUBLE SPOT**
>
> **court**, (n). = Gericht, Hof
> **court** (v) = umwerben, den Hof machen

LADY ANNE	Didst thou not kill this king?	
GLOUCESTER	I grant ye.	
LADY ANNE	Dost grant me, hedgehog? then, God grant me too	
	Thou mayst be damned for that wicked deed!	
	O, he was gentle, mild, and virtuous!	5
GLOUCESTER	The fitter for the King of heaven, that hath him.	
LADY ANNE	He is in heaven, where thou shalt never come.	
GLOUCESTER	Let him thank me, that holp to send him thither;	
	For he was fitter for that place than earth.	
LADY ANNE	And thou unfit for any place but hell.	10
GLOUCESTER	Yes, one place else, if you will hear me name it.	
LADY ANNE	Some dungeon.	
GLOUCESTER	Your bed-chamber.	
LADY ANNE	Ill rest betide the chamber where thou liest!	
GLOUCESTER	So will it, madam till I lie with you.	15
LADY ANNE	I hope so.	
GLOUCESTER	I know so. But, gentle Lady Anne,	
	To leave this keen encounter of our wits,	
	And fall somewhat into a slower method,	
	Is not the causer of the timeless deaths	20
	Of these Plantagenets, Henry and Edward,	
	As blameful as the executioner?	
LADY ANNE	Thou art the cause, and most accursed effect.	
GLOUCESTER	Your beauty was the cause of that effect;	
	Your beauty: which did haunt me in my sleep	25
	To undertake the death of all the world,	
	So I might live one hour in your sweet bosom.	
LADY ANNE	If I thought that, I tell thee, homicide,	
	These nails should rend that beauty from my cheeks.	
GLOUCESTER	These eyes could never endure sweet beauty's wreck;	30
	You should not blemish it, if I stood by:	
	As all the world is cheered by the sun,	
	So I by that; it is my day, my life.	
LADY ANNE	Black night o'ershade thy day, and death thy life.	
GLOUCESTER	Curse not thyself, fair creature; thou art both.	35
LADY ANNE	I would I were, to be revenged on thee.	
GLOUCESTER	It is a quarrel most unnatural,	
	To be revenged on him that loveth you.	
LADY ANNE	It is a quarrel just and reasonable,	
	To be revenged on him that slew my husband.	40

2 **grant** admit, allow
6 **the fitter** the better
8 **holp** (past tense) helped
    tither there
12 **dungeon** dark underground prison
14 **Ill rest betide the chamber** may there be no peace and quiet to be had in the room
18 **keen encounter of our wits** our fierce argument
20 **timeless** too early
23 **accursed** damned
25 **haunt** follow, chase, stalk
29 **rend** rip, pull
30 **endure** tolerate
31 **blemish** ruin
40 **slew** (past tense) killed

The Power of Words – from Shakespeare to Today Chapter 4

4 Part A

41 **bereft thee of sb.** made you lose sb.
55 **toad** *Kröte*
58 **basilisk** mythical animal that could cause death by looking at a person
62 **shamed ... of childish drops** made me feel ashamed as I cried like a child
63 **sued to** appealed to, was attractive to
64 **smoothing** nice, flattering
65 **fee** reward
67 **scorn** ridicule, sarcasm
68 **contempt** hate, disrespect
70 **Lo** *(archaic)* Look!
74 **humbly** modest, moderately
77 **nay** no
  dispatch send away

GLOUCESTER He that bereft thee, lady, of thy husband,
            Did it to help thee to a better husband.
LADY ANNE   His better doth not breathe upon the earth.
GLOUCESTER He lives that loves thee better than he could.
LADY ANNE   Name him. 45
GLOUCESTER Plantagenet.
LADY ANNE   Why, that was he.
GLOUCESTER The selfsame name, but one of better nature.
LADY ANNE   Where is he?
GLOUCESTER Here. 50

She spitteth at him.

            Why dost thou spit at me?
LADY ANNE   Would it were mortal poison, for thy sake!
GLOUCESTER Never came poison from so sweet a place.
LADY ANNE   Never hung poison on a fouler toad. 55
            Out of my sight! thou dost infect my eyes.
GLOUCESTER Thine eyes, sweet lady, have infected mine.
LADY ANNE   Would they were basilisks', to strike thee dead!
GLOUCESTER I would they were, that I might die at once;
            For now they kill me with a living death. 60
            Those eyes of thine from mine have drawn salt tears,
            Shamed their aspect with store of childish drops: [...]
            I never sued to friend nor enemy;
            My tongue could never learn sweet smoothing word;
            But now thy beauty is proposed my fee, 65
            My proud heart sues, and prompts my tongue to speak.
            Teach not thy lips such scorn, for they were made
            For kissing, lady, not for such contempt.
            If thy revengeful heart cannot forgive,
            Lo, here I lend thee this sharp-pointed sword; 70
            Which if thou please to hide in this true bosom.
            And let the soul forth that adoreth thee,
            I lay it naked to the deadly stroke,
            And humbly beg the death upon my knee.
            Nay, do not pause; for I did kill King Henry, 75
            But 'twas thy beauty that provoked me.
            Nay, now dispatch; 'twas I that stabb'd
                young Edward,
            But 'twas thy heavenly face that set me on.

Here she lets fall the sword. 80

Take up the sword again, or take up me.

From: *Richard III*, Act 1, Scene 2

The scene ends with Anne allowing Richard to place his ring on her finger and agreeing to meet him after the burial of Henry VI.

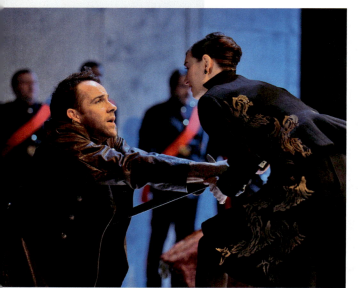

80 Chapter 4 The Power of Words – from Shakespeare to Today

Shakespeare's Power of Language

The opening of Richard the Third in the First Folio of Shakespeare, 1623

───────────────────────────── COMPREHENSION ◀

1 Understanding the content
   a Outline the gist of the fight between Lady Anne and Gloucester.
   b Describe Lady Anne's feelings for her dead husband and for Gloucester.

───────────────────────────── ANALYSIS ◀

2 A word fight
   a Look closely at how one speaker takes up a particular word or concept from the other and changes it according to their own purposes. Make notes.
   b Discuss your findings with a partner or in class.

3 Working with imagery
Work with a partner. Identify the images each speaker uses. Explain them with the help of the annotations and from the context they are used in.

SUPPORT ▶ p. 206

4 Persuasive words and actions
   a Note down words and phrases that Gloucester uses to change Lady Anne's feelings towards him.
   b Discuss if her reactions show the desired effect.
   c Point out the effect of Gloucester offering Lady Anne his sword to kill him on the spot.

───────────────────────────── LANGUAGE AWARENESS ◀

5 Language Awareness
Look at the Fact File on p. 77 again. Analyse the use of 'thou' and 'you' forms as an indicator of the relationship of the speakers. Examine and interpret their forms of addressing each other.

6 Understanding character
   a On the basis of your analysis, describe the speakers' characters.
      SUPPORT ▶ p. 206
   b Discuss how these characters could be presented on stage.

───────────────────────────── BEYOND THE TEXT ◀

7 Performing the scene
In small groups, practise reading the dialogue out loud with appropriate *emphasis and gestures. Then perform your reading in front of the class.

Part B

Shakespeare's Words Updated

B1 My future wife

The following extract is taken from William Shakespeare's The Taming of the Shrew[1]. *Petruchio has gone to Padua to find a wealthy wife. On hearing of the shrewish elder daughter of the wealthy Baptista Minola, who so far has driven any potential husband away with her sharp tongue, he decides that she is just the right woman for him. The following extract is from their very first meeting.*

[1] **shrew** widerspenstiges, zänkisches Weib

PETRUCHIO	Good morrow, Kate; for that's your name, I hear.	
KATHARINA	Well have you heard, but something hard of hearing:	
	They call me Katharina that do talk of me.	
PETRUCHIO	You lie, in faith; for you are called plain Kate,	
	And bonny Kate and sometimes Kate the curst;	5
	But Kate, the prettiest Kate in Christendom	
	Kate of Kate Hall, my super-dainty Kate,	
	For dainties are all Kates, and therefore, Kate,	
	Take this of me, Kate of my consolation;	
	Hearing thy mildness praised in every town,	10
	Thy virtues spoke of, and thy beauty sounded,	
	Yet not so deeply as to thee belongs,	
	Myself am moved to woo thee for my wife.	
KATHARINA	Moved! In good time: let him that moved you hither	
	Remove you hence: I knew you at the first	15
	You were a moveable.	
PETRUCHIO	Why, what's a moveable?	
KATHARINA	A joined-stool.	
PETRUCHIO	Thou hast hit it: come, sit on me.	
KATHARINA	Asses are made to bear, and so are you.	20
PETRUCHIO	Women are made to bear, and so are you.	
KATHARINA	No such jade as you, if me you mean.	
PETRUCHIO	Alas! good Kate, I will not burden thee;	
	For, knowing thee to be but young and light –	
KATHARINA	Too light for such a swain as you to catch;	25
	And yet as heavy as my weight should be. [...]	

She strikes him.

PETRUCHIO	I swear I'll cuff you, if you strike again.	
KATHARINA	So may you lose your arms:	
	If you strike me, you are no gentleman;	30
	And if no gentleman, why then no arms. [...]	
PETRUCHIO	[...] 'Twas told me you were rough and coy and sullen,	
	And now I find report a very liar;	
	For thou are pleasant, gamesome, passing courteous,	
	But slow in speech, yet sweet as spring-time flowers:	35
	Thou canst not frown, thou canst not look askance,	
	Nor bite the lip, as angry wenches will,	
	Nor hast thou pleasure to be cross in talk,	
	But thou with mildness entertain'st thy wooers,	
	With gentle conference, soft and affable. [...]	40

2 **something hard of hearing** you must be slightly deaf
5 **bonny** fair
  curst *(past tense)* cursed
7 **dainty** sweet
8 **dainties are all Kates** a pun on 'cate', an Elizabethan sweet
9 **consolation** Trost
11 **sounded** proclaimed, reported
13 **woo** court sb.
14 **hither** to this place, here
15 **hence** away from here
18 **joined-stool** piece of furniture
20 **ass** Esel
21 **bear** Lasten tragen; gebären
22 **jade** worthless person
23 **Alas!** expression of sadness, Ach!
25 **swain** lover, wooer
28 **cuff sb.** hit sb.
29 **arms** Wappen
32 **coy** shy
  sullen unfriendly
34 **gamesome** playful
  passing very, exceedingly
  courteous polite
36 **frown** look displeased
  askance verächtlich
37 **wench** girl
40 **conference** talk
  affable likeable

Shakespeare's Words Updated

> Thus in plain terms: your father hath consented
> That you shall be my wife; your dowry 'greed on;
> And, will you, nill you, I will marry you.
> Now, Kate, I am a husband for your turn;
> For, by this light, whereby I see thy beauty,   45
> Thy beauty, that doth make me like thee well,
> Thou must be married to no man but me;
> For I am he am born to tame you Kate,
> And bring you from a wild Kate to a Kate
> Conformable as other household Kates.   50
> Here comes your father: never make denial;
> I must and will have Katharina to my wife.
>
> From: *The Taming of the Shrew*, Act 2, Scene 1

42 **dowry** *Mitgift*
   'greed agreed
43 **will you, nill you** if you want or not
44 **for your turn** just right for you
50 **conformable** *angepasst, fügsam*
   household Kates wives by the name of Kate
51 **make denial** refuse

COMPREHENSION

1 YOU CHOOSE Understanding the dialogue

a Create a *cartoon summarizing the scene. Draw 1–2 frames with speech bubbles and captions.

OR

b Write a short modern English version of the dialogue. Practice reading it with a partner, and then present it to the class.

ANALYSIS

2 Comparing dialogues

Compare the way Petruchio woos Katharina to the way Gloucester woos Anne (A2, pp. 79–81). Evaluate what each man reveals about himself and how effectively they each use words to achieve their aims. **SUPPORT** p. 206

LANGUAGE AWARENESS

3 Playing with words

a Look at ll. 7–31 again. Describe the changes in meaning, grammar or form that occur to certain words.

b Translate those words into German. Explain why in some cases the word-play does not work and in others it works the same as in English.

c Think of three more words that have at least two meanings (= homonyms). Write six appropriate sentences.

BEYOND THE TEXT

4 Modernizing the play

a Imagine the scene is going to be adapted for a modern film version. With a partner, discuss a suitable setting and which actors should take the leading roles. Consider in particular which elements from the original scene should be kept and which removed. Share your ideas in class.

b **CHALLENGE** Create a storyboard for the scene you are planning.

My scene

Storyboard text

The Power of Words – from Shakespeare to Today   Chapter 4

Part B

▶ SF 23: Analysing a film

VIEWING FOCUS ON SKILLS

Evaluating a modern Shakespeare adaptation

Kate in a Lift
The film sequence you are about to watch is from a BBC series in which Shakespeare plays were modernized. It represents the same scene from The Taming of the Shrew *that you have studied in* **B1**.

1 Before viewing
Before watching the film clip, speculate which aspects might have been modernized. Look at your notes from **B1**, task **3** again.

📀 DVD

2 Viewing without sound
You will watch the film extract without sound. Split the class in two groups, with one half doing task **a** and the other doing task **b**.
  a Concentrate on the places shown in the scene. While viewing, make notes on them and the atmosphere they create. Explain why the director may have chosen them.
  b Examine the body language and facial expressions of the two main characters. While viewing, make notes about what they tell you about their characters.
  c Share your findings first with a partner, then report them to the class.

quid *(BE slang)* British pound
clap eyes on sb. see sb. for the first time
trout *(slang)* unpleasant woman
chord Akkord
take the mick make fun of sb.
certifiable lunatic crazy person
bugger sth. up *(slang)* ruin sth.
put your cards on the table say what you really want
alluring attractive
arousing sexy
snarl make an angry noise when talking
lewd sexually vulgar
obnoxious very annoying
plucky having courage and spirit

3 Viewing with sound
  a Watch the film with sound. With your partner from task **2**, discuss if you get new information from the dialogue. List elements of the dialogue that surprised you.
  b View the extract again and concentrate on the music. Describe how it is used, and to what effect.

4 Viewing for the final time
Before viewing the extract for the final time, look at ▶ SF 23 Analysing a film on p. 276. Then, in groups of four, examine the camera work. Two of you concentrate on the part in front of the flat, the other two on the part in the lift. Explain how the camera work affects you as a viewer. Share your findings in your group, then in class.

5 Evaluation
Evaluate how successful the director has been in adapting the material. Describe the elements that were changed and the effect the scene has on you. **SUPPORT** ▶ p. 207

'Modernizing Shakespeare'

84   Chapter 4   The Power of Words – from Shakespeare to Today

Shakespeare's Words Updated

4

B2 Responding to a sonnet

Before reading: Appointment task
- Make an appointment card with the names of three partners.
- Discuss the statements on the right and make notes on your appointment card.
- Discuss your conclusions in class.

Now read the sonnets. Concentrate on the different images the words create in your mind.

1 *Love for someone does not change, even if the person you love changes.*
2 *Love can be between anyone, no matter what age, gender, race or religion.*
3 *Love is not a physical but a spiritual experience.*

Sonnet 116   *William Shakespeare*

Let me not to the marriage of true minds
Admit impediments. Love is not love
Which alters when it alteration finds,
Or bends with the remover to remove:
O no! It is an ever-fixèd mark   5
That looks on tempests and is never shaken;
It is the star to every wandering bark,
Whose worth's unknown, although his height be taken.
Love's not Time's fool, though rosy lips and cheeks
Within his bending sickle's compass come: 10
Love alters not with his brief hours and weeks,
But bears it out even to the edge of doom.
If this be error and upon me proved,
I never writ, nor no man ever loved.

1 **Let me not** May I never
2 **admit** accept
  impediment *Hindernis*
3 **alter** change
4 **remover** person who goes away
5 **mark** landmark or star that helps a sailor to navigate
6 **tempest** storm
7 **wander** travel
  bark ship
10 **bending** curved
  sickle *Sichel*
  compass *Reichweite*
12 **bear out** endure
  edge of doom end of time
13 **upon** against
14 **writ** (have) written

In 1971, Northern Irish poet James Simmons (1933–2001) wrote a series of 'Marital Sonnets'. No. 4 reads like a modern response to Shakespeare's Sonnet 116.

Marital Sonnet 4   *James Simmons*

We murmured passionate language in that trance
when each was famished for the mutual kiss;
but we have altered, and it spoils all chance
of happiness, comparing that with this.
Displays of fireworks were put on by lust,   5
romantic symphonies, unholy wars:
now contraceptives, unworn, gather dust,
in which we once soared gleaming towards the stars.
In age's Leamington our joys last longer,
the libraries are good, the tea-rooms neat,   10
good arguments aren't broken off by anger,
new appetites are fed, we are replete.
Let's call this love, that alters when it finds
alteration, the marriage of two minds.

2 **famished** very hungry
  mutual *gegenseitig*
7 **contraceptive** *Verhütungsmittel*
8 **soar** rise high
  gleam shine
9 **Leamington** a spa town in Warwickshire, England
12 **replete** very full

From: James Simmons, *Poems 1956–1986*, 1986

The Power of Words – from Shakespeare to Today   **Chapter 4**

85

4 Part B

- SF 29: Writing a formal letter or email
- SF 34: Argumentative writing
- SF 37: Doing a creative writing task
- SF 38: Writing a well-structured text

◀ COMPREHENSION

1 Brief summaries
Summarize each poem's message in one sentence.

◀ ANALYSIS

2 Comparing the sonnets
GALLERY WALK Compare the two sonnets. Examine structure, development of the idea and style. Present your findings on posters and evaluate them in a gallery walk. SUPPORT ▶ p. 207

◀ BEYOND THE TEXT

3 Creative writing
Write a response to one of the sonnets. This can take the form of an email or a letter to a friend, an essay, or even a short poem. Refer to your notes from the pre-reading discussion.

CULTURE SPOT

Shakespeare for the masses

1 Comment on the T-shirt. Consider what wearing it would mean to you.

2 What do objects like this tell you about Shakespeare's place in British culture?

3 Design a Shakespeare object. Choose a picture, pun, quote or slogan and present your idea to the class.
   ▶ SF 24: Giving a presentation

Part C | 4

The Powerful Words of Today's Poets

C1 Performance poetry

> **FACT FILE**
>
> **Performance poetry**
> During the 1980s, the term 'performance poetry' came into popular usage to describe poetry written or composed for performance before an audience rather than for print distribution. Before the invention of the printing press, all poetry was performed orally, and in many cultures outside our Western traditions, oral poetry and story-telling are still more important than reading. In the West poetry has become a very individual form of culture. With the rise of new media and technology, the interest in poetry on the page faded, but the spoken word remained important. Punk, reggae and hip hop all had an effect on how the spoken word was perceived. Many contemporary poets took up these influences and started to 'perform' their poetry rather than just read it.
>
> 1 Discuss why you think oral poetry came into existence and what role it has played in society.
>
> 2 Do you prefer to listen to poetry or to read it? Give reasons for your answer.

Benjamin Zephaniah

Dis poetry Benjamin Zephaniah

Benjamin Zephaniah is well known in Britain for his oral renditions of his poems. Watch him perform. ▶ LANGUAGE HELP

────────────────────── **COMPREHENSION** ◀

1 First impressions
  a Watch the performance. Make notes of your first impression and of what you hear. Exchange notes with a partner.
  b Listen and watch again. Add to your notes.

2 A first attempt at understanding
  Choose the sentences that correspond with how you understand the poem.
  A The speaker is saying that his poetry is an essential part of his life.
  B The speaker is saying that rhythm is all that matters.
  C The speaker is saying that poetry needs to be written with love.
  D The speaker is saying that poetry needs to be chanted.

3 Understanding the poem
  Now use the webcode to download the text. Read the poem.
  a List the various descriptions of 'dis poetry' given in the poem.
  b Sum up what his poetry means for the poet himself.

────────────────────── **ANALYSIS** ◀

4 Looking at the language
  Discuss why the poet decided to spell some of the words as he did.

5 Looking at rhythm and rhyme
  One of the key words of the poem is 'riddim'. Analyse how the length of the lines and the rhymes contribute to the rhythm.

▶ **DVD**
▶ SF 22: Listening
▶ SF 23: Analysing a film

> **LANGUAGE HELP**
> • He uses rhythmic gestures / body gestures / his hands to / while …
> • He moves his hands along with the rhythm to …
> • His vivid / lively facial expressions show / underline …
> • He keeps his eyes closed / open when / while …
> • His slow / rapid speech / tone of voice is …

Find the poem here:
 Webcode context-00

▶ SF 21: Analysing poetry
▶ SF 36: Writing a text analysis

The Power of Words – from Shakespeare to Today | Chapter 4

4   Part C

▶ SF 27: Having a discussion
▶ SF 34: Argumentative writing

▶ SF 32: Writing a review

6 The meaning of the poem
Discuss the meaning of the last 7 lines with a partner. Use your findings to write down your interpretation of the poem.

——————————————————————————— BEYOND THE TEXT ◀

7 Reviewing a poetry performance
Watch the performance again. Pay special attention to the speaker's gestures. Then write a review for the English pages of your school magazine.
SUPPORT ▶ p. 207

Famous for what?   Hollie McNish

*Discuss what being famous means to you.
Then watch Hollie McNish perform her poem.*

——————————————————————————— COMPREHENSION ◀

🎬 DVD
▶ SF 27: Having a discussion

Hollie McNish

Webcode context-00

1 Discussing your first reactions
Discuss your first impressions of the performance. Consider aspects like the poet herself, the manner of delivery, the type of poem, and the poem itself.

2 Understanding the poem
Describe the situation in the poem briefly and state what you think the message is.

3 Re-examining the message
Now use the webcode to download the text. Read the poem and then look at your answer to task **2** again. If necessary, change your statement.

——————————————————————————— ANALYSIS ◀

4 Analysing the style
Explain what makes this a poem. Examine the rhythm, sound of words, rhyme and imagery.

——————————————————————————— BEYOND THE TEXT ◀

🎧 CD1 10
▶ SF 41: Mediation of written and oral texts

5 Mediation (German → English)
Listen to the poem on the CD. Imagine that an English friend sent you a link to Hollie McNish performing her poem. You want to show him or her that Germans do poetry performances too, and send an email with a link to the poem from the CD. Tell your friend what the subject of the poem is and how it is similar or different to the performance by Hollie McNish. Write about 150 words.

6 YOU CHOOSE ▶ **Creative writing**

▶ SF 29: Writing a formal letter or email
▶ SF 37: Doing a creative writing task

a   Imagine you are a careers advisor at school. Write a letter to the girl addressed in Hollie McNish's poem.

b   Imagine the person addressed in Hollie McNish's poem was a boy. What parts of the poem might be changed? Rewrite those lines using new phrases and ideas.

4 The powerful words of today's poets

C2 The psychological power of words

All poets rely on the power of their words to make an impression on listeners and readers. On a different level, some poets write directly about the impact of words in our lives. The following two poems are examples – one by a British writer of Pakistani origin, the other by an American with a Chinese background.

Before reading
Before reading or listening, list situations in which the impact of words plays a decisive role.

The right word   *Imtiaz Dharker*

Listen to Imtiaz Dharker reading her poem.

Imtiaz Dharker

— COMPREHENSION ◀

1 **Giving an initial reaction**
  a Talk about your impression of the poem with a partner. Then agree on one sentence that states its message.
  b Now read the poem.

Outside the door,
lurking in the shadows,
is a terrorist.

Is that the wrong description?
Outside that door,   5
taking shelter in the shadows,
is a freedom fighter.

I haven't got this right.
Outside, waiting in the shadows,
is a hostile militant.   10

Are words no more
than waving, wavering flags?
Outside your door,
watchful in the shadows,
is a guerrilla warrior.   15

God help me.
Outside, defying every shadow,
stands a martyr.
I saw his face.

No words can help me now.   20
Just outside the door,
lost in shadows,
is a child who looks like mine.

One word for you.
Outside my door,   25
his hand too steady,
his eyes too hard
is a boy who looks like your son,
too.

I open the door.   30
Come in, I say.
Come in and eat with us.

The child steps in
and carefully, at my door,
takes off his shoes.   35

---

2 **Understanding the general idea**
  a List the different descriptions of the people standing outside the speaker's door. **SUPPORT** ▶ p. 207
  b Add *connotations that go with each description as well as the mental image it conveys.
  c In one sentence, state the idea that the speaker is developing in the course of the poem.

— ANALYSIS ◀

3 **Analysis and interpretation**
Interpret the poem by analysing its structure and images. Evaluate whether the poet gives an answer to her question about words being 'no more than waving, wavering flags'. Conclude your interpretation by considering whether she found 'the right word'.

---

2 **lurk** wait secretly, not wanting to be seen
12 **wave** (v) move a hand or a flag up and down, usually in greeting
waver (v) move in an unsteady or uncertain way
17 **defy sth.** einer Sache trotzen

▶ SF 17: Analysing stylistic devices
▶ SF 21: Analysing poetry

The Power of Words – from Shakespeare to Today   Chapter 4

4 Part C

You should've stopped there   William Marr

While reading, imagine the setting and context in which these lines are spoken. Try to 'see' what is going on here.

2 **uppercase** in capital letters
  bold *fett gedruckt*
4 **hiss** *zischen*
6 **scatter** move quickly into different directions
16 **shatter** fall to pieces suddenly
19 **crumble** fall to pieces slowly

```
              first I see words coming out of your mouth
                  black words all UPPERCASE and bold
       they become so dark and dense that I think they are bullets
         wait a second they ARE bullets now all streaming hissing
                      smoking burning toward us                      5

            we scatter and run for cover waiting for something
           to happen but are surprised to hear a sudden silence
                          explode in our ears
                 I look up and find you just standing there
                        with your mouth wide open                   10
                    as if you are running out of ammunition
                   but from the expression on your twisted face
                      and out-stretched tongue there must still be
                      something inside that wants to come out

              for a few seconds you remain in your frozen posture   15
            then right before our eyes your body shatters and breaks up
                     we slowly rise and gather around
         trying to pick up the pieces but find they are so badly burned
                        that they crumble at a touch

                      you should've stopped there really            20
                         before you opened your mouth
```

From: William Marr, *In this 21st century: New Poems from William Marr*

LANGUAGE HELP

- Get lost / out of my sight / out of here!
- Go to hell!
- … someone as lazy/crazy/ … as you!
- You never listen to me / get anything right!
- I'm done with / fed up with …
- I never want to … again!
- I've had enough of …
- I've had it up to here with …
- I can't believe what/that you …
- You have no idea how …
- I really didn't mean what … / to …
- I wish you / I hadn't …
- I was just being honest/frank about …
- I just feel like …
- Can you forgive me / hear me out, please?
- How do we carry on / ever get over …?
- Let's try and start over / be honest …

▶ SF 17: Analysing stylistic devices
▶ SF 21: Analysing poetry

COMPREHENSION ◀

1 Understanding the situation
Say in one sentence what kind of situation the poem deals with, including the relationship between the speaker and the person addressed.

ANALYSIS ◀

2 Analysing imagery
  a There are two main images used in this poem. Analyse them and say what they have in common.
  b From your personal experience explain whether you find the imagery appropriate.

BEYOND THE TEXT ◀

3 YOU CHOOSE Creative writing

  a Write a poem from the point of view of the person addressed.

  b Write a dramatic scene based on the poem. Add a few stage directions to the dialogue. ▶ LANGUAGE HELP

Chapter Task

'I can't wait to see the reviews in the newspaper to find out whether I like the movie or not.'

Writing a review

Reviews are written by critics to inform other people about the positive and negative aspects of a particular book, film, etc. But increasingly ordinary people write reviews on the internet not just about films and books, but also about general products.

For the task at hand, you are going to be the critic of a weekly magazine for young adults. You have been asked to hunt for some 'good stuff' in literature or film and write a review explaining to readers of your own age group why you like the material you have chosen.
When you have finished the task, your teacher will give you an assessment sheet.

1 Get hold of one of your literary favourites. This can be a novel, a short story, a play (that you have either read or watched on stage), a poem or a collection of poems, a song or a film.

2 Take a fresh look at your chosen material and read/view it for analysis.

3 Write a catchy beginning for your review.

4 State what the text/film is about and what happens. Don't reveal anything that might ruin the pleasure for someone else (e.g. the ending).

5 Write the main body, which includes the reasons you have decided on. Include quotes from the text/film that reveal the power of its language.

6 Write a suitable ending in which you recommend your item.

7 a When you are satisfied with your review, type a neat copy and present it in a gallery walk.
   b Move around and read all the reviews. Take a vote on which three should be printed.

▶ Focus On Skills, Close reading, p. 78
▶ SF 19: Analysing narrative prose
▶ SF 20: Analysing drama
▶ SF 21: Analysing poetry
▶ SF 23: Analysing a film
▶ SF 8: Structuring ideas
▶ SF 32: Writing a review
▶ SF 40: Proofreading

5 The UK – a Kingdom United?

Download a chronological word list here:

 Webcode context-00

▶ SF 3: Using a dictionary

1 Getting to know the British
  a Choose four red words and four blue words from the flag. Explain them to a partner and say why you think they are part of 'Britishness'.
  b Choose four words you do not know and look them up in a monolingual dictionary. Guess why these words are considered typically British.
  c Find three words on the flag that you do not think are typically British. Compare your words with those chosen by a partner.

2 Looking at your own country
   What's typically German? Collect your ideas and make up a German flag in the same way as the British flag above. Present your German flag to your partner. Explain your choices and discuss the words that are different.

Lead-in

Prince George benefits rugby fish & chips Ascot
haggis David Beckham hypocrisy Republic booze
House of Lords complain fashion newspaper Queen
The Empire Wales values rain lager
music monarchy James Bond Marmite
Giant's Causeway football drink Jason Statham
Kate together
humour culture England cuppa Northern Ireland
weather manners class queuing Commonwealth
resilience posh tea Shakespeare pound sterling NHS
integrity One Direction
rambling
bank holiday Keira Knightley Jamie Oliver accents
Scotland irony Plymouth
cider heritage cynicism traffic
prude Monty Python Downton Abbey Diamond Jubilee
Westminster multiculturalism Union
J. K. Rowling xenophobia Wimbledon
community tolerance

PREVIEW

In this chapter you will gain an insight into British culture and learn about problems faced by people in Britain today.

Main topics

- Politics and traditions .... p. 98
- Multiculturalism in the UK .... p. 103
- Future challenges .... p. 110

Focus on Skills: LISTENING

- Listening for gist and detail .... p. 99

Chapter Task:

Listening to a podcast and using it as a model to make a podcast of your own .... p. 111

The UK – a Kingdom United? **Chapter 5**

93

5 Words in Context

Listen to an audio version of the text on the CD or download it here:
Webcode context-00

Character of a country

A political state

The terms Great Britain, Britain, England and the UK are often mistakenly used as synonyms. Great Britain is the largest island of the British Isles (and also the largest island in Europe); England is a country on this island. The United Kingdom (also called 'Britain') includes England, Scotland, Wales and Northern Ireland and is a state with a population of about 62 million people.
The Union Flag, also known as the Union Jack, has been the national flag of the United Kingdom since 1908 and represents the powerful community and strong individual identities of the different nations.
Characteristically, Scotland has always been seen as a separate nation and since the late 20th century, many Scots have wanted to be fully independent. However, in a 2014 referendum, 55% of the voting population voted to stay in the UK.
Even in the 21st century, the royal family remains a very important British institution. Events like the opening ceremony of the 2012 Olympic Games (in which one scene showed the Queen jumping out of a helicopter with James Bond), the Queen's Diamond Jubilee, Prince William's marriage to Kate Middleton and the birth of Prince George all saw the British population celebrate the fresh and modern image portrayed by their monarchy.

Multiculturalism

As head of the British Empire, the UK was once a colonial superpower with territories in many countries, like India, Australia, New Zealand and small island nations like the Seychelles, Mauritius and the Maldives. Today there is still a strong bond between many former states of the British Empire and most of these nations are members of the Commonwealth of Nations. Together, they work towards world peace, promotion of democracy worldwide, and ending racism, sexism, poverty, ignorance, and disease.
Partly due to its history, immigrants from all over the world have settled in the UK, shaping the culture and adding to the nation's diversity with their food, religions and music. The result is a very multicultural society with the aim that everyone, regardless of colour, race or culture, should feel at home.

An uncertain future

The UK plays a significant role in world politics as a member of the EU and has permanent representation on the UN Security Council and in NATO. Furthermore, the UK has one of the largest and most influential economies in the world.
However, the financial crisis of 2007–2008 did not leave the UK unaffected and has led to economic problems, increased unemployment, social inequality and poverty. Anti-immigration feeling has also increased in some parts of the population and politicians who oppose the EU and Britain's membership have become more and more popular.

Character of a country

1 Using your own knowledge
For each of the three parts of the text, try to think of one piece of information which is not mentioned. Write them down and compare your findings with a partner.

2 Words in use
  a Find a highlighted expression from the text that describes or names the following:
  1 the name of the national flag of the UK
  2 a person who joins a team, a union or an organisation
  3 relatives of the monarch of the United Kingdom
  4 something that connects people or things, keeping them firmly together
  5 a country that governs many other countries
  6 an institution made up of countries that were once under the leadership or control of the British crown
  7 having a strong effect on somebody or something

  b Give definitions or use examples to explain the following terms from the text:

  1 multicultural society   5 former
  2 referendum   6 diversity
  3 image   7 crisis
  4 shape   8 social inequality

▶ SF 10: Working with closed test formats

In the 2014 referendum, Scottish inhabitants had to vote 'Yes' or 'No' over whether Scotland should leave the UK and become an independent country.

3 Phrases into English
In each of the following sentences, a useful phrase from the text is missing. Copy and complete the sentences. If you aren't sure how to translate the German words, look at the text again.
  1 The royal family aims to *(ein frisches, modernes Erscheinungsbild vermitteln)*.
  2 People with roots all over the world *(tragen zur Vielfalt der Nation bei)*.
  3 Everyone should feel safe in the country they live in *(unabhängig von Hautfarbe, Rasse oder Kultur)*.
  4 Events that began on Wall Street in New York *(haben das Vereinigte Königreich nicht unberührt gelassen)*.
  5 Politicians *(die die EU ablehnen)* are gaining more popularity in some parts of the UK.

4 Writing
Create a slogan for an educational course on the UK's history and traditions, culture or politics. Write a short explanation for your slogan and use as many highlighted words from the text above as possible. Present your slogans in a gallery walk and decide on the best three.

▶ SF 1: Dealing with unknown words
▶ LP 20: Choosing the right translation
▶ LP 18: Avoiding Germanisms

■ **FACT FILE**

Slogans should be easy to understand and memorable. Good slogans play with language (e.g. rhyme or rhythm and puns) to make you think.

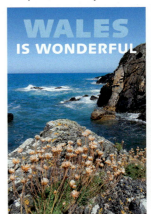

The UK – a Kingdom United?   Chapter 5

95

5 Part A

A crowned nation

A1 Dangerous books Alan Bennett

- In three sentences, state why you think reading is or isn't important. Share your answers in class.
- Discuss whether you think reading plays a part in a typical day in the Queen's life. What other duties might be on her agenda?

In the following extract from the *novel The Uncommon Reader, *the Queen has developed an intense passion for literature. This starts to affect the way she carries out her public duties and what people think of her.*

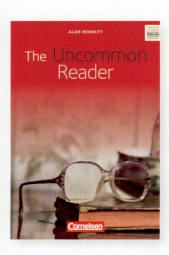

One of the Queen's recurrent royal responsibilities was to open Parliament, an obligation she had never previously found particularly burdensome and actually rather enjoyed: to be driven down the Mall on a bright autumn morning even after fifty years was something of a treat. But not any more. She was dreading the two hours the whole thing was due to take, though fortunately they were in the coach, not the open carriage, so she could take along her book. She'd got quite good at reading and waving, the trick being to keep the book below the level of the window and to keep focused on it and not on the crowds. The duke didn't like it one bit, of course, but goodness it helped.

Which was all very well, except it was only when she was actually in the coach, with the procession drawn up in the palace forecourt and ready for the off, that, as she put on her glasses, she realised she'd forgotten the book. And while the duke fumes in the corner and the postillions fidget, the horses shift and the harness clinks, Norman is rung on the mobile. The Guardsmen stand at ease and the procession waits. The officer in charge looks at his watch. Two minutes late. Knowing nothing displeases Her Majesty more and knowing nothing of the book, he does not look forward to the repercussions that must inevitably follow. But here is Norman, skittering across the gravel with the book thoughtfully hidden in a shawl, and off they go.

Still, it is an ill-tempered royal couple that is driven down the Mall, the duke waving viciously from his side, the Queen listlessly from hers, and at some speed, too, as the procession tries to pick up the two minutes that have been lost.

At Westminster she popped the offending book behind a cushion in the carriage ready for the journey back, mindful as she sat on the throne and embarked on her speech of how tedious was the twaddle she was called on to deliver and that this was actually the only occasion when she got to read aloud to the nation. 'My government will do this … my government will do that.' It was so barbarously phrased and wholly devoid of style or interest that she felt it demeaned the very act of reading itself, with this year's performance even more garbled than usual as she, too, tried to pick up the missing couple of minutes.

It was with some relief that she got back into the coach and reached behind the cushion for her book. It was not there. Steadfastly waving as they rumbled along, she surreptitiously felt behind the other cushions.

The Queen and the Duke of Edinburgh making a journey in the royal carriage

2 **burdensome** implying hard work
3 **the Mall** road leading to Buckingham Palace
14 **draw up** position yourself
ready for the off ready to go
16 **fume** be very angry
17 **postillion** driver of a coach with horses
fidget make nervous movements
Norman fictional character in *The Uncommon Reader* who works as the Queen's servant
18 **stand at ease** relax *(military)*
21 **repercussion** negative consequence
skitter run in a funny way
24 **viciously** angrily
listlessly without energy or enthusiasm
28 **twaddle** *(infml)* silly speech
30 **barbarously** in a very unpleasant way
31 **devoid of sth.** without sth.
demean sth. make people have less respect for sth.
36 **surreptitiously** in a subtle way

96 Chapter 5 The UK – a Kingdom United?

A crowned nation 5

'You're not sitting on it?'
'Sitting on what?'
'My book.'
40 'No, I am not. Some British Legion people here, and wheelchairs. Wave, for God's sake.'
When they arrived at the palace she had a word with Grant, the young footman in charge, who said that while ma'am had been in the Lords the sniffer dogs had been round and security had confiscated the book. He thought it had probably been 45 exploded.
'Exploded?' said the Queen. 'But it was Anita Brookner.'
The young man, who seemed remarkably undeferential, said security may have thought it was a device.
The Queen said: 'Yes. That is exactly what it is. A book is a device to ignite the 50 imagination.'
The footman said: 'Yes, ma'am.'
It was as if he was talking to his grandmother, and not for the first time the Queen was made unpleasantly aware of the hostility her reading seemed to arouse.
'Very well,' she said. 'Then you should inform security that I shall expect to find 55 another copy of the same book, vetted and explosive free, waiting on my desk tomorrow morning. And another thing. The carriage cushions are filthy. Look at my gloves.' Her Majesty departed.
'Fuck,' said the footman, fishing out the book from where he had been told to hide it down the front of his breeches. But of the lateness of the procession, to everyone's 60 surprise nothing was officially said.

From: *The Uncommon Reader*, Alan Bennett, 2008

40 **British Legion** organisation that helps ex-soldiers
44 **confiscate sth.** take sth. away
46 **Anita Brookner** British novelist and art historian (1928–)
47 **undeferential** showing no respect
49 **ignite sth.** etw. entzünden
55 **vet sth.** check sth.
59 **breeches** *(pl)* Reiterhose

COMPREHENSION

1 Identifying key points
  a Point out how the Queen's reading habit interferes with her duties.
  b Compare the Queen's day as shown in the passage to your ideas about a typical day in her life from **1b**.

▶ SF 19: Analysing narrative prose

LANGUAGE AWARENESS

2 Analysing direct speech
Analyse the language used in direct speech by the Queen, the duke and the footman. Assess its effect on your impression of their characters.

ANALYSIS

3 Analysing *humour
Analyse the *humour in this passage. Take into consideration how the *plot, certain aspects of the language and the imagery contribute to the humorous effect.

▶ SF 17: Analysing stylistic devices
▶ LP 21: Writing about texts

BEYOND THE TEXT

4 YOU CHOOSE ▶ **Creative writing**

  a Imagine another situation (e.g. naming a ship / attending a pop-concert / on a state visit) in which the Queen does not fulfil her duties because of her new hobby and write a similar passage. Try to include elements of *humour.

  OR

  b After the incident, the footman tells his wife about his encounter with the Queen. Write their dialogue and include the events that probably took place while the Queen was opening the Parliament.
  SUPPORT ▶ p. 208

Find out more about British royal family here:
 Webcode context-00

▶ EE 4: Talking about sensitive issues

The UK – a Kingdom United? Chapter 5

5 Part A

■ FACT FILE

The Palace of Westminster, London

Parliamentary system

The head of state is the king or queen, who has many ceremonial functions and social duties but no real power. The monarch's duties include opening Parliament and officially appointing the Prime Minister after his or her election.

The UK Parliament is known as the 'Mother of Parliaments' because it has served as a model for many governments all over the world. It dates back to the year 1215, when a group of noblemen forced King John of England to respect certain rights. Among these, set down in the Magna Carta, was their right to be consulted before the king could make them pay new taxes. Over the centuries, this group of noblemen evolved into today's Parliament.

Members of Parliament attending a session of Parliament in the House of Commons

The two houses of Parliament, the House of Lords and the House of Commons meet in the Palace of Westminster. Thus journalists often refer to 'Westminster' when they mean Parliament, especially if they are talking about the House of Commons. There are currently over 700 members of the House of Lords, but their power is limited. Although both houses of Parliament must, in theory, approve laws before they are submitted to the king or queen, the Lords can only delay a bill that has passed in the House of Commons. Traditionally, a committee of the House of Lords was also the highest court in the land, but that function has been moved to the newly created Supreme Court.

Real power lies with the House of Commons, which is elected for up to five years (although the Prime Minister can call a general election any time before that). Each Member of Parliament (MP) represents one of 650 constituencies (electoral districts) in the UK. In each constituency, the candidate with the most votes wins, and that person then sits in the Commons. In the UK's so-called 'first-past-the-post' system, all other votes are worthless. This effectively prevents smaller parties being elected to Parliament and can potentially lead to a majority in Parliament that does not always reflect the total number of votes. For example, in the 2005 general election, the Labour party won 55% of the seats in the House of Commons with just 35% of the votes.

Her Majesty's Government consists of the Prime Minister (PM) and the Cabinet, which is made up of the MPs who run the different government departments. The most important ministers are the Chancellor of the Exchequer, who is in charge of finance, the Foreign Secretary and the Home Secretary, who is responsible for the country's internal affairs. In the press, the Prime Minister's office is often referred to as 'Number 10', after its address at 10 Downing Street, and the ministries are known as 'Whitehall', after the street in London where most of them are located.

1. *Describe the roles of the following people and groups to a partner using one sentence for each:*
   Partner A: ▪ the Prime Minister ▪ the Cabinet
   Partner B: ▪ an MP ▪ the monarch

2. *In a table, list what you now know about one of the houses of the UK Parliament. Present your list to your partner.*
   Partner A: The House of Lords
   Partner B: The House of Commons

3. *List differences and similarities to the German system of government.*

A crowned nation

5

LISTENING **FOCUS ON SKILLS**
Listening for gist and detail

Listening is the key to successful oral communication. It requires focus, preparation and practice.

What do Brits think of the royal family?

1 Before listening
You are going to hear two short interviews about people's opinions of the British monarchy. What might people say? Write 2–3 sentences.

2 Dealing with different accents
When listening to native English speakers, you will often hear people speak with different accents. When somebody's accent is difficult to understand, you should focus on words you can understand and use the context to figure out the rest of the sentence. As you listen, you will probably get used to the accent.
  a Listen to a short excerpt of an interview. The interviewer and the interviewee have different accents. Try to write down exactly what both men say, then compare your answers with a partner.
  b Discuss which man was easier to understand and why.

3 First listening: listening for gist
  a Skim through the task below and note down keywords that you can listen out for. Compare your notes with a partner.
  b Listen to the extract, then choose the right answers.
   1 The first interviewee …
     … considers the institution of the monarchy a brilliant idea.
     … isn't really sure what he thinks about the monarchy.
     … completely rejects the monarchy.
   2 The young couple …
     … think the royal family should be abolished.
     … have generally positive opinions about the royal family.
     … think the royal family is mainly a bad thing for the UK.

4 Second listening: listening for detail
Again, skim through the questions to find out what *specific* information you will have to listen out for.
  a Listen to the first interview again. Are the sentences below true or false? Correct the false answers.
   1 The first interviewee understands why some people would like to have an elected president instead of a monarch.
   2 The Queen is his favourite member of the royal family.
   3 He was born during the Queen's reign.
   4 He does not think that Charles will become King.

▶ SF 22: Listening

FACT FILE
A regional accent is determined by where a speaker is from and where they live.
A social accent is often determined by a speaker's socio-economic status, i.e. their level of education, how wealthy their family is, and their family's level of education. People from the same region can have different accents if they are from different socio-economic groups.

🎧 CD 13

🎧 CD 14

▶ SF 15: Marking up a text / Making and taking notes

Buckingham Palace, home of the Queen in London

The UK – a Kingdom United? Chapter 5

99

5 Part A

b Listen to the second interview and finish the sentences.
1 The young woman says that the royal family does a lot of good for …
2 The young man mentions … as two examples of the stereotypical English image.
3 The young man says that the … has been lost.
4 The young man's favourite member of the royal family is …
5 The young man thinks that Kate has …

c Compare and discuss your results with a partner.

5 Evaluating the listening procedure

a Compare your initial expectations which you wrote for Task **1** with what you actually heard.
b Discuss the listening procedure with a partner. To what extent were your anticipations useful? Which tip or strategy was most helpful to you?

CD 15
▶ SF 22: Listening

A2 Does Britain still need the monarchy?

— COMPREHENSION ◀

1 Listening for gist
Listen to part two of the podcast and decide which of the following statements best expresses the main ideas of the speakers.
a 1 The first interviewee would keep the monarchy, but doesn't like them very much.
2 The first interviewee thinks the media hates the royal family.
b 1 The second interviewee quite likes William and Harry.
2 The second interviewee thinks Australia should no longer be a member of the Commonwealth.

2 Listening for detail
Listen to the first interview again. Match the arguments given in the box to those of the interviewee. There are more arguments than needed.

do a lot of charity • very expensive • outdated institution • symbol of Britain • attracts tourists • good role mode • a tradition to keep • too many scandals • arrogant and snobby family • close to the people • loved by the media

— BEYOND THE TEXT ◀

3 Preparing for a discussion
a Look again at the arguments put forward by all of the speakers in both parts of the podcast. Divide their arguments into two columns: 'in favour of' and 'against' the monarchy.
b Together with a partner, add further arguments to your list.

4 Having a discussion
a In groups of 4–5, discuss whether the monarchy in Britain should be abolished. ▶ LANGUAGE HELP
b **CHALLENGE** ▶ Make notes on the different arguments raised during your discussion and present the three most convincing ones to the rest of the class.

LANGUAGE HELP
Stating your opinion:
- In my opinion … / The way I see it …
- As far as I'm concerned / If you ask me …
- I'm absolutely convinced that …

Agreeing:
- I couldn't agree with you more.
- Exactly! / Precisely! / Certainly! / Definitely!

Disagreeing:
- I'm not so sure, really.
- I'm not convinced that …
- I strongly disagree / I don't agree with you at all.

▶ SF 27: Having a discussion

Chapter 5   The UK – a Kingdom United?

Part B

5

The multicultural face of the UK

FACT FILE

From Empire to Commonwealth

The British Empire was the largest colonial empire in the world covering nearly one fifth of the land worldwide during the late 19th and early 20th centuries.

Since the 16th century, Britain had established colonies all over the world including settlement colonies like Canada, Australia and New Zealand, trading colonies (e.g. India) as well as strategically important naval bases in the Mediterranean (e.g. Gibraltar). It was said that the sun never set on the Empire, so great was its power and territory. However, the effects of a decolonization movement and two world wars led to the decline of the British Empire and the foundation of the Commonwealth of Nations. The Commonwealth of Nations was founded in 1931 and is a voluntary association of 53 countries of the former British Empire.

Queen Victoria (1819–1901) ruled over almost a quarter of the world's population by the end of her reign.

The Head of the Commonwealth is the British monarch. The states are united by language (English), culture, history and in their values, such as democracy, economic development, the rule of law and the guarantee of human rights.

The Commonwealth includes about two billion people, which is 30 per cent of the world's population. Every four years, athletes from the member countries take part in the Commonwealth Games. These include classic olympic sports as well as typical sports played in Commonwealth countries (e.g. netball).

The three key values of the Commonwealth Games movement are Humanity, Equality and Destiny.

Explain and comment on the quote 'The sun never sets on the British Empire.'

B1 The British Empire report

The video you are about to watch presents the rise, dominance and fall of the British Empire.

▶ SF 23: Analysing a film

1 Before viewing
Before you watch the video, speculate about how the filmmaker might deal with the subject of colonialism. Take into consideration the Fact File 'From Empire to Commonwealth'.

📀 **DVD**
peak highest point
leap big jump
shift sth. move sth.
spell trouble be a problem

─────────────── ANALYSIS ◀

2 Viewing for the first time
Watch the video and describe it with two adjectives which you find most suitable: e.g. funny, informative, exaggerated, annoying, innovative, childish, surprising, etc. Explain your choices.

3 Examining how material is presented
  a Watch the video for a second time. Describe the different methods that are used to present information. Consider how the events are visualized and supported by film excerpts, still pictures, sound effects and music.
  b Compare your findings and discuss their effect on the viewer. To what extent do the presenter and the different material that is shown support the viewer's understanding of the Empire's history?

Map of the world showing in red the extent of the British Empire in 1901

The UK – a Kingdom United?   Chapter 5

101

5 Part B

▶ SF37: Doing creative writing tasks

━━━━━━━━━━━━━━━━━━━━━━━━━━━━━━━━━━━ BEYOND THE TEXT ◀

4 Beyond the video
a List five important dates and events in German history. With a partner compare your lists and decide on the 4 most important events.
b **CHALLENGE** Write the script for a video report aimed at an English audience in which you show and comment on important dates in German history. If you want to, you can use *irony and humour or you can make it informative and objective.

B2 Between two cultures   *Mike Bartlett*

In the play Artefacts *by Mike Bartlett, Kelly is a teenage girl living in Great Britain with her mother Susan. In the following scenes, she meets her father Ibrahim for the first time since he left the family when Kelly was a child to live in his home country Iraq.*

Read the two extracts and imagine what the *scenes would look like on a stage.

Extract 1

IBRAHIM	Do you think we look alike?
KELLY	You and my uncle?
IBRAHIM	You and me.
KELLY	Uh … No.
IBRAHIM	You're passionate.
KELLY	I'm English.
IBRAHIM	You are half Iraqi. You can have an Iraqi passport now.
KELLY	That's not much use.
IBRAHIM	Would you prefer it if I had been an American?
KELLY	No.
	Well, yeah. That would be better though, wouldn't it? Cos an American passport's worth loads. I could go there and work and stuff. But I told you I'm not going to go to Iraq, am I?

After a short pause when Kelly's mother Susan enters, Kelly continues.

KELLY	This afternoon when I was bored I looked in the mirror cos, apparently, I'm half Iraqi.
SUSAN	Are you sure you're both all right?
KELLY	But which bits?
SUSAN	Up here?
KELLY	Hips. Hands.
IBRAHIM	Kelly?
KELLY	I've got English legs. Iraqi breasts.
IBRAHIM	I wish we could've met earlier.
KELLY	But my stomach is slightly potted.
IBRAHIM	Kelly? […]
KELLY	I have a little pot belly. Maybe this is the point they mix. The two countries. Where my genes got confused. This belly is not Iraqi or English. It's Engraqi. Iringlish. I like my belly. Yeah. […] Am I what you expected?
IBRAHIM	I tried not to expect anything.
KELLY	But you did.

5

10

15

20

25

30

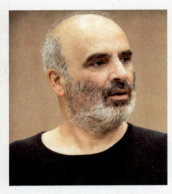

Actor Peter Polycarpou played the role of Ibrahim in Artefacts *in 2008.*

11 **cos** *(sl)* because
25 **potted** *(here)* larger than usual

102   Chapter 5   The UK – a Kingdom United?

The multicultural face of the UK 5

	IBRAHIM	I imagined you might look like Kate Winslet.
	KELLY	This isn't going very well, is it?
35	IBRAHIM	I don't know.
	KELLY	Bit of a fucking disappointment for you.
	IBRAHIM	No.
	KELLY	If you were after –
	IBRAHIM	You are better than Kate Winslet.
40	KELLY	What do you want?
	IBRAHIM	You are you.
	KELLY	Why are you here? Now, what do you *want*?
	IBRAHIM	That we meet.
	KELLY	Just that.
45	IBRAHIM	Yes.
	KELLY	You don't want money?
	IBRAHIM	I run the National Museum of Iraq. In Baghdad. A number of our artefacts were stolen. During the war. I was invited to come and give a lecture at the British Museum about the current state of our collection.
50		That is where I have been today.
	KELLY	So I'm not actually why you came at all.
	IBRAHIM	It is expensive to fly here. I will probably never come back to Britain. So I thought it best we meet.

Extract 2
On her first visit to Iraq, Kelly meets her father's other family. One of Ibrahim's daughters has been kidnapped and Kelly asks her father about this incident.

	IBRAHIM	Why? Why are you asking? Why do you want to know?
55	KELLY	I've got a right to know.
	IBRAHIM	A right? You have no right to know about my family.
	KELLY	She's my sister.
	IBRAHIM	And I'm your father.
	KELLY	Apparently.
60	IBRAHIM	You should trust me that I will do the right thing. But you don't. Do you? You think you know better. You have not been here a day yet. What makes you think you will know better than me.
	KELLY	Maybe I don't trust you. Not hard to work out why is it? [...]
	IBRAHIM	What makes you think what I am doing is a mistake?
65	KELLY	You are that kind of man.
	IBRAHIM	Weak.
	KELLY	Careless.
	IBRAHIM	And why do you think I am *careless*? I will tell you.
	KELLY	Yeah, all right then, tell me what I think.
70	IBRAHIM	You come here and you see this city and you see me and my normal house. You see how poor we are and we don't have things you have. And you see on your news how the country is fighting itself. And you think we are all careless. No, not just careless, you think we are stupid. So this is why you're asking what is going on, because you want to make
75		sure that I am being civilised in what I am doing. That I am being intelligent – *reasonable* in how I am behaving. Because we Iraqis, you think, we tend to get things wrong all the time. We allow our girls to be kidnapped.

Actress Lizzie Watts performing in a production of Artefacts *at the Bush Theatre in London*

77 **tend to do sth.** do sth. regularly

5 Part B

₇₉ **tend to do sth.** do sth. often
mess sth. up do sth. very badly

	We tend to mess things up.
	That is really why you do not trust me.
KELLY	Cos I'm racist.
IBRAHIM	Because you are English. And you don't know any better. When you are a child in England you are still taught underneath that you should rule the world. How in the end Britain has always made the world better.
KELLY	You told me I'm half Iraqi.
IBRAHIM	I hoped you were.
KELLY	I am. Whether I like it or not. I can't choose.
IBRAHIM	Yes, you can. You can choose where you belong.

From: *Artefacts*, Mike Bartlett, 2008

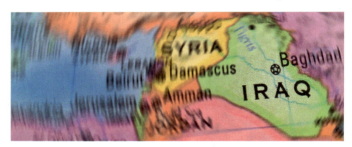

▶ SF 14: Reading strategies

▶ SF 20: Analysing drama
▶ LP 21: Writing about texts

FACT FILE

In literature, **colloquialism** is the use of informal words and expressions in conversations to underline the speaker's social status, level of education, relationship with others etc. The opposite of colloquialism is standard or formal English.
Examples:
wanna want to
gonna going to
go nuts go insane

▶ SF 37: Doing creative writing tasks

▶ SF 27: Having a discussion

▶ LP 14: Emphasizing your message

COMPREHENSION
1 Looking for the main idea
a Describe how Kelly tries to find out which culture she belongs to.
b Point out which prejudices towards the Iraqi and English cultures are discussed in the text.

ANALYSIS
2 Analysing character relationships
Analyse the relationship between Kelly and her father Ibrahim. Reflect on what they talk about and how they speak to each other. SUPPORT ▶ p. 208

LANGUAGE AWARENESS
3 Studying colloquial language
a Read the explanation of colloquialism on the left and find examples of colloquial language in the conversation between Kelly and Ibrahim.
b Rewrite the examples you found in the text in formal English.

BEYOND THE TEXT
4 YOU CHOOSE ▶ **Creative writing**

a Write an email Kelly sends to her best friend in Britain after she has met her father in Iraq.

b Together with a partner, write a dialogue between Kelly's father Ibrahim and her mum Susan after the first meeting of father and daughter.

5 Thinking about cultural identity
a Together with a partner, discuss whether 'You can choose where you belong' (l. 88). Who or what influences you in your choice? Think about family, culture, education and list concrete examples for and against the quote.
b CHALLENGE ▶ Write a *comment on Ibrahim's idea that 'You can choose where you belong.' (l. 88)

104 Chapter 5 The UK – a Kingdom United?

The multicultural face of the UK — 5

B3 The British and their tea

The British are famous for their love of tea. In the following podcast, you will get to know more about this tradition.

Before listening
Brainstorm in class what you know about the British tradition of drinking tea.

► COMPREHENSION ◄

1 **Listening for gist**
   In one sentence, summarize what the podcast is about.

2 **Listening for detail**
   a Complete the following statements about the history of tea.
      1 The British made their first cup of tea sometime in the middle of the … century.
      2 In the 19th century, tea became popular among … people.
      3 Tea drinking has a much longer history in …, where people have drunk tea for thousands of years.
      4 Nearly everyone in Britain puts … in their tea, and about a third of people add … to make the tea sweet.
   b CHALLENGE ► While working on **2a**, take notes on how to make a nice cup of tea the British way.

3 **Analysing style**
   How does the speaker of the podcast try to hold the audience's attention and entertain his listeners? SUPPORT ► p. 208

► SF 22: Listening

 CD 16
rich *(here)* dark; strong

■ TROUBLE SPOT
drunk *(v)* = getrunken
drunk *(adj)* = betrunken
drunk *(n)* = Betrunkene

► SF 17: Analysing stylistic devices

◉ CULTURE SPOT

The Fourth Plinth is one of four pillars in Trafalgar Square in London, which was built in 1840. As there wasn't enough money to make a statue for it, it stood empty for 150 years. In 1999 a commission decided to display contemporary artworks on it and in 2010 the artwork *Nelson's Ship in a Bottle* by Anglo-Nigerian artist sculptor Yinka Shonibare was unveiled.

Yinka Shonibare

The Fourth Plinth

1 Comment on the idea to use the fourth plinth as a display for art.

2 Research other artworks that have been featured on the Fourth Plinth. Present the one you like best to the class. Give reasons. ► S5: Doing research

5 Part B

B4 Halal food festival

'Britishness' is influenced by the many different cultures found in the UK. One such influence is Britain's large Muslim population.

The first ever to be held in the UK and the world's largest, the Halal Food Festival is a three day consumer food show dedicated to foodies who eat halal, or haloodies as they have been coined by festival events director Norman Khawaja. [...]

Visitors can look forward to over 100 exhibitors from across the globe showcasing the most innovative and delicious halal food and drink products, restaurants and street-food stalls. In addition, there is a cooking school and live demonstration kitchen featuring top chefs. [...]

Halal is an Arabic word meaning lawful or permissible. It not only covers food and drink but also all matters of daily life. Followers of Islam (Muslims) must follow a dietary requirement that does not permit pork or pork products or alcohol and only allows meat slaughtered in accordance to strict guidelines in the Qur'an. Halal food is not a cuisine or a style of cooking in its own right. Therefore any cuisine or style can become halal provided it is cooked using halal ingredients and prepared in a halal manner.

With a growing UK Muslim population currently standing at 2.7 million (Census 2011) with a £20.5 billion a year spending power and expected to rise to 5.5 million people by 2030 (Pew Report, The Future of the Global Muslim Population 2011) access to delicious halal food in the UK is becoming increasingly important. [...]

Improving the range, availability and quality of halal foods and restaurants drives the Halal Food Festival's founder Imran Kausar, who comments: 'The growing British Muslim middle classes have greater needs and demands from food producers, retailers and restaurateurs, and command significant spending power.'

From: Halalfocus, 2013

Haloodies at the Halal Food Festival in London

TROUBLE SPOT

chef = Koch / Köchin
boss = Chef / -in

---

2 **foodie** person who is interested in food culture
3 **coin sth.** name sth.
5 **innovative** using new ideas
10 **dietary** related to what people eat
11 **slaughter** killing of animals for their meat
28 **command** *(here)* have

LANGUAGE HELP

- Halal food is delicious/interesting/exotic/important.
- Are YOU interested in / excited by trying new food?
- Come to the Halal Food Festival for …
- Want to meet top chefs / taste good food / try cooking something new?
- Come and see us at …

▶ SF 24: Giving a presentation

You can find a tool to make your flyer here:
 Webcode context-00

▶ COMPREHENSION ◀

1 Finding key points
  a Explain the concept of halal.
  b Create an electronic flyer for the halal festival in which you inform the public about the key details of the event. ▶ LANGUAGE HELP

▶ BEYOND THE TEXT ◀

2 YOU CHOOSE ▶ **Thinking about other food cultures**

  a What other ideas for festivals to integrate different cultures can you think of? Choose one example and write an outline for an event similar to the text above.

   OR

  b Prepare a short oral presentation about similar food festivals in Germany.

---

106 | Chapter 5 | The UK – a Kingdom United?

The multicultural face of the UK

B5 Eastern Europeans in the UK *Amelia Gentleman*

Many Polish migrants want to work in the UK, but success is not guaranteed.

The UK remains a promised land in popular Polish mythology. When someone returns from a stint working there, they are expected to come home driving an expensive car, with a suitcase full of savings. For some, like Michal Novak, 30, the return was triumphant. He came back after 14 years in Britain with enough money to buy a
5 smart flat in a good part of Warsaw, and the prospect of a good job in Poland, paying almost the same salary as he had received in London.

Even so, friends and colleagues were puzzled by his decision to return. 'People asked me 'Why did you come back? It's so horrible here.' As if it is a dogma that living in the UK is better. And it's not true,' he said.

10 Less triumphant will be the return of Lukasz Z, 24, and Adam B, 22, due to travel back by coach imminently, their fare paid for by the Polish charity Barka, that seeks out Poles sleeping rough in London, and encourages them to abandon their attempt to make it in the UK. It gives them tickets to get home and offers them somewhere to live once they arrive.

15 Adam has spent the past six months since he lost his factory job sleeping in parks, railways stations and squats, stealing food to survive. Lukasz has spent several chunks of the past year in Pentonville prison, sentenced for stealing and carrying a knife, after work as a painter and decorator dried up.

Neither man had been in trouble with the police at home, and neither has anything
20 positive to say about their time here.

Their stories illustrate the successes and failures of UK-Polish migration, a phenomenon that exploded on an unexpected scale with Poland's accession to the EU in 2004. [...]

Whilst the vast majority have found work in the building industry, or as carers,
25 cleaners or waitresses, not everyone has been happy. [...]

'I used to come across so many similar stories in London – of young Polish people with economics degrees working as waiters,' [Novak] said.

'Typically, they left Poland five years ago because they couldn't find any work here, but they fail to find anything proper there. So they got jobs much below what their
30 education has prepared them for, and they spent four or five years of their lives, working in a bar, not getting any experience. What can you do here after four years as a waiter in the UK?'

From: *The Guardian*, 6 April 2011

FACT FILE
Since the end of World War II, there has been a continual flow of **migrants from Poland** to the UK. After the fall of Communism in 1989 and the relaxing of travel restrictions within Europe, Polish immigration increased sharply. The expansion of the EU to include Poland in 2004 also paved the way for more Polish workers to relocate to the UK, as citizens from EU member states could work there legally. However, after 2007, Polish migration to the UK began to decrease as economic growth and less unemployment in Poland made it more attractive for Poles to stay in there for work.

2 **stint** *Arbeitsperiode*
8 **dogma** an unquestioned belief
11 **imminent** happening very soon
16 **squat** *besetztes Haus*
   chunk a large part

◀ COMPREHENSION

1 Summarizing key parts of an article
Summarize the stories of Lukasz and Adam and present them to a partner.

2 Mediation (English → German)
You are writing a post for a political *blog aimed at German teens. Your post is about the successes and failures of immigrants in the UK. Write a short text, comparing the lives of the three Polish men named in the article.

◀ BEYOND THE TEXT

3 YOU CHOOSE **Writing**

a Write a *comment on the idea of Britain as 'a promised land' (l. 1) for migrants.

OR

b Write a letter from either Lukas or Adam to friends or relatives in Poland, explaining what happened to them in the UK and why they are returning.

▶ SF 31: Writing a summary

▶ LP 4: Present perfect or simple past?

▶ SF 41: Mediation of written and oral texts

▶ SF 34: Argumentative writing

5 Part C

Where do we go from here?

C1 A referendum on the EU

You are going to listen to a speech by British Prime Minister David Cameron about the UK's membership in the EU.

🎧 **CD 17**
disillusionment no longer feeling enthusiasm
ensure sth. make sure that something happens

▶ SF 22: Listening
▶ SF 12: Analysing charts and graphs

1 Before listening
Describe the statistics on the left.

◀ COMPREHENSION

2 Listening for gist
Which of these topics does David Cameron talk about?
- reasons for the British to be sceptical about the EU
- arguments why he wants a referendum right now
- the right time for a referendum

3 Listening for detail
a Complete the sentences taken from Cameron's speech.
1 They resent the … in our national life by what they see as unnecessary rules and …
2 But I don't believe that to make a … at this moment is the right way forward, either for Britain or for Europe as a …
3 And when the referendum comes let me say now that if we can … such an arrangement, I will … for it with all my heart and …
b **CHALLENGE** Explain the reasons for the anti-EU feeling mentioned by Cameron in your own words.

◀ ANALYSIS

4 Analysing style
Listen again. Analyse how Cameron tries to convince his listeners. Focus on language and content. Is he successful? **SUPPORT** ▶ p. 209

ON THE UK'S MEMBERSHIP OF THE EU

Thinking about the UK's membership of the European Union, would you say that this is generally a good thing or a bad thing?

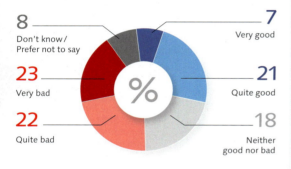

- 8 Don't know / Prefer not to say
- 7 Very good
- 23 Very bad
- 21 Quite good
- 22 Quite bad
- 18 Neither good nor bad

Total: Bad thing 45%   **28% Total: Good thing**

Opinium Research carried out an online survey of 1,957 GB adults aged 18+ from 13 to 15 November 2012. Results have been weighted to nationally representative criteria.

▶ SF 17: Analysing stylistic devices

■ **TROUBLE SPOT**
eine Rede halten =
give / deliver / make a speech
Not: ~~hold a speech~~

C2 Merkel's speech in London

In February 2014, Angela Merkel gave a speech in London to both Houses of the British Parliament on the future of Europe. British expectations concerning her speech were high – perhaps too high, as Merkel said herself at the beginning of her address.

BERLIN – Es ist eine Geste besonderer Wertschätzung für die Bundeskanzlerin: Erst als dritte deutsche Politikerin nach Willy Brandt und Richard von Weizsäcker hielt Angela Merkel an diesem Donnerstag eine Rede vor beiden Kammern des britischen Parlaments. Die Regierungschefin selbst sprach zu Beginn ihres Auftritts von einer „großen Ehre", die ihr zuteil werde. Die Einladung sei „Ausdruck der engen Verbundenheit zwischen unseren Ländern".

Die Kanzlerin erinnerte an ihren ersten Besuch in London im Frühjahr 1990. Mit ihrem Mann sei sie durch den Hyde-Park zum dortigen Speakers Corner gegangen. Dies sei gerade für sie als Ostdeutsche ein „Symbol der freien Rede" gewesen.

5

108   Chapter 5   The UK – a Kingdom United?

Where do we go from here? 5

10 Merkel begann ihre Rede auf Englisch, wechselte erst nach einigen Minuten ins Deutsche.

Die Kanzlerin wies selbst darauf hin, dass ihr Auftritt in der britischen Öffentlichkeit im Vorfeld mit hohen Erwartungen verbunden wurde. Die konservative Regierung um Premierminister David Cameron erhofft sich
15 Schützenhilfe von Deutschland in der Europapolitik. Cameron will im Rahmen von Vertragsreformen unter anderem die Arbeitnehmerfreizügigkeit innerhalb der EU begrenzen und die Arbeitszeitrichtlinie beschneiden. Bis 2017 will er das Volk über den Verbleib in der EU abstimmen lassen.

„Einige erwarten, dass meine Rede den Weg für eine fundamentale
20 Reform der europäischen Architektur ebnet, die alle angeblichen oder tatsächlichen britischen Wünsche zufriedenstellt", sagte Merkel. „Ich fürchte, ich muss Sie enttäuschen." Dies gelte aber auch für jene, die darauf setzten, dass sie den Briten in ihrer Rede klarmachen würde, dass man keinen Preis zahlen werde, um das Vereinigte Königreich in der EU zu halten. „Großbritannien
25 braucht seine europäische Berufung nicht zu beweisen", sagte die CDU-Politikerin und zitierte damit aus der Rede von Weizsäckers an gleicher Stelle im Jahr 1986.

Merkel blieb in ihrer Rede beim Grundsätzlichen. „Wir brauchen den Mut zur Veränderung, um die Erfolgsgeschichte der europäischen Einigung fort-
30 zusetzen", sagte die Kanzlerin. „Wir brauchen starke europäische Institutionen und starke Nationalstaaten." Das Subsidiaritätsprinzip müsse in Europa wieder mehr Beachtung finden, mahnte sie.

Gerade letzteren Satz werden die Briten gerne gehört haben. Großbritannien will bei einer EU-Reform über eine Rückverlagerung von Kompetenzen von europäischer
35 Ebene in die Nationalstaaten verhandeln. Merkel hatte zuletzt zwar ihre Bereitschaft dazu angedeutet – über das Ausmaß allerdings gehen die Vorstellungen weit auseinander. Das hatte Außenminister Frank-Walter Steinmeier (SPD) jüngst bei seinem Besuch in London klargemacht.

Merkel unterstrich denn auch die Grundwerte der EU, die nicht angetastet werden
40 dürften: der freie Handel, die Arbeitnehmerfreizügigkeit und ein „Europa ohne Grenzen". Zugleich betonte sie, dass sie Großbritanniens Platz in der EU sieht. Die EU brauche „ein starkes Vereinigtes Königreich mit einer starken Stimme in der Europäischen Union". Hintergrund ist die anhaltende britische Debatte über eine Renationalisierung und sogar einen Austritt des Landes aus der EU. „Unsere Vorstel-
45 lungen der künftigen Entwicklung der Europäischen Union mögen sich in Details immer wieder unterscheiden, aber wir, Deutschland und Großbritannien, teilen das Ziel einer starken, wettbewerbsfähigen Europäischen Union, die ihre Kräfte bündelt."

From: *Spiegel Online*, 27 February, 2014

Angela Merkel shakes David Cameron's hand in front of Number 10 Downing Street.

1 Mediation (English → German)
A Spanish follower of your *blog wants to find out about Merkel's speech. Summarize chancellor Merkel's future visions regarding the EU in general and the position of Great Britain in the EU in English for him.

2 YOU CHOOSE ▶ Writing

a Taking into account what you already know about Cameron's attitude towards the EU (from **C1**), write his reply to Merkel's speech.

 OR

b Write a dialogue between an anti-EU journalist and Merkel that takes place directly after the speech.

▶ LP 4: Present perfect or simple past?
▶ SF 41: Mediation of written and oral texts

▶ SF 37: Doing creative writing tasks
▶ SF 34: Argumentative writing
▶ CC 6: Talking about sensitive issues
▶ CC 3: The language of politeness

The UK – a Kingdom United? Chapter 5

5 Part C

Bastian Schweinsteiger at the 2014 World Cup Final

1 **dip into** examine or read something casually or superficially
blogosphere the blogs on the Internet
muse think or say sth. in a thoughtful way
twitterati frequent users of the social media website Twitter
5 **cloak** cover, hide
begrudging missgünstig
6 **ruthless** having no pity, merciless
7 **inanimate** not living
8 **by implication** as a consequence / effect
9 **resentful** having or showing a feeling of anger
13 **at the expense of** auf Kosten von
15 **root for** applaud for / encourage
Messrs plural of Mr
19 **bonnet** Schutzkappe
21 **R&D** research and development

▶ SF 29: Writing a summary

▶ SF 18: Analysing non-fiction

▶ SF 31: Writing a formal letter or email

▶ LP 12: Using the right register

C3 It's OK to like the Germans Stewart Wood

Many Britons cheered for Germany in the 2014 World Cup final. But one journalist argues that there is a lot the Britons can learn from the Germans in the world outside the football stadiums.

Dip into the weekend papers, the blogosphere & the musings of the twitterati, and you'll see multiple variants on a similar sentiment: 'I can't quite believe it, and I never thought this would happen, but I find myself supporting Germany. Fancy that!'

Usually our praise for German football is similar to our praise for Germans in other spheres of life where they lead the world. We cloak it in begrudging virtues: 'efficient', 'clinical', 'ruthless'. Germans are applauded in the language we use to describe well-functioning inanimate objects, such as Mercedes cars, or Miele dishwashers. And characteristics of good cars and dishwashers are, by implication, characteristics of people that you admire in a slightly resentful way.

So we are impressed with Germany, but we don't have any particular affection for it or its people. We have respect for Germany, but we don't want to spend much time there. We applaud Germans' economic success, but we resent their dominance of the European Union. We make lots of jokes at their expense, but we say they have no sense of humour.

Maybe a day on which millions of Brits find themselves rooting for Messrs Müller, Hummels and Schweinsteiger is a good moment to challenge this approach to all things German. Because the truth is that there is much to like and admire about Germany. And – whisper it softly – there is a lot we can learn from them too. [...]

Take the state of Britain's economy. Underneath the bonnet of our recovery lies an economy characterised by low productivity, a poor record in technical skills, low levels of savings and investment and relatively weak performance in R&D. In the long run, we will simply not be able to compete internationally, or solve the cost of living crisis we face, without addressing these challenges. We cannot copy the German economy, or transplant the culture in which it is embedded. But we can learn much from the institutions and policies that have helped produce the most successful high-wage, high-skill economy of the modern era. [...]

Of course Germany has its share of problems, blind spots and policy failures too. And taking inspiration from German success does not mean wanting Britain to be become Germany [...] But surely it is time for us as a country to take a collective deep breath, and tell ourselves: it's OK to like, admire and even learn lessons from Germany. And you never know: once we do, we may be on the long road to finally winning another World Cup.

From: *The Guardian*, 13th July 2014

— COMPREHENSION ◀

1 Summarizing
Summarize the writer's main points concerning Britons' relationship to Germany. SUPPORT ▶ p. 209

— LANGUAGE AWARENESS ◀

2 Analysing key vocabulary
Analyse the three 'begrudging virtues' in ll. 5–6 and explain what they tell us about how some Brits view German people.

— BEYOND THE TEXT ◀

3 Responding to the article
a Write an email to *The Guardian's* editor in response to this article.
b CHALLENGE ▶ Write an article on what Germany can learn from Britain.

Chapter 5 The UK – a Kingdom United?

Chapter Task

5

A podcast on British culture

In this Chapter Task you will listen to a report on a British TV show and use what you learn to create your own podcast on an aspect of British culture.

> ■ **FACT FILE**
>
> **Downton Abbey** is a well-known and popular British TV series that is broadcast by ITV in the UK and PBS in the USA. The period drama series, set in Yorkshire, England, follows the wealthy Crawley family through life's events as they are impacted by history. Some of the major historical events include the sinking of the Titanic, World War I and the Spanish influenza pandemic. Julian Fellowes is the creator, executive producer and writer of this series that is co-produced by Carnival Films and Masterpiece. *Downton Abbey* has won several awards, including a Golden Globe and a Primetime Emmy.

1 Understanding an example podcast
  a Read the Fact File and look at the picture. Collect ideas about the setting and the characters of the series.
  b Listen to the podcast and complete the sentence: In the interview …
    1 … the executive producer summarizes the *plot of *Downton Abbey* for those who do not know the series.
    2 … *Downton Abbey's* success in the UK and worldwide is mentioned.
    3 … the executive producer announces the final season of the series and gives hints about its ending.
  c Listen again. Which statements are true? Correct the wrong statements.
    1 *Downton Abbey* is set around the time of the Second World War.
    2 *Downton Abbey* is a uniquely English *genre that cannot be produced anywhere other than in Great Britain.
    3 *Downton Abbey* portrays the class system and shows how aristocrats lived in a very contemporary way.
    4 The fourth series and the Christmas special have to be cancelled since many key stars are leaving the series for Hollywood.

2 Thinking about podcasts
  Collect ideas about what makes a podcast interesting.

3 Creating a podcast
  Go back to the flag on the Lead-in pages. Choose a topic connected to the UK and discuss it in your own short podcast, between three and four minutes long. Organize your work, make an outline, write your script, practise and record it.

4 Evaluating a podcast
  Present your podcast to the class. While listening to your classmates' podcasts, take notes on their content as well as their strengths and weaknesses. Give feedback, praising the aspects that you liked and giving clear, constructive advice for the aspects your classmates could improve. Your teacher will give you an assessment sheet.

🎧 **CD** 18
▶ SF 22: Listening

▶ SF 6: Doing project work
▶ SF 8: Structuring ideas

▶ SF 27: Having a discussion
▶ LP 14: Emphasizing your message

Find recording tools here:
 Webcode context-00

6 India – a Kaleidoscope

- India is the largest democracy, the 2nd most populous country and the 9th largest economy in the world.
- Four world religions originated in the Indian subcontinent: Hinduism, Buddhism, Jainism and Sikhism.
- 50 % of all Indians are below the age of 25.

Download a chronological word list here:
 Webcode context-00

▶ SF 11: Analysing pictures

1 A first glimpse of India: photos and facts
Work with a partner. Choose one picture and speculate about the people you see and where and when the photo might have been taken. Link your photo to the facts about India. Present your picture in class, saying what you find most interesting and surprising.

2 Presenting India
Form groups. Imagine you are going to produce a short video clip about India for a multicultural festival at your school. Brainstorm ideas about what your audience might want to know about India, and discuss how you would present them in your clip. Share your ideas in class. Use them when you work on the chapter task (cf. p. 131).

Lead-in

- The literacy[1] rate in India is 65% among women and 82% among men.
- India is about 31% urban (as compared to 82.4% in the USA and 73% in Germany).
- Mumbai (21 million), Delhi (16 million) and Kolkata (14 million) are among the world's biggest metropolitan areas.

[1] **literacy** the ability to read and write

PREVIEW

In this chapter you will learn about India as a modern society and about its history. You will gain an insight into India's development from a former British colony into an independent nation and learn about Indian communities abroad.

Main topics
- India's past, the legacy of the British Empire and Mahatma Gandhi .... p. 116
- Aspects of Indian life today .... p. 123
- Indians abroad .... p. 127

Focus on Skills: LISTENING and VIEWING
- Listening to a radio interview .... p. 122
- Watching a film trailer .... p. 124

Chapter Task: Putting together a multi-media presentation about India for a multicultural festival at your school .... p. 131

India – a Kaleidoscope   Chapter 6   113

6 Words in Context

CD2 02

Listen to an audio version of the text on the CD or download it here:

Webcode context-00

> ■ **TROUBLE SPOT**
> **Hindi** = one of the official languages spoken in India
> **Hindu** = a person whose religion is Hinduism

In 2001, Shahrukh Khan starred as Ashoka in the Bollywood blockbuster movie of the same name.

The 1982 biopic *Gandhi* retells Gandhi's life from his time in South Africa to his assassination. The movie won eight Oscars.

India then and now

India before the arrival of the Europeans

Mark Twain once referred to India as 'the cradle of the human race'. Indeed, India can look back on a long history. As early as 2500 BC large cities emerged along the Indus River. This civilization traded with Mesopotamia and Egypt and developed a distinctive culture, from which Hinduism emerged. The Mauryan Empire, the first and largest empire on the Indian subcontinent, reached its peak in the 3rd century BC. Under its ruler Ashoka, Buddhism spread throughout the region. Arts and science flourished again in the 4th century AD during the Golden Age of the Gupta emperors. The concepts of zero and infinity are believed to have been developed by Indian mathematicians during this era.
In the 12th century AD Islamic invaders conquered northern India. Islamic rule reached its zenith during the Mughal period, which began in 1526 and led to the unification of large parts of India. It was during the Mughal era that many magnificent buildings such as the Taj Mahal were built.

India and the British Empire

When European trading companies arrived in India in the early 17th century to gain access to the country's wealth, the decline of the Mughal empire was accelerated. A century later, the British East India Company had become the dominant force in the subcontinent. After a massive revolt against the British in 1857, the last Mughal emperor was disposed, and the British Crown took over control, turning India into the largest and most profitable colony of its empire, its 'Jewel in the Crown'. British rule in India, also known as 'the Raj', lasted until 1947. During this era, the British modernized the country, but mismanagement, food shortages and diseases also led to the deaths of millions of people and resentment against the colonial power. The Indian struggle for independence, led by Gandhi and Nehru, culminated in 1947, when the former colony was divided into two separate countries, Hindu-dominated India and Muslim-dominated Pakistan. After Partition widespread displacement of Hindus and Muslims and sectarian violence between the two groups followed. Until today, the relationship between India and Pakistan remains tense.

India today

India is often described as a land of contrasts and paradoxes. It is home to ten percent of the world's millionaires, but also to one third of the world's poor. It is the world's largest democracy, but millions of its citizens are still illiterate. India is the largest country in southern Asia, yet it is densely populated with a population exceeding 1.2 billion people, half of them under the age of 25. India is also one of the world's most promising new markets, but the benefits of economic growth have not yet reached all Indians. In fact, India's growth poses many new challenges. India will need to feed, house and educate the next generation of Indians, who will both contribute to and benefit from the country's success. In the next two decades, India will see a massive migration from rural areas to the cities. The demand for energy will increase as future city dwellers will need electricity, water and mass transit. Today 400 million Indians are not connected to the electricity grid. The Indian government aims to increase power generation by 700% in the next 25 years. Will the new India manage to meet these challenges successfully?

Chapter 6 — India – a Kaleidoscope

India then and now

1 Paraphrasing key terms
Paraphrase the following key terms, which are used frequently when talking about India:

1. Indian subcontinent
2. colonial power
3. the Jewel in the Crown
4. the Raj
5. Independence
6. Partition

2 Words in use
Find the highlighted words in the text to match the definitions:
1. the act of joining parts of a country together
2. a situation when people do not have enough to eat
3. the act of forcing people to leave the area where they live
4. a violent confrontation between different groups in society
5. increase in business activities
6. movement of a large number of people

3 Prepositions
▶ LP 23: Collocations

Complete the following sentences about India with the correct prepositions. Look at the text if necessary:
1. Gandhi united millions of Indians in their struggle … independence.
2. India is home … about 1.56 million millionaires.
3. There is great demand … highly-skilled IT professionals.
4. Indian citizens have started to show growing resentment … inequality.

4 Verbs and nouns
▶ LP 23: Collocations

a Many verbs in English have a tendency to form partnerships with nouns (as in *make a decision* or *find a solution*). These are called 'collocations'. Scan the text for the noun *challenge*: which verbs does *challenge* collocate with?

b Search for more examples of verbs collocating with *challenge* using a monolingual dictionary or a corpus, e.g. the British National Corpus (BNC). Illustrate each collocation with an example sentence.

c Do the same for the nouns *access* and *control*.

5 Images of India
▶ SF 38: Writing a well-structured text

India has been described as 'the cradle of the human race' and as 'a land of contrasts and paradoxes'. Write two paragraphs in which you explain the two images. Choose appropriate vocabulary from the text and the tasks above.

India – a Kaleidoscope   Chapter 6   115

Part A

India's past: echoes and reflections

A1 India's UNESCO World Heritage sites

The following WebQuest will take you on a virtual journey across India through time and space.

Qutb Minar

Mountain Railways of India

Sanchi

Taj Mahal

Ellora Caves

Chola Temples

▶ SF 5: Doing research

1 A WebQuest
  a Form six groups. Each group works on one site. Go to the UNESCO World Heritage website and find information, videos, etc. there about the history and cultural significance of your site. Present your findings in class, explaining what makes them places of outstanding universal value.
  b Together create a timeline of Indian history based on the information you have collected.

Chapter 6   India – a Kaleidoscope

6 India's past: echoes and reflections

A2 Colonizers and colonized

'To feel that somewhere among those millions you have left a little justice or happiness or prosperity, a sense of manliness or moral dignity, a spring of patriotism, a dawn[1] of intellectual enlightenment[2] or a stirring[3] of duty where it did not before exist – that is enough, that is the Englishman's justification in India.'

Lord Curzon, Viceroy[4] of India from 1899 to 1905, in his farewell speech on leaving India.

[1] **dawn** time of day when light first appears
[2] **enlightenment** process of understanding sth.
[3] **stirring of sth.** beginning of sth.
[4] **viceroy** person representing the British monarch in India

► SF 11: Analysing pictures

— ANALYSIS ◄

1 Comparing a quote and photos
Study the photos and the quote carefully. Then prepare an oral statement in which you explain what they tell you about the relationship between the British and the Indians during the British Raj. SUPPORT ► p. 210

A3 The British Empire from an Indian perspective
Gurcharan Das

In this text you will learn about the impact of the British Empire from an Indian perspective. Certain parts of the text have been left out (cf. Gap A, etc.) – don't worry about them on your first reading.

[A] Britain gave us democracy, the rule of law, an independent judiciary and a free press. It built railways, canals, and harbors, but it could not bring about an industrial revolution. It could not raise economic growth or lift people out of poverty. It could not avert famines. The truth is the Raj was economically incompetent. It just did not
5 know how to 'develop' a country. Had it known it, Britain could have gained much from having a larger market for its manufactures. It introduced modern education and helped create a small middle class, but it did not educate the mass of the people. This was its other failure and linked to the first, for development is not possible without mass literacy.

10 [B] Had India remained united, billions could have been saved in defense expenditures and invested instead in improving the lives of ordinary people in both countries. Whether an undivided India could have survived the Muslim-Hindu animosity is another counterfactual of history.

[C] Many Indians despair over the divisiveness of caste and would prefer to wish it
15 away. However, the hold of the Indian way of life is also a bulwark against the onslaught of the global culture. The British gave us the English language, which allowed us to converse with our compatriots in a country with 16 official languages. However, English also divided us into two nations – the 10 percent elite who learned English and shut out the 90 percent who did not. Knowing English today,
20 though, gives Indians a competitive advantage in the global economy and is an important factor in our nascent success in the information economy.

[D] In school we had learned that the Indian subcontinent was a triangle with the Himalayas, the Arabian Sea, and the Bay of Bengal as its sides. The Himalayas ran from east to west and cut off the cold winds from the north. This allowed agriculture

[4] **avert sth.** prevent sth.
famine long period of time without food
[6] **manufactures** *(here)* goods made in large numbers
[10] **expenditure** amount of money spent
[12] **animosity** strong feeling of hatred
[13] **counterfactual** sth. that has not happened but might have under different conditions
[14] **divisiveness** force that splits people into different groups
[17] **16 official languages** 23 languages are now recognized for official use at state level
[21] **nascent** ['neɪsənt] beginning to exist

India – a Kaleidoscope Chapter 6

117

6 Part A

to prosper and created wealth, but it also attracted barbarian invaders from the north. It gave us a warm climate so that no one who came wanted to leave. First came the Aryans, then the Turks, the Afghans, and the Mughals. They came, they stayed, and they merged and became Indian. To accommodate them we merely created a new sub-caste each time and they became part of our diversity. The British did not. But now that they have been gone for more than fifty years, our confidence is restored, especially among the young. Our infuriating diversity may also be of some value. Because we have always learned to live with pluralism, it is possible that we might be better prepared to negotiate the diversity of the global economy.

From: Gurcharan Das, *India Unbound*, 2001

27 **Aryans** ancient race that moved into India from Central Asia around 1500 BC
Mughals Muslim dynasty that conquered northern India in the 16th century
31 **infuriating** making you extremely angry

Statue of Queen Victoria in Kolkata.

[1] **aloof** distant, impersonal

▶ SF 9: Paraphrasing

▶ SF 40: Mediation of written and oral texts
▶ SF 15: Making notes

— COMPREHENSION ◀

1 Filling in gaps
Four passages from the text above have been omitted. For each of the four gaps (A, B, C, D) select the most appropriate passage from the list below. Note that there are six passages to choose from. Compare with a partner.
1 Although Indians gloss over it, the British Raj was the most important event in the making of modern India – for better and for worse.
2 As a subdivisional officer, my father was an important official of the British Raj.
3 The British gave us a hundred years of peace – the so-called Pax Britannica – but they also consciously pursued a divide-and-rule policy which made Hindus and Muslims conscious of their separate identities. This led to a tragic division of the country.
4 The British were different from our other invaders. They did not merge with us and remained aloof[1] to the end. This shook our self-confidence.
5 The Raj gave us modern values and institutions, but it did not interfere with our ancient traditions and our religion. India has therefore preserved its spiritual heritage and the old way of life continues.
6 Western education provided the stimulus for the most dramatic change in the minds of Indians in a thousand years.

2 Examining British rule
Make a T-chart and list the positive and the negative aspects mentioned by Gurcharan Das about British rule in India.

— ANALYSIS ◀

3 A critical view of British rule in India
a Work with a partner. Paraphrase the following quotes from the text:
'The Raj was economically incompetent.' (l. 4)
'Had India remained united, billions could have been saved in defense expenditures.' (ll. 10–11)
'English ... divided us into two nations.' (l. 18)
'Our infuriating diversity may ... be of some value.' (l. 32)
b Then take turns to explain their relevance for understanding the legacy of the British Raj.

4 Mediation (English ➔ German)
In your History class, India is one of the topics you are discussing. You read this text and offer to summarize the main points raised in the text in German. Make notes and practise your talk.

Chapter 6 India – a Kaleidoscope

6 India's past: echoes and reflections

▶ BEYOND THE TEXT ◀

5 CHALLENGE ▶ **The legacy of the Raj**
Discuss whether the British Raj was a good thing for India, both during the Raj and following Independence. Refer to the texts you have examined.
SUPPORT ▶ p.210

A4 Gandhi remembered *Chetan Bhagat*

- 3-2-1 BRAINSTORMING Write down three things you know about Mahatma Gandhi, two reasons why he is considered very important today, and one question you have about him. In class, share your ideas and create a mind map about Gandhi.
- Read the fact file about Gandhi and add more details to your mind map.
- Use the mind map to give a one-minute speech about Gandhi.

FACT FILE

Gandhi and India's struggle for independence

Mohandas Karamchand Gandhi was born in Porbandar in Gujarat in 1869 to Hindu parents. At the age of 19, he was sent to London to become a barrister.

He returned to India in 1891 to practice law. Two years later, he moved to Durban, South Africa, where he accepted a job at an Indian law firm.

Gandhi was shocked at the way Indians were treated there. He became actively involved in fighting for their rights and developed his philosophy of non-violence, *satyagraha* ('devotion to truth'). After 20 years of fighting for the rights of Indians and Africans, Gandhi returned to India in 1915.

Gandhi continued his fight against colonial rule in India by organizing peaceful protests.

India celebrates Independence Day.

Millions of Indians followed him. His campaigns for independence ultimately led the British to withdraw from India in 1947.

But independence from British rule came at a price: the Partition of the subcontinent. In 1948 Gandhi, who had been opposed to Partition, was shot by a young Hindu fanatic who was angry at him for his tolerance towards Muslims.

Gandhi's philosophy of non-violent resistance has inspired millions of people around the world, and even today the Mahatma ('Great Soul') is admired for his courage, willpower, strength and determination in fighting for a just cause.

TROUBLE SPOT
fanatic = noun (person who is extremely enthusiastic about sth.)
fanatical = adjective (enthusiastic)

The following letter to Gandhi was written by Chetan Bhagat, one of the most popular Indian novelists writing in English today.

Dear Gandhiji,
You left us more than sixty years ago. If you were still around, you would have been more than 140 years old. However, we have not forgotten you. You are on every banknote and most stamps. There are many statues of you. Prestigious roads in almost
5 every city are named after you. Our politicians try to model themselves on you. They wear the fabric you promoted, they quote you at every instance, they've got a photograph of you in their offices and some even eat and live like you. There are books, TV

1 **Gandhiji** in many Indian languages '-ji' can be added to names to show respect

TROUBLE SPOT
fabric = material from which clothes are made
Fabrik = company, firm

India – a Kaleidoscope   Chapter 6   119

6 Part A

> **TROUBLE SPOT**
> **programme** = sth. that people watch on TV or listen to on the radio
> **Fernsehprogramm** = TV channel

programmes and movies about you. Seriously, you'd be impressed at how much we still adore you. However, there are things that won't make you feel proud. The India you spent all your life making free is far from free. True, the white guys are gone. But there are still millions of poor people. After sixty-plus years, we are still among the poorest nations on earth. This lack of money leads to a lot of problems in healthcare, infrastructure and education. Many children still don't go to a good school. Those who do don't get into good colleges. And those who go to college don't get good jobs. We need to get rich, and fast. Not only to make more schools and colleges, but also because most Indian problems are linked to the lack of money. Yet, it is considered un-Indian to think that way. The young generation, which thinks like that, is considered materialistic and greedy. The older generation takes the moral high ground – slowness in work is termed patience, non-stop discussion and no action is called careful consideration and lack of improvement in standards of living is countered with claims about the need to live with austerity. And yes, in many cases, politicians who speak like this claim to be your fans.

The younger generation wishes you could come down for one day and clarify these points. Is progress un-Indian? Is change bad? Is a desire to see my country as rich as some other nations materialistic? Is getting things done fast impatience? If you blessed our purpose of building a developed India, the job would become so much easier.

Election campaign in India.

The young generation needs you down here for something else, too. We have a new battle here just like the one you fought with the British. The enemy is not as clear as it was in your case – the white people. Our enemy is the old school of thought, or rather, the people who defend the old school of thought. They do this in the name of antique Indian policies, culture and values. You could help identify this enemy more clearly. Many people who are at the helm of affairs now have served India for decades, maybe with good intentions.

But obviously they don't want to accept they screwed up. We wish they would, though, and we'd have a national day of shame. It won't be easy, but from there we could make a new beginning. But they won't, for they are in power. And to defend themselves and their ways, they don't mind crushing the aspirations, ideas and talent of an entire generation.

Yes, there is a lot of talk of India being a young nation and about youth power. However, youth power is the biggest myth going around India right now. Of course, the youth has spending power – we can buy enough SIM cards, sneakers and fizzy drinks to keep many MNCs in business. But we do not have the power to change things. Can the youth get a new college set up? Can the youth ask the government to provide tax incentives to MNCs to relocate jobs to smaller towns? No way. We are wooed, used, but seldom heard. If you came down, you could unite us. You used religious festivals as social events and propagated your cause. You understood that people need entertainment to bind them. Perhaps we could integrate colleges in the same way, link all colleges maybe for their annual festivals and the message of change could be

---

16 **lack of sth.** state of not having sth.
18 **greedy** wanting more money
take the moral high ground claim that your arguments are morally better than other people's arguments
22 **austerity** situation when people do not have a lot of money
40 **at the helm of** in charge of
42 **screw up** (infml) do sth. badly
50 **MNC** = (abbr) **multinational company** a company operating all over the world
51 **tax incentive** Steueranreiz
52 **woo sb.** try to get sb.'s support
54 **propagate your cause** spread your ideas

120 Chapter 6 India – a Kaleidoscope

India's past: echoes and reflections   6

channelled through them. We have amazing technology such as the Internet now. You would use it so well. If the youth unites, there could actually be youth power.

With our purpose blessed, enemy identified and youth united, we could take the
60 first steps towards the new Indian revolution. After all, China had one and only after that did they get on the path of true progress.

But if it is not feasible for you to come back, we'll have to try to bring about change ourselves. If we can be inspired to do that, we can say we have not forgotten you and understand the meaning of your birthday. We hope you had a good one up there!
65 Lots of love, The Younger Generation

62 **feasible** that can be achieved

From: Chetan Bhagat, 'Letter to Bapu from Generation Next on His Birthday', *What Young India Wants*, 2012

▶ COMPREHENSION ◀

1 True/false statements
Write six true/false statements on a piece of paper. Swap your statements with a partner. Check your partner's statements, correct the false ones and check each other's solutions.

2 Finishing sentences
Finish the sentences with ideas from the text.
1 If Gandhi lived in India today, he would be shocked to hear that …
2 Young Indians need Gandhi to …
3 Gandhi's message to young Indians would be …

▶ LANGUAGE AWARENESS ◀

3 Informal style
Chetan Bhagat often uses informal language in his letter.
a Put the following examples of informal English into formal English:
'If you were still around.' (l. 2)
'True, the white guys are gone.' (l. 10)
'But obviously they don't want to accept they screwed up.' (l. 42)
'No way.' (l. 52)
b Scan the letter for at least three more examples of informal style and put them into formal style.
c Explain why Bhagat uses informal diction in this text.

▶ BEYOND THE TEXT ◀

4 Youth empowerment   ▶ LANGUAGE HELP

YOU CHOOSE   Choose one of the following writing tasks:

a An Indian newspaper has asked young people to write about their Indian Dream and contribute a text for their online blog. Imagine you are a teenager growing up in India. Write a blog entry. Use ideas for your blog from Bhagat's letter. You could start like this: 'I dream of an India that …, a country that stands up to …, an India Mahatma Gandhi would be proud of …'

 OR

b '[Young people] do not have the power to change things.' (l. 50) Comment on this statement with reference to the community *you* live in.

LANGUAGE HELP
• What I would like to see is …
• If we put all our efforts together …
• We have the potential to …
• One major obstacle is …
• If we want to see improvements, we have to …
• Our main contribution could be …

▶ SF 37: Doing a creative writing task
▶ SF 38: Writing a well-structured text

India – a Kaleidoscope   Chapter 6   121

6 Part A

🎧 CD2 03

Ela Gandhi

▶ SF 22: Listening

FACT FILE

Nelson Mandela (1918–2013) was a civil rights activist in South Africa who fought against apartheid. Inspired by Gandhi, he became a leader of the African National Congress (ANC) and was sent to prison after protesting against racial inequality. When he was released in 1990 after 27 years in prison, he continued his fight – and succeeded. In the 1994 presidential elections all races were finally allowed to vote, and Nelson Mandela won the election and became president. Like Gandhi, Mandela is regarded as a role model of tolerance and reconciliation around the world today.

LISTENING FOCUS ON SKILLS

Listening to a radio interview

In this section you are going to focus on how to listen to a radio interview. Ela Gandhi, Mahatma Gandhi's granddaughter, is a peace activist and politician. She grew up in Durban, South Africa, and knew both Mahatma Gandhi and Nelson Mandela personally. You are going to listen to part of a radio interview with her.

1 Before listening
Sometimes you may have an idea what a radio report or an interview you are about to listen to might be about. In this case it is useful to collect some words that you might expect to hear. This will make it easier to understand the interview.
Before you listen to the interview with Ela Gandhi, read the fact file below and brainstorm what an interview with someone who knew both Gandhi and Mandela might be about. Make a list of key words you expect to hear.

2 Listening for gist
Listen to the interview for the first time to get the gist. Before you do, read the task below carefully so you know what information to listen out for.

What is Ela Gandhi speaking about? Choose the correct answers:
Ela Gandhi is speaking about:
1. Her childhood memories in South Africa.
2. Nelson Mandela's visit to India.
3. Similarities between Mahatma Gandhi and Nelson Mandela.
4. The situation in South Africa when Mandela was released from prison.
5. The political situation in South Africa after Nelson Mandela's death.

3 Listening for detail
Listen to the interview again and pay attention to details. In the task below you will be asked to complete sentences while listening. When doing a task like this, you are usually not expected to write down exactly what you have heard. You may use your own words to show that you have understood that particular part of the text.

Listen again and complete the sentences:
1. Gandhi and Mandela were capable of inspiring people because …
2. Both Gandhi's and Mandela's ideal was to …
3. When Mandela visited Gandhi's home in India, he refused to … because …
4. The fact that Nelson Mandela invited the man who had demanded the death penalty for him symbolizes …
5. When Mandela was released from prison, South Africans hoped that … despite the fact that … .

Part B 6

Tales from modern India

B1 Urbanization in India: the big picture

[1] **net new employment** *Nettoneu-beschäftigung (= Differenz aus der Anzahl neu geschaffener Arbeitsplätze und der Anzahl beendeter Arbeitsverhältnisse)*
[2] **residential space** area consisting of houses rather than offices

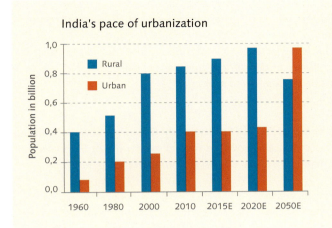

FACT FILE

India in 2030
- **590** million people will live in cities, nearly twice the population of the USA today.
- **70**% of net new employment[1] will be generated in cities.
- **91** million urban households will be middle class, up from **22** million today
- **68** cities will have a population of 1 million plus, up from **42** today; Europe has 35 today
- **700–900** million m² of commercial and residential space[2] will be built – or a new Chicago every year
- **2.5 billion** m² of roads will be built, 20 times the amount added in the past decade
- **7,400 km** of metros and subways will be constructed – 20 times the capacity added in the past decade.

From: the website of Equitymaster, 10 October 2012

COMPREHENSION

1 Bar chart
Use the bar chart above to describe the process of urbanization in India.
SUPPORT p. 210

▶ SF 12: Analysing charts and graphs

ANALYSIS

2 Key figures
Work with a partner and analyse the consequences of urbanization for the future of India. One partner focuses on the opportunities that urbanization provides, one on the dangers. Use the key figures provided in the fact file as a starting point. Exchange your ideas with each other afterwards and discuss them.

B2 Life in a megacity

Kolkata is one of the fastest-growing megacities in the world. The documentary film The Revolutionary Optimists *(2013) follows several young children growing up in Kolkata.*

ANALYSIS

1 Film poster
Study the film poster on the right. Speculate about who the girl is and what she might be fighting for. Use the data and facts from **B1**.

BEYOND THE TEXT

2 Creative writing
Use your ideas to write the girl's speech.

▶ SF 11: Analysing pictures
▶ SF 37: Doing a creative writing task

India – a Kaleidoscope   Chapter 6   123

6   Part B

 DVD

[1] **feature film:** a main film with a story

▶ SF 23: Analysing a film

VIEWING   **FOCUS ON SKILLS**

Watching a film trailer

In the previous section you examined a poster. Now you are going to watch the trailer for the documentary film The Revolutionary Optimists *(2013). A film trailer is a short film advertising a feature film[1] or documentary. A trailer introduces audiences to the film it advertises and tries to get them interested in watching the whole film. Trailers use various techniques to create interest and grab the viewers' attention. When dealing with a film trailer you should therefore pay special attention not only to the story of the film and the actors, but also to camera work, visual elements, sound and music.*

1 Before viewing
Before you watch the trailer for *The Revolutionary Optimists*, speculate about what you expect to see in it and how the subject matter might be presented. Use the notes you made when you discussed the poster (cf. p. 123).

2 While viewing: first impressions
 a While watching the first time, take notes on the following aspects:
   - characters and setting (who do you see? where are they?)
   - actions (what are people doing in the film?)
   Share your findings.
 b What would you say the documentary film is about?

3 While viewing: camera work
 a Watch the trailer again, this time without sound so that you can concentrate on the camera work. Choose the correct answers:

1 The field size predominantly used in the trailer is			
a long shots	b full shots	c medium shots	d close-ups

2 The camera angle predominantly used in the trailer is		
a high angle	b low angle	c eye level

3 The type of camera movement predominantly used in the trailer is			
a zooming	b tilting	c tracking	d panning

 b Explain the function of each of these techniques in this trailer.

4 Analysing the voice-over
Watch the trailer a third time, this time with sound. Concentrate on the intertitles and the voice-over. Make notes on the information they provide and explain how they contribute to the trailer.

5 Evaluating the trailer
Look through your findings in tasks **1–4** and discuss whether the trailer is successful in creating interest in the film.

Chapter 6   India – a Kaleidoscope

Tales from New India

B3 Celebrating Indian culture

Sanjeev Bhaskar is a well-known British comedian and broadcaster. In 2007 he made a four-part television series for the BBC, *India with Sanjeev Bhaskar*, in which he travelled back to the country of his ancestors.

▶ DVD

▶ SF 23: Analysing a film

— BEFORE VIEWING ◀

1 The importance of Holi
The President of India, Shri Pranab Mukherjee, published the following message on 15 March 2014 on the occasion of one of the most important festivals celebrated in India, Holi:

> On the happy occasion of Holi, I extend my greetings and good wishes to all my fellow citizens. As spring arrives, this festival of colours brings with it a joyous celebration of the rejuvenation of nature and ushers in renewed faith in peaceful co-existence. Holi not only brings joy and gaiety in our lives but also provides an opportunity to strengthen the bonds of friendship and brotherhood among people of all faiths. May this festival reinforce the multi-coloured hues of our extraordinary heritage and bring peace and prosperity to our Motherland.
>
> From: the website of the President of India, 16 March 2014

Why are religious festivals important to people around the world? Generate ideas in a placemat activity. Include ideas from President Mukherjee's message to the Indian people.

— COMPREHENSION ◀

2 First viewing: no sound
You are going to watch a scene from *India with Sanjeev Bhaskar* showing Bhaskar celebrating Holi. Watch the clip without sound first and make notes on how Holi is celebrated.

3 Second viewing: with sound
Watch the clip again, now with sound, and make notes on how Bhaskar explains the importance of Holi today.

— ANALYSIS ◀

4 Third viewing: analysing camera work and sound
Watch the clip for a third time and analyse how the camera work and the soundtrack contribute to creating Bhaskar's perspective of Holi.

— BEYOND THE TEXT ◀

5 The meaning of Holi
Research the religious side of Holi and explain its origins and meaning.

▶ SF 5: Doing research

6 Mediation (German → English)
Holi has become a global phenomenon in recent years. It is even celebrated in Germany today. An Indian friend of yours wants to know why. You have come across the following interview with Maxim Derenko, who started organizing Holi festivals in Germany in 2011. Write an email to your friend answering his question based on this interview. **SUPPORT** ▶ p. 210

▶ SF 40: Mediation of written and oral texts

India – a Kaleidoscope   Chapter 6

6 Part B

Wie kam die Idee, das indische Holi-Festival in Deutschland zu veranstalten?
Mein Kollege und Mitveranstalter, Jasper Hellmann, war 2011 in Indien auf Durchreise. Er war beim ursprünglichen Holi Festival selbst vor Ort und war total begeistert davon. Bei seiner Rückkehr steckte er mich und Max Riedel, den dritten Mann im Bunde, mit der Idee an, ein Holi-Festival in Deutschland zu veranstalten.

In Indien ist das Holi-Fest ein hinduistisches Frühlingsfest. Wie kommt es, dass es trotz fehlenden traditionellem Hintergrunds in Deutschland so gut aufgenommen wird?
Die Reaktionen und Erfahrungen aus dem letzten Jahr haben gezeigt, dass die Kernelemente des Holi-Festes [...] bei den Leuten gut ankommen. Bei dieser Festlichkeit steht die Gleichheit aller Menschen im Vordergrund, denn in Indien werden die sogenannten Kasten aufgehoben. In Deutschland gibt es zwar keine Kasten, jedoch soziale Unterschiede. Des Weiteren wird Toleranz und gegenseitiger Respekt groß geschrieben. Die vielen bunten Farben spielen einen weiteren Faktor beim Festival. Die Symbolik für die Gleichheit und die Besonderheit dieses Festivals sind die Farben, diese sollen alle Menschen gleich (bunt) machen.

Habt ihr mit dem Erfolg der ersten Holi-Festivals im letzten Jahr gerechnet?
Wir haben natürlich nicht mit einem so durchschlagenden Erfolg gerechnet. Eigentlich war die Idee ein kleines Open-Air-Festival für einige Leute zu machen, in diesem Bereich haben wir auch schon Erfahrungen in Berlin gesammelt. Ein solches Festival gab es zuvor noch nie in Deutschland. [...]

Wird sich das Holi-Festival etablieren können oder handelt es um einen aktuellen Trend?
Die Resonanz des letzten Jahres hat gezeigt, dass der Hype ungebrochen ist und die Nachfrage immer noch sehr hoch ist. Wir haben unsere Tour für dieses Jahr durchgeplant, und waren innerhalb weniger Stunden in fast allen Städten ausverkauft.

From: 'Holi Festivals – der neue Trend?!', ARTikel, 1 July 2013

CULTURE SPOT

'[Indian truck art is] an art form that makes journeys through the dusty highways of India incredible in more ways than one. With a kaleidoscope of bright paints, motifs, typography and some unique couplets, these Indian trucks take you on a rather colourful journey of diverse cultures and beliefs of the country.'

From: the website of Horn Please, 2012

Indian truck art

1 Describe the trucks in the photos.
2 Explain how Indian truck art relates to what you have learned about India in this chapter so far.

126 Chapter 6 India – a Kaleidoscope

Part C 6

Indians abroad

C1 The Indian diaspora

1 Brainstorming
Work in pairs and brainstorm possible reasons why people move to foreign countries today.

2 Locating the Indian diaspora
The word 'diaspora' describes communities of people who live outside their country of origin. India has the second largest diaspora comprising around 30 million ethnic Indians living in more than 100 countries.
  a Work in pairs. Each pair focuses on one of the regions or countries on the right. Research the history, size and role of the Indian diaspora in the area you are dealing with and make a poster summarizing your findings.
  SUPPORT ▶ p. 211
  b Present your posters in a gallery-walk activity.

> **Countries/regions**
> - United Kingdom
> - United States
> - Canada
> - The Middle East (UAE, Saudi Arabia, Oman, Kuwait)
> - South Africa
> - East Africa (Tanzania, Kenya)
> - South-East Asia (Malaysia, Singapore)
> - South America and the Caribbean (Guyana, Suriname, Trinidad)
> - Pacific Islands (Fiji)
> - Indian Ocean Islands (Mauritius, Reunion)
>
> Find a map showing the regions here:
>
> **Webcode** context–00

C2 A taste of the Indian diaspora   *Michelle Warwicker*

When it comes to food, the Indians of the diaspora have not only absorbed influences from the countries they live in but have also influenced the cuisine of their new countries.

Bunny chow has nothing to do with rabbits. [...] It is made with a half or a quarter loaf of bread, hollowed out and filled with steaming curry cooked with meat or beans. A traditional bunny chow (or simply 'bunny' if you are in Durban in South Africa where the dish originated) is made with mutton,
5 chicken, mince, lamb or kidney beans. The loaf is crusty enough to hold the saucy filling in a parcel, and the bread from the centre is placed on top to keep the curry warm and provide diners with something to scoop with. Cheap, tasty and filling, bunny chow is one of the most popular takeaway meals in its home city. It is sold in small
10 diners and takeaway kiosks and is rarely even served with a fork. [...]
   Durban is home to a very large population of people of Indian ethnic origin, and the dish fuses Indian and African influences. Bunny chow may owe its origins to the Indian immigrants who arrived in South Africa in the second half of the 19th century to be put
15 to work on sugar plantations. One theory is that they began to use a sturdy bread loaf so they could transport curry to the plantations to eat during the day. Today bunny chow has spread to other South African cities, but the original and for many people the best is still found in Durban.

From: 'What its bunny chow?', the website of the BBC, 20 January 2014

1 **chow** [tʃaʊ] feed

Bunny chow.

─────────────────────────────── COMPREHENSION ◀

1 Thinking about food
Explain how bunny chow reflects the Indian diaspora experience.

─────────────────────────────── BEYOND THE TEXT ◀

2 Fusion cuisine
Discuss to what extent fusion food is an integral part of modern society.

India – a Kaleidoscope   Chapter 6   127

C3 English lessons   Shauna Singh Baldwin

Shauna Singh Baldwin is an Indo-Canadian author. Born in Montreal, she grew up in Delhi and went to the USA to study. The following short story is about an Indian woman who has moved to the USA.

I told Tony – that is what he likes me to call him in America – I told Tony I will take English lessons till my green card comes. Valerie says there are English teachers who will teach me for free and she will find a good one who will come to the apartment so that I do not have to go outside. Tony says OK, and then he leaves for work at the cardboard factory.

I pick up the breakfast dishes and Suryavir's toys. No one can say his name here – I will tell them at the school to call him Johnny, like Tony's Johnny Walker whisky.

The phone rings and my heart starts to pound – *dharak dharak*. Our answering machine message has Valerie's voice, and I follow the words with her accent.

'We're naat here right naow, but if you leeev a mehsej, weell get right baak to you.' But it is only Valerie herself. 'Pick up the phone, Kanwaljit. I want to know if you're home so I can drop the kids off for the day.'

'Hello,' I say. 'I am here. You come.'

Valerie is a nice person, but you cannot be too careful. Tony says we cannot meet anyone from India till my green card comes, so Valerie is the only one who sees me. I call her Grocery Store Valerie to myself, because she answered my card in the grocery store, and now I babysit her two strong and unruly boys. What farmers they would have made in Punjab. My son is not so strong. More than two years of women's company. I spoilt him while we were waiting for Tony to get his citizenship, but what was I to do? If I had disciplined him, Tony's parents would have been angry – he is their only grandson.

Valerie's boys don't listen to love or scolding. But they go to school, and Valerie says it is the law. I have to send Suryavir to school. So I went there with her to register him and on the form I wrote the address I had memorized from Valerie's cheques, not ours. Still, Tony was worried in case anyone who might report us saw me. He makes me dress in pants so that I look Mexican, and says it is only a short while now. I hope so.

But first I will learn English. It's not that I don't understand it, but it has too many words. Get it. Put it. I am stuffed. Pick up your stuff. On the other hand. Hand it to you. I learned English in school, passed my matriculation examination, too. We learned whole passages of translation by heart – I had a good memory. Now Tony says I must speak English to pass my immigration interview and to memorize my amnesty story.

A knock. Someone is standing far away from the peephole – why are they doing that? Oh, it's Valerie; she was bending down to tie a shoelace for little Mark.

'Hello, hello. Come in. How are you?'

Valerie has found an English teacher who will come to the apartment and teach me for free. But Tony and I are afraid. This English teacher is from India and we didn't want to meet any people from India.

Valerie said she told the teacher I am Tony's girlfriend and that Suryavir is our son. She said the English teacher was surprised. Indian couples do not usually live together, she told Valerie. Tony says to tell Valerie we don't need this teacher. But I took her phone number to please Valerie. I may call her just to speak in Punjabi for a while.

I told Valerie I will change my name. I asked her to call me Kelly. No one here can say Kanwaljit. And Kanwaljit is left far away in Amritsar before the fire.

---

2 **green card** document that allows sb. to work legally in the USA
7 **Johnny Walker whisky** US brand of whisky
18 **Punjab** region in north-western India, largely populated by Sikhs
22 **scold sb.** speak angrily to sb. who has misbehaved
29 **stuffed** full from eating
30 **matriculation examination** exam taken in the final year of school

Indians Abroad

Some nights I lie next to Tony, here in America where I live like a worm avoiding the sunlight, and I wonder if he knows. And is it only because it was his brother that he does not sense that another man's body has come between us, or is it that he cannot remember the fire we felt in those early days? We only had three weeks in which Suryavir was made. Then he was gone.

If I had been able to return to my parents until he told me to come to America, I would not have been so weak. But to do so would have smelled of disgrace, and I am not shameless. Nor was it a matter of a month or two. Tony told me after six months, when I was becoming big with his son; it would take him two more years.

I tell myself it is not only another man's body that invades our bed, but another woman's too. And yet, that is different. I hear her tearful voice on our answering machine. Her anger follows us from city to city – Fremont, Dallas, Houston, Miami, New York, Chicago – threatening to report us to Immigration. He lived with her for two years, shared her bed, paid her our life savings for a marriage certificate. I will ask the English teacher how to say, 'Is not two years of our life enough? Is not my worm existence, my unacknowledged wifehood, enough for you? Enough that I call myself his girlfriend, my son his bastard?'

But she does not have form, no substance in our bed, I cannot imagine him with her black body – and if I can, what of it? Many men pay prostitutes. This one's price was higher and she lasted longer. And he got his green card after two years. Thus am I here.

The other man in bed with us – he has form. He looks like Tony, only younger. And he still laughs at me, waving pictures of Tony with her. Telling me Tony left me for an untouchable, a *hubshi*. Threatening to tell my parents if I would not open my legs to him.

I did. *Rubba-merey*, I did.

I thought some force would come upon us then and tear him from my flesh before the act was done. Save me, as the virtue of Dropadi was saved. And it did. Too late for virtue but soon enough for vengeance.

The police came looking for him. Oh, not for my protection – no. They were rounding up all Sikh boys between the ages of fifteen and twenty-five for 'questioning'. Tony's parents knew what was in store and they hid him in the servant's quarter, a concrete room on the flat roof of the house.

They told the police he was with Tony in America. That made them angry. One sinewy fellow with a whisky smell took a can of gasoline and slowly, as we marched from the rooms around, and as Suryavir's eyes grew larger, poured it in a steady dribble all round the centre courtyard. They all walked to the door and, almost as an afterthought, the sinewy policeman threw a lit match and the world exploded from silence into horror.

I took no chances. I gave Suryavir to Tony's mother and then climbed out of the back window. His father was blinded by tears and I pushed him after them. Then I ran up the narrow steep staircase to the servant's quarter on the roofs.

And I locked it.

And ran back through lung-searing smoke and purifying flame. I was given vengeance, and I took it as my due. But still he comes between us – the half-dead only half a world away.

I called the English teacher today. She speaks Punjabi with a city accent. I will have to ask Tony, but I think it will be, like Americans say, 'fine, fine' for her to come and teach me.

> **FACT FILE**
>
> **The Sikhs**
> Since the formation of India, many Sikhs have demanded a separate Sikh state in Punjab. During the 1980s militancy reached a peak, leading to an attack by Indian forces on the Golden Temple of Amritsar, Punjab – the Sikhs' holiest temple – and the subsequent assassination of the prime minister, Indira Gandhi.
>
>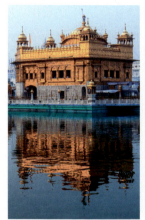
>
> *The Golden Temple of Amritsar*

52 **disgrace** loss of respect
61 **unacknowledged** not publicly recognized
69 **hubshi** *(here)* black (originally Punjabi/Hindi for 'Ethiopian')
71 **rubba-merey** (Punjabi/Hindi) oh my God
73 **Dropadi** a popular heroine in Hindu mythology who is regarded as a role model of virtue, bravery and resilience
74 **vengeance** revenge
80 **sinewy** having a thin body
89 **searing** so strong that it burns you
89 **purify sth.** make sth. pure

India – a Kaleidoscope   Chapter 6   129

Part C

Her family on her father's side is from Rajasansi, just outside Amritsar. And she is married to a white guy so she is probably not part of the Gurdwara congregation; they have all heard of Tony's Green-Card Wife. (These matters travel faster than aeroplanes fly between cities.) I will tell Tony I will take English lessons, and that she will be my teacher. 95

Tony was finishing breakfast when Mrs Keogh, the English teacher, arrived. She knocked and I let her in. Then I asked her to sit down, offered her some tea and listened while she and Tony spoke English. 100

'Thank you very much. My girlfriend is just new from India. As soon as her green card comes we will be getting married, so till then I think English lessons will help her pass the time.' 105

The English teacher did not remark on 'my girlfriend'. Good. Not a prying woman. She said, 'I am glad to help you and your fiancée.'

Tony continued, 'I will not like it if you teach her more than I know. But just enough for her to get a good-paying job at Dunkin' Donuts or maybe the Holiday Inn. She will learn quickly but you must not teach her too many American ideas.' 110

The English teacher smiled at me.

Tomorrow, I will ask her where I can learn how to drive.

From: Shauna Singh Baldwin, *English Lessons, and Other Stories*, 1996

96 **Gurdwara** building in which Sikhs worship
100 **Keogh** [ˈkiːəʊ]
106 **pry** find out
109 **Holiday Inn** US hotel chain

▶ SF 19: Analysing narrative prose

▶ COMPREHENSION ◀

1 Characters and plot
  a Read up to l. 45 and collect facts about the narrator, her husband, her son and Valerie.
  b Read on up to l. 91 and summarize what the narrator's dark secret is.
  c Read the last part of the story and point out the meaning of the English lessons for the narrator and for her husband.

▶ ANALYSIS ◀

2 The protagonist's identity
  a Work with a partner and identify the different facets of Kawaljit's identity. Consider the following aspects: her personality, family, friends, relationships, cultural background, feelings and thoughts, language. Visualize your findings.

▶ SF 5: Doing research

  b CHALLENGE ▶ Do research on the concept of 'hybrid identities', and then use the term to analyse Kawaljit's identity.

▶ LANGUAGE AWARENESS ◀

3 Language awareness
  Oral and written storytelling is traditionally done in the past tense. This story also uses the present tense and the future tense for *narration. Analyse the use and functions of the different narrative tenses in the story.
  SUPPORT ▶ p. 211

▶ GOING BEYOND THE TEXT ◀

▶ SF 37: Doing a creative writing task

4 Writing a letter about your life
  Imagine you are Kanwaljit in three years' time. Write a letter to your parents in which you tell them about your new life.

130

Chapter 6   India – a Kaleidoscope

Chapter Task

Presenting your case

After working on this chapter, gather ideas for a multi-media presentation on the topic 'India – a kaleidoscope' for a multi-cultural festival at your school. You could include some of the following aspects in your presentation:

Germans in India – the Indian diaspora in Germany – the global importance of India in the 21st century – Indian festivals – Indian foods – Indian classical and popular music – Indian literature – Indian movies – reasons to visit India – traces of India in your community (e.g. food, music, clothes) – ways to promote intercultural relations between India and Germany (e.g. exchange programs, business cooperation, etc.)

Form groups. Each group picks one topic. Think about interesting ways of presenting it, e.g. interviews, slide shows, showing a film, making your own film, or reading out poetry or stories you like. Use ideas from this unit and choose at least one audio file (e.g. a radio interview or report) or video clip (e.g. an excerpt from a feature film or documentary, a trailer, song) for your presentation.

With the use of an assessment sheet, which your teacher will give you, evaluate the work of the different groups.

India

भारत

ଭାରତ

ভারত

7 The USA – Still the Promised Land?

Download a chronological word list here:
 Webcode context-00

Download further information on the pictures and the dates on the timeline here:
Webcode context-00

1. **GROUP PUZZLE The American experience**
   a Form six groups. Give each group a letter A–F.
   In your group, talk about the picture that matches your letter: What situation does it show? What do you know about this episode in American history? Share your knowledge.
   b Use the webcode to access further information on the story behind your picture. Share the new information in your group.
   c Form new groups of at least six members each; all six letters must be represented in each group. Tell each other about your pictures. Discuss what makes them part of the American experience.

Timeline of American history

| 1607 | 1620 | 1775–1783 | 4 July 1776 | 1789 | 1803 | 1861–1865 | 1890 |

Chapter 7   The USA – Still the Promised Land?

Lead-in

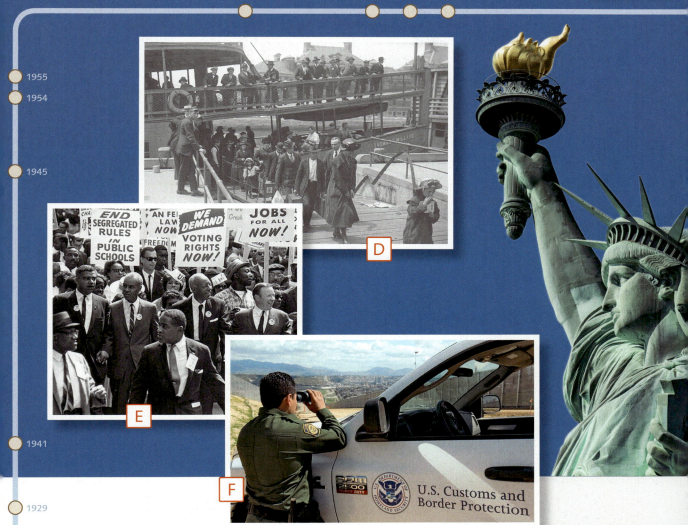

2 **Putting yourself in the picture**
   a Choose one person from any of the six pictures.
      Write an *interior monologue for your person: How (or why) did you get into your present situation? How do you imagine your future?
   b Form groups of 4–5. Read your monologues to each other. The listeners try to guess which person you have chosen.
   c Discuss the different motives of the people you have talked about, and how they are connected with the idea of America as 'the Promised Land'.

PREVIEW

In this chapter you will examine America's image at home and abroad and learn more about some of the challenges facing the USA today.

Main topics
- The American dream today .... p. 136
- The challenge of diversity .... p. 141
- Equality and inequality .... p. 148
- America's role in the world .... p. 152

Focus on Skills: SPEAKING
- Speaking in front of an audience .... p. 146

Chapter Task: Giving a speech in which you explain why you would like to be given the opportunity to visit the United States .... p. 155

The USA – Still the Promised Land?   Chapter 7

7 Words in Context

 CD2 04
Listen to an audio version of the text on the CD or download it here:
Webcode context-00

A country like no other

A nation founded on principle
Most nations are held together by a common history, language and culture. America is different: it is a nation united solely by the shared values of equality, democracy, and individual freedom. The Founding Fathers, inspired by the ideas of the Enlightenment, created a self-governing republic without social barriers. The crowned heads of Europe expected the young nation to collapse in chaos; instead, it grew and prospered, ultimately rising to the status of a world power.

Land of opportunity
While the promise of freedom from religious and political persecution played and continues to play a major role in attracting immigrants to America's shores, it became clearer as the United States expanded westward that the continent also held vast stores of natural resources. In the first half of the 19th century, it was mainly the availability of cheap farmland that drew millions to try their luck in the New World; later, huge supplies of coal and iron ore powered the growth of industry, attracting further waves of immigration. The economic vitality of the young nation gave rise to the material side of the American dream, expressed in slogans like 'from rags to riches' or 'the sky's the limit'. In a country so rich in opportunity, success was believed to lie in the hands of the individual. A culture arose that honoured personal material success; as long as upward mobility guaranteed equality of opportunity for all, the majority felt that the self-made millionaire had a right to his wealth.

'Remember, gentlemen, we aren't here just to draft a constitution. We're here to draft the best damned constitution in the world.'

The American century – and beyond
The 20th century saw America rise to a position of economic and military leadership in the world. America viewed itself as a beacon of democracy, which it strove to export to other countries. With the collapse of the Soviet Union and the end of the Cold War (1989), the USA was seemingly the only superpower left standing. Yet since the turn of the century, America has increasingly been forced to cope with doubts and difficulties. The attacks of 11 September 2001 left Americans with a deep-seated feeling of insecurity. The official response – two undeclared wars and an unprecedented expansion of surveillance operations – cost America sympathy abroad and contributed to the heavy debt burden. Economic turmoil, the massive loss of jobs in the manufacturing sector, a housing crisis that cost millions their home, and a widening gap between rich and poor that undermines the equality of opportunity – all of these factors cause Americans today to wonder if the American dream still holds true for their generation. It remains to be seen if this extraordinary nation, which has in the past so often demonstrated its ability to reinvent itself, will once more rise to the challenges of a new era.

> ■ **TROUBLE SPOT**
> *the USA* (l. 32) + singular verb
> *The USA is/was/has ...*

Chapter 7   The USA – Still the Promised Land?

A country like no other

7

1 Words in use
Replace the underlined words with highlighted expressions from the text:
1 In the 20th century America became the most powerful country in the world.
2 Americans believe that everyone should have the same chance in life.
3 We don't know yet if America will remain the leading world power.
4 The availability of cheap land was an important factor attracting Europe's rural poor to America's shores.
5 The growing difference between rich and poor is without parallel.

2 Collocations with prepositions
▶ LP 19: Collocations

a Complete the underlined collocations with the correct prepositions. If you need help, look at the text again:
1 By 1900, the USA had risen ... the status of a major industrial country.
2 America became known as the land of promise, a country rich ... opportunity.
3 Hundreds of different ethnic groups have all contributed ... American culture.
4 Stories of successful immigrants gave rise ... the saying that in America the streets were paved with gold.
5 For many European Jews, freedom ... persecution made America the new Promised Land.
6 The American dream didn't hold true ... everyone; African Americans and Native Americans, for example, were long excluded.
b Find four more collocations with prepositions in the text and write a quiz for your partner. Then do the quiz your partner gives you.

3 Connotation
Most people react positively to the word *freedom* and negatively to *slavery*. This emotional aspect of language is called *connotation.

a Sort the words in the list on the right into two groups (positive/negative connotation). Compare results with your partner.
b Together, find three more words from the text for each of the two groups.

values • persecution • doubts • prosper • opportunity • insecurity • undermine • equality

4 General terms ('Oberbegriffe')
a Find general terms to describe each of the five (groups of) examples. Choose the terms from the highlighted expressions in the text.
1 George Washington and Benjamin Franklin
→ **general term:** *the Founding Fathers*
2 coal, oil, water, farmland → **general term:** ...
3 Free public schools are available to everyone. → ...
4 A factory worker rises to become the director of a large firm. → ...
5 Only landowners are allowed to vote. → ...
b Choose three more general terms from the highlighted words in the text. Write an example illustrating each of them. Swap examples with a partner and find the correct terms from the text.

5 Your view
The USA – still 'a beacon of democracy' (l. 30) for the rest of the world? State your opinion in a short text (ca. 200 words).

The USA – Still the Promised Land?   Chapter 7

135

7 Part A

Pulitzer Prize-winning journalist Liz Balmaseda

▮ FACT FILE
Pulitzer Prize
The Pulitzer Prizes were established in 1917 by the American publisher Joseph Pulitzer. They are awarded annually in the fields of journalism, literature and musical composition.

The American dream

A1 Viva America! *Liz Balmaseda*

Liz Balmaseda (born 1959) is a Cuban-American journalist who has worked for various Miami newspapers as well as for Newsweek and NBC News. She won Pulitzer Prizes for journalism in 1993 and 2001. Balmaseda contributed this text to an online collection of immigrant stories.

I grew up in America's most Cuban city – Hialeah, Florida. The municipality's tagline, 'The City of Progress', far more often was quoted in Spanish. The cheering section at local football games brought conga drums. The Catholic saint statues that often adorned front lawns concealed Afro-Cuban alter egos. And the 'fries' at fast-food drive-thru joints were made of yuca.

But the city was fiercely American, just as my parents were fiercely American. Having fled Cuba shortly after its Communist regime took hold of the island, they brought me to Florida when I was 10 months old and raised me to cherish the American dream. Cuba lingered only in the flavor notes of my mother's cooking, the rhythms on our stereo, and the bottomless sense of yearning for loved ones stranded on the island. The rest of it was all-American: The stray threads I pulled off my mother's clothes when she returned each night after a grueling day at her clothing factory job. The snazzy ties my dad wore to work as a car salesman. His religious attention to Election Day, when he'd leap out of bed to cast his vote. The pride I sensed in my parents after I brought home the miniature trophy that declared me the winner of the first-grade spelling bee, in the year I learned to speak English.

I could say it was by magic that a loving and supportive community emerged around our family. But that village force of good neighbors, church friends, American-born school teachers who took the initiative to visit our home and offer a word of praise and encouragement – that doesn't happen by magic. It happens in response to a life embraced, a life that is often turbulent, painful and imperfect. This is what I learned from my mother, may she rest in peace. This is what I continue to learn from my father. At 84, he is stricken with Parkinson's. Last Election Day, I sat with him at the polling place and, at his direction, filled out the ballot. I watched as he slipped the ballot into the box and gave the poll worker a smile of great accomplishment. It's an image I'll carry with me always.

My Cuba is now buried in a Miami cemetery. But my America resounds in all its glory, like a hundred conga drums playing beneath Friday night lights in Hialeah.

From: *The Huffington Post*, 19 July 2013

1 **municipality** [mjuːˌnɪsɪˈpæləti] town
   tagline motto, slogan
3 **conga drum** kind of African drum
4 **adorn sth.** *etwas schmücken*
   conceal sth. hide sth.
   alter ego [ˌæltərˈiːgəʊ] alternate identity
5 **joint** *(infml)* small restaurant
   yuca *(Spanish)* Cassava *(Wurzel der Maniokpflanze)*
6 **fiercely** passionately, intensely
8 **cherish sth.** love sth.
9 **linger** [ˈlɪŋgə] remain
10 **yearning** [ˈjɜːnɪŋ] *(fml)* feeling of wanting sth. badly
11 **stray threads** *einzelne Fäden*
12 **grueling** *(AE)* = *(BE)* **gruelling** very hard
13 **snazzy** *(infml)* showy
   religious *(here)* taking sth. very seriously
14 **leap** *(v)* jump
16 **spelling bee** spelling contest
17 **supportive** offering support
   emerge come into existence
21 **embrace sb.** take sb. into your arms
23 **be stricken with sth.** *an etwas erkrankt sein*
24 **polling place** place where voters can cast their vote in an election
25 **accomplishment** [əˈkʌmplɪʃmənt] feeling of having achieved sth.
27 **resound** [rɪˈzaʊnd] *ertönen*

Hialeah City Hall

136 | Chapter 7 | The USA – Still the Promised Land?

The American dream

COMPREHENSION

First reactions
1 Talk about your reactions to the text. Why do you think Balmaseda chose to submit her family's story to the immigrants website?

ANALYSIS

2 **From Havana to Hialeah**
Balmaseda uses many images to describe life in Hialeah. Name some examples and talk about why they are important to her.

LANGUAGE AWARENESS

3 **Words that convey emotion**
   a Collect words from the text that express the *author's (or someone else's) feelings (e.g., 'fiercely', l. 6). Examine how they influence the effect of the text.
   b The following text sounds bland because it lacks words that convey feelings. Rewrite it to give it more emotional impact. ▶ LANGUAGE HELP
   My father thought that his life would change for the worse if Castro came to power in Cuba. He applied to the American Embassy in Havana for an immigration permit. He waited three months. Then a letter arrived saying we could leave for the USA. My parents packed their belongings and said goodbye to their friends and relatives in Cuba. On March 11th, 1958, on board a small passenger ship bound for Miami, they had their first glimpse of the American mainland.
   SUPPORT p. 212

LANGUAGE HELP
• anxious
• be ~ to do sth.
• excited
• fear (n, v)
• hope (n, v)
• nervous
• overjoyed
• relieved
• sad
• tearful
• thrilled
• with a feeling of ~
• with trembling hands

BEYOND THE TEXT

4 GROUP INTERVIEW **One family's American dream**
   a Form groups of four. One of you is Liz Balmaseda, another is her father, and the third member is her mother. The fourth member of the group is a journalist who is interviewing the family on the subject 'Our American dream'. Prepare your roles using the role cards that can be downloaded via webcode. Then carry out the interview.
   b Summarize the aspects of the American dream that were named in your group and present them to the rest of the class.

Download the role cards here:
 Webcode context-00

A2 Reinventing the American dream   *June Sochen*

June Sochen is professor emerita of history at Northeastern Illinois University.

• Speculate on the title: Why might the *author think that the American dream needs reinventing?

Given the uncertain economic conditions, a contentious presidential campaign and the high cost of a college education, it is difficult to know how the traditional definition of the Dream can be applied for the younger generation. [1] Answering the question looking backward is easier than looking forward.

5   For the generation that fought to free the American colonies from Great Britain, it meant freedom of religion and speech and the liberty to pursue your own path. Contrary to the experience of most people across the Atlantic in the 1700s, Americans looked to a bright future. Children benefited from public school education, hardworking parents, and seemingly endless land to be purchased and cultivated.

10   If things were not favorable for you in Boston, you could pack your belongings, hitch your wagon, and take your family to the West. [...]

7 **contentious** full of conflict
8 **benefit** ['benɪfɪt] (v) profitieren
9 **purchase sth.** ['pɜːtʃəs] (fml) buy sth.
10 **favorable** (AE) = (BE) **favourable** günstig
11 **hitch your wagon** (here) attach your wagon to horses

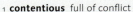

The USA – Still the Promised Land?   Chapter 7   137

7 Part A

The popular press and penny novels heralded the 'rags to riches' stories of ordinary Americans. This country could fulfill both the ideals and the material aspirations of all newcomers, or so the rhetoric promised. For much of the 19th Century, upward mobility became a constant theme in all political pronouncements, sermons, and business proposals. If you worked hard, you could achieve the American Dream of more education than your parents, greater economic success than your parents, and a larger home than your parents.

There were enough measurable examples of success to make most Americans believe that the American Dream was attainable for them. [2] Though the Civil War surely set back the hopes and plans of a generation, the post-war generation looked forward to a brighter future.

The 20th Century, though promising much of the same, had more obstacles in its path. Two world wars, the worst depression in American history, the Cold War, Korea and Vietnam all slowed down the belief, and the actuality, of inevitable progress toward everyone's fulfillment of the American Dream. Indeed, the seeming certainty that each generation would do better than the last one, has been dashed in recent years.

The 21st Century started with a new threat: September 11, 2001 and the attack on the World Trade Center. [3] The dot.com bubble burst early in the century followed by the Great Recession of 2007; though the recession is formally over, it has left us five years later with high unemployment and great uncertainty about the future.

The divide between the generations is dramatic. [4] Recent college graduates find their career hopes unrealized in the current job market. Wages have stagnated in the last 30 years with manufacturing and service industries going overseas.

Only a small segment of the economy – the banks and insurance companies, for example – seem[s] to be thriving.

[5] This country remains a desirable destination for immigrants from all over the world. Just as new immigrants believe in the American Dream, most Americans, according to the polls, also appreciate the multiple benefits offered by this country and have no desire to live elsewhere. The current economic troubles are seen as challenges to overcome, not as insuperable obstacles. Home ownership remains a goal as does job security.

Despite our troubles, the original meaning of the Dream, the ideological portion, remains vibrant while the material promises are harder to obtain. The freedoms enjoyed in this country cannot be taken for granted as there are still many places on the globe where repression describes daily life for many people. Though surely the material aspect of the Dream continues to be a goal – a home [...], a yearly vacation, and a job that pays all the bills – preserving the ideals of the American Dream is more important than ever before.

From: *Naples Daily News*, 8 August 2012

12 **herald sth.** ['herəld] (v, fml) call attention to sth.
14 **rhetoric** ['retərɪk] (fml) (here) speech-making
15 **pronouncement** public statement
16 **proposal** plan, idea
20 **attainable** within reach
21 **set sth. back** etwas zurückwerfen
24 **obstacle** ['ɒbstəkl] sth. that is in the way
26 **inevitable** [ɪn'evɪtəbl] unvermeidlich
28 **dash sth.** destroy sth.
30 **dot.com bubble** period from ca. 1997–2000, when the value of internet start-ups rose sharply and then collapsed
33 **divide** (n) gap
38 **desirable** [dɪ'zaɪərəbl] attractive
40 **appreciate sth.** [ə'priːʃieɪt] know the value of sth.
   benefit (n) advantage
42 **insuperable** [ɪn'suːpərəbl] (fml) unüberwindlich
45 **vibrant** ['vaɪbrənt] alive
46 **take sth. for granted** etwas als selbstverständlich ansehen
47 **repression** Unterdrückung

COMPREHENSION

1 Filling the gaps

a Five sentences have been removed from the text; the gaps are marked and numbered. Choose the right sentence for each gap from sentences A–G below (there are two sentences that don't belong to the text):

A Workers over 50 who lost their jobs may never recover the earnings and positions they once had.
B But the American Dream continues to live.

---

138 | Chapter 7 | The USA – Still the Promised Land?

The American dream 7

   C In particular, African Americans and many women felt excluded from the Dream.
   D There was little government on any level to help or hinder individual accomplishment.
   E Americans have always believed in the power of the individual to shape his or her own life.
   F Indeed, all future generations may have to reinterpret the Dream.
   G International terrorism became a new concern.

   b Compare solutions with your partner and discuss points where you differ. You can download the complete text via webcode to check your answers.

Download the text here:
 Webcode context-00

2 The main idea
Sum up the main reasons Sochen gives why the American dream needs to be reinvented. Compare her reasons with the ideas your class had before reading the text.

— ANALYSIS ◀

3 Exploring the American dream
   a Form small groups. Each group will need a blank poster. Your task is to present the information on the American dream contained in the text in the form of a mind map. Follow these steps:
   1 Divide the subtopics from the list on the right among the members of your group. Each member makes notes on their subtopic.
   2 Pool your results and create a mind map that presents your information in a clearly structured form.

   b Display your posters on the walls of your classroom. Compare the mind maps created by your classmates and discuss their pros and cons.

- *political ideals*
- *economic opportunity*
- *upward mobility*
- *threats to the dream*
- *state of the dream today*

— BEYOND THE TEXT ◀

4 YOU CHOOSE Comparing interpretations

   a Reread **A1** (Viva America!) in the light of what you have learned about the American dream. Then write a comment of ca. 200 words on the topic: 'The Balmasedas – an American dream come true'.

    OR

   b Write a comment comparing June Sochen's views on the American dream (**A2**) and the cartoon below.

▶ SF 34: Argumentative writing
▶ SF 13: Analysing cartoons

The USA – Still the Promised Land?   Chapter 7

7 Part A

CULTURE SPOT

Flag (1954)

is a painting by the American artist Jasper Johns (born 1930). It is on display at the Museum of Modern Art in Manhattan, New York City.

1. Describe your reaction to the work of art above. Would you react the same way to a painting of the German flag in a German art museum? Explain.

CD2 05

2. Listen to a recording of two American teenagers talking about the picture. How does what they say influence your reaction to the painting?

3. The photo on the right shows a small section of the painting in detail. Describe what you can recognize in the painting, and discuss why you think the artist chose this technique.

4. Jasper Johns's 'Flag': a statement on the American dream? Discuss.

Chapter 7   The USA – Still the Promised Land?

Part B 7

Dealing with diversity

FACT FILE

Ethnic neighbourhoods

Because of its history America is a racially and ethnically diverse nation. With immigrants pouring in from all over the world, it was only natural that newcomers to America's shores flocked to neighbourhoods where they could speak their own language and live their culture. They often had networks of friends and relatives from the Old World who helped them find work and a place to live. By 1900, Polish, Irish, Italian, Jewish and Asian quarters had arisen in virtually every American city.

Although **ghetto** is technically just another word for 'ethnic neighbourhood', in the USA it is used mainly for the – usually undesirable – quarters of a city in which African Americans formerly were forced to live. Black families wishing to move to a better part of town found that no landlord would rent them an apartment and no bank would give them credit to buy a house. White homeowners feared that the appearance of black faces in their street would send property values into a downward spiral. It was only after the Civil Rights Act of 1968 prohibited discrimination in housing that the situation of African-American families slowly began to improve.

List the 'push and pull factors' that lead to the creation of ethnic neighbourhoods. Do they exist in Germany too?

B1 The new neighbours   Bruce Norris

September 1959. Karl comes to visit his neighbours Russ and Bev, who have just sold their inner-city house (where the *scene takes place) and bought a new one in the suburbs. Jim is a young clergyman who has come to talk to Russ. Ted Driscoll is the real estate agent[1] who has sold the house for Russ and his wife. Betsy is Karl's wife.

- While you are reading the *dialogue, form a mental image of the situation, i.e. the *characters and what they may be doing while they are speaking.

Stuart McQuarrie (Russ) and Sophie Thompson (Bev) in a performance of **Clybourne Park**

KARL […] I take it, Russ, you're aware that the Community Association meets the first Tuesday of each month? And as I'm sure you know, Don 5 Skinner is part of the steering committee. And somehow it came to Don's attention at this late juncture that Ted Driscoll had found a buyer for 10 this house and I have to say it *did* come as something of a shock when Don told us what sort of people they were.

RUSS What sort of people are they? 15 *(Beat. Karl stares at Russ.)*

KARL Well. *(Chuckles.)* Uhh … Huh. I suppose I'm forced to consider the possibility that you actually don't *know*. 20

RUSS Don't know *what*?

KARL Well, I mean. That they're colored.

RUSS Who are?

KARL The family. It's a colored 25 family. *(Pause.)* So: I contacted the family –

JIM Wait wait wait.

KARL *(To Russ.)* You're saying Ted never 30 bothered to tell you?

RUSS We, uhh … sort of gave Ted free rein on the –

JIM I don't think you're right on this one, Karl. 35

KARL Oh, but I am. Oh, I've spoken with the family.

RUSS Bev?

JIM On the *telephone*? 40

[1] **real estate agent** Immobilienmakler/in
1 **I take it** (infml) I assume
6 **steering committee** [kəˈmɪti] Steuerungskomitee
9 **juncture** [ˈjʌŋktʃə] (fml) moment in time
16 **beat** (n) brief pause
17 **chuckle** laugh briefly and quietly
25 **colored** (AE) = (BE) **coloured** (used for black people until the late 1950s, now an old-fashioned or offensive word)
32 **bother to do sth.** [ˈbɒðə] think it necessary to do sth.
33 **give sb. free rein (on sth.)** [reɪn] jdm. freie Hand geben (in einer Sache)

141

The USA – Still the Promised Land?   Chapter 7

7 Part B

45 c'mere = come here

65 Negro (used for black people up until 1966, now an old-fashioned or offensive word)

▶ CC6: Talking about sensitive issues (Fact File: Political correctness)

68 common courtesy [ˈkɜːtəsi] standard politeness

70 interchangeable austauschbar

73 conduct one's business [kənˈdʌkt] behave

78 pull a stunt (infml) play a trick

88 one hundred percent (here) pure African American

92 unsavory (AE) = (BE) **unsavoury** unpleasant looking

117 love thy neighbor (AE)/**neighbour** (BE) *allusion to the Bible („Liebe deinen Nächsten")

118 principled basing our behaviour on moral principles

KARL Oh, no. As a matter of fact, Betsy and I've just come directly from … *(Beat, for effect.)* well, from *Hamilton Park.*

BEV *(To Russ.)* What is it?

RUSS C'mere a second. 45

KARL Now, Russ. You know as well as I do that this is a progressive community.

BEV *(To Russ as she joins them.)* What's he talking about?

KARL If you take the case of Gelman's grocery: That's a fine example of how we've all embraced a different way of thinking – 50

RUSS Slow down a second. Bev, get Ted Driscoll on the phone. 55

BEV *(To Russ.)* What for?

RUSS Karl says. Karl is *claiming* –

KARL Russ, I have met *personally* with the family, and –

BEV What family? 60

RUSS He claims this family. The family to whom Ted sold the house.

KARL It's a colored family. *(Jim shakes his head.)*

JIM *(To Karl.)* Sorry, don't we say *Negro,* now? 65

KARL *(Irritated.)* I *say* Negro. –

JIM *(Overlapping.)* Well, it's only common courtesy, and I'm –

KARL *(Continuous.)* – I say them inter-changeably – 70

JIM *(Overlapping.)* – not trying to tell you how to conduct your business.

KARL *(Continuous.)* – and of course I said *Negro* to them – No I think we both know what you're doing. 75

JIM And furthermore, I don't think Ted would pull a stunt like that.

KARL Yes. We all admire Ted. But I don't think any of us would accuse him of putting the community's interests ahead of his own. [...] 80

BEV Waitwaitwait. Karl, are you *sure?*

KARL I was sitting with them not two hours ago. 85

BEV But isn't it possible that they're … I don't know, *Mediterranean,* or – ?

KARL Bev, they are *one hundred percent.* And I don't know how much time any of you have spent in Hamilton Park, but Betsy was waiting in the car and I can tell you, there are some *unsavory* characters. [...] 90

Now, some would say change is inevitable. And I can support that, if it's change for the better. But I'll tell you what I *can't* support, and that's disregarding the needs of the people who *live* in a community. 95

BEV But don't they have needs, too? 100

KARL Don't who?

BEV The family.

KARL Which family?

BEV The ones who –

KARL The *purchasers?* 105

BEV I mean, in, in, in, in *principle,* don't we *all* deserve to – shouldn't we *all* have the opportunity to, to, to –

KARL *(Chuckles with amazement, shakes his head.)* Well, *Bev.* 110

JIM In *principle,* no question.

KARL But you can't *live* in a principle, can you? Gotta live in a *house.*

BEV And so do they.

KARL Not in *this* house, they don't. 115

JIM But here's the real question:

KARL And what happened to *love thy neighbor*? If we're being so principled.

BEV They would *become* our neighbors.

KARL And what about the neighbors you already *have,* Bev? 120

BEV I care about them, too!

KARL Well, I'm afraid you can't have it both ways.

RUSS Okay. Assuming – 125

BEV Wait. Why not? [...]

JIM But the key question is this:

BEV No. Why *not* have it both ways?

KARL Darling, I came to talk to Russ. [...]

BEV Why not, if it would *benefit* someone? 130

JIM But *would* they benefit?

BEV If we could make them our *neighbors.*

KARL But they won't be *your* neighbors, Bev. *You're* the ones moving *away*!

From: Bruce Norris, *Clybourne Park,* 2010 – Act One

Chapter 7   The USA – Still the Promised Land?

Dealing with diversity

7

COMPREHENSION ◀

1 Sum up the main topic of the conversation in one sentence.

2 **True or false?**
Check each of the following statements. If you think it is true, point to evidence in the dialogue. If you think it is false, correct it.
1 A black family has bought Ted Driscoll's house.
2 Karl has just phoned the people who bought the house.
3 Russ didn't know that the house had been sold to African Americans.
4 Karl is upset about a black family moving into the neighbourhood.
5 Karl thinks that Hamilton Park is a progressive community.
6 Bev believes that everyone should be given a chance.

ANALYSIS ◀

3 **Working with a *dramatic text**
a In groups of four, each of you chooses one of the four roles in the scene. Listen to a recording of the text and concentrate on 'your' character while listening. Try and imagine what your character is doing, and where he/she is standing, etc.
b 'Playback': In your group, decide where you want to stand while you are playing your roles. Then practise playing your part in pantomime while the recording is on.

4 **Examining the characters**
Copy and complete the table. For the second column, choose phrases from the box on the right, or make up your own. ▶ LANGUAGE HELP

	behaviour / character traits	evidence from text (line numbers)
Karl		
Russ		
Bev		
Jim		

5 **The dramatic conflict**
At the heart of every *drama is a *conflict that is usually embodied by two of the characters. Choose the two characters that you think most clearly stand in conflict in this scene. Contrast their points of view in a text of 100–150 words.

BEYOND THE TEXT ◀

6 **The other side of the coin**   **SUPPORT** ▶ p. 212
Form groups of four. Two of you are Bev and Russ, the other two are the African-American couple who have bought the house in Clybourne Street. Imagine that after Karl has left, the black couple come to look at the house. How would Russ and Bev behave? How might the black couple explain their wish to move to an all-white neighbourhood? Discuss the issues at hand, then prepare role cards for your parts. Practise the scene, then perform it for your class.

▶ SF 10: Working with closed test formats

🎧 **CD2** 06

LANGUAGE HELP
- naïve
- shocked
- angry
- hypocritical
- idealistic
- wants to appear liberal
- self-confident
- tries to mediate
- embarrassed
- bossy

▶ SF 20: Analysing drama

Find help and detailed instructions for this task here:
🖰 **Webcode** context-00

▶ SF 37: Doing a creative writing task

The USA – Still the Promised Land?   Chapter 7   143

7 Part B

Bill Clinton,
42nd President of the USA

B2 The changing face of America   William J. Clinton

Looking back on American history at the end of the 20th century, Clinton, President of the United States from 1993–2001, points out how the lessons of the past can help America cope with the challenges of the future. His message still rings true[1] in the second decade of the 21st century. Clinton made the *speech from which this excerpt is taken to graduating students at Portland State University.

Today I want to talk to you about what may be the most important subject of all, how we can strengthen the bonds of our national community as we grow more racially and ethnically diverse. [...]

The driving force behind our increasing diversity is a new, large wave of immigration. It is changing the face of America. And while most of the changes are good, they 5
do present challenges which demand more, both from new immigrants and from our citizens. Citizens share a responsibility to welcome new immigrants, to ensure that they strengthen our Nation, to give them their chance at the brass ring. In turn, new immigrants have a responsibility to learn, to work, to contribute to America. If both citizens and immigrants do their part, we will grow ever stronger in the new global 10
information economy.

More than any other nation on Earth, America has constantly drawn strength and spirit from wave after wave of immigrants. In each generation, they have proved to be the most restless, the most adventurous, the most innovative, the most industrious of people. Bearing different memories, honoring different heritages, they have 15
strengthened our economy, enriched our culture, renewed our promise of freedom and opportunity for all. [...]

But now we are being tested again by a new wave of immigration larger than any in a century, far more diverse than any in our history. Each year, nearly a million people come legally to America. Today, nearly one in ten people in America was born in 20
another country; one in five schoolchildren are from immigrant families. Today, largely because of immigration, there is no majority race in Hawaii or Houston or New York City. Within five years, there will be no majority race in our largest State, California. In a little more than 50 years, there will be no majority race in the United States. No other nation in history has gone through demographic change of this 25
magnitude in so short a time.

What do the changes mean? They can either strengthen and unite us, or they can weaken and divide us. We must decide.

Let me state my view unequivocally. I believe new immigrants are good for America. They are revitalizing our cities. They are building our new economy. They are 30
strengthening our ties to the global economy, just as earlier waves of immigrants settled the new frontier and powered the Industrial Revolution. They are energizing our culture and broadening our vision of the world. They are renewing our most basic values and reminding us all of what it truly means to be an American. [...]

My fellow Americans, we descendants of those who passed through the portals of 35
Ellis Island must not lock the door behind us. Americans whose parents were denied the rights of citizenship simply because of the color of their skin must not deny those rights to others because of the country of their birth or the nature of their faith.

---

[1] **ring true** be valid
2 **strengthen sth.** make sth. stronger
7 **ensure** make sure *(sicherstellen)*
8 **the brass ring** *(AE, infml)* the opportunity to be successful
14 **industrious** [ɪnˈdʌstriəs] hard-working
15 **heritage** [ˈherɪtɪdʒ] cultural tradition
26 **magnitude** *Größenordnung*
29 **unequivocally** [ˌʌnɪˈkwɪvəkli] *unmissverständlich*
30 **revitalize sth.** [ˌriːˈvaɪtəlaɪz] give sth. new life
32 **energize sth.** [ˈenədʒaɪz] give sth. energy
35 **descendant** [dɪˈsendənt] *Nachkomme*
36 **Ellis Island** N.Y. centre for new immigrants, 1892–1954
38 **faith** religion

New York doorbell nameplate

144 Chapter 7   The USA – Still the Promised Land?

Dealing with diversity

7

We should treat new immigrants as we would have wanted our own grandparents
40 to be treated. We should share our country with them, not shun them or shut them
out. But mark my words, unless we handle this well, immigration of this sweep and
scope could threaten the bonds of our Union.

Around the world, we see what can happen when people who live on the same land
put race and ethnicity before country and humanity. If America is to remain the
45 world's most diverse democracy, if immigration is to strengthen America as it has
throughout our history, then we must say to one another: Whether your ancestors
came here in slave ships or on the Mayflower, whether they landed on Ellis Island or
at Los Angeles International Airport, or have been here for thousands of years, if you
believe in the Declaration of Independence and the Constitution, if you accept the
50 responsibilities as well as the rights embedded in them, then you are an American.
Only that belief can keep us one America in the 21st century.

From: William J. Clinton, 'Commencement Address at Portland State University', 13 June 1998

> **TROUBLE SPOT**
>
> **treat sb.** (l. 40) = jdn. behandeln (auch als Arzt/Ärztin)
> **deal with a topic** = ein Thema behandeln
> **handle a situation/problem** (l. 41) = mit einer Situation / einem Problem o. Ä. umgehen, zurechtkommen

40 **shun sb.** avoid sb.
41/42 **sweep, scope** Größenordnung
44 **ethnicity** [eθˈnɪsəti] ethnische Zugehörigkeit

COMPREHENSION

1 Clinton's message
Summarize Clinton's position on diversity in no more than four sentences.

LANGUAGE AWARENESS

2 Political vocabulary
a Clinton's speech contains many words and phrases related to the idea of a country and the people who live in it, e.g. *our national community* (l. 2). Collect more examples from the text.

b Compare lists with a partner and add any words or phrases that are missing from your list.

c **YOU CHOOSE**

Arrange the terms you have found in the form of a mind map. Use at least five of the terms you have found in sentences of your own.

New York street sign

The USA – Still the Promised Land?   Chapter 7

145

7 | Part B

SPEAKING FOCUS ON SKILLS

Speaking in front of an audience

*Before you speak in front of an audience, you should consider how to make your
*speech more effective. Analysing a professional speech is a good way to examine
rhetorical devices and their effect.

Analysing a speech

1 Analysing the structure

   a Identify the following parts of Clinton's speech (pp. 144–145) by putting
     them in the correct order and giving line numbers:

     1 ▪ Statement of the main topic
     2 ▪ Appeal to the audience to be fair in dealing with the consequences
     7 ▪ Appeal to the audience to make a commitment
     4 ▪ Description of historical developments
     5 ▪ Statement of the challenge
     6 ▪ Description of the present situation
     7 ▪ Statement of opinion

   b Examine how Clinton links the parts of his speech to make it easier for his
     listeners to follow his ideas. List the different ways of linking ideas for your
     own later use.

2 Analysing the rhetorical devices

   a Examine the language of the speech. Point out passages where Clinton
     1 catches his listeners' attention
     2 emphasizes his message
     3 creates a feeling of unity with his audience
     4 conveys a positive or negative attitude to his subject
     5 appeals to his listeners' sense of fairness.
     Make notes on your findings (including line numbers).

   b Compare notes with your partner. Analyse your examples and explain the
     techniques used. The terms you may need are in the list on the left.

   c Team up with another pair and give Clinton's speech an 'effectiveness
     rating' (on a scale from 1 to 6).

Preparing your own speech

1 Choosing a topic

  Choose one of the following topics to prepare and deliver your own speech
  modelled on the one you have just analysed:

   ▪ *Living together in our multicultural school*
   ▪ *The world is changing – let's change with it!*
   ▪ *The challenges of freedom in a diverse society*

2 Collecting and organizing ideas

   a Brainstorm what ideas/associations/aspects of your topic come into your
     head.

   b Sort the ideas, keeping in mind that your speech will need a clear structure.

   c Prepare an outline that includes suitable linking phrases and signpost
     words, e.g. 'for one thing …', 'In addition …', 'above all …'.

Find help with this task here:
Webcode context-00

---

anaphora [əˈnæfərə] ▪
contrast ▪ *direct address* ▪
enumeration ▪ *metaphor* ▪
parallelism ▪
personal pronoun ▪
repetition ▪
rhetorical question ▪
simile ▪ *wordplay*

▶ Glossary, p. 323

Chapter 7   The USA – Still the Promised Land?

Dealing with diversity

3 **Writing a first draft**
   a Decide on a good opening sentence. Choose from the following list, or phrase your own:
   - Today I would like to talk to you about what we can do to make life easier for all of us at this school.
   - Last night I went to a multicultural community event, and that gave me the idea of talking to you about how our world is changing and what we can do to change our attitudes.
   - The other day I saw a sign that said 'Freedom is never free', and I started thinking about the price of freedom in our democracy. Today I would like to tell you my thoughts on this subject.

   b Remember to use rhetorical devices like those you identified in Clinton's speech in order to
   - catch your listeners' attention: *Do you know how many nations are represented by the students at our school?*
   - emphasize your message: *Cheap air travel, the internet, the end of the Cold War – all of these developments have made our world smaller and more connected than it has ever been before.*
   - create a feeling of unity with your audience: *Together, we can find a solution.*
   - convey a positive or negative attitude: *Tolerance and respect lead to understanding and cooperation; intolerance and distrust to conflict and violence.*
   - appeal to your listeners' sense of fairness: *Imagine how you would feel if this happened to you.*

   c Take special care with your closing sentence(s), because this is what will stick in your listeners' minds.

4 **Revising your draft**
   Read your draft aloud to a partner to test its effect as a spoken text. Mark the places that don't 'work' and note what changes you want to make. Then write a revised version, always keeping in mind that it is a speech with which you want to make an impact on your listeners.

Rehearsing and delivering your speech

1 Decide how you want to deliver your speech, and take the necessary precautions to ensure you don't get mixed up and can be seen and understood clearly:

Method	Position
Speaking freely from notes on index cards	Standing in front of the class
Reading aloud from a manuscript	Sitting at a desk in front of the class

2 Practise your speech until you feel comfortable with it. You can make a recording of the speech and then listen to yourself speaking to get an 'outside impression'. Practise speaking in front of a full-length mirror to monitor your eye contact and body language. Refer to the Skills File (p. 280) for additional tips on how to deliver a speech.

▶ SF 25: Giving a speech

The USA – Still the Promised Land?   Chapter 7

7 Part C

▶ SF 22: Listening

Equality and inequality

C1 The danger to the dream   Barack Obama

The extract you are about to hear is taken from a *speech made by President Barack Obama on 4 December 2013.

— COMPREHENSION ◀

1 Listening for gist
After listening to the excerpt once, decide which of the following statements best summarizes the main idea:
1 America has always rewarded success.
2 The present imbalance between poor and rich threatens the American dream.
3 The task of the government is to ensure that everyone has a fair share of America's wealth.

2 Listening for detail
YOU CHOOSE ▶ Together with your partner, choose either task **a** or task **b** before listening to the speech a second time.

US President Barack Obama

🎧 **CD2** 07

premise [ˈpremɪs] assumption (*cf.* German *Prämisse*)
land-grant college college funded with money from the sale of state-owned land
bust (*v*) break up
Medicare, Medicaid state-supported healthcare programs
New Deal, War on Poverty, Great Society slogans of social policy under (F. D.) Roosevelt and Johnson
prosperity [prɒˈsperəti] *Wohlstand*
confine sb. to sth. limit sb. to sth.
blue-collar job factory job
debt [det] money you owe sb.
consistently [kənˈsɪstəntli] regularly
unravel [ʌnˈrævl] fall apart
automate [ˈɔːtəmeɪt] become automated
leverage [AE: ˈlevərɪdʒ, BE: ˈliːvərɪdʒ] negotiating power
begrudge sth. *etwas missgönnen*
aspire to sth. strive to reach sth.
handsomely [ˈhænsəmli] generously
offend sb. upset sb.

a **Looking backward**	OR	b **Then and now**
1 Obama begins by pointing to four former presidents: Abraham Lincoln, Theodor ('Teddy') Roosevelt, Franklin D. Roosevelt ('FDR'), and Lyndon B. Johnson ('LBJ'). Take notes on each of them while listening.		1 Take notes on the following points: • the American attitude to success • upward mobility • factors that limited upward mobility in the past • the threat to upward mobility in the present.
2 Compare notes with your partner. Together, decide what these presidents had in common and why Obama mentions them.		2 Compare notes with your partner. Make any necessary additions or corrections.
3 Link up with a pair that chose task **b**. Tell each other what you have learned.		3 Link up with a pair that chose task **a**. Tell each other what you have learned.

— BEYOND THE TEXT ◀

3 More success stories
Choose one American person who you regard as a success story. Research this person's *biography and report back to your class.

Steve Jobs	Steven Spielberg	Henry Ford
Bill Gates	Lady Gaga
Oprah Winfrey	Hillary Clinton	…

148

Chapter 7   The USA – Still the Promised Land?

Equality and inequality   7

C2 How to become homeless

You are going to watch an excerpt from the 2009 documentary Capitalism: A Love Story. *In it, film-maker Michael Moore explains how millions of Americans lost their homes following the financial crisis of 2008.*

■ FACT FILE

Home ownership
As few people can afford to pay cash for a house, the usual procedure is to borrow the money you need from a bank. The so-called **mortgage** ['mɔːgɪdʒ] (a kind of loan) can have either a fixed **interest rate** (e.g., for a 10-year period) or a floating rate that varies with the money market. If the borrower cannot pay the monthly rate, the bank **forecloses**, meaning it cancels the mortgage and tries to sell the house to get its money back. In a **boom market**, this is usually no problem, but if housing prices fall, the bank can be left with a loss.

Make sure you understand the four terms **in bold print**. *Then shut your book. Together with your partner, take turns asking each other to explain each of the terms in bold.*

📺 DVD

hunky-dory *(infml)* state in which everyone is happy
tap sth. *etwas anzapfen*
home equity ['ɛkwəti] net value of your house
refinance your home pay back old loans by taking out new ones
scam dishonest plan for making money
down payment *Anzahlung*
approved [ə'pruːvd] accepted (as customers)
demeanor *(AE)* = *(BE)* **demeanour** way sb. looks or behaves
pitch sales talk
subprime used to describe loans to people who are considered bad risks
on disability receiving disability payments *(Erwerbsunfähigkeits-rente)*
foreclosure notice letter stating that your mortgage has been cancelled

---

◀ COMPREHENSION

1 Writing conference: First reactions (first viewing)
Form small groups. Write down your first reaction to the video. Then pass your paper to the right. Add comments to the papers you are given.

2 Understanding the background
Copy and complete the following text using words from the list on the right:

American *homeowners* were persuaded to … from banks to finance …. The new … had a … interest rate. When the interest rate …, many … were unable to pay the … rates. They lost the … of their houses and were forced to ….

borrow money •
consumer spending •
floating • homeowners •
monthly • mortgages •
move out • owners •
ownership • rose

◀ ANALYSIS

3 Film technique (second viewing)
a Make notes on the effect of the film while watching it for the second time. Fill in the missing information on the worksheet that can be downloaded via webcode.
b Discuss how effective the film is at helping people to understand the housing crisis.

Download the worksheet here:
 Webcode context-00

◀ BEYOND THE TEXT

4 YOU CHOOSE **Michael Moore: an American institution**

a Research Moore's career and report back to your class.

OR

b Read a few online reviews of 'Capitalism: A Love Story' and report back to your class: What did the critics praise or criticize about the film?

Film-maker Michael Moore

7 Part C

C3 A politics lesson   Todd Strasser

In Todd Strasser's 2014 *novel No Place, the *narrator Dan Halprin, a popular high-school athlete in his final year, is forced to move in with relatives when both his parents lose their jobs. For some weeks, a student activist has been trying to recruit him for a protest march on Washington.

One day the following week I was leaving the cafeteria with Noah and some friends from the team, talking and laughing when the ratty-haired kid at the table in the hall called out, 'Hey, Dan, ready to sign up?'

I felt myself tense. All my friends, plus a couple of kids at the sign-up table, were watching and listening. 'Why do you ask?' 'Seems like a good time,' he said.

Had he heard that we'd lost our home? Did he think that would make me more sympathetic to his cause? 'Why's that?' I gave him a hard look.

Some kids will back down when you give them that look, but this kid kept his eyes steadily on mine. 'Just figured for once I had your undivided attention.'

It took a second to realize that for the past few weeks I'd been with Talia every time I'd passed him, and he probably remembered that time she'd pulled me away before he had a chance to lay out his spiel. But Talia wasn't feeling well and had stayed home that day. Still, it had to take guts to stand up in front of senior athletes and call one out. I looked at the posters on the wall behind him.

> 400 Americans have more than half the wealth in this country.
>
> Why is it easier to believe that 150,000,000 Americans are being LAZY rather than that 400 Americans are being GREEDY?
>
> STOP THE WAR ON THE POOR!
>
> Bail out schools, not banks!

'People are suffering,' the kid said. 'They can't find work, or get a decent education. You think it's fair that someone dies because he can't pay for adequate medical care while someone else with the same disease lives because he can?'

My friends started to drift away. Meanwhile, I thought of Meg's family living in Dignityville because her mom and brother had to spend practically everything they earned on medicine for Mr. Fine. I used to think that life was like sports: Things were rarely fair. The other team cheated. Your best player got hurt. You threw a perfect strike and the ump called it a ball.

But that's a game, not life.

In sports people don't die because they can't afford medicine.

They don't become homeless because a company goes out of business or moves jobs overseas.

I gestured at the posters. 'You really think marching's gonna make a difference?'

The ratty-haired kid looked surprised. 'You don't think protests changed the war in Vietnam or segregation in the South?'

Anti-bank bailout protests on Wall Street in 2008

4 **tense** *(v)* become tense
7 **be sympathetic to sth.** [ˌsɪmpəˈθetɪk] einer Sache gegenüber aufgeschlossen sein
   cause Sache, Anliegen
9 **figure** [AE: ˈfɪɡjər, BE: ˈfɪɡə] *(v) (infml)* think, believe
10 **Talia** Dan's girlfriend
12 **lay out a spiel** *(infml)* make a speech
13 **guts** *(infml)* courage
   call sb. out jdn. namentlich ansprechen
21 **bail sb. out** rescue sb. from a difficult situation

■ TROUBLE SPOT
decent [ˈdiːsnt] *(l. 22)* = anständig
But: *dezent* =
1. **subdued, soft** (colours, music, etc.);
2. **tactful, discreet** (behaviour)

25 **Meg Fine** girl in Dan's class. Her father has cancer.
26 **Dignityville** name of tent city for the homeless in Dan's town
28 **You threw a perfect strike and the ump called it a ball.** The ball you threw was in the valid zone but the umpire (Schiedsrichter/in) said it wasn't.

150   Chapter 7   The USA – Still the Promised Land?

Equality and inequality 7

I couldn't say. We may have studied those events in school, but those old protest movements were about as real to me as trigonometry. You learned what you needed to ace the test. And not for an instant did it feel like it had any actual meaning in your
40 life.

'If we don't do something, it's only going to get worse,' the kid said. 'And it's not the kind of thing one person can do. Marches show strength. They tell politicians that we have the numbers and the votes to change elections.'

I was more than three years away from being able to drink legally, but only months
45 from being able to vote. Sure, voting may have been way more important, but given the choice, I would have switched those two age requirements in a heartbeat.

The kid was still waiting for me to respond.

'Can I ask you something personal?' I said. 'Why do you care? You homeless or something?'
50 The kid gave me a long, curious look, then said, 'No, I care ... because I'm *not* homeless.'

From: Todd Strasser, *No Place*, 2014

39 **ace a test** get a good mark on a test

TROUBLE SPOT
actual ['ækt∫uəl] (l. 39) = *real, concrete*
But: *aktuell* = **current**

COMPREHENSION

1 Mediation (English → German)
Tell your parents / little brother/sister at the dinner table in two German sentences what the novel extract is about.

▶ SF 41: Mediation of written and oral texts

2 Interviews
Write five interview questions for Dan Halprin based on the text you have just read. Ask your partner your questions, then answer your partner's questions. Discuss any points on which you differ.

▶ SF 26: Taking part in an interview

ANALYSIS

3 Dan's political development
Point to examples from the text that show how Dan's interest in politics and political action is changing. Name the factors that influence him.

LANGUAGE AWARENESS

4 Uses of the progressive form
  a Collect examples of the past progressive from the extract. Compare lists with your partner. Together, formulate a rule explaining when the past progressive is used.
  b In the following text, no progressive forms have been used. Rewrite the text, deciding which verbs should be put in the past progressive:
  When Mr Purcellen arrived home that evening, I sat next to Talia on the front porch. It was a warm evening; the moon shone behind the trees, and a soft wind blew. Mr Purcellen got out of the old pickup he always drove to work. He walked across the dark lawn and stopped about ten yards from the house. I think he watched us, but I couldn't guess what he thought.
  c CHALLENGE Examine the text on the poster (in the middle of the opposite page). The second sentence uses a progressive form of the verb *be* twice. Explain how this form differs in meaning from the simple form of the verb.

▶ LP 1: Simple and progressive verb forms
▶ SF 4: Using a grammar book

BEYOND THE TEXT

5 YOU CHOOSE Creative writing

a Retell the episode described in the extract from the point of view of the student activist.

b Write a continuation of the extract, in which Dan decides whether he wants to sign up for the protest march.

▶ SF 37: Doing a creative writing task

The USA – Still the Promised Land? Chapter 7

151

7 Part D

America's place in the world

D1 Facts and figures

	USA	China	Germany	Brazil	Russia	India
1 GDP	16,244,600	8,277,103	3,428,131	2,252,664	2,014,775	1,841,710
2 Military spending	682,478	166,107	45,785	43,576	90,749	46,125
3 Balance of trade	–784,775	155,142	219,938	19,169	198,760	–154,401

All figures are in millions of US dollars and are from 2012, except (3), which contains data from 2011.

■ FACT FILE

GDP (**Gross** [grəʊs] **Domestic Product**) is defined as the total value of goods and services produced in a country. The **balance of trade** is the difference between the total value of exports from a country and imports into the same country. A negative balance (**deficit** ['defɪsɪt]; opposite: **surplus** ['sɜːpləs]) means the country imports more than it exports.

▶ SF 12: Analysing charts and graphs

— COMPREHENSION ◀

1 Analysing numbers
   a Write eight sentences comparing the figures in the table. **SUPPORT** ▶ p. 212
   b Compare sentences with your partner. Check each other's information to make sure you have both got the facts right.

— BEYOND THE TEXT ◀

2 The facts behind the figures
Link up with another pair and discuss what influence the facts from the table above could have on the balance of power in the world.

🎧 CD2 08

D2 The German view *Michael Hochgeschwender*

Mediation (German → English)
In the podcast you are about to hear, historian Michael Hochgeschwender is asked if the USA is still the leading world power. When you mention this interview to your American penfriend, she wants to know what the professor says about America's status in the world. You will hear the interview twice.

▶ SF 41: Mediation of written and oral texts

— COMPREHENSION ◀

1 While listening
Listen to what Hochgeschwender says about America's position in the world. Take notes on the following aspects:
- what the historian says about America's world status
- his reasons for his opinion
- his views on the future development of America's role.

▶ SF 22: Listening

2 After listening
   a Compare notes with your partner.
   b Use your notes to write an email of ca. 150 words explaining Hochgeschwender's position to your penfriend.

— BEYOND THE TEXT ◀

3 CHALLENGE ▶ Commenting
Add a further paragraph to your email from **2b** in which you comment on the historian's views and ask your American penfriend for her opinion.

▶ CC 6: Talking about sensitive issues

152   Chapter 7   The USA – Still the Promised Land?

America's place in the world

D3 Better than its reputation   *Anne Applebaum*

The 20th century is sometimes called 'the American century'. Collect reasons why this might be. How do you think historians will refer to the present century?

LONDON – In Beijing a few months ago, I met a young Filipina journalist who did video interviews for a Chinese website. She seemed clever and competent. She spoke perfect American English, which she learned growing up near a U.S. base. She was very pleased to be in China: Her job in Beijing was interesting, well-paid, and gave her a future. I asked whether she thought her career might take her to the United States. She shrugged. She would never get a visa, let alone a job. Not worth trying.

At the time, I thought this conversation rather ominous. It seemed another reminder that the American dream is looking rather tarnished these days, and not only to Americans. To much of the outside world, the United States appears unpromising and unwelcoming, especially compared with the largest economy in East Asia, the new land of opportunity. We are growing far more slowly than China. Our middle class is downwardly mobile. U.S. news organizations are not scouring the world for talent, whereas China's apparently are. [...]

And yet, when a disaster unfolds and resources have to be rapidly mobilized, it's as if nothing has changed. One of the largest typhoons on record hit the Philippines last week. The extent of the damage isn't yet known. But the American response is already larger – by a factor of hundreds – than that of the largest economy in East Asia. The United States is sending an aircraft carrier to the worst-hit regions and has promised $20 million in emergency aid. Millions more will be raised by U.S. charities. The British are sending a warship and $16 million. Even the Vatican has promised $4 million. And the government of China, the new land of opportunity? $100,000.

There are politics behind China's stinginess. China has recently made claims on Philippine territory, citing historical documents that date to the fifth century. The Philippine government has responded with anger, a lawsuit, and an invitation to the U.S. Navy to reopen some bases closed in the 1990s. There are also politics behind American generosity, which partly reflects the renewed warmth and military cooperation between Washington and Manila.

But these differing responses to the typhoon also signify a different set of attitudes to power, and not just to 'soft power': Americans, like Europeans, have long believed that strength and wealth entail responsibility. That's why two American ex-presidents voluntarily coordinated the international response to the 2004 tsunami, even though Indonesia was not the site of a U.S. naval base. That's why massive amounts of U.S. aid went to victims of the 2005 earthquake in Kashmir, even though relations between the United States and Pakistan were deteriorating at the time.

That's also why an American president who is actively uninterested in engaging with the Syrian conflict has pledged more than $1 billion in humanitarian aid to Syrian refugees, accounting for nearly 30 percent of all such aid; European contributions as a whole make up a good percentage of the rest. China's contribution, meanwhile, comes to $3 million, less than that of Luxembourg. China plays an enormous

Members of the U.S. and Philippine army unload U.S. aid as part of relief efforts after Typhoon Haiyan

6 **let alone** *geschweige denn*
8 **tarnished** *(here)* no longer attractive
12 **scour sth.** ['skaʊə] search sth. intensely
14 **unfold** *(here)* happen
16 **on record** [BE: 'rekɔːd, AE: 'rekərd] *seit Menschengedenken*
17 **extent** *Ausmaß*
21 **aircraft carrier** *Flugzeugträger*
24 **charity** organization that helps people in need
28 **stinginess** ['stɪndʒɪnəs] *Geiz*
31 **lawsuit** *(juristische) Klage*
37 **entail sth.** have sth. as a consequence
41 **deteriorate** [dɪ'tɪəriəreɪt] become worse
42 **engage with sth.** get involved in sth.
43 **pledge sth.** promise to give sth.
44 **account for sth.** *etwas ausmachen*

7 Part D

48 sidelined unable to take action
obligated ['ɒblɪɡeɪtɪd]
verpflichtet
51 counter sth. deal with the
effects of sth.
facilitate sth. [fə'sɪlɪteɪt] *(fml)*
make sth. easier
53 for its own sake *als Selbstzweck*
57 elaborate [ɪ'læbərət] long and
complex
59 wane become less
60 taper off become less

political role in Syria – the Chinese veto has helped keep the United Nations firmly sidelined there – but clearly does not feel obligated to help those affected by its decisions.

The Chinese do give development aid, but differently: not in response to tragedies, not to counter disaster, but to facilitate the export of raw materials to China. There is merit to some of China's efforts, especially in Africa. But the Chinese state is not, for the most part, interested in generosity for its own sake. Nor do many Chinese billionaires believe that new wealth brings new obligations. Several of them refused even to meet Bill Gates a few years ago, apparently because they were afraid he might ask them to give away some of their money. 50 ... 55

All of which is not an elaborate excuse for messy American foreign policy, or the still-weak American economy, or the indecisive American president. It's just a little reminder: U.S. strength may be waning, U.S. status may be fading, and U.S. attraction for talented foreigners may soon taper off. But there will be reasons to be sorry if America isn't a superpower anymore, perhaps more than America's critics think. 60

From: Anne Applebaum, 'Why America's Critics Will Miss the U.S. Superpower',
Slate (magazine), 13 November 2013

COMPREHENSION ◀

1 Summarizing the text
Summarize the *author's views in no more than four sentences.

► SF 31: Writing a summary

2 Collecting information
a Copy and complete the table with information from the text:

	China	America
strong points		
weak points		

b Compare tables with your partner; add any missing information.

ANALYSIS ◀

► SF 18: Analysing non-fiction

3 The author's bias
a Examine the author's bias: whose side is she on?
b Point to examples from the text that illustrate her bias (selection of facts, word choice, use of *emphasis, *juxtaposition, sentence structure, etc.).
   SUPPORT ▶ p.213
c Use your results from tasks 1–3 to analyse the author's strategy: How does she 'package' her views on America's position in the world?

LANGUAGE AWARENESS ◀

► LP 20: Word formation
► SF 3: Using a dictionary

4 Word formation
a Form eight word pairs (either 'noun – adjective' or 'noun – verb') using words from the text. Example: *generosity – generous; contribution – contribute*. Consult a monolingual dictionary if necessary.
b Use the words that don't appear in the text in sentences of your own.

BEYOND THE TEXT ◀

5 WRITING CONFERENCE The next ten years
Form small groups. Write down your ideas on the topic: Will America still play a major role in the world ten years from now? Share your ideas with your group, and discuss the reasons for your opinions.

Chapter 7   The USA – Still the Promised Land?

Chapter Task   7

Giving a speech on why you would like to visit the USA

▶ SF 25: Giving a speech

Imagine you discover this *advert on the internet:

> ## The Chance of a Lifetime!
>
> The German-American Friendship Organization is offering ten stipends for German teenagers aged 18 or older. Winners will spend three months in the United States, living with American families, visiting schools, businesses and places of interest, talking to politicians, business people, and just plain Americans of all ages.
>
> To apply to our program, send us a video of not more than five minutes in which you make a speech on the subject: 'Why I want to learn more about America.'

Excited at the prospect of an all-expenses-paid stay in the USA, you decide to apply.

1 **Getting started**
   Collect your ideas using a suitable method: What do you find fascinating, irritating, or intriguing about America and the Americans? What kinds of people would you like to talk to? What questions would you ask them?

2 **Writing your speech**
   a Organize your ideas in the form of an outline. Use the outline to write a first draft.
   b Read your drafts aloud in small groups and discuss them, suggesting improvements where needed.
   c Prepare a revised version. Make sure it is not longer than five minutes. Practise reading your speech in front of a friend or a mirror until you feel confident with it. Then make a video of yourself delivering your speech.

3 **Evaluation**
   Form small groups. In your group, let the others watch your video (or you can deliver it 'live'). The others give you feedback. They fill in assessment sheets given out by your teacher.

The USA – Still the Promised Land?   Chapter 7

8 Beyond the Nation – Europe and a Globalized World

Download a chronological word list here:

Webcode context-00

▶ SF 41: Mediation of written and oral texts

1 **Displaying one's national identity**
During great sports events, above all soccer world championships, people often display their national identity and patriotism by carrying flags or singing their national anthem.
   a THINK Describe your attitude to this behaviour, referring to the pictures above and your own experience.
   b PAIR Compare and discuss your ideas with a partner.
   c SHARE Present your most interesting findings to the class.

2 YOU CHOOSE **Researching flags and anthems**

   a Use German sources to find out about the history of the German flag and the national anthem. Prepare a short presentation for English-speaking visitors to your school. b Choose a country and do some research into the history of its anthem and flag. Present your findings to the class.

3 **Understanding national symbols**
Define the function of national symbols such as flags and anthems.

156   Chapter 8   Beyond the Nation – Europe and a Globalized World

Lead-in

4 **Finding out about international institutions**
   a Find out about the roles of the following institutions: UN, UNESCO, WHO, Commonwealth, EU. Describe and explain their logos.
   b Say why institutions that cut across national boundaries might be necessary.

5 **Thinking about your sense of identity**
   a Complete this sentence: 'I rather see myself as (1) a German or other national citizen, (2) a European, (3) a cosmopolitan citizen, (4) none of the above.' Say why.
   b Find out how the majority of your class see themselves and why.

PREVIEW

In this chapter you will learn what living in a globalized world means for the individual and the world.

Main topics
- Personal identities in a global world .... p. 156
- The historical peacekeeping merits of the EU and its current challenges .... p. 160
- Promises and challenges of globalization .... p. 166
- The role of English in a global world .... p. 171

Focus on Skills: MEDIATION and READING
- Mediating texts in oral communication .... p. 165
- Using reading strategies .... p. 170

Chapter Task:
Preparing an exhibition on the topic 'Slavery? Not today, not in Germany!' .... p. 175

Beyond the Nation – Europe and a Globalized World   Chapter 8

157

8 Words in Context

 CD2 09

Listen to an audio version of the text on the CD or download it here:
 Webcode context-00

> ■ **TROUBLE SPOT**
>
> Preis = **prize** (award given to sb. for an achievement)
> = **price** (the money you have to pay for sth.)

Globalization: Europe, the World

European integration as a model?
Political experts say that the power of nation states has been declining and that today the most important decisions are taken on an international level. The European Union, which connects independent nation states, is a good example. Since its foundation, the European Union (or its predecessors) was meant to serve two principal purposes: to secure peace and promote economic growth. In 2012, the European Union was awarded the Nobel Peace Prize for overcoming the hostility among European countries after the Second World War and for advancing reconciliation and peace. At the moment of the award, however, Europe was and still is challenged by a monetary crisis, which forced many member states to make massive cuts in their budgets. As a result, unemployment rates increased and many young people, especially those from Spain or Greece were forced to leave their countries and find occupation elsewhere.

Chances and risks of globalization
Globalization can be described as a process in which barriers, especially trade barriers, between nations are removed. This process accelerated when modern communication technologies came into play and transport costs decreased. It made international collaboration and competition possible: Companies in the developed countries were able to outsource their production and services to countries whose labour force was prepared to work for significantly lower wages.

This international division of labour may have freed many people in the developing countries from extreme poverty; however, many of them have to work under poor working conditions with low safety standards. In the traditional industrialized countries, globalization has resulted in redundancies in the domestic workforce.

The threats and opportunities of globalization can be illustrated well through the example of international sports. Top soccer clubs pay enormous sums for the best players from all over the world, allowing for extraordinary labour mobility. Yet, only the richest clubs can participate in this 'leg-drain' and if players are frequently being bought and sold they may feel uprooted and unable to develop a sound sense of identity.

English as a global language
The cultural impact of globalization is illustrated most clearly by the role of English as a global language. Today, English is not only the native language of more than 3 million speakers worldwide, but it is also used as a lingua franca between non-native speakers of English in international business, science and technology, and popular culture. On the one hand, this makes international communication easier, but on the other hand, it threatens local languages and thus cultural and linguistic diversity.

Globalization: Europe, the World

1 Words in use: synonyms
Find a highlighted word or expression that means the same as …
1 the aim or function of something.
2 the percentage of people in a country without a job.
3 the readiness of people to work in different places.
4 not feel at home anywhere.
5 give a job to external workers, often in another country.
6 language spoken all over the world.

2 Word formation
For each gap in the sentences below choose a suitable word from the list on the right, turn it into the required word class (e.g. a verb into a noun) and adjust its grammatical form if necessary (e.g. the plural form).
1 Some European countries had an extremely … relationship for centuries.
2 With the Treaty of Friendship (1963) France and Germany were officially …
3 In our times of globalization, individuals world-wide have to … and …
4 Since the EU was …, lasting peace has been one of its aims.
5 Today, the EU is facing great …

collaboration • competition • challenge • foundation • hostility • reconciliation

▶ LP 20: Word formation

3 Activating your vocabulary
Translate the following passage. The underlined words and phrases are taken from the text, but you should try to translate them without looking at the text again. Paraphrase if you do not know the exact word or expression. Revise your version with the help of the text and a dictionary.

▶ SF 9: Paraphrasing
▶ SF 3: Using a dictionary

> Globalisierung ist ein Prozess voller Chancen und Risiken. Kritiker befürchten, dass sie Arbeitsplätze in den traditionellen Industrieländern gefährdet und Arbeiter in den Entwicklungsländern ausbeutet, die oft unter sehr schlechten Arbeitsbedingungen arbeiten müssen. Befürworter der Globalisierung glauben, dass sie extreme Armut in vielen Ländern besiegen kann. Der Abbau von Handelsschranken sei von Vorteil für alle.

▶ LP 16: Avoiding Germanisms

4 The future of nation states
You are asked to briefly inform your politics course in German on the future of nation states as described in this text. Prepare and give a short oral presentation. Make visual aids if necessary.

▶ SF 7: Making visual aids
▶ SF 24: Giving a presentation

Beyond the Nation – Europe and a Globalized World   Chapter 8

8 Part A

European integration as a model?

A1 A great achievement of the past Herman Van Rompuy

Since 1901 the Nobel Peace Prize has been awarded annually (with few exceptions) to individuals and institutions who have sought to establish or keep peace. During the award ceremony, the winner is required to give the Nobel Lecture, a lecture on a subject related to the topic of the prize. When in 2012 the European Union was awarded the prize, the Nobel Lecture was given by Herman Van Rompuy, President of the European Council, and José Manuel Barroso, President of the European Commission.

1 Before listening
Look at the picture below and describe the setting and the general atmosphere of the ceremony.

COMPREHENSION

2 Listening for gist
Listen to the audio file, which contains Van Rompuy's part of the Nobel Lecture. From the following statements choose the one that best describes the speaker's intention.
1 Peacekeeping is Europe's ongoing goal.
2 Lasting peace has been established in Europe.
3 Current challenges are threatening to seriously destabilize the EU.

3 Listening for detail: part 1
Listen to the first part of the speech, then decide whether the following statements are true or false according to the speaker.
1 The Nobel Prize belongs to Europe's political elite, who united Europe after World War II.
2 War used to be a constant feature of European history.
3 Van Rompuy still has wartime memories of his own.
4 Europe would not have gained peace without the European Union.
5 Konrad Adenauer was awarded a French medal in 1951.

> **TROUBLE SPOT**
> *etwas verleihen* = (a prize)
> **award sth. (to sb.)**
> = (allow sb. to use sth. and return it afterwards)
> **lend sb.** *sth.*

▶ SF 11: Analysing pictures

 CD2 10, 11, 12, 13

Herodotus *(ca. 484–425 BC)* Greek historian
Winston Churchill *(1874–1965)* British Prime Minister (1940–1945 and 1951–1955)
founder person who starts an institution or organization
ceasefire time when enemies stop fighting
reconciliation situation where two people or groups become friendly again after a disagreement
Konrad Adenauer *(1876–1967)* first post-war Chancellor of West Germany (1949–1963)
Treaty of Rome founding document of the European Economic Community from 1957
Willy Brandt *(1913–1992)* West German Chancellor (1969–1974)
Gdansk Danzig, Polish seaport
François Mitterand *(1916–1996)* French President (1981–1995)
Helmut Kohl *(born 1930)* West German Chancellor (1982–1998)
Tallin, Riga, Vilnius capitals of the Baltic states Estonia, Latvia and Lithuania, respectively
Jean Monnet *(1888–1979)* French diplomat, considered to be one of the founding fathers of the European Union
perpetual continuing for a long period of time with no interruption
Srebrenica town in Bosnia, site of a massacre during the Balkan War (1995)
Abraham Lincoln *(1809–1865)* President of the United States (1861–1865)

160 Chapter 8 Beyond the Nation – Europe and a Globalized World

European integration as a model?

4 Listening for detail: part 2
Say which historical events depicted in the photos are mentioned by Rompuy. Give the photos headings.

5 Listening for detail: part 3
Choose the correct statement.
- **a** Rompuy mentions the example of Srebrenica to prove that …
    1. … there is no European post-war generation.
    2. … some young Europeans have experienced war themselves.
    3. … Soviet rule in Eastern Europe was responsible for massacres.
- **b** According to the speaker, the economic crisis …
    1. … does not put the European Union to the test.
    2. … mainly affects young academics.
    3. … reduces the feeling of solidarity.

— LANGUAGE AWARENESS ◀

6 A non-native accent
- **a** Listen to the speech once more and examine Van Rompuy's English. Identify elements that show that English is not his native tongue.
    ▶ LANGUAGE HELP
- **b** Do you think it's a disadvantage to speak with an accent? Say why or why not.

— BEYOND THE TEXT ◀

7 YOU CHOOSE Research on the EU
Do some research on one of the topics below, then present your results:

- **a** Describe the status of English in the European institutions. Discuss whether the use of other languages, e.g. German, should be promoted within European institutions.

OR

- **b** Outline the events that led to European unification and describe their context and consequences. Add more 'historical moments' that helped to unite Europe.

LANGUAGE HELP
- pronounce … as …/ say … instead of …
- not pronounce … properly
- use voiceless/voiced consonants
- long/short vowel / diphthong

▶ SF 24: Giving a presentation

Beyond the Nation – Europe and a Globalized World   Chapter 8

Part A

A2 Young, educated – and leaving the country

Liz Alderman

The following extract from an article illustrates the consequences of the European financial crisis for individuals.

Soon after her 23rd birthday four years ago, Melissa Abadía made a wrenching decision: She would leave her close-knit family in Spain, where the grinding fallout from the 2008 financial crisis had made securing a good job impossible, and move to the Netherlands, where employers were still hiring.

'When I got on the plane, I was crying,' Ms. Abadía, a bright, ebullient woman, 5 recalled. 'But I had to decide: Should I fight for something back home that makes no sense, or get out of there and make a life for myself?'

Despite five years of training in nursing in her hometown, Castellón de la Plana, in eastern Spain, she now works in a windowless stockroom in Amsterdam organizing purses, socks and other accessories at a clothing store. 10

It is a sign of the plight of her generation that simply having a job and a measure of independence makes her one of the lucky ones – never mind homesickness, dashed dreams of a very different career and a gradual acceptance that her life will probably never be the one she expected to live.

'Of course, I hate the fact that I have to do this,' she said, speaking in somber tones. 15 'Leaving your country should be a decision, not an obligation.'

Finding only unpaid nursing internships and a temporary nightclub job in Spain, Ms. Abadía scoured the Internet for work in Europe's more prosperous north. She quickly found employment as an au pair in Amsterdam.

For the first time, she experienced the shock of being an immigrant. Having arrived 20 in Amsterdam as part of an influx of young Spanish, Greek, Italian and Portuguese men and women all searching for any employment, 'I now know what it's like to be seen as someone who's coming to steal jobs,' she said.

She soon found better-paying work at the clothing shop, near the Royal Palace. The store was crowded with at least 10 other young Spaniards who had migrated for 25 employment.

She spent two years bouncing between short-term contracts, which employers have sharply increased during the crisis to cut costs and avoid the expensive labor protections granted to permanent employees.

In some countries, especially those with the highest youth unemployment rates, 30 short-term contracts are nothing more than opportunities for employers to take advantage of the weak labor market.

But when used by employers as intended – to give experience to young people who otherwise could not get a start – they can lead to steady work. That was the case with Ms. Abadía, whose employer eventually turned her temporary job into a permanent 35 contract with benefits overseeing the store's biggest stockroom.

On one level, having even that kind of employment is a victory in today's Europe. Her salary of €1,200 a month (about $1,600) was nearly twice what she could have expected to make in Spain.

'The day I signed a permanent contract was the best day of my life,' she said one 40 recent weeknight, beaming as she sipped a Coke at a bustling pub.

'It is almost impossible to get one now in Spain,' she said. 'Here, they trust me, a Spanish girl, and give me responsibilities. I can pay my rent, save money and be independent. I'm even writing a book.'

Working in a clothes shop

1 **wrench** *(adj)* very difficult and painful
2 **grinding** never ending or improving
fallout *(here)* long-term consequences of a disaster
5 **ebullient** *(fml)* full of energy
9 **stockroom** room where goods are kept in a shop
11 **plight** difficult and sad situation
15 **somber** *(AE = BE sombre)* serious and a little sad
17 **internship** ['- - -] temporary job, often for little or no pay, especially done by newcomers to a job
27 **bounce between jobs** move from one job to another
36 **benefits** advantages given to an employee in addition to their salary (e.g. sick pay, health insurance)
contract ['- -] formal document containing an agreement, e.g. between employer and employee
oversee sth. *(here)* be the manager of sth.
41 **beam** *(v)* smile broadly

European integration as a model?

45 But because of her work hours, she still does not qualify for the Netherlands' monthly minimum wage of €1,477 (about $2,000), and her new career was a long way from where she had always hoped to end up.

Discussing the path that had brought her to this point, Ms. Abadía became suddenly pensive. Adjusting to a life far from home in a job beneath her skills has been harder
50 than she imagined.

'I gave up the thought of working as a nurse long ago,' she said. 'With this job, I'm so tired sometimes that I can't move. I don't know what a weekend is anymore.'

Above all, Ms. Abadía still yearns for Spain. [...]

'Recently, I heard criticism that people like us are running away,' Ms. Abadía said.
55 'We didn't run away. We left because the economic situation and the politicians pushed us.'

'If they don't fix things, they are going to lose a couple generations of smart, young people,' Ms. Abadía added as her friends nodded in agreement. 'And then what will happen to the country that's left behind?'

60 That question is weighing on European leaders. An estimated 100,000 university graduates have left Spain, and hundreds of thousands more from Europe's crisis-hit countries have gone to Germany, Britain, and the Nordic states for jobs in engineering, science and medicine. Many others have gone farther afield to Australia, Canada and the United States.

65 The current migration 'is mostly the skilled part of the population,' said Massimiliano Mascherini, a research manager at Eurofound, a European Union research agency. 'It is alarming for the countries that young people are leaving, and it should be a big source of concern for their governments.'

From: *The New York Times*, 15 November 2013

> **TROUBLE SPOT**
> *career* = beruflicher Werdegang
> = erfolgreiche Karriere

49 **pensive** thinking deeply, worrying about sth.
49 **beneath sth.** lower than sth., not good enough for sth.
60 **weigh on sb.** make sb. worried
63 **farther afield** far way from home

◄ COMPREHENSION

1 Understanding Ms. Abadia's situation

a Point out why Ms. Abadia left Spain, how her working life developed in Amsterdam and which consequences youth unemployment in Europe has in general.

b Write a summary of the text in no more than 150 words.

▶ LP 4: Present perfect and simple past

◄ LANGUAGE AWARENESS

2 Transforming direct into indirect speech

a Choose two quotations by Ms. Abadia and turn them into indirect speech.

b Explain what changes you have to make when turning direct into indirect speech. What role does the introductory verb play?

◄ ANALYSIS

3 Examining the use of direct and indirect speech

a Go back to your results from task **2** and compare the effect of direct speech and indirect speech respectively.

b Analyse the effect the writer achieves by using many direct quotations.

c **CHALLENGE** ▶ Explain why direct statements are used frequently in reports and feature articles.

◄ BEYOND THE TEXT

4 Creative writing **SUPPORT** ▶ p. 214

Form groups of four. Each select one important moment of Ms. Abadia's immigrant experience and write a diary entry. Read out your entries to your group and join your texts to form one coherent diary entry.

▶ SF 37: Doing a creative writing task

Beyond the Nation – Europe and a Globalized World   Chapter 8

▶ LP 6: Infinitive or gerund after certain nouns

Part A

A3 Hunting for personnel *Sascha Schmierer*

In some European countries many young people face the problem of unemployment. In others, employers in some areas have great difficulty filling their job vacancies. Read this text from a German newspaper about a way to solve both problems.

Es steht nicht zu befürchten, dass die Krankenschwestern im Ludwigsburger Klinikum ihre Patienten beim Weckruf am Morgen künftig mit einem fröhlichen „Buenos Dias" begrüßen. Und das Küchenteam wird statt leckerer Tapas wohl auch weiterhin salzarm zubereitete Krankenhauskost servieren. Dennoch bricht für den Klinikenverbund Ludwigsburg-Bietigheim nächsten Mittwoch eine „spanische Ära" an.

Pünktlich um 9.30 Uhr wird die Medizindirektorin Andrea Grebe im Konferenzraum an der Erlachhofstraße mehr als 30 neue Pflegekräfte von der Iberischen Halbinsel begrüßen. Nach einem ambitionierten Sprachkurs sollen die hoch qualifizierten neuen Mitarbeiter den eklatanten Personalmangel in der Intensivmedizin in den drei Häusern in Ludwigsburg, Bietigheim und Neuenbürg beheben – olé im OP sozusagen.

> **TROUBLE SPOT**
> jdn. / etwas pflegen = (a sick person) **nurse sb. / care for sb.**
> = (an animal) **look after sth.**
> = (a garden, a plant) **tend sth.**

„Fachkräfte für Intensivstationen und den OP-Bereich sind in Deutschland fast nicht zu finden, der Markt ist leergefegt", erklärt der Kliniken-Sprecher Alexander Tsongas den für ein schwäbisches Spital bisher noch eher ungewöhnlichen Schritt. Weil bei der Suche nach qualifiziertem Personal allerdings weder regionale Berufsmessen noch die Werbeaktionen in angrenzenden Bundesländern erfolgreich waren, wichen die Stellenbesetzer des Kliniken-Verbunds nach Südeuropa aus.

Auf die in Spanien geschalteten Anzeigen für OP-Pflegekräfte meldeten sich binnen weniger Tage zahlreiche Bewerber, mit 60 Kandidaten führten die Personalchefs ein Vorstellungsgespräch.

Ergebnis ist, dass bereits nächste Woche mehr als 30 spanische Pflegekräfte ihren Dienst in Ludwigsburg antreten. Bevor die neuen Mitarbeiter – bis auf wenige Ausnahmen handelt es sich um junge Frauen – auf die Tochterkliniken verteilt werden, steht ein je nach Vorkenntnissen zwischen vier und sechs Monaten dauernder Intensivsprachkurs auf dem Lehrplan. Parallel zum Deutschlernen sind Arbeitspraktika in den Krankenhäusern vorgesehen. Für das erste halbe Jahr sind die neuen Pflegekräfte mit einem Praktikantenvertrag ausgestattet. Nach der Probezeit winkt ein unbefristeter Arbeitsvertrag – schließlich hofft die Chefetage des Kliniken-Verbunds, dass die neuen Mitarbeiter aus dem Süden im kalten Deutschland nicht gleich das Weite suchen.

From: *Stuttgarter Nachrichten*, 12 October 2012

1 Comparing situations
Compare the information presented in the the article with Ms. Abadia's situation (cf. p. 162).

European integration as a model? 8

MEDIATION FOCUS ON SKILLS
Mediating texts in oral communication

*Imagine the following situation: On a trip to Amsterdam you meet Ms. Abadia (cf. **A2**, p. 162) in a pub and she tells you her story in English. You remember the article about job vacancies in Germany (cf. **A3**, p. 164) and decide to tell her about it.*

▶ SF 41: Mediation of written and oral texts

1 Choosing the relevant information
   a Examine the situation closely, then look at the following keywords from text **A3**. Which of them do you think would be relevant to Ms. Abadia?

TROUBLE SPOT
information (sing)
Not: ~~informations~~

1 Um 9.30 werden die neuen Pflegekräfte in Ludwigsburg begrüßt.	4 In Deutschland gibt es nicht genügend Pflegekräfte für Intensivstationen.
2 Auf Messen und durch Werbeaktionen konnte kein zusätzliches Pflegepersonal gewonnen werden.	5 Die neuen spanischen Pflegekräfte sind vor allem Frauen.
3 Pflegekräfte müssen einen Sprachkurs absolvieren.	6 Sie sind zunächst als Praktikanten angestellt.

   b Note down any other information you consider useful to Ms. Abadia.

2 Explaining specific terms
   When mediating information from German into English, you will have to paraphrase or explain words, either because you (or the person you are talking to) don't know their English equivalents or because your partner has a different cultural background.
   a Imagine you knew the translations for the words below. Which of them would you explain to Ms. Abadia all the same? Say why.

▶ LP 16: Avoiding Germanisms

LANGUAGE HELP
- continue/conclude/cancel/end a contract
- a contract expires after …
- dismiss sb.

1 Intensivstation	4 Praktikantenvertrag
2 Arbeitspraktikum	5 unbefristeter Arbeitsvertrag
3 Sprachkurs	6 Probezeit

   b Paraphrase or explain the words from **a**. ▶ LANGUAGE HELP

▶ SF 9: Paraphrasing

3 Choosing the correct *register
   The place where a conversation takes place and your relationship to the addressee influence the way you speak to them. Read the two beginnings of the conversation with Ms. Abadia and decide which of them would be more appropriate in the given situation. Say why.

▶ LP 11: Using the right register

'Well, actually, I read an article just a few days ago and I think it might interest you. Basically it was all about how Germany really needs nurses and …'	'Bearing in mind the situation you have been telling me about I would like to inform you about the opportunities that have opened in Germany for qualified nurses.'

4 Speaking to the addressee
   a Structure your ideas and prepare your side of the conversation, bearing in mind your results from tasks **1–3**.
   b Work with a partner to role-play the conversation. Answer their questions and pay attention to their facial expression or gestures to find out whether they have understood you. Rephrase your statements if necessary. Then swap roles.

▶ CC 4: Meeting and greeting

▶ LP 12: Avoiding German-sounding sentence patterns

Find a recording tool here:

Webcode context-00

Beyond the Nation – Europe and a Globalized World   Chapter 8   165

8 Part B

Chances and risks of globalization

B1 How big is the impact?

Globalization is a complex process that affects various aspects of life. The video you are going to watch explains how it works.

▶ LP 7: The passive

1 Identifying the players in globalization
Describe the aspects of globalization that are presented in the picture below. Based on what you already know about globalization try to say how they are connected.

DVD

▶ SF 15: Marking up a text / Making and taking notes

— COMPREHENSION ◀

2 Defining globalization
a Watch the video and note down the main topics mentioned in it. Compare notes with a partner.
b Watch the video for a second time and add information on the topics from **a**.
c Compare your notes in a group and add to them if necessary.
d As a group give a short presentation on globalization with each group member contributing 1–2 sentences on each topic.

▶ SF 24: Giving a presentation

— ANALYSIS ◀

▶ SF 23: Analysing a film

3 Examining the video
a Describe the devices that are employed in the video. ▶ LANGUAGE HELP
b Assess their suitability for the purpose and topic of this video.

LANGUAGE HELP
- explainer video / instructional video
- hand-crafted drawings showing … / scraps of paper
- put sth. on screen / remove sth.
- use audio effects to …

— BEYOND THE TEXT ◀

4 YOU CHOOSE Illustrating globalization

a Comment on the quotation below and find examples that illustrate it further.

OR

b Find a picture that illustrates your personal view on the impact that globalization has on people. If necessary, collect background information about it. Present your findings in class.

'Globalization isn't something that just happens to economies. It happens to people.'
— Kelsey Timmerman

166 Chapter 8   Beyond the Nation – Europe and a Globalized World

Chances and risks of globalization

B2 The need for a new label Lucy Siegle

- What information do the labels on the right give? What information might be missing?

Imagine a label, one that reads: 'An actual, living, breathing human used their own hands to help make this product.' This is just what the (western) world needs, a label affixed to consumer goods. We need this urgent reminder because in those seconds when we decide to purchase another piece of life's apparatus we are strikingly effect-
5 ive at suppressing any ethical doubt over its provenance.

The first thing we do (with varying levels of awareness) is convince ourselves that – from the hottest bits of sleek hi-tech gadgetry to highly embellished fashion garments – these were made by very clever robot arms that can apply toxic chemicals to a touch screen or expertly sew a sequin or bead. But as today's Observer report on
10 Apple products lays bare, our consumer goods still arrive courtesy of the blood, sweat and tears of many human beings. [...] The habitual use of unpaid, enforced overtime is common across many sectors. In the fashion industry, garment workers are effect- ively set up to fail. When a multinational places an order at the behest of a buyer the workers are set quotas to meet the order. Professor Doug Miller, an expert on the
15 garment supply chain and workers' rights, has identified a discrepancy between the estimated and real time taken for a garment worker to complete an order. So the multinational buyer's calculations are based on standard minute values (SMVs) – virtual minutes based on a factory that operates at near 100% efficiency. However, in countries such as Cambodia (the British high street is heavily reliant on Cambodian
20 production), the efficiency of factories rarely rises above 30%. Garment workers can therefore work flat out without any hope of meeting their targets within their paid working hours. At this point, they are forced to work overtime and sometimes gates may be shut or locked (including the fire escapes). [...] As consumers, we still tend to be most receptive to the voices of brand spokespeople. Time after time, we trust their
25 soothing words: 'We're working on these challenges', 'We've been let down badly by a supplier', 'These are not our values' etc. and placated by their corporate social responsibility reports. Robert Reich warns in his recent book, *Supercapitalism*, corporate social responsibility is 'as meaningful as cotton candy'. But Reich's ultimate position is that we should stop expecting corporations to do the right thing. And I can't
30 see any way of absolving the consumer of responsibility. I used to advocate going through a sort of consumerist catechism before making any consumer purchasing decision. Who made this product? Why did they make it? Why do I need it? I feel as if I urgently need to return to this way of buying. An understanding of the provenance of the product is key.

From: the website of *The Guardian*, 1 May 2011

5 **provenance** place that sth. has come from
7 **sleek** elegant, shiny
 gadgetry collection of modern devices/tools
9 **sequin** small shiny disc sewn onto clothes as decoration
 bead small piece of wood or glass that can be put on a string and worn as jewellery
10 **lay sth. bare** *(fml)* make sth. known that was a secret
 courtesy of sth. as the result of sth.
11 **overtime** time that you spend at your job after the normal work hours
13 **at the behest of sb.** because sb. has ordered it
14 **quota** amount of sth. that sb. needs to achieve
21 **flat out** *(adv)* completely
26 **supplier** Lieferant
 placate sb. make sb. worry less about something
28 **cotton candy** Zuckerwatte
30 **absolve sb.** state formally that sb. is not responsible for sth.
 advocate sth. advise/recom- mend sth.
31 **catechism** set of questions and answers used to instruct people about Christian beliefs

---

◀ COMPREHENSION

1 **Collecting information**
   Collect information from the article about the situation in the garment industry, how we consumers deal with it and what we *should* do. Write down 5–9 keywords for each of these topics, then present your results.

◀ ANALYSIS

2 **Examining the text**
   Describe and analyse the tone of the text.

◀ BEYOND THE TEXT

3 **Promoting transparent labelling**   SUPPORT ▶ p. 214
   a Design a clothing label that helps buyers make responsible choices.
   b Write an article for a magazine in which you promote this new label.

B3 The Dutch footballer from Japan *Elko Born*

- Skim the text. Within 1–2 minutes find out the gist of the text.

Some scholars argue that the process of 'globalization' (broadly defined as the global integration of various aspects of culture) started in the 16th century, when maritime empires such as Portugal and the Dutch Republic started colonizing parts of Asia and the Americas, setting up trade routes and kickstarting modern capitalism along the way.

Others argue that it wasn't Columbus who 'discovered' the Americas, that the ancient Greeks and the Romans used the so-called 'Silk Route' to trade with China, and that the process of 'globalization' started when humans first started interacting with others of their kind.

Nonetheless, it's fair to state that in recent decades, the process of globalization – whenever it may have started – reached a new phase: the phase of automatization and the gradual diminishing of the relevance of national borders. Just think of the Internet, the EU, and of eating Kettle crisps whilst crossing the border between France and Belgium without showing anyone your passport.

An early example of globalization: 13th century merchants on the silk route

The birth of modern football, of course, largely coincided with this new phase in globalization. During the 1960s, when politicians were negotiating the supranational perimeters of the European Union (dubbed by some as the modern day Habsburg Empire), football produced its first superstars.

The fame of footballers like Pelé reached far beyond Brazil, and across the world, people took time off to sit in front of their black and white television sets to watch the South American legend play. Indeed, when Pelé jokingly put himself ahead of Jesus Christ by telling a reporter that 'there are parts of the world where Jesus Christ is not so well known', he wasn't even being absurd.

In modern day football, we see different manifestations of the ongoing process of globalization. National leagues filled with foreign players provide the obvious example: so far in 2013/2014, only 32.26% of minutes in the Premier League – an 'English' league, but followed intensely by people from all over the world – were completed by English players, with a remarkable 8.1% completed by players from France.

Another obvious example of globalization in football is the Champions League: an international competition, deemed as one of the most important and prestigious in the world. And it's not just international competitions that make football fans and stadium-goers travel outside the borders of their countries. To name just one example: this season Championship-side Leicester City was pleasantly surprised by a large contingent of R.S.C. Anderlecht fans showing up at the King Power Stadium to sing songs in praise of their former player Marcin Wasilewski – a Polish player – on multiple occasions. Unconstrained international travel and the internet make it all possible. [...]

▶ SF 14: Reading strategies

2 **maritime** (fml) near the sea
4 **trade routes** routes that people used to follow to buy and sell things
kickstart sth. make a process or project start more quickly
13 **recent** in the near past
decade ['dekeɪd] period of ten years
16 **gradual** step by step, slow
diminish sth. reduce sth.
18 **Kettle crisps** particular kind of crisps
21 **coincide with sth.** happen at the same time as sth.
22 **negotiate sth.** arrange something by formal discussion
supranational referring to more than one nation
23 **perimeter** outside edge of an area of land
dub sth. sth. else call sth. sth. else
25 **Pelé** (born 1940) former Brazilian footballer, often considered the best football player of all time
32 **Premier League** English professional football league
36 **Champions League** annual continental football competition organized by the UEFA, the Union of European Football Associations
37 **deem sth. to be sth. else** consider sth. to be sth. else
prestigious [preˈstɪdʒəs] having a lot of prestige
41 **contingent** [-ˈ- -] group of people who share sth., usually the place they come from

Chances and risks of globalization

Back in the early-modern period, trading diasporas functioned as communities of merchants living in foreign lands. They were semi-permanent residents. Not quite Dutch, English or Portuguese, but not quite native either. Often, these diasporas would be linked: with the mother-country, but with other diasporas as well.

Diasporas, and the people living in them, were 'stateless': they lived in the world's twilight-zone, more or less unconfined by regionalism or primitive nationalism. In many ways, football clubs are today's world's trading diasporas, employing footballers as merchants. They travel around, performing their profession.

But while we might be able to typify some of Vitesse's players as 'merchants', we would do well to rid the term of some of its negative connotations. The Arnhemmers' flirt with globalization has manifested itself in wonderful things as well. Take Mike Havenaar, a 6 foot 4 striker who looks Dutch, sounds Dutch, plays in the Dutch league … but is Japanese.

Mike was born in 1987 in Hiroshima, where his father, the Dutch goalkeeper Dido Havenaar, played for Mazda FC (now called Sanfrecce Hiroshima). Dido had initially planned to only stay in Japan for a short while, but the months became years and the years became a decade, until finally, the family decided to stay forever: 'When I was little, I spoke Dutch with my parents but Japanese with all of my friends. Initially I felt somewhat torn between the two countries but as I got older, my love for the country where I was born grew. When I had to make a decision about my nationality, there was never any doubt', Havenaar told Fifa.com in an interview in 2013.

Havenaar, who conducts his interviews in English rather than Dutch, has a Japanese passport, and as such, he plays for the Japanese national team, making his debut in 2011 and scoring 3 goals in 16 matches.

Besides his name and his appearance, there's little to reveal his Dutch roots. Indeed, when Havenaar first moved to The Netherlands, he felt like a foreigner. 'At first I had trouble acclimatising,' he told Fifa.com, 'but since then the Dutch in me – which I had kind of forgotten – has really come to the fore. Today I feel great, just like at home actually.'

In this regard, the humility he displayed after injuring Stijn Schaars in Vitesse's 6–2 defeat of PSV in December 2013 spoke volumes. Havenaar visibly apologized about ten times, and his whole demeanour contrasted starkly with the reaction of the Dutch on and off the pitch.

Indeed, while merchants travel around and perform their profession, they not only take things, they leave things behind as well. Wonderful things, in the case of Mike Havenaar. The ongoing process of globalization, driving people as well as culture to travel from The Netherlands to Japan and back again, allows for the birth of the hybrid and unique.

Who knows, maybe one day Havenaar will move on to yet another league, and maybe he'll decide to stay there for a long time. Maybe he and his kids will stay there forever.

From: the website of The False Nine, 9 January 2014

Mike Havenaar

45 **trading diaspora** community of merchants who live in foreign countries
46 **semi-permanent** living in the same place for most of the time
resident person living in a certain place
47 **native** (here) born in the country you live in
50 **twilight** time between day and night
unconfined by sth. not held back by sth.
53 **Vitesse** football club based in the Dutch city of Arnhem
71 **acclimatize** (here) start feeling at home
72 **come to the fore** start playing an important role
74 **humility** quality of not thinking that you are superior to others
display sth. show sth.
75 **PSV** (= PSV Eindhoven) football club from Eindhoven in the Netherlands
speak volumes tell a lot about sb./sth.
76 **demeanour** [dɪˈmiːnə] behaviour
stark obvious, easy to see
77 **pitch** football field
81 **hybrid** mix of two or more different things

8 Part B

- LP 5: Infinitive or gerund after certain verbs

- SF 14: Reading strategies

READING · FOCUS ON SKILLS

Using reading strategies (non-fictional texts)

Reading strategies help you to read more effectively. They can help you to find information quickly, to see if a text is relevant for you or to come to an in-depth understanding of the content.

Before actually reading the text **B3***, you were asked to skim it to find out what it's about. Now practise your scanning and close reading techniques.*

1 Scanning
 a Scan the text on p. 168f. to find the answers to the following questions. For each question decide what keyword, name or number you are going to look out for in the text.
   1 What are the characteristics of people living in diasporas?
   2 What has Pelé got to do with a globalized world?
   3 How does Mike Havenaar feel about his nationality?
 b Locate the following ideas in the text and say in which order they appear. What keyword, name or number are you going to look for?
   1 Unconstrained international travel and the internet allow fans to visit football matches outside their country.
   2 Mike Havenaar felt like a foreigner when he first moved to the Netherlands.
   3 Mike Havenaar's father worked as a goalkeeper in Hiroshima.
   4 Globalization has reached the phase of automatization.
   5 In 2013/2014 less than half of the minutes in the Premier League were completed by English players.

A global sport: football

2 Close reading I: content and structure
 a Read the text carefully and make notes on the content of each paragraph.
 b Write a summary of the text.
 c Read the text again and examine its structure. Add the words below to your notes from **a** where they fit. You can also add own categories.
   thesis – example – cause – detail – background information – result – quotation – opposite viewpoint – conclusion – outlook – …

- SF 31: Writing a summary

- SF 16: Identifying text types (non-fiction)

3 Close reading II: identifying the text type
 Explain what type of text this is and analyse its *tone.

170 | Chapter 8 | Beyond the Nation – Europe and a Globalized World

Part C

8

English as a global language

C1 Keeping the accent   *Aoife Mannix*

- What do you expect after reading the title of the poem?

> The barman makes me repeat my order
> three times before he finally understands me.
> Heads turn and stare, I can feel my hands sweat
> and my throat close over the way it did years ago.
> Then he tells me my accent is so cute,   5
> he's going to give me one of the drinks for free.
> And all the people at the bar smile at me.
> And it doesn't make up for the way
> they laughed at me at school,
> repeating how I said the word potato   10
> over and over like a needle in my ear,
> or Alexis Fortgang dropping a worm in my hair
> and telling me to fuck off back to the little hole
> in the ground I crawled out of.
> But still, now that the way I speak is sweet,   15
> I swallow my bitterness
> and try not to think about how opening my mouth
> used to feel like a betrayal.
> The words sounding out of tune,
> a fork dropped on a china plate.   20
> Suddenly it's interesting and cool
> and everyone wants to go there.
> But I still hide behind my pride,
> the way I used to long to talk
> like everybody else.   25

From: Aoife Mannix, *The Elephant in the Corner: New & Selected Poems*, 2005

COMPREHENSION ◄

1 Understanding the situation
Describe the speaker's experience in the bar and the memories it provokes.

LANGUAGE AWARENESS ◄

2 Examining the present participle
  a Identify the present participles in ll. 8–14, then reformulate these lines without using participles.
  b Compare with the original and explain why the participle constructions are especially helpful in the poem.

ANALYSIS ◄

3 Examining the poem
  a Subdivide the poem by introducing *stanzas, which may vary in length. Explain the structure you have chosen. Compare it to the original version.
  b Examine the *stylistic devices used in this poem and their effect. Focus on the choice of words and the *imagery used.

FACT FILE

The term ***third culture kid*** (TCK) is applied to children who spend a considerable time of their childhood or adolescence outside their parents' home country, usually because their parents work abroad. Third culture kids experience the culture they are living in plus the culture from which their parents originated – without really belonging to either of them: they belong to a third culture, which is a mix of the other two cultures. In the era of modern globalization, the number of third culture kids has increased: global job mobility, proximity to neighbouring countries, international school attendance, multi-ethnic homes and worldwide adoption are on the increase and bring with them not only cultural, but also linguistic opportunities and challenges.

Compile possible advantages and challenges of early cross-cultural education.

---

1 **order** *(n)* request for food or drinks in a pub or restaurant
4 **throat** *Kehle*
  close over become very narrow
5 **cute** sweet, nice
8 **make up for sth.** do sth. that corrects a bad situation
19 **out of tune** not be singing/playing the correct notes to sound pleasant
20 **fork** *Gabel*
  china *Porzellan*

► LP 18: Writing about texts

► SF 21: Analysing poetry
► SF 17: Analysing stylistic devices

171

Beyond the Nation – Europe and a Globalized World   Chapter 8

8 Part C

▶ SF 37: Doing a creative writing task

BEYOND THE TEXT ◀

4 **YOU CHOOSE** Creative writing **SUPPORT** p. 214

a Write a *short story based on the poem. **OR** b Write a scene based on the poem.

C2 English as a global language   *David Crystal*

- Try to define the term *global language* and collect reasons why a language might become a global language.

🎧 CD2 14

▶ SF 22: Listening

COMPREHENSION ◀

1 **Understanding the main idea**
Listen to David Crystal and then decide which of these statements fits the text best.
1 English-speaking nations are powerful because they speak the global language English best.
2 Throughout the centuries people have had the power to decide which language is the global language.
3 The global language is the language of the people who have the most power globally.

2 **Connecting language and power**
Listen again and describe the connection between power and language as seen by Crystal.

BEYOND THE TEXT ◀

3 **Thinking about global languages of the future**
Discuss when and how the four types of power mentioned by David Crystal might one day be dominated by other languages. Which languages might they be? Give examples.

C3 Linguistic diplomacy: the Eurovision Song Contest   *R. L. G.*

- Do you prefer listening to songs in English or in your mother tongue? Explain what difference it makes for you.

Last Saturday saw Denmark win the Eurovision Song Contest, the country's third win in the contest's history. A prototypically apple-cheeked blonde took the trophy for her country, but she did so with the rather un-Danish name of Emmelie de Forest and the equally un-Danish title, 'Only Teardrops'.

The contest has always been about more than music. Every year comes a slew of articles about the political nature of the voting. Countries that share ethnic or political friendships routinely give each other high marks: Greece and Cyprus typically give each other the maximum of 12 points while stiffing Turkey with nul points, for example. Estonia and Latvia this year gave Russia 12 points, no doubt because those countries' large Russian populations voted for their neighbour.

Language, of course, plays a role in this as well. 'Ethnicity' in Europe is often linguistic: an ethnic Russian is not apparent on the streets of Riga until he opens his mouth. Linguistic neighbours will tend to be generous to one another. Finland and Estonia are friendly not only because they are nearby but because their Finno-Ugric languages resemble each other, while being utterly unrelated to their neigbours'. 5

10

15

Emmelie de Forest, winner of the 2013 Eurovision Song Contest

2 **apple-cheeked** having cheeks (= *Wangen*) the colour of apples
5 **slew** (*ifml*) large number
8 **stiff sb. with sth.** (*here*) reject / mildly insult sb.
   nul points [nyl pwɛ̃] (*French*) nil (= *no*) points
11 **ethnicity** fact of belonging to a particular race
12 **Riga** capital of Latvia

172   Chapter 8   Beyond the Nation – Europe and a Globalized World

English as a global language

(Hungarian is also Finno-Ugric.) Each country can give 12 points to only one other country, and this year Denmark and Sweden gave their 12's to Norway, Norway its 12 to Sweden, as befits the Scandinavian language continuum.

20 But the Scandinavians share something else besides apple-cheeked blondes and North Germanic languages: their tendency to sing in English. In that, they are like most countries nowadays. But some interesting variation clouds the picture.

The French, of course, overwhelmingly prefer French. (France has, however, sent two entries in Corsican and one, in 2008, mostly in English.) Spain nearly always opts for Spanish, and Italy for Italian. But it isn't true that big countries sing in their
25 own languages while small ones opt for English. Germany has sung just one German title ('Frauen regieren die Welt', or 'Women Run the World') in the past ten years. And a few small countries opted for linguistic pride over Anglophone Euro-cheer this year. Iceland's EyþórIngi offered up a dreary ballad in Icelandic, the perfect accompaniment to an official video in which he glumly fillets a fish in the rain. The highest-rank-
30 ing song not sung in English this year was technically Greece's 'Alcohol is Free', an upbeat ska tune in which the verses were in Greek and only the three-word chorus in English. It came in 6th place. The highest-ranking song entirely devoid of English was Italy's 'L'Essenziale' (7th).

Songs mostly in English have won 24 times, while songs in French have won 14.
35 That leaves just about a third of the contests won in any other language. This is despite two periods (1956–1965 and 1977–1999) in which contest rules required countries to sing in their own languages. [...]

It is clear that pop is just another area in which English is taking over Europe, alongside business and the politics of the European Union. French is holding a solid second
40 place, as it does elsewhere. The rest of Europe's many language communities divide up what remains. Whether you find this linguistic convergence cheerful as an Abba foot-stomper or depressing as an Icelandic fishing trip will say as much about your politics as it will about your views on language.

From: *The Economist*, 20 May 2013

18 **befit sb.** *(fml)* be suitable for sb.
21 **cloud sth.** make sth. unclear
23 **entry** *(here)* song that takes part in a competition
24 **opt for sth.** choose sth.
28 **dreary** sad and boring
accompaniment music that is played to support singing
29 **glum** quiet, sad, unhappy
31 **upbeat** *(ifml)* cheerful / enthusiastic
ska fast and rhythmic music, related to Reggae
chorus part of a song that is sung after each verse
32 **devoid of sth.** without sth.
41 **convergence** process of moving towards each other and meeting at a point
ABBA Swedish pop band that won the ESC in 1973
42 **foot-stomper** lively music that makes you move your feet

---

◀ **COMPREHENSION** ◀

1 Understanding the content
Structure the text, then make notes on the content of each paragraph.

2 Mediation (English ➔ German)
You are watching the song contest together with a friend who claims that language does not play any role in the ESC today since almost all songs are sung in English. In German, tell him why he is not quite right using information from the text (200 words).

▶ SF 15: Marking up a text / Making and taking notes

▶ SF 41: Mediation of written and oral texts

◀ **ANALYSIS** ◀

3 Examining the tone
a Analyse the *tone of the text and illustrate how neutral it is. Give examples.
b Identify the text type.

▶ SF 18: Analysing non-fiction
▶ SF 16: Identifying text types

◀ **BEYOND THE TEXT** ◀

4 Reacting to a statement
Explain the last sentence and comment on it.

5 Discussion SUPPORT ▶ p. 215
In groups of five prepare and hold a panel discussion in which you discuss the question of whether each country should be obliged to enter songs in their national language only. One student is the moderator, the others argue either for or against the topic.

▶ SF 27: Having a discussion

Find a recording tool here:
 Webcode context-00

8 Part C

CULTURE SPOT

Keeping our language clean?

🎧 CD2 15   1 You're skyping with an Irish friend of yours and talking about music. She has just come across a song by the Wise Guys that she doesn't understand. Listen to the song, then tell her what it's about and what message you think it conveys.

2 Collect other examples of English (or pseudo-English) words often used in German. State for each example whether you accept it and use it or whether you avoid using it.

3 What does this use of English tell you about the role of English in German culture?

4 Radio stations, e.g. in France and Italy, are obliged to play a considerable number of songs in French or Italian respectively. What do you think of this attempt to promote the native language?

Chapter Task

'Slavery? Not today, not in Germany!' Preparing an exhibition

For the project week at your school, you are preparing an exhibition on the topic 'Slavery? Not today, not in Germany!' As a lot of visitors from your foreign partner schools will be attending, posters and presentations will be in English.

Work in groups of five.

1 Planning your work
   a Do some research to get a general idea of the topic and to identify suitable subtopics. SUPPORT ▶ p. 215
   b Divide the work up among yourselves.

2 Preparing your poster
   a Research your part. Make sure to use German publications, too. Notes, articles, books or worksheets you read at school, also in other subjects (e.g. History or Latin) may also be helpful. Make notes.
   b Organize your findings and prepare your poster. SUPPORT ▶ p. 215
   c In your group, swap posters and check each other's.

3 Preparing and giving your presentation
   a In your group, organize and practise your presentation.
   b Give your presentation in class.

4 Assessing presentations
   Using the assessment sheet your teacher will give you, assess the other groups' presentations. In class, discuss how they might be improved.

Find some helpful links here:
Webcode context-00

▶ SF 6: Doing project work

▶ SF 5: Doing research

▶ SF 7: Making visual aids
▶ SF 40: Proofreading

▶ SF 24: Giving a presentation

Find a webtool to help you create your poster here:
Webcode context-00

Beyond the Nation – Europe and a Globalized World   Chapter 8

9 Work and Business – Careers and Perspectives

A

B

Download a chronological word list here:
 Webcode context-00

▶ SF 11: Analysing pictures
▶ SF 13: Analysing cartoons

1 Talking about pictures

a Choose one of the pictures A–E. Think about the situation it shows and prepare to talk about your response to it. Find other students who have picked the same picture and exchange your thoughts. Select one spokesperson for your group to report back to your class.

b Work with a partner and choose another picture. Think of a question raised by this picture and write it on the board or on a strip of paper that you attach to the board. Take a class vote about the two most interesting questions and start discussing them.

176 Chapter 9 Work and Business – Careers and Perspectives

Lead-in

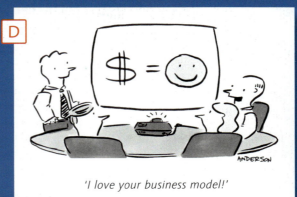

'I love your business model!'

'I really enjoyed my job. Management found out about it and fired me.'

Career decisions: priorities and consequences

- You enjoy doing it.
- Poor but happy
- Just a dream
- The perfect job
- You're good at it.
- Rich but unfulfilled
- It's well-paid.

FACT FILE

Venn diagrams – named after John Venn (1834–1923), a British logician, philosopher and mathematician – use over-lapping circles to illustrate all possible logical relations between a number of sets.

2 Talking about charts and diagrams

With a partner, explain the Venn diagram above with regard to business and entrepreneurs. Try and find an example of a person and a business idea that fits the field in the centre.

▶ SF 7: Making visual aids
▶ SF 12: Analysing charts and graphs

PREVIEW

In this chapter you will learn about today's challenges and prospects of entering the world of work and business.

Main topics
- Work and business then and now .... p. 180
- Job aspirations and job satisfaction .... p. 185
- Applying for your first job .... p. 192
- Job interviews by telephone or face-to-face .... p. 196

Focus on Skills: SPEAKING and WRITING
- From informal to formal dialogues .... p. 186
- Writing a letter of motivation .... p. 195

Chapter Task:
Writing an application letter (a 'personal statement') to a university .... p. 197

Work and Business – Careers and Perspectives   Chapter 9

177

9 Words in Context

CD3 02
Listen to an audio version of the text on the CD or download it here:
Webcode context-00

The world of work and business

The right to a job – the right job
World economy has two faces. Many countries are recovering from a difficult period of recession. In many countries, average wages have risen so that many people have been lifted out of poverty. Despite minimum wage and unconditional basic income being under discussion, there is a global rise in income inequality – the rich are getting richer, and the poor are getting poorer. The fact that budget cuts have claimed many jobs makes the situation even more tense: people collecting unemployment benefits often have to face tough odds.

Stepping into the world of work
Building a career is not always easy nowadays. In some university courses competition among students is unusually high – for some the job hunt is already on. And once people get into their dream job, more often than not they are expected to move around the world and to adapt to new situations quickly. Furthermore, it is not unusual to change jobs often.

To get your career on track, it is therefore essential to access career advice and gain work experience. Career advisers can do you a huge service, e.g. by telling you which applicants are really needed out there because they are in short supply. Too often there is a massive mismatch between young people's career expectations and the realities of the market.

In a paid or unpaid internship you can catch up on missing experience: schools do not, for example, tell you how to deal with difficult customers – this is what you learn best in an internship. Once you know that you have a head for, say, numbers, or that you have a passion for languages, you can narrow down your job sector or employment area.

Applying for a job
Research the companies that have caught your interest and start your application. For example, report on your ability to solve problems and showcase your skills in a professional letter of motivation.

Job interviews
Even though face-to-face interviews are still most popular, you might also be invited for a telephone interview or an assessment centre. As applicants come from a wide range of backgrounds, it is important that you leave a positive impression on the interviewer. Successful candidates convince employers not only with their interview responses but with professional body language and demeanour too. Don't spoil your chances by right away asking about the salary package!

178 Chapter 9 Work and Business – Careers and Perspectives

The world of work and business

1 Words and phrases
Complete these phrases (1–6) with the help of the highlighted words from the text and match them with the correct German equivalent (a–f).

1 income …   a Durchschnittsgehalt
2 … package   b Etatkürzungen
3 job…   c Berufsberatung
4 … advice   d Arbeitserfahrung
5 … cuts   e Gesamtgehalt
6 average …   f Einkommensgefälle

2 Prepositions
Test yourself: do you know the right prepositions?
- recover … recession
- be lifted … poverty
- a rise … inequality
- be … short supply
- deal … customers
- report … your skills
- a mismatch … expectations and reality

▶ LP 25: Using collocations: prepositions

3 Opposites
Find the opposites of these words and expressions:
- have no particular talent for sth.
- employee
- do sb. a disservice
- hide sb./sth.

4 Collocations
Which words usually go together? From the three words offered, choose the correct one.
- make/build/form a career
- gain/make/find work experience
- from a big/great/wide range of backgrounds
- the elected/successful/winning candidate

▶ LP 23: Using collocations: verb + noun

5 The situation in Germany
Using the text as background information, describe the situation for (young) job hunters in Germany. You may draw on the experiences of people you know.

6 Showcase your skills
Think about a talent that you have, or that you have always dreamed of possessing. Talk to your partner about how you can use this talent to start a unique career.

'I see under "special talents" that you always land on your feet. Tell me about that.'

Work and Business – Careers and Perspectives   Chapter 9

9 Part A

The right to a job – the right job

A1 The second Bill of Rights   *Franklin D. Roosevelt*

In his State of the Union address of 11 January, 1944, US President Franklin D. Roosevelt suggested that an 'economic bill of rights' be adopted to complement the political rights guaranteed by the US Constitution and the Bill of Rights of 1791.

We have come to a clear realization of the fact that true individual freedom cannot exist without economic security and independence. 'Necessitous men are not free men.' People who are hungry and out of a job are the stuff of which dictatorships are made.

In our day these economic truths have become accepted as self-evident. We have accepted, so to speak, a second Bill of Rights under which a new basis of security and prosperity can be established for all – regardless of station, race, or creed. Among these are:

- The right to a useful and remunerative job in the industries or shops or farms or mines of the nation;
- The right to earn enough to provide adequate food and clothing and recreation;
- The right of every farmer to raise and sell his products at a return which will give him and his family a decent living;
- The right of every businessman, large and small, to trade in an atmosphere of freedom from unfair competition and domination by monopolies at home or abroad;
- The right of every family to a decent home;
- The right to adequate medical care and the opportunity to achieve and enjoy good health;
- The right to adequate protection from the economic fears of old age, sickness, accident, and unemployment;
- The right to a good education.

All of these rights spell security. And after this war is won we must be prepared to move forward, in the implementation of these rights, to new goals of human happiness and well-being.

America's own rightful place in the world depends in large part upon how fully these and similar rights have been carried into practice for all our citizens.

For unless there is security here at home there cannot be lasting peace in the world.

From: the website of the Franklin D. Roosevelt Presidential Library and Museum

---

FACT FILE

The **State of the Union address** is an annual *speech by the US president delivered to the US Congress in January in which she or he describes the condition of the nation and outlines the administraive policies.

▶ Historical documents:
The Bill of Rights (1791), p. 345

2 **necessitous** (*fml*) [nəˈsesɪtəs] poor, needy
5 **self-evident** obvious, needing no proof or further explanation
7 **prosperity** success, material or financial well-being
  station (*fml*) social position
9 **remunerative** (*fml*) [rɪˈmjuːnərətɪv] well-paid
11 **recreation** *Freizeit, Erholung*
13 **decent** [ˈdiːsnt] of a sufficient standard or quality
26 **implementation** realization of sth. that has been officially decided
28 **rightful** correct, appropriate, legal

FACT FILE

F. D. Roosevelt giving his State of the Union address on 11 January 1944

Franklin D. Roosevelt [ˈrəʊzəvelt] (1882–1945), commonly known by his initials FDR, was the 32nd president of the United States (1933–1945). Not to be confused with Theodore Roosevelt (1858–1919), US president of the United States 1901–1908, FDR lead the US during times of worldwide economic depression and during World War II. He was a strong supporter of social welfare programs and work projects, by which the US government created many jobs.

 COMPREHENSION ◀

1 Looking at the text
  a In your own words, give a brief description of each of the eight rights that Roosevelt wants guaranteed.
  b Explain what Roosevelt means by 'People who are hungry and out of a job are the stuff of which dictatorships are made' (ll. 3–4).

Chapter 9   Work and Business – Careers and Perspectives

The right to a job – the right job

LANGUAGE AWARENESS

2 Finding the 'right' constructions

a Collect all the expressions from the text which contain the word 'right' followed by a preposition. Write them down in a table like this:

the right of … to + *verb*	the right to + *noun (phrase)*
the right of every farmer to raise …	the right to a useful and remunerative job …

b Find a simple rule explaining how you can use the prepositions *of* and *to* in connection with the noun *right*.

▶ SF 4: Using a grammar book
▶ LP 25: Using collocations: prepositions

ANALYSIS

3 Examining the text

a Show how Roosevelt attempts to convince his audience in this excerpt. Take the language and the line of argument into account.
b Explain why the realisation of the rights listed is essential for Roosevelt.

▶ SF 17: Analysing stylistic devices
▶ SF 25: Giving a speech

BEYOND THE TEXT

4 Reacting to the text

Choose the three rights which you consider most important and explain your choice to your partner. After listening to your partner's reasons, work together to decide which in your opinion are the three most important rights.

5 YOU CHOOSE **Commenting or giving a speech**

'Necessitous men are not free men.' (ll. 2–3)

a Prepare a three-minute speech on the basis of this quote. **OR** b Write a *comment of 200–300 words.

▶ SF 25: Giving a speech
▶ SF 34: Argumentative writing

A2 Moving on after recession   *Barack Obama*

This is an excerpt from President Barack Obama's State of the Union address, delivered on 28 January, 2014. Obama presents an America that is still struggling but gradually recovering from a difficult period of recession.

Over more than three decades, even before the Great Recession hit, massive shifts in technology and global competition had eliminated a lot of good, middle-class jobs, and weakened the economic foundations that families depend on.

5 Today, after four years of economic growth, corporate profits and stock prices have rarely been higher, and those at the top have never done better. But average wages have barely budged. Inequality has deepened. Upward mobility has stalled. The cold, hard fact is that even in the midst of recovery, too many Americans are working more than ever just to get by – let alone get ahead. And too many still aren't working at all. […]

10 I'm also convinced we can help Americans return to the workforce faster by reforming unemployment insurance so that it's more effective in today's economy. But first, this Congress needs to restore the unemployment insurance you just let expire for 1.6 million people.

Let me tell you why.

15 Misty DeMars is a mother of two young boys. She'd been steadily employed since she was a teenager. She put herself through college. She'd never collected unemployment benefits, but she'd been paying taxes. In May, she and her husband used their

Job seekers wait to attend a job fair.

4 **corporate** [ˈkɔːpərət] of or belonging to a large business company
stock prices *Aktienpreise*
6 **budge** *(v)* move
stall *(v)* stop suddenly

Part A

₁₈ **claim sth.** *(here)* cause the loss of sth.
₂₉ **shake sth. up** change sth., e.g. an organization, to make it more efficient
₃₀ **incentive** *Anreiz*
₃₁ **price sb. out of sth.** prevent sb. from having sth. by making it expensive
₃₂ **cap sth.** *eine Obergrenze für etwas festlegen*
₃₄ **reach out to sb.** show sb. that you are interested in them
₃₅ **corporation** large company or group of companies
₃₈ **Ronald Reagan** *(1911–2004)* US President 1981–1989
₃₉ **Tom Harkin** US Senator (Demokrat, Iowa)
George Miller US Representative (Democrat, California)

Graduation ceremony

life savings to buy their first home. A week later, budget cuts claimed the job she loved. Last month, when their unemployment insurance was cut off, she sat down and wrote me a letter – the kind I get every day. 'We are the face of the unemployment crisis,' she wrote. 'I am not dependent on the government … Our country depends on people like us who build careers, contribute to society … care about our neighbors … I am confident that in time I will find a job … I will pay my taxes, and we will raise our children in their own home in the community we love. Please give us this chance.' […]

Of course, it's not enough to train today's workforce. We also have to prepare tomorrow's workforce, by guaranteeing every child access to a world-class education. […] We're working to redesign high schools and partner them with colleges and employers that offer the real-world education and hands-on training that can lead directly to a job and career. We're shaking up our system of higher education to give parents more information, and colleges more incentives to offer better value, so that no middle-class kid is priced out of a college education. We're offering millions the opportunity to cap their monthly student loan payments to ten percent of their income, and I want to work with Congress to see how we can help even more Americans who feel trapped by student loan debt. And I'm reaching out to some of America's leading foundations and corporations on a new initiative to help more young men of color facing tough odds stay on track and reach their full potential. […]

Of course, to reach millions more, Congress needs to get on board. Today, the federal minimum wage is worth about twenty percent less than it was when Ronald Reagan first stood here. Tom Harkin and George Miller have a bill to fix that by lifting the minimum wage to $10.10. This will help families. It will give businesses customers with more money to spend. It does not involve any new bureaucratic program. So join the rest of the country. Say yes. Give America a raise.

From: the website of the White House, 28 January 2014

COMPREHENSION

1 Close reading
Decide whether the following statements about this text are true, false or whether the information is not given. Give line numbers to support your answer and correct the statement where necessary.
1 The elimination of good jobs began with the Great Recession.
2 On average, wages have fallen despite economic growth.
3 If the current system of unemployment insurance is changed, it will speed up many Americans getting back to work.
4 There is not enough training for today's workforce.
5 School buildings will be redesigned.
6 Misty DeMars and her husband had to sell their home.
7 People who are out of work do not have to pay taxes.
8 Since Ronald Reagan's presidency, wages have fallen by 20%.

ANALYSIS

2 Comparing two State of the Union addresses
Make a list of the issues that Obama wants to tackle. Compare it with the problems mentioned by Roosevelt (cf. **A1**). Point out similarities and differences in the promises made by the two presidents.

3 Political *speeches: convincing the audience
Look at Obama's style and language and show how he tries to convince his audience. **SUPPORT** p.216

▸ SF 17: Analysing stylistic devices
▸ SF 25: Giving a speech

182 | Chapter 9 | Work and Business – Careers and Perspectives

9 The right to a job – the right job

▶ BEYOND THE TEXT ◀

4 Reacting to the text
Imagine Misty DeMars is invited to the local TV station for an interview. Choose a partner. One of you is Misty, the other a reporter.
a Before getting together, work on your own:
   Misty prepares herself for the kind of questions she might be asked.
   The reporter thinks of questions the local audience might be interested in.
b With your partner, decide which questions should be in the interview.
c Together, practice your interview. Prepare to present it in class.

A3 Income inequality and guaranteed income

Felix Oberholzer-Gee

The idea of an unconditional basic income has many supporters in western Europe, but also among Americans. Felix Oberholzer-Gee, professor at Harvard Business School, seeks an explanation for this.

In Western Europe, there is a lively debate about proposals to guarantee every citizen a basic income. The idea, which has a long history dating back to the 1920s (at least), is increasingly popular in policy circles and the broader population. The German and Spanish parliaments explored it. The Swiss will soon vote on an initiative that would
5 guarantee everyone $2,800 each month — no questions asked, irrespective of whether a person works. Early polls indicate that more than 45 percent of Swiss voters will support the initiative.
  The supporters of a guaranteed income are a varied lot. They range from unreconstructed communists to humanists with a strong sense of dignity and the
10 wealthy. One concern that many of them share, however, is the global rise in income inequality. In the past few decades, economic growth lifted hundreds of millions out of poverty. But, at the same time, the distribution of income became increasingly skewed in favor of wealthy individuals.
  The current situation is exceptional from a historical point of view. For example, the
15 top 10 percent of earners in the U.S. captured 35 percent of income through the 1950s and 1960s. Today, this share stands at 50 percent. Rising inequality reflects gains at the top in all sources of income: salaries and business income, as well as capital income and capital gains.
  There are many reasons why income inequality has risen. One is technology, which
20 tends to benefit the well-educated. Machines increasingly take over routine tasks, leaving low-paid service jobs for unskilled workers. As a result, U.S. employment and wages tend to grow at the very bottom and at the very top of the distribution in skills. The middle is hollowed out.
  Import competition from poorer countries is a second reason. Chinese imports, for
25 example, explain about one quarter of the decline in U.S. manufacturing from 1990 to 2007.
  Third, globalization produces so-called superstar effects. In a flat world, top talent is handsomely rewarded for its broad appeal. The Brazilian soccer player Pelé, the best ever, earned $1.1 million in 1960 (adjusted for inflation). The Portuguese forward
30 Cristiano Ronaldo made $17 million this past year. Pelé played for 350,000 television sets in Brazil. At the [2010] World Cup, 700 million people watched Ronaldo, as Eduardo Porter writes in *The Price of Everything*.

From: the website of PBS Newshour, 7 April 2014

Protesting against income inequality

■ FACT FILE

In his bestselling book *The World Is Flat: A Brief History of the Twenty-First Century* (2005), Thomas L. Friedman analyses the globalization of markets and the resulting challenges and opportunities both for societies and for individuals. The term **flat world** has become a widely-used catchphrase.

5 **irrespective of sth.** regardless of sth.
9 **unreconstructed** (adj) (derog) hartnäckig, unverbesserlich
   dignity sense of your own importance
13 **skewed** (adj) not accurate or correct, distorted
23 **hollow sth. out** (fig) diminish sth.
27 **flat world** cf. Fact File above

Work and Business – Careers and Perspectives   Chapter 9   183

9 Part A

▶ SF 15: Marking up a text / Making and taking notes
▶ SF 40: Mediation in written and spoken interaction

◀ COMPREHENSION

1 Looking at the text
  a Outline the concept of an unconditional basic income.
  b Point out references to the following countries in the text: Brazil, China, Germany, Portugal, Spain, Switzerland, the USA.
  c Using keywords, sum up the three reasons given for America's current problem of income inequality.

◀ ANALYSIS

2 Money and motivation
Analyse the *article using the information in the Venn diagram on p. 177 as a backdrop to your analysis.

◀ BEYOND THE TEXT

3 Mediation (English → German)
The topic of income inequality comes up in your Social Studies class. You offer to give a talk in German about the situation in the USA and its causes as presented in this article. Sum it up for a presentation of about three minutes. Make notes and practice the talk.

4 An unconditional basic income for all?
Suppose Germany adopted the concept of an unconditional basic income for all citizens. Think of possible consequences …
  a … for employees.
  b **CHALLENGE** … for self-employed people and businesses.
Write an article for your school magazine.

> ■ **FACT FILE**
>
> The concepts of **minimum wage** and an **unconditional basic income** (UBI) are essentially different from each other. While one stipulates a certain level of pay to all employees, the other guarantees an income to all, whether they are currently holding a job or not, in addition to any other income they might receive. In Switzerland, there have been initiatives for both concepts. In May 2014, a majority of voters rejected the proposal for a minimum wage of 22 Swiss francs per hour.
> Preparations for another, more far-reaching referendum began in September 2013, when activists advocating the introduction of UBI collected around 130,000 signatures from supporters. As this is the first referendum of its kind anywhere in the world, it requires thorough preparation and is not expected to be held before 2019.
>
>
>
> *Basic-income activists dumped eight million Swiss coins – one for each citizen – in front of the parliament building in Bern in the autumn of 2013.*
>
> Make appointments with two students and exchange your views about the idea an unconditional basic income.

184 Chapter 9 Work and Business – Careers and Perspectives

The right to a job – the right job

A4 Teenagers' career aspirations   *Sean Coughlan*

In March 2013, a survey listed young Britons' job ambitions according to popularity. Before you read the summary of findings, look at the table below and do task **1** on page 186. Then read the text and continue with tasks **2–4**.

Most popular jobs	Percentage 15–16	Least popular jobs	Percentage 15–16
Teacher/Lecturer	4.4%	Locksmith	0.2%
Lawyer (barrister/solicitor)	4.2%	Welder[2]	0.2%
Accountant[1]	4.0%	Surveyor[3]	0.2%
Actor/Actress	3.7%	Speech therapist	0.2%
Police	3.6%	Personnel/HR	0.2%
IT consultant	3.4%	Miner	0.1%
Doctor	3.4%	Call centre	0.1%
Sportsman/woman	3.3%	Audiologist	0.1%
Army/Navy/Airforce/Firefighter	3.2%	Factory worker	0.1%
Psychologist	3.1%	Glazier[4]	0.00%

From: Nothing in Common report, Education and Employers Taskforce, UK Commission for Employment and Skills, B-Live

> **TROUBLE SPOT**
> *Schauspieler* = **actor**; *Schauspielerin* = **actor** (also: **actress**)
> *Gastgeber* = **host**; *Gastgeberin* = **host** (also: **hostess**)
> *Kellner/in* = **waiter, waitress, server**
> *Flugbegleiter/in* = **flight attendant** (not: ~~stewardess~~)
> *Polizist/in* = **police officer**
> *Schriftsteller/in, Autor/in* = ***author**
> *Dichter/in* = ***poet**

There is a 'massive mismatch' between young people's career expectations and the reality of the jobs available, a major survey of teenagers suggests. [...]
    The study, based on a survey of 11,000 13- to 16-year-olds, is an attempt to map the job ambitions of teenagers against the employment market up to 2020. It shows teen-
5 agers have a weak grasp of the availability of jobs – and that large numbers will be aiming for jobs that are in short supply.
    For instance, there are 10 times as many people aiming for jobs in the culture, media and sports sector than there are jobs likely to be available. And even though almost a quarter of jobs are in the distribution, hotels and restaurant category, only
10 about one in 40 youngsters are considering careers in these industries. Fewer than one in 30 young people are considering jobs in banking and finance, even though one in five jobs are expected to be in this sector.
    This 'misalignment' could mean long-term problems for young people, the report says, because they are making decisions about qualifications and subjects with little
15 awareness of the jobs market ahead of them. And the report warns it can be difficult in later years to catch up with missing qualifications. This lack of informed choices fuels the problem of employers struggling to find suitably skilled staff, even though there are high levels of youth unemployment.
    The report also looks at the perceptions of young people about types of employ-
20 ment. Among the 10 least preferred occupations are jobs such as surveyor and speech therapist, even though they are likely to earn above-average pay. The two least preferred jobs, as identified by teenagers, are factory work and glaziers. The most preferred employment areas, from the perspective of teenagers, include teaching, the law, the police, psychology and sport. These might be influenced either by role models
25 such as teachers at school – or else by media images. But the report says it suggests the narrowness of young people's view of the types of work available – and the failure of employers to present a broader picture of opportunities. [...]

[1] **accountant** sb. who keeps or checks financial accounts
[2] **welder** *Schweißer/in*
[3] **surveyor** *Landvermesser/in*
[4] **glazier** ['gleɪzɪə] sb. who fits glass into the frames of windows, etc.
[5] **grasp of sth.** understanding of sth.
[6] **in short supply** not available in great numbers, scarce
[13] **misalignment** state of not being in the correct position to sth. else
[17] **fuel sth.** increase sth.
[19] **perception** belief or opinion

Work and Business – Careers and Perspectives   Chapter 9   185

9 Part A

Education and Employers Taskforce director Nick Chambers said: 'As a country we are doing our young people a huge disservice if we don't give them enough information to allow them to make proper informed decisions about their futures.' This charity has campaigned to improve the quality of careers education, highlighting the link between social mobility and access to career advice and work experience.

From: the website of the BBC, 19 March 2013

▟ **LANGUAGE HELP**
If you don't know the English term for a certain job or profession, describe in your words what duties and responsibilities this job involves in order to arrive at a more general job description for the class survey. You can also check in a dictionary.

1 Popular and unpopular job aspirations
  a The table on p. 185 shows the ten most popular as well as the ten least popular jobs according to a UK survey among young Britons aged 15–16. Do you find anything surprising? Talk to your partner. ▶ LANGUAGE HELP
  b Carry out a class survey: What kind of job(s) do you want to do later? Make a list, ranking jobs according to popularity. Then compare the results with the UK survey, pointing out similarities and differences.

 COMPREHENSION ◀

2 The central message
  a Spot these percentages in the text and explain what they stand for:
   ca. 2.5%   less than 3.3%   20%   nearly 25%
  b List the consequences of the 'massive mismatch' (l. 1) as mentioned in the text and explain who is most affected by it.
  c Sum up the main message of the text in one sentence.

ANALYSIS ◀

▶ SF 15: Marking up a text / Making and taking notes

3 Examining and reflecting
Find reasons why the jobs at the top of the list are so popular and why the ones further down are unpopular among teenagers. Work on your own and make notes, then compare with your partner.

BEYOND THE TEXT ◀

▶ SF 34: Argumentative writing

4 Writing
Should you pursue the career of your choice or should you consider only those careers where job demand is fairly certain?
Write an argumentative text in which you consider both sides and state your own view. **SUPPORT** ▶ p. 216

SPEAKING FOCUS ON SKILLS
From informal to formal dialogues

In any form of successful conversation, you should stick to the topic and contribute to a pleasant atmosphere. Moreover, you should adapt your style, vocabulary and your reactions to the situation in general and to the other person's social and professional standing. Sometimes you can be informal and sometimes you have to be more formal, depending on the situation.

▶ CC 5: Making small-talk

1 An informal conversation
  a Imagine you meet somebody your age at a party. You talk to each other about your career aspirations and your dreams about the future.
  Before you start, scan **A4** (cf. pp. 185–186) again for phrases and words you might need for this conversation. Then talk to a partner for at least three minutes.

186 | Chapter 9 | Work and Business – Careers and Perspectives

The right to a job – the right job

b You probably talked to your partner in a rather colloquial way.
THINK Assess your conversation and make notes on the following aspects:
- style of language
- phrases that you used repeatedly
- sentence structures
- the way you adapted to the given situation
- problems, mistakes, breaks

PAIR Exchange your findings with your partner and add to your notes and your list of phrases.
SHARE Share your most interesting findings with your class. Explain how you could have improved your conversation.

2 A formal conversation

a Imagine you have to have a similar conversation in a more formal context and with somebody older than you and in a different position, e.g. a guidance counsellor at school, an advisor at university or a board member of an organization that awards scholarships, internships or something else you are very interested in. What would you have to change in this form of discourse? Make notes.

b Match the following sentences and phrases with the stages of a formal conversation in the box below. Pick out the ones you consider too blunt or even impolite to be used in such a conversation.

Bye. – It's very convenient for me to meet you here. – I absolutely hate that kind of job. – I actually think I am quite good at working in a team as … – Oh, really, you studied at ABC University! I have heard a lot about it. – I don't think I'm qualified for such a career. – Excuse me for taking up some of your time, but … – Hi, my name is Tom. – It was very nice talking to you. Thank you for devoting some of your time to me. – I actually always wanted to talk to you in person. – I don't care for other people's experience. – You can't be serious! – It was a pleasure meeting you. Thank you very much for your advice. – Would you mind me asking you a few questions?

> - Introducing yourself
> - Getting into the conversation
> - Showing interest in the other person
> - Talking about your qualities, likes and dreams
> - Expressing dislikes and rejections politely
> - Saying thank you and goodbye

▶ CC 1: Cultural awareness
▶ CC 2: Polite behaviour
▶ CC 3: The language of politeness
▶ CC 5: Making small-talk
▶ LP 12: Using the right register

In groups of 3–4, collect more ideas and phrases and add them to your list.

3 Role play

Talk to a partner about your plans and career aspirations as described in task **2** for at least five minutes.
Partner A: You are a student. You have plans and career aspirations, but you are not sure how to go about them.
Partner B: You are an influential older person and you are willing to give Partner A some help or advice.
After five minutes swap partners and take over the other role.

Part A

Satisfaction at work – what does it take?

A5 Do you love your job? *Uwe Jean Heuser*

In a job interview you may be asked about your ideas of your future workplace and how you can achieve satisfaction at work. The following excerpt from an *article in the German weekly DIE ZEIT *gives an insight into job satisfaction and its implications.*

Lange gingen Ökonomen davon aus, dass Arbeit reine Last sei: Statt ihre Freizeit zu genießen, litten die Menschen acht oder zehn Stunden am Tag – und für dieses Übel würden sie bezahlt. Eine traurige Theorie war das und gottlob eine falsche. Heute erforschen Wirtschaftswissenschaftler, in welchem Maße der Beruf ihr Lebensglück beeinflusst und wie zufrieden Menschen sind. Und siehe da: Menschen, die sich als hochzufrieden bezeichnen, werden von anderen auch so wahrgenommen. Sie sind offener für positive Einflüsse, nehmen leichter Kontakt auf und blicken optimistischer in die Zukunft. Sogar ihre Immunabwehr ist besser, sie sind selten krank. [...]

Nach einer Umfrage der Beratungsfirma Gallup sind mehr als 90 Prozent der Arbeitnehmer mit ihrem Job zufrieden, aber fast 25 Prozent spüren keine innere Bindung an ihr Unternehmen. Manchmal liegt das an ihnen, oft aber an Firmenkultur und Chefs. Wo Kollegen kooperationswillig sind, wo Führungskräfte schwelende Konflikte rasch lösen und die Mitarbeiter beruflich unterstützen, entsteht Zufriedenheit. Umgekehrt geht es den meisten auf die Nerven, wenn Streitigkeiten ungelöst bleiben, niemand Apathie oder Mobbing entgegentritt. Noch schlimmer ist es nur, wenn Angestellte – zu Recht oder Unrecht – ihren Job permanent für gefährdet halten und keine Möglichkeit für einen Wechsel sehen.

Produktiv ist dieses Gefühl des Ausgeliefertseins nicht, auch wenn umgekehrt ein Wohlgefühl bei den Angestellten noch keine gute Leistung garantiert. Die Wirtschaft braucht eine Atmosphäre, in der sich zufriedene Mitarbeiter über den Dienst nach Vorschrift hinaus engagieren. Und sie schafft umso mehr Wohlstand, je treffsicherer sich die Menschen erst ihren Beruf und später ihre Jobs aussuchen.

Die Bedingungen in der Wirtschaft ändern sich heute rasant, also müssen sich Erwerbstätige öfter fragen, ob die Arbeit ihre Erwartungen erfüllt. Gerade diejenigen, die sich im Job aufzehren, stellen sonst irgendwann fest, dass das übrige Leben leidet. [...] Kein Wunder, dass auch flexible Tätigkeiten und Phasen von Teilzeit das Glück des Einzelnen beflügeln. Und sei es nur, weil er merkt: Ich habe mein Leben selbst in der Hand.

From: *DIE ZEIT*, 23 Oktober 2013

1 Translating or paraphrasing?
Not every word or phrase can be directly translated; sometimes you have to find a paraphrase.
a Find out whether *luck* or *happiness* are both good translations for *Glück* in the context of this article (cf. l. 26). Likewise, check whether *binding* for *Bindung* (l. 11), and *wellness* for *Wohlgefühl* (l. 19) are suitable translations.
b Describe in German what is meant by the following expressions, then paraphrase them in English: 'dieses Gefühl des Ausgeliefertseins' (l. 18), 'Dienst nach Vorschrift' (ll. 20–21), 'sich im Job aufzehren' (l. 25).

2 Mediation (German → English)
An English friend of yours thinks that the importance of job satisfaction is overrated. Sum up the main ideas of the article for her in English (ca. 150 words).

▶ SF 3: Using a dictionary
▶ LP 18: Avoiding Germanisms
▶ LP 21: Choosing the right translation

▶ SF 41: Mediation in written and oral texts

The right to a job – the right job

3 A tricky question in your job interview

a Some of the aspects of job satisfaction mentioned by Heuser should not be brought up in a job interview. List them, then compare with your partner.
SUPPORT ▶ p. 216

b Work with your partner again. One of you acts as the interviewer and asks 'How can you contribute to a healthy working atmosphere?', the other tries to answer this question. Then swap roles and ask or answer the question again.

⚲ CULTURE SPOT

Corporate Head (1991)

The joint work of Terry Allen (sculpture) and Philip Levine (*poem on the plaque next to the sculpture), 'Corporate Head' is located outside the Los Angeles offices of the professional services firm EY (previously Ernst & Young).

> They said
> I had a head
> for business.
> They said
> to get ahead
> I had to lose
> my head.
> They said
> be concrete
> & I became
> concrete.
> They said,
> go, my son,
> multiply,
> divide, conquer.
> I did my best.

1 Describe 'Corporate Head'.

2 How do the sculpture and the poem relate to the topic of this chapter?

3 Discuss why the company EY may have commissioned 'Corporate Head'.

Stepping into the world of work

B1 Mitch's first glimpses of the world of work
Carl Deuker

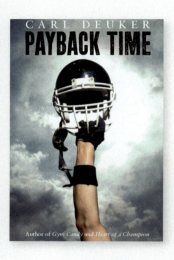

In the *novel Payback Time (2010), Mitch True, a not-too-popular high-school student, is a reporter for the school magazine. He has reluctantly accepted the responsibility for the sports section. In the following excerpt, Mitch is on his way to his first interview with the coach of the Lincoln Mustangs – his former PE-teacher McNulty.

I parked my mom's Ford Focus by the gym, eased out of the front seat, and looked around. When I spotted McNulty loading tackling sleds into a school van, I tensed. To him, I'd always be a fat loser and nothing more. But a reporter has to have the courage to approach people, ask them questions, and get them to talk. 'I'm Mitch True,' I said as I neared him. 'I'm the school sports reporter. I'd like to ask you some questions.'

'I was hoping you'd come around,' he said. 'Step into my office.'

I gaped, dumbfounded. He was hoping I'd come around? When I recovered, I nearly had to run to catch up as he strode across the field and into the coaches' office in the gym. He took a seat behind a neatly organized desk while I squeezed into a wobbly blue plastic chair across from him.

'What's your name again?'

I told him again.

'You were in my gym class last year, right?'

'Two years ago.'

'Well, Mr. True, you are now an important member of the Lincoln Mustang football family.'

I smiled.

'What's funny?' McNulty said, his blue-gray eyes glittering like shiny stones.

Like an idiot, I patted my jiggly belly. 'Me? An important member of the football family. How?'

He leaned forward, pointing his pencil at me. 'You are the person who sends in a game recap to the Seattle Times. You write exciting articles, and the Times will push them to the top of the high school page. That happens, and other newspaper will pick them up, which translates into publicity for the players and for me. It also means a byline for you, some cash, and a summer internship to boot. You remember last year's sports writer, Boyd Harte. He interned at the Bellevue Journal.'

I hadn't thought about the connections I'd be making, but as a sports stringer, I'd be dealing with editors of real newspapers, something that would not have happened if I'd remained the news reporter for the Lincoln Light – unless the big dailies suddenly become interested in the accomplishments of Lincoln High's chess club. 'Sounds great,' I said. 'In fact, it sounds fantastic.'

McNulty leaned back. 'See. We're all part of one big family.'

I cleared my throat. 'How about we get started? I've got some question. First –'

'No, no, no,' McNulty said, pointing the pencil at me again. 'No questions – not today, not ever. This job takes forever and pays peanuts. Here's how it works. You write down or tape what I tell you. When I'm done, jazz it up whatever you want, but never make me, my coaches, or my players look bad. Understand?'

---

2 **tackling sled** „Angriffsschlitten" (schweres Trainingsgerät im American Football)
7 **gape** (v) stare with your mouth open
dumbfounded [dʌmˈfaʊndɪd] (adj) very surprised and unable to speak
19 **pat sth.** touch sth. gently
22 **game recap** summary of a game
24 **translate into sth.** change into sth.
25 **byline** line at the beginning or end of a newspaper article that gives the writer's name
to boot (adv) (old-fashioned/ humorous) obendrein
26 **intern** [ˈ- -] (v) be on an internship (Praktikum)
27 **stringer** [ˈstrɪŋə] freelance journalist
36 **jazz sth. up** (infml) make sth. more interesting or attractive

Stepping into the world of work

Mr. Dewey had warned us about people like McNulty, but this was my first time dealing with one. 'A reporter who lets himself be pushed around is a traitor to his
40　profession.' That's what Dewey had said.

I could feel myself trying to say: 'Coach, I will ask the questions I want to ask, and I will write what I want to write.'

In the classroom, practicing with bald, bowtied Mr. Dewey, I had spit out similar words like a machine gun spits out bullets. But McNulty's eyes were scary. I squirmed
45　as he stared at me, feeling like a snot-nosed preschooler who'd been caught marking a wall with crayons. 'Understood?' he said again, a threat in his voice, as though he might force me to do cartwheels in front of the football team if I argued.

'Yes, sir!'

From a drawer he took three sheets of paper covered with black type and showed
50　them at me. 'Here's the information for the football preview. Horst Diamond will be the focus, and you'll be leading every game story with his name, too. He's a lock for a D-I scholarship. UW is drooling over him, but he's got a shot at a bigger school – Notre Dame, or even USC. Your job is to get him publicity.'

I scanned the three sheets. 'But what if somebody else has a better game?'

55　'Nobody's going to have a better game. Run or pass – everything we do goes through Horst. I want a swarm of college coaches around here. They'll see him, and they'll see me and the program I run. I do not intend to spend my life coaching high school.

McNulty stood. 'Read those pages, prepare a few questions, and before practice tomorrow you can interview Horst. He'll be at the field fifteen minutes early. Have
60　your photographer come along for that.' He paused. 'You've got a photographer, right?'

'A photographer?'

'Every sports story needs pictures. Either you've got to take them yourself, or you've got to get a photographer. Didn't you know that?

From: Carl Deuker, *Payback Time*, 2010

> **TROUBLE SPOT**
>
> **intern** ['--] *(n)* = Praktikant/in
> **intern** ['--] *(v) (l. 26)* = ein Praktikum machen
> **internship** ['---] *(l. 25)* = Praktikum
> **apprentice** = Auszubildende/r, Lehrling
> **apprenticeship** = Ausbildung, Lehre
> **trainee** [-'-] = Auszubildende/r, Trainee
> **hand** = Helfer/in (z.B. in einer Fabrik)
> **employee** [--'-] = Mitarbeiter/in, Angestellte/r
> **employer** = Arbeitgeber/in
> **superior** = Vorgesetzte/r
> **boss** = Chef/in, Vorgesetze/r
> **chief** = Leiter/in, Chef/in

43　**bowtied** *(adj)* wearing a bow tie (Fliege)
44　**squirm** *sich winden*
46　**crayon** ['--] *Buntstift*
51　**lock** *(n) (infml)* sure thing, certainty
52　**D-I = Division I** in the USA, highest level of college and university athletics
UW = University of Washington
drool over sb./sth *für jdn./ etwas schwärmen*
53　**USC** = University of Southern California

COMPREHENSION ◀

1 Who said it?

Using the text, point out who says the following and what is being talked about or what is happening at that particular moment: 'I'd like to ask you some questions.' / 'What's funny?' / 'Sounds great.' / 'How about we get started?' / 'Understood?' / 'Nobody's going to have a better game.'

ANALYSIS ◀

2 Power relations

Work on your own first, then tell each other about your findings.

Partner A: Analyse the meeting between Mitch and McNulty and explain how one of them shows his power and superiority through non-linguistic means (e.g. facial expressions). **SUPPORT** ▶ p. 217

Partner B: Analyse the meeting between Mitch and McNulty and explain how one of them uses language to demonstrate his power and superiority. **SUPPORT** ▶ p. 217

BEYOND THE TEXT ◀

3 Writing about Mitch's experiences

a　Outline what Mitch has learned about the world of work. Make notes.

b　In an email to a friend Mitch writes about the experience he has gained. Write his email using your notes from **a**.

▶ SF 15: Marking up a text / Making and taking notes

Work and Business – Careers and Perspectives　　Chapter 9

9 Part B

B2 Ten things not to say in a job interview *Mark King*

Getting invited to an interview is a big step on the way to getting a job. Now it's important not to spoil one's chances by saying something stupid. The Guardian's Mark King has some useful advice.

With the jobs market more competitive than ever it can be hard work just to get an interview, so once you're actually in front of potential employers you don't want to ruin your prospects with an ill-chosen comment.

Sadly, some job hunters still do speak before they think. Corinne Mills, managing director of Personal Career Management, says she can recall many instances of interviewees saying the wrong thing. 'I remember when one man was asked why he wanted the job, he replied, "Because my mum thought it was a good idea",' she says.

She adds that some job hunters have also been known to say they've applied for a job 'because it will pay the rent while I look for a job I really want to do', and a common response to a question about what candidates like to do in their spare time is 'go to the pub'.

Richard Nott, website director at CWJobs.co.uk, says candidates should avoid discussing religion and politics. 'Employers like people who can talk passionately about their own interests as it helps them to get to know you as a person. But we would always advise against sharing your views on these two topics without knowing if the interviewer shares that point of view.'

We asked Nott, Mills and Nik Pratap of Hays Senior Finance for their list of the top things to avoid saying at a job interview:

1. 'Sorry I'm late.' It goes without saying that punctuality is key. Your interviewer doesn't want you to arrive for work 20 minutes late every morning.
2. 'What's your annual leave and sickness policy?' It doesn't look good if, before you've even been hired, you're planning your absence from the company.
3. 'I'll just take this call.' Mills says a large number of candidates think it is OK to take telephone calls, texts etc during an interview. It isn't.
4. When asked, 'Where do you see yourself in five years?' never say, 'Doing your job.' As much as this might be a genuine answer, Nott says candidates should 'try to build a response around the experience they would like to have gained and the level of responsibility they'd like to have, rather than threatening the interviewer's job.'
5. 'My previous employer sucked.' No matter how mind-numbingly boring those roles might have been, 'speaking badly of a previous employer is not only unprofessional, but also reflects on your character,' Pratap says. Your new employer will contact your former employer for references following an interview, so it's never wise to burn your bridges.
6. 'You make widgets? I thought you made cricket bats.' Failing to research your prospective employer fully is a big faux pas. 'Saying you've looked at their website is only marginally better – employers expect far more research,' Mills explains.
7. 'Bloody hell.' Never swear in your interview. It can happen, especially if your interviewer is themselves prolific with the profanities, but don't let them set the standard of the interview and remain professional at all times.
8. 'I was very good at sorting out PEBs by using ARCs.' Don't fall into the industry jargon of your previous employer or assume the interviewer knows anything about your experience, Pratap advises. Instead, speak clearly about your skills and experience to avoid any confusion or misunderstanding.

TROUBLE SPOT

apply to sb. for sth. *(l. 18)* = sich bei jdm. um/für etwas bewerben
applicant ['---] = Bewerber/in
applicable [-'---] = anwendbar
application = Anwendung

---

21 **leave** *(n)* time away from work, holiday
30 **suck** *(v) (sl)* be very bad
mind-numbingly boring very boring
34 **burn one's bridges** *(idiom)* do sth. that makes it impossible to return to the previous situation
35 **widget** simple software application
36 **faux pas** [ˌfəʊ 'pɑː] (French: 'wrong step') embarrassing action or remark
37 **marginally** *(adv)* very slightly
39 **prolific** producing a lot
profanity *(usu. pl)* swear word

Chapter 9 — Work and Business – Careers and Perspectives

Stepping into the world of work

45 9. 'Do I really have to wear that uniform?' Any criticism of staff uniform will go down like a lead balloon. Do you think your interviewer enjoyed wearing that fluorescent green ensemble when they performed your role?
10. When asked, 'What do you expect to enjoy most about this role?' never reply with any of the following: the perks, the pay, lunchtimes, my co-workers or the holidays,
50 Nott says.

From: the website of the *Guardian*, 10 May 2012

47 **ensemble** [ɒnˈsɒmbl] set of clothes that are worn together
49 **perk** *(usu. pl.)* Vergünstigung

COMPREHENSION

1 Understanding the rules
In groups of three or four, discuss which of the mistakes in the list (cf. ll. 19–50) are ones that are easily made and which ones you are sure you would never make.

ANALYSIS

2 The language of the text
a Explain how King tries to amuse the reader. SUPPORT p. 217
b Explain how King makes his advice easy to understand and to remember.

▶ SF 17: Analysing stylistic devices

BEYOND THE TEXT

3 Your five golden rules
King gives tips for people being interviewed – but what about those asking the questions? In a group, think of five golden rules for interviewers.

B3 The best job in the world is back! *Emanuel Wetterqvist*

In order to promote the Great Barrier Reef as an international tourist attraction, Australia launched a competition for 'the best job in the world'. The winner of the contest would live on a Queensland island, explore and enjoy the area and write a blog about it.
In 2013, the second round of 'the best job in the world' was announced.

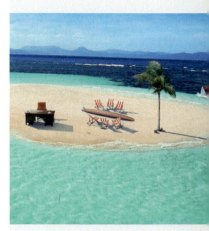

Yes, you read right. As our ex-island caretaker is regretfully handing over the keys to his island hacienda we're looking for someone to take his place.
As our Park Ranger you will be exploring the world's oldest rainforest, watching whales migrate on the Great Barrier Reef, and showcase our five World Heritage areas
5 to the world through blogs and social media.
This is the perfect opportunity for an outdoor lover with a sense of adventure to promote some of the world's most awe-inspiring natural wonders to an international audience. The position is a six-month contract attracting a generous salary package of AUD $100,000 and a free jar of vegemite.

10 **Your responsibilities**
• Patrol the beaches – you have 7,400 kilometres of palm and beach-fringed coastline within your jurisdiction, but you only need to show us your favourites.
• Swim, dive and snorkel the world's biggest aquarium. With 600 islands and 1,500 species of fish to hang out with, we're sure the 30 °C water will keep you
15 occupied.
• Feed the fish, and meet and greet with local wildlife, including kangaroos, crocodiles and the short-tempered cassowary.
• Get up close and personal with hatching turtles and migrating whales and share your experience with the world.
20 • Showcase the best of our 300 national and marine parks and state forests. Like a well-paid Tarzan.

2 **hacienda** [ˌhæsɪˈendə] large farm
4 **showcase sth.** show the best aspects of sth.
7 **awe-inspiring** impressive
8 **attract sth.** *(here)* be worth sth.
9 **vegemite** type of food paste, very popular in Australia
17 **short-tempered** *(adj)* getting angry easily
cassowary Kasuar (Laufvogel)

Work and Business – Careers and Perspectives   Chapter 9   193

9 Part B

TROUBLE SPOT

Conventions for writing currencies (cf. l. 9) vary. Sometimes symbols, sometimes standard abbreviations are used. In English-speaking countries, these are usually placed before, not after, the amount, e.g.
Euros: *€100 / EUR 100 / 100 euros* (~~euro~~)
British pounds: *£200 / GBP 200*
US dollars: *$300 / US$300* (to avoid confusion, e.g. with Canadian dollars) / *USD 300*
Australian dollars: *$400 / A$400 / AUD 400*
Indian rupees: *₹400 / INR 400*

37 **gadget** small and useful device
38 **commence** (v) start
40 **boast sth.** have sth. you can be proud of
array [–'–] large collection of things

▶ SF 16: Identifying text types (non-fiction)

▶ LP 12: Using the right register

- Report on your adventures through photo blogs, social media channels and media interviews.

Who we're looking for – We will consider applicants from a wide range of backgrounds, but believe you should possess these traits: 25
- Excellent oral and written English communication skills
- Be adventurous by nature and willing to try new things
- Have a passion for the outdoors and nature
- Good swimming skills and enthusiasm for snorkelling and/or diving

About the job package – The position of Park Ranger attracts a AUD $100,000 salary 30 package (AUD $50,000 salary and AUD $50,000 to cover living expenses) for the six-month contract.
The successful candidate will live amongst the stars with a range of rent-free accommodation. You might spend one night camping on an island and the next in a bunk on a luxury yacht. 35
You'll receive return airfares from your nearest capital city (in your home country), travel insurance and the cameras and gadgets required to show the world a good time. The six-month contract commences on 1st August 2013.

About your new office – Queensland is regarded as having one of the world's richest natural environments and boasts a rich and diverse array of World Heritage areas 40 including the Great Barrier Reef, Daintree Rainforest and Fraser Island.
The state is home to hundreds of national parks, conservation areas, resource reserves and state forests.

How to apply – The position is open to adventure-hungry outdoor lovers from Australia and overseas. Apply online at http://bestjo.bs/Park_Ranger. 45

From: *Hello Sunshine*, the official travel blog of Queensland, 5 March 2013

COMPREHENSION ◀

1 Making sense of numbers
Pick three numbers from the text and ask your partner explain them. Then swap roles. *Example: '6.' – 'The contract is valid for six months.'*

ANALYSIS ◀

2 *Text type and target group
a Name characteristic aspects of the text type 'job advertisement' and illustrate them with examples from the text. **SUPPORT** ▶ p. 217
b Identify the target group of this text and explain which aspects of the advertisement are likely to appeal to them most.

LANGUAGE AWARENESS ◀

3 Language and target group
Show how the *tone and language of the ad aim at its target group.
Pay special attention to humorous and colloquial elements.

BEYOND THE TEXT ◀

4 What's your opinion?
THINK Is the above text about proper work or a leisure activity? About a real application process or a casting show? Find evidence to support your argument.
PAIR Exchange your ideas and arguments with your partner. Try and agree on a position.
SHARE Tell your class about your view(s).

Chapter 9   Work and Business – Careers and Perspectives

Stepping into the world of work 9

WRITING **FOCUS ON SKILLS**

Writing a letter of motivation

When applying for any type of position – an internship, a place at a university, a job – you are usually expected to write a letter of motivation, in which you explain why you are interested and what recommends you for the position. Such letters, which may also be called personal statements, cover letters, statements of purpose or letters of intent, are mostly formal letters.

*Imagine you want to apply for the 'best job in the world' (cf. **B3**, pp. 193–194).*

▶ SF 29: Writing a formal letter or email
▶ SF 30: Writing an application
▶ LP 12: Using the right register

1 Thinking about your motivation
   a Reread the 'job ad' on pp. 193–194. ▶ LANGUAGE HELP
   b THINK List three reasons that motivate you to apply for this job. If you are not really interested in the job, list the reasons of an invented other person who is.
   c PAIR AND SHARE Work with one or two partners and exchange your ideas from **b**. Add convincing ideas to your list.

2 Presenting your assets
Of course, it is not enough to just write that you have all the requirements as listed in the job ad – you must prove it, either by presenting convincing arguments or by handing in relevant certificates.
   a List arguments and certificates proving that you answer the description given in the section 'Who we are looking for'.
   b Work with a partner you know well. Exchange your lists and give feedback to each other.

3 Writing your first draft
   a Turn your lists from **1** and **2** into a text. Stick to the conventions of formal letters.
   b Add typical application phrases to your text.

4 Typing your final version
   a Reread your first draft after one or two days.
   b Type it up on a computer and use your spellchecker to correct it.

5 The winner's application
Watch the application video of Elisa, the young woman who was eventually chosen for the 'best job in the world'. Discuss similarities and differences in content between her video and your letter of motivation.

LANGUAGE HELP
- I have a strong interest in …
- I was particularly impressed by …
- I understand that this position requires …
- I have demonstrated the desired qualities through …
- I would value the opportunity to gain experience in …
- I am very keen to …
- I see that this position offers … In respect to this, one of my key strengths is the ability to … I recently demonstrated this quality through …
- This experience taught me the importance of …
- I have developed skills in …
- My experience in …
- As you can see from the attached CV …
- In addition, my role as …
- My responsibilities included …

▶ SF 40: Proofreading

 DVD
▶ SF 23: Analysing a film

Work and Business – Careers and Perspectives   Chapter 9

9 Part B

🎧 **CD3** 03

▶ SF 22: Listening

▶ SF 26: Taking part in an interview

📺 **DVD**

▶ SF 11: Analysing pictures

▶ SF 26: Taking part in an interview

B4 Surviving a telephone interview

Telephone interviews have become increasingly popular in the business world. Easy as they might seem, there are practical dos and don'ts applicants should be aware of, as the audio explains.

— COMPREHENSION ◀

1 Expectations
Before listening, arrange the following headings in the order of appearance you expect from the listening text:
Thank your interviewer / Research the company / Practice responses for your phone interview / Keep notes about your work experience / During the phone interview
Then listen to the audio and check whether you were right.

— ANALYSIS ◀

2 After listening
Explain what the following have to do with telephone interviews:
paper, sticky tape, voice recorder, water, letter.

— BEYOND THE TEXT ◀

3 Act out an interview
  a Here are some typical questions asked by interviewers. With a partner, add three more questions:
    What is important to you in a job? How would you describe your present work place? How do you handle stress and pressure? What motivates you? Where do you see yourself in three years' time? In what kind of company do you enjoy working? What does success mean to you?
  b Let your partner interview you.

B5 Look them in the eye – the job interview

Though the most frequent type of interview, a face-to-face meeting between an employer and a job seeker, has its pitfalls. This video gives helpful advice.

— COMPREHENSION ◀

1 First looks are (not) deceiving
Look at the still on the left and talk to your partner about how this person might come across in a job interview.

— ANALYSIS ◀

2 Pieces of advice
Watch the video. With your partner, list and rank the given dos and don'ts of job interviews: Which pieces of advice do you consider most important?
SUPPORT ▶ p. 217

— BEYOND THE TEXT ◀

3 Good body language – and bad
  a Compare Lauren Ferrara's body language to that of the presenter.
  b Take your own pictures in which you show good and bad examples of body language in job interviews and/or the oral exams of the *Abitur*.

Chapter 9 Work and Business – Careers and Perspectives

Chapter Task

Writing your personal statement

'Personal statement' is the term commonly used for a letter of motivation that you send to the university at which you want to study. In this letter you present yourself and explain why the university should offer you a place to study. A standard *text type in the English-speaking world, personal statements are becoming increasingly popular with German universities too. They may also be required when applying for an internship, for volunteer work or for a year abroad.

▶ SF 30: Writing an application

1 Think about yourself
   a Imagine you want to apply to a university for a particular course or subject. Alternatively, think of what kind of internship or volunteer work you are interested in.
   Then study the table below and make notes on the points in the left column ('What?').

▶ SF 15: Marking up a text / Making and taking notes

Your personal statement	
What?	**How?**
• reasons why you are choosing higher education • reasons for your interest in the subject • things you already know about your subject • the subject and its connection to your education, work experience and to your hobbies	• catchy introduction • coherent main part • concise conclusion • max. 600 words • perfect grammar, spelling and punctuation • reader-friendly layout

   b Add some notes as to why you think you should be offered a place. Describe your skills, your knowledge and your experience.
   c Finally, add any other achievements and attributes that you might mention in your personal statement.

3 Ask for feedback
Work with a partner you know well. Let your partner read your notes and ask if there are any aspects of your personality that you forgot to mention. Then swap roles.

4 Get down to work
Now write out your personal statement for a course of your choice. Make use of your partner's advice and of the phrases given on p. 195. Your teacher will give you an assessment sheet.

Work and Business – Careers and Perspectives   Chapter 9

197

Context Task

global warming

qualification

literature

nationalism

communication

knowledge

civil rights

lingua franca

ethnicity

language awareness

skills

future plans

literacy

analysis

power

multiculturalism

happiness

visions

culture

rhetoric

application

stereotypes morals

going abroad

role models

talents

word power

responsibility

disappointments

research

environmental awareness

immigration

intercultural learning

dreams

globalization

leadership

identity

Context Task

This context task gives you the opportunity to consider the topics you have dealt with in class again and to think about their relevance for your future life.

▶ YOU CHOOSE

1 Giving a presentation I
Work on your own or in a group. Choose 3–5 items from the word cloud on the left and prepare a presentation on the topic 'Skills and insights I got from my English course that might be helpful for my future life'. Your presentation should be 5–7 minutes long if you are working on your own or 10–12 if you're in a group. You may want to add examples from your course work to illustrate your statements.

▶ SF 6: Doing project work
▶ SF 24: Giving a presentation

2 Giving a presentation II
Work on your own. Think of 3–5 items that are not in the word cloud and use them as the basis of a presentation as explained in **1**.

▶ SF 24: Giving a presentation

3 Making an advertisement
Work on your own, in pairs or in a group. Make an advertisement for your English class that tells younger students what to expect and/or what to look forward to. Choose a suitable form (e.g. leaflet, poster, electronic presentation, blog …) and present it in class (and, if possible, on the school website).

▶ SF 6: Doing project work
▶ SF 37: Doing a creative writing task

4 Having a debate
Work in a group. Prepare and conduct a debate on the motion 'This house believes that English is the most important subject at school'.

▶ SF 28: Having a debate

5 Writing a quiz
Work in a group.
a Choose five chapter topics or items from the word cloud and write a quiz consisting of three questions/tasks for each topic/item, e.g.
Example *lingua franca*:
1 Name three situations in which English is used as a lingua franca.
2 Why is a lingua franca so important in a country like India?
3 Name two possible disadvantages of using a lingua franca.
b Ask fellow students to do your quiz.

▶ SF 6: Doing project work

Support Pages

Chapter 1 Modern Media – Tools or Tyrants?

A1 Lonely friends   p. 14

4 Poetic devices
Examine the means which the poet uses to draw our attention to the influence of social media on our lives.
Poetic devices are tools used by the poet to emphasize the meaning of a poem.
These questions might help you to do the task:
- What effect does the title have on the reader?
- What is striking about the endings of the lines?
- What means does the poet use to make the content appear more vivid and appealing to the reader?
- How does the poet involve the reader in the poem?
- What is the tone of the poem, and what effect does this tone have on the reader?

A2 Online learning in 2044   p. 17

2 Telling names ('Sprechende Namen')
Refer to the annotations on pp. 16–17 and analyse what the names reveal about the *character and the *setting.

Step 1: Gather and structure the relevant information given in the text, using a grid like this one.

	Public school	OASIS Incipio	OASIS Ludus
Quality of the facilities			
Quality of education			
Wade's attitude and status			

Step 2: Relate your findings to the names and explain their significance in the story.

B1 Should classrooms have video cameras?   p. 23

3 Discussing the pros and cons of surveillance at school
  c Present your concept to the school board (i.e. the class).
   Step 1: Make notes for each of the following steps.
    1 Address the members of the school board.
    2 State your group's attitude towards surveillance at school.
    3 Give reasons for your opinions and provide examples to illustrate your points. Present your concept in a clearly structured way with your most substantial argument at the end.
    4 Briefly sum up your main points.
    5 Invite the school board to ask questions or comment on your concept.
   Step 2: Plan how to present your reasons visually on the board/smartboard.
   Step 3: Use your notes to present your concept.

Support Chapter 1

C1 Big Brother out of this world   p. 27

2 What makes the text engaging for readers?
Analyse the methods the *author uses to make the text engaging for the reader (e.g. heading, *register, *stylistic devices, use of quotes, objective/biased?).

Step 1: Copy the table below. Examine the aspects listed and find more examples from the text to illustrate each aspect. Look at all the examples again and try to identify what the author has done to make the text engaging. Add a few notes in the 'Methods' column.

Aspects you should examine	Example from the text	Methods used by the author
Ways of attracting the reader's attention from the very beginning beginning	• Big Brother out of this world • Not only will they require mental and physical strength, but now, they will also need to have the makings of the next reality-TV star.	…
Style / Use of words	• The ticket is one-way. • 'the world's toughest job interview'	…
Structure	…	• The different stages of the project are described chronologically. • …
Way(s) of presenting the content	• The applicants have now been short-listed to 705 candidates – 418 men and 287 women.	…
Author's attitude towards the topic	…	…

Step 2: Use your points to organize your analysis of the methods used by the author to make the text engaging for readers.

C2 The ultimate reality TV show   p. 28

2 Lally's mode of argumentation
a Explain Lally's line of argumentation to convince the reporter and the audience of his idea.
Answer the following questions:
1 What historical reason does Lally mention to support his view of broadcasting prisoners' executions? What conclusion does he draw from this argument for society?
2 What political reason does he put forward? What would be a positive effect of his idea?
3 What economic reason does he state? Who might profit from the show?
4 What legal and ethical reasons does he present? In what way would the prisoners benefit from the reality TV show?

Now go back to **2b**.

201
Support Pages

Support Chapter 2

Chapter 2   Science – Enhancing Life?

A1 A saviour sibling   p. 34

3 Argumentative structure
1 Structure the text by finding headlines for each paragraph, e.g.

ll. 1–2	Introduction: sibling was saved
ll. 3–6	Medical history of first sibling
ll. 7–12	Problems facing a second sibling
ll. 13–23	Medical treatment

2 Examine the direct quotes: Who is quoted and what do they say? Are the quotes in favour or against the procedure?
3 Examine the indirect quotes: Who is quoted and what do they say? Are the indirect and direct quotes from the same person? If so, decide how the direct quotes relate to the indirect quotes.

A4 At the lab   p. 38

4 Practising speaking
- In order to grab your audience's interest, think of a catchy introduction to your speech, e.g. start with a provocative statement like 'designer babies are the future' or 'a child has to be smart, intelligent, healthy and cute'.
- State your opinion on the topic clearly: In my opinion …, the point is that …, the way I see it …, my point is …, what I'm trying to say is …
- Make sure you have at least three good arguments in favour or against the topic:
  Pro: reduced risk of genetic diseases, better chances to succeed in life, the child can get better genes than his or her parents
  Con: imperfect embryos are killed, no more individuality, only the rich can afford the perfect child, altering a human being is unethical
- Summarize your points at the end of your speech and clearly state your opinion:
  'To sum up …', 'That's why I think …', All things considered …', 'All in all …'

Support Chapter 2

B4 Gene doping   p.43

4 Examining the tone
It may be useful to look at these quotes when deciding on the writer's attitude:

- a battle like no other in sport (l. 1)
- The authorities are so concerned, they have been preparing for it for more than 10 years. (ll. 1–2)
- as anyone who had a vague brush with professional cycling in the 90s knows (l. 14–15)
- the illicit dope of choice for competitors (ll. 17–18)
- the wonder drug (l. 18)
- Could this be an undetectable way of improving oxygen delivery? (ll. 23–24)
- even better for the would-be doper (l. 29)
- So what is the World Anti-Doping Agency (Wada) doing about it? (ll. 30–31)
- it could be lethal (l. 33)
- your blood thickening into sludge (ll. 34–35)

C4 Biofuels – the green alternative   p.50

3 Conducting a debate
Discussion boxes for a debate:

Agreeing with and supporting an argument

Exactly!
Definitely!
I couldn't agree more!
That's right!
I agree with …
What … said is (absolutely) right.
I'm of the same opinion (as …)
I would like to support what … said.
You've got a good point there.

Disagreeing

I can't agree with you …
I think you're (absolutely) wrong there!
I (completely) disagree with you!
Do you really mean to say that?
But you just said that now.
I'm sorry, but that can't be right!
But what you've just said is …
I must contradict you …
lie in wait, as if for an attack (negative)

Interrupting – Asking for clarification

Sorry to interrupt, but …
I would like to add something here.
What do you think about …?
What is your opinion on …?
Could you explain that again, please?

Support Chapter 3

Chapter 3 Living One's Life – Individuals in Society

A2 Successful children p. 57

3 What if …?
a Here are some hints which will help you with conditional sentences of all three types:
- Conditional sentences type I refer to the future:
  – If her daughters are not honor students, Amy Chua will …
  – If Amy Chua ever has grandchildren, she will …
- Conditional sentences type II refer to present or future unreal situations. Using type II, Louisa's might express her dreams and wishes:
  – If I had a part in the school play, I would …
  – If my mother were not a Chinese mother, I could …
- Conditional sentences type III refer to the past. Looking back, Amy Chua might think:
  – If my parents had not been Chinese immigrants, I would not have …
  – If I had been less strict with my daughters, they would never have …

A3 Childhood – the 21st century p. 60

3 Formal elements
Do the following tasks and after each decide whether the poet is using traditional style or is using innovative elements or is using free rhyme:
1 Count the number of stanzas and lines within the stanzas.
2 Then work out the rhyme scheme.
3 Read it aloud to yourself: how does the rhythm sound?
Decide which of the following stylistic devices the poet uses:
simile – metaphor – rhetorical question – personification – anaphora
How does the use of the stylistic device(s) affect you?

Support Chapter 3

B1 Stereotypes in Los Angeles p.61

6b **Discuss the function of stereotypes in everyday life.**
Consider the following questions. This can also be done as pair or group work.
1 How do stereotypes develop?
2 How do they influence our perception of others, and what are the consequences?
3 Are stereotypes only negative or can stereotypes be positive too?
4 How should we deal with stereotypes?

C1 Volunteering in the wake of the Olympics p.66

1 Pre-viewing
a First, write a definition of volunteering in your own words.
Then, consider the following phrases and say which are part of volunteering:

> *giving money to a charity* · *altruism* · *helping others* · *no financial gain* · *getting life experience* ·
> *helping sb. secretly* · *helping raise money for a charity* · *gaining self-respect* · *making contacts* ·
> *helping the community* · *doing a sponsored run* · *working full-time for a charity*

Now examine each photo in turn, deciding if it shows people volunteering. Some obviously don't, others may.

C2 Volunteering in Germany p.66

1 Mediation (German ➔ English)
- Read the German article, find keywords and note them down in English.
- Find English headings for each paragraph and write an introductory sentence which tells your friend not only about the author, source and topic of the article at hand, but also about the writer's attitude towards his topic. Is he biased or neutral?
- With the help of your collection of keywords and your headings make your first draft. Concentrate on central statements and try to sum up and shorten the article.
- Revise your first draft. Improve its style by using participle constructions and connectives.
(Length: about 1/3 of the original article.)

You may start your e-mail like this:
Dear ...,
We recently talked about the volunteering campaign initiated by the mayor of London, Boris Johnson.
I have just read a thought-provoking article in a German online newspaper and would like to tell you about it.

C4 The Hunger Games: an individual in a utopian society p.68

2 A volunteer
b 1 First of all, consider what volunteering is. You have already encountered it in this chapter, so look back at your work in **C1**, Tasks **1a** (if you have not done it, then look at the support information at **C2** above) und **2a**, and the description of a volunteer in **C2**, in order to form a definition in your own words of a volunteer.
2 Examine the word 'volunteer' and where it comes from, and what different meanings it has. In the extract Katniss says 'I volunteer'. What does she mean in the context of the film. What does volunteering possibly mean for her?
3 Now relate the two ideas of volunteering: what similarities do they share?

Support Pages

Support Chapter 4

Chapter 4   The Power of Words – from Shakespeare to Today

A2   Richard courts his enemy   p. 81

3 Working with imagery
Work with a partner. Identify the images each speaker uses. Explain them with the help of the annotations and from the context they are used in.
It is useful to become aware of your personal mental images when reading any text, and in particular a poetic passage like the one you are dealing with here.
Consider:
- names that Lady Anne calls Gloucester and whether these are straightforward or evoke certain images
- personification of abstracts or of body parts
- *similes
- *metaphors

6 Understanding character
a On the basis of your analysis, describe the speakers' characters.
Gloucester (= Richard) keeps twisting Anne's insults around to make them say something flattering to her in response – which she does not seem to accept, at least verbally. In this context you have analysed her response to Richard's offering her his sword to kill him.
All these things are indicators of what kind of people these two dramatic characters are.
When describing them, consider
- what motivations they have for acting as they do.
- what emotions they display while they are speaking.
- what their actions reveal about them.
- if their original emotions change and what that tells you about their characters.

B1   My future wife   p. 83

2 Comparing dialogues
Compare the way Petruchio woos Katharina to the way Gloucester woos Anne (A2, pp. 79–81). Evaluate what each man reveals about himself and how effectively they each use words to achieve their aims. First look at your answers to A2, tasks 4 and 5 on p. 79. Then use the following questions to help you examine Petruchio.
1 How does Petruchio respond to Kate telling him that her name is Katharina? (ll. 4–8)
2 What does he say he has heard about her from others? (ll. 4–14)
3 How does he respond to her attempts to make fun of him? (ll. 20–24)
4 How does Katharina come across?
5 How does Petruchio describe Katharina? (ll. 34–40 and ll. 49–50)
6 How does he propose to her? (ll. 41–52)

Now consider what sort of person Petruchio is, and whether you think he is successful at wooing Katharina. Then find similarities and differences between Richard and Petruchio, considering the context of each man's wooing and the emotions involved. Finally, decide which of the two men will be more successful.

206   Support Pages

Support Chapter 4

B1 VIEWING FOCUS ON SKILLS   p. 84

5 Evaluation

Evaluate how successful the director has been in adapting the material. Describe the elements that were changed and the effect the scene has on you. Use the following categories to create a table in which you contrast the play and the film:

setting *(What is the setting in each genre?)* • **characters** *(How did they come across in the play/film?)* • **relationship** *(What was the characters' relationship like in each genre?)* • **changes** *(What elements were added to / missing in the film?)* • **extras** *(How did the film maker use lighting, music, noise?)*

B2 Responding to a sonnet   p. 86

2 Comparing the sonnets

Compare the two sonnets. Examine structure, development of the idea and style. Present your findings on posters and evaluate them in a gallery walk. These steps may be useful:

1 Look at the structures of the poems by examining the rhyme scheme.
2 State the main idea presented in each poem.
3 Divide each poem up according to the images in it.
4 Examine how the idea of alteration is addressed in each poem.
5 Examine how Simmons uses phrases and ideas from Shakespeare in his own poem.

C1 Performance poetry   p. 88

7 Reviewing a poetry performance

Watch the performance again. Pay special attention to the speaker's gestures. Then write a review for the English pages of your school magazine. In order to write a review, first consider what your opinion of the poetry performance is.

1 Describe the performance.
2 Decide what you think about how Zephaniah performs his poem.
3 Decide whether the performance helped you to appreciate the poem, or whether you would have preferred just reading it.
4 Write the review by following these steps:
   - Find a suitable introductory sentence.
   - When writing the body of the review, remember to combine elements of description and of comment, and consider both the poem itself and the performance by the poet.
   - Finish by giving either a recommendation or a short statement that summarizes why you are not recommending the poem or the performance.

C2 The psychological power of words   p. 89

2 a + b Understanding the general idea

Draw a table like the one below. It will help you to examine the verbs and their connotations and to understand the images that the poem conveys.

person	verb/phrase	connotation	image
terrorist	lurk in the shadows	lie in wait, as if for an attack (negative)	dangerous person
freedom fighter …	take shelter …	wait somewhere safe until a danger has passed (neutral) …	person who needs safety and protection …

Support Pages

Support Chapter 5

Chapter 5 The UK – a Kingdom United?

A1 Dangerous books   p. 96

5 Creative writing
Write the dialogue between the footman and his wife and include the events that probably took place while the Queen was opening the Parliament.
The following questions might help you to collect ideas:
- How did the footman experience the incident?
- What is probably the most important aspect for him?
- Imagine the footman's feelings during his encounter with the Queen. Do you think he was embarrassed, frustrated, angry, unhappy, etc.? How could he express this in his conversation with his wife?

Don't forget: You are going to write a dialogue. So the footman and his wife should refer to each other and react to what the other person says.

A royal footman waits for the Queen to arrive in the royal carriage

B2 Between two cultures   p. 102

2 Analysing character relationships
Analyse the relationship between Kelly and her father Ibrahim. Reflect on what they talk about and how they speak to each other.
Read the following quotes that Kelly and Ibrahim say to each other. How do you imagine the actors are meant to say them? What emotions are being portrayed?

IBRAHIM	Would you prefer it if I had been an American?
IBRAHIM	I wish we could've met earlier.
IBRAHIM	I imagined you might look like Kate Winslet.
IBRAHIM	Because you are English. And you don't know any better.
KELLY	But I told you I'm not going to go to Iraq, am I?
KELLY	This isn't going very well, is it?
KELLY	Why are you here? Now, what do you want?
KELLY	Yeah, all right then, tell me what I think.

B3 The British and their tea   p. 105

2 Analysing style
How does the speaker of the podcast try to hold the audience's attention and entertain his listeners? First make notes on the following aspects of the podcast. What further examples can you find? What effect do they have on you as a listener? Use your points to organize your analysis.

Aspect	Example	Effect
Statistics	By the end of the day, the counter will reach 165 million – that is three cups of tea per person per day.	…
Interesting facts	And it is well-known that the Queen likes a nice cup of tea, as well.	…
Personal facts	Yukk! I cannot stand tea with sugar!	…
Exaggeration	… in the interests of international harmony and understanding I shall now explain …	…

Support Chapter 5

C1 A referendum on the EU   p. 108

4 Analysing style

Listen again. Analyse how Cameron tries to convince his listeners. Focus on language and content. Is he successful?
- a First fill in the 'Explanation' column of the table. What are the different stylistic devices?
- b List examples of the different devices you can hear in the text.
- c Describe the effect they have on you as a listener.
- d Use your points to organize your analysis of the speaker's style.

Stylistic device	Explanation	Example from the speech	Effect
Alliteration	- ...	- Rules and regulations - ...	- ...
Empathy	- ...	-	- ...
Antithesis, contrast	- ...	- Some people say ... but the question mark is already there. - They say, but I don't believe	- ...
Parallelism Repetition Anaphora	- The same word / structure is repeated	- It will be ... - ...	- ...
Rule of three	- ...	- Weeks, years and months - ...	- ...

C3 It's OK to like the Germans   p. 110

1 Summarizing

Summarize the writer's main points concerning Britons' relationship to Germany.
In the text, there are several main ideas you need to communicate in your summary.
Choose the seven most important facts from the list below:
- name of the text, author, date and source
- main idea: how British people feel about Germans
- background: the 2014 World Cup final
- quote: "I can't quite believe it ... but I find myself supporting Germany."
- stereotypes about German people
- the state of Britain's economy
- what Britain cannot copy from Germany
- what Britain can learn from Germany
- German problems
- The chance of a British team winning the World Cup

Now go back and summarize the text.

Support Chapter 6

Chapter 6 India – a Kaleidoscope

A2 Colonizers and colonized p. 117

1 Comparing a quote and photos
When studying the quote, you could consider the following:
- Who spoke the words?
- What is the speaker's view of colonialism?
- What is the speaker's view of the colonized people?
- What is the main message?

When studying the photographs, you should take the following aspects into account:
- When and where was the photo probably taken?
- Who can you see in the picture?
- What does body language reveal about the relationship of the people in the picture?
- What can you deduce from the picture about India under British rule?

Lord Curzon and the Maharajah of Patiala

A3 The British Empire from an Indian perspective p. 117

5 The legacy of the Raj
When discussing this, consider the following points in **A2**:
- What does Curzon say that he hoped he gave the Indians? Consider whether some of these might have been given to the Indians, and whether the Indians needed what he hoped to give.
- How might the Indians in the photos feel? Has their lives changed much since the Empire?

When discussing this, consider the following points in **A3**:
- The positive elements listed in ll. 1–2, 6–7, 16–21
- The failures of the Empire in ll. 2–9, 10–14, 18–19

B1 Urbanization in India: the big picture p. 123

1 Bar chart
When describing a graph, or diagram, start out by mentioning the topic, the type of presentation used (e.g. a bar chart, a line graph, etc.), the span of time it covers and its source and date of publication (if available). Then describe the diagram in detail by turning the graph into words. In the end summarize what you have learned.

B3 Celebrating Indian culture p. 125

6 Mediation (German → English)
Before writing your email, have a look at the following opening and closing formulas and decide which of them are best used in formal, which ones in informal emails (or letters). Decide on the best for your email.

Dear Dr. Smith, • Dear Madam, • Dear Ms. White, • Dear Prof. Smith, • Dear Sir or Madam, • Dear Mike, • Dear Sir(s), • Dearest • Hello, Mike! • Hey, babe! • Hi, • Tony,	Best regards • Best wishes • Hugs and kisses • Lots of love • Love • Regards • Sincerely yours • With best wishes • With kind regards • Yours ever • Yours faithfully • Yours sincerely • Yours truly • Yours

Now choose the most appropriate opening and closing formulas for your email.

Support Chapter 6

C1 The Indian diaspora   p. 127

2 Locating the Indian diaspora

When designing your poster, take the following points into consideration:
- Overall appearance: Does the poster attract your attention? Is it informative? How creative is the work that went into its making?
- Title: Does the poster have a title banner? Is the title clear? Is it eye-catching? Can it be read easily from 3 m away?
- Layout: Is the text large enough to be read from 2 m away? Is there sufficient 'resting space for the eye' (i.e. blank space)? Are colours and graphic highlighting used effectively? Are texts and illustrations/ photographs integrated in a meaningful way?
- Writing: Is the writing concise? Is the information included in the texts relevant? Can the texts be read easily? Is language used correctly (e.g. vocabulary, grammar, spelling)?

C3 English lessons   p. 128

2 Language awareness

The following passages from 'English Lessons' illustrate the use of the narrative past, narrative present and narrative future tenses in the story:

> **narrative past:**
>
> The police came looking for him. Oh no, not for my protection – no. They were rounding up all Sikh boys between the ages of fifteen and twenty-five for 'questioning'. Tony's parents knew what was in store and they hid him in the servant's quarter, a concrete room on the flat roof of the house. (ll. 75–78)
>
> **narrative present:**
> The phone rings and my heart starts to pound – *dharak, dharak*. Our answering machine message has Valerie's voice, and I follow the words with her accent. (ll. 8–9)
>
> **narrative future:**
> I will tell Tony I will take English lessons, and that she will be my teacher. (ll. 98–99)

Find more examples like this in the story to illustrate each type of narration, then answer the following questions:
- Which type of narration lends the story a sense of immediacy?
- Which type of narration has a distancing effect?
- Which type of narration could be said to add a prophetic tone to the story?

Go back to 'English Lessons' and use your findings to interpret the story: Why are there so many tense switches in 'English Lessons'? What do they reveal about the first-person narrator? And what is their effect on the reader?

Support Chapter 7

Chapter 7   The USA – Still the Promised Land?

A1 Viva America!   p. 137

3 Words that convey emotion

b The following text sounds bland because it lacks words that convey feelings. You can give it more emotional impact by adding the words from the box.

> anxious · feared ·
> hastily · hoping ·
> nervously · overjoyed ·
> tearfully · thrilled

My father … that his life would change for the worse if Castro came to power in Cuba. He … applied to the American Embassy in Havana, … for an immigration permit for himself and his family. After waiting three … months, he was … to receive a letter saying we could leave for the USA. My parents … packed their belongings and … said goodbye to their friends and relatives in Cuba. On March 11th, 1958, on board a small passenger ship bound for Miami, they were … to have their first glimpse of the American mainland.

When you have finished, compare texts with someone who did not use the Support option. Talk about different ways of modifying sentences to give them more emotional appeal.

B1 The new neighbours   p. 143

6 The other side of the coin

Form groups of four. Two of you are Bev and Russ, the other two are the African-American couple who have bought the house in Clybourne Street. Imagine that after Karl has left, the black couple come to look at the house. How would Russ and Bev behave? How might the black couple explain their wish to move to an all-white neighbourhood? Discuss the issues at hand, then prepare role cards for your parts.

Step 1:   Give the black couple names (e.g. Francine and Albert). Each member of your group chooses one of the characters. Read the list below and decide whether the attitude would better fit the white couple or the black couple:

- a bit embarrassed by the situation
- looking forward to changing neighbourhoods
- want a better life for their children
- feel guilty about their behaviour
- worried about the reaction of the neighbours
- believe in equality and progress
- avoid talking about race and skin colour
- want their share of the American dream

Step 2:   Now work together in 'couples' to prepare your role cards. Write down (in keywords) questions your person might ask and statements they might make.

Now practise the scene, then perform it for your class.

D1 Facts and figures   p. 152

1 Analysing numbers

a Compare the figures in the table by completing the eight sentences on the opposite page with phrases from the box.

	USA	China	Germany	Brazil	Russia	India
1 GDP	16,244,600	8,277,103	3,428,131	2,252,664	2,014,775	1,841,710
2 Military spending	682,478	166,107	45,785	43,576	90,749	46,125
3 Balance of trade	−784,775	155,142	219,938	19,169	198,760	−154,401

Support Pages

Support Chapter 7

1 The GDP of the USA is almost … as that of China, the country with the … largest economy.
2 The Russian GDP is only about … as China's.
3 China's GDP is … that of Germany, Russia and Brazil together.
4 Russia's GDP is … that of Brazil.
5 No country spends … money on the military as the USA.
6 Germany ranks only … in terms of GDP, but … in terms of balance of trade.
7 Russia has a healthy trade surplus, whereas India imports … it exports.
8 China's trade surplus is almost … India's trade deficit.

> as many • as much • first • fourth • half as big • larger than • (slightly) less than • more than • one quarter as big • second • the same size as • third • twice as big

■ FACT FILE
GDP (**Gross** [grəʊs] **Domestic Product**) is defined as the total value of goods and services produced in a country. The **balance of trade** is the difference between the total value of exports from a country and imports into the same country. A negative balance (**deficit** ['defɪsɪt]; opposite: **surplus** ['sɜːpləs]) means the country imports more than it exports.

D3 Better than its reputation   p. 154

3 The author's bias

b Point to examples from the text that illustrate the author's bias (selection of facts, word choice, use of *emphasis, *juxtaposition, sentence structure, etc.). Match the words and expressions that have been highlighted to one or more of the categories in the box and describe the effect they have on the reader. ▶ Glossary, p. 322

> comparison • *juxtaposition / selection of facts • *contrast • word choice (e.g. positive / negative *connotations) • *emphasis • *repetition / *anaphora

But the American response is already larger – by a factor of hundreds – than that of the largest economy in East Asia. The United States is sending an aircraft carrier to the worst-hit regions and has promised $20 million in emergency aid. Millions more will be raised by U.S. charities. The British are sending a warship and $16 million. Even the Vatican has promised $4 million. And the government of China, the new land of opportunity? $100,000.
(Lines 18–27 of the text on p. 153)

Journalist Anne Applebaum

Americans, like Europeans, have long believed that strength and wealth entail responsibility. That's why two American ex-presidents voluntarily coordinated the international response to the 2004 tsunami, even though Indonesia was not the site of a U.S. naval base. That's why massive amounts of U.S. aid went to victims of the 2005 earthquake in Kashmir, even though relations between the United States and Pakistan were deteriorating at the time.

That's also why an American president who is actively uninterested in engaging with the Syrian conflict has pledged more than $1 billion in humanitarian aid to Syrian refugees, accounting for nearly 30 percent of all such aid; European contributions as a whole make up a good percentage of the rest. China's contribution, meanwhile, comes to $3 million, less than that of Luxembourg. China plays an enormous political role in Syria – the Chinese veto has helped keep the United Nations firmly sidelined there – but clearly does not feel obligated to help those affected by its decisions.

The Chinese do give development aid, but differently: not in response to tragedies, not to counter disaster, but to facilitate the export of raw materials to China.
(Lines 36–51 of the text on pp. 153–154)

Now go on to **3c**; if possible, choose a partner who has not made use of the Support option.

213
Support Pages

Support Chapter 8

Chapter 8 Beyond the Nation – Europe and a Globalized World

A2 Young, educated – and leaving the country   p. 162

4 Creative writing
Form groups of four. Each select one important moment of Ms. Abadia's immigrant experience and write a diary entry. Read out your entries to your group and join your texts to form one coherent diary entry.
1 Look for the description of an important moment in the text.
2 Make notes on what happened and how Ms. Abadia felt at that moment.
3 If necessary add other events and feelings Ms. Abadia may have had.
4 Write your diary entry.

B2 The need for responsible globalization   p. 167

3 Promoting transparent labelling
a Design a clothing label that helps buyers make responsible choices when buying clothes. Present it to the class.
  1 Make a list of aspects that are important for responsible clothing production.
  2 Choose the most important points and think of a system to evaluate them.
  3 Write the text for a clothing label that contains information about these aspects.

Now go back to task **3b** on p. 167.

C1 Keeping the accent   p. 172

4 Creative writing
a Write a short story based on the poem.
  1 Outline the events and emotions you would like to include in your story.
  2 Decide from which character's point-of-view to tell the story – the speaker of the poem, the barman or other people in the bar.
  3 Decide what type of narrator to use.
  4 Start writing. Do not write an introduction, but start in the middle of the scene, e.g. 'I can feel their looks piercing my back'.
  5 Do not write a clear, conclusive ending, but leave it open, even a bit vague.
  6 Hold writing conferences among four or five students to improve your texts.
b Write a scene based on the poem.
  1 Decide on how you are going to convey the speaker's feelings or memories. You might make her speak a *soliloquy or you might have a second actor who acts as the speaker's 'shadow', articulating her feelings and thoughts.
  2 Write your scene, starting the action right in the middle of the action, e.g. with the barman saying 'Sorry, what was that?'.
  3 Imagine the actors' gestures or movements and write stage directions.

Support Chapter 8

C3 Linguistic diplomacy: the Eurovision Song Contest p. 175

5 Discussion

In groups of five prepare and hold a panel discussion in which you discuss the question of whether each country should be obliged to enter songs in their national language only. One student is the moderator, the others argue either for or against the topic.

Moderator:
- Think of possible arguments and their counter-arguments.
- Collect questions or remarks that might make the participants put these arguments forward.

Discussion participants:
- Think of arguments for your position and collect examples to illustrate your point.
  Don't just talk about the very obvious topics, but search for arguments and examples the others might not have thought about.
- Collect arguments that your opponents might put forward and think about ways to refute them.

Chapter Task p. 175

1 Planning your work
  a Do some research to get a general idea of the topic and to identify suitable subtopics.
   1 Don't forget to provide a definition of slavery.
   2 Define the areas you want to focus on:
     a You might want to give a short historical survey of slavery. Consider e.g. the situation in Ancient Greece or Rome, the Middle Ages and/or the Americas.
     b You might also want to outline the grievances that have led to slave rebellions throughout history.
     c When considering modern-day slavery, think of e.g. the catering trade or agriculture, the construction industry, private households, the entertainment industry (football) or sexual slavery.
   3 Decide whether you want to present a case study or general aspects of slavery.

Now go back to task **1b** on p. 175.

2 Preparing your poster
  b Organize your findings and prepare your poster.
   1 Structure your text and visual aids in a way that guides the reader of your poster through it:
     Use symbols, lines, arrows, colours, and fonts in a clear and meaningful way.
   2 You may use pictures and/or quotations taken from films and/or literature dealing with slavery.

Now go back to task **2c** on p. 175.

Support Pages

Support Chapter 9

Chapter 9   Work and Business – Careers and Perspectives

A2 Moving on after recession   p. 181

3   Political speeches: Convincing the audience
Look at Obama's style and language and show how he tries to convince his audience. Pay attention, for instance, to how Obama appeals to the audience by
- varying sentence lengths,
- referring to historical events,
- …

Also, observe the effect the story of Misty DeMars has on the audience.

Now go back to task **4** on p. 183.

A4 Teenagers' career aspirations   p. 185

4   Preparing a discussion
Should you pursue the career of your choice or should you consider only those careers where job demand is fairly certain? Write an argumentative text in which you consider both sides and state your own view. For ideas *for* wanting to pursue your preferred career / studies programme, i.e. *against* considering only those careers where job demand is projected, consider
- motivational aspects,
- your talents,
- achieving the goals you set yourself,
- potentially good results in examinations etc., if you are diligent and hardworking.

For ideas *against* wanting to pursue your preferred career / studies programme, i.e. *for* considering only those careers where job demand is projected,
- look for arguments, facts and figures from the article for support,
- think of the possibility of combining talents and interests with promising career paths.

A5 Do you love your job?   p. 188

3   A tricky question in your job interview
   a Some of the aspects of job satisfaction mentioned by King should not be brought up in a job interview. List them, then compare with your partner. Remember, for instance: Your future employer is interested in your well-being and job satisfaction, but also wants employees who can work in a team.

Now go back to task **3** on p. 189.

B1 Mitch's first glimpse of the world of work   p. 190

2   Power relations
Partner A: Analyze the meeting between Mitch and McNulty and explain how one of them shows his power and superiority through non-linguistic means (e.g. facial expressions). Focus and take notes on
- Mitch and McNulty on their way to the coach's office,
- where and how they are sitting in the office,
- McNulty's eyes and voice,
- McNulty's pencil.

216

Support Pages

Support Chapter 9

Partner B: Analyze the meeting between Mitch and McNulty and explain how one of them uses language to demonstrate his power and superiority. Focus and take notes on
- who is asking the important questions,
- who is using imperatives,
- who is trying to be funny,
- who controls the conversation.

Now go back to task **3** on p. 191.

B2 Ten things not to say in a job interview   p. 192

2 The language of the text
  a Explain how King tries to amuse the reader. Consider the following stylistic devices used by King: absurd example, exaggeration, metaphor. Find examples of these devices in lines 30, 35 and 46–47.

Now go back to task **2b** on p. 193.

B3 The best job in the world is back!   p. 193

2 Text type and target group
  a Name characteristic aspects of the text type 'job advertisement' and illustrate them with examples from the text. The subheadings of the text give you a first idea about typical elements of job ads. Match the subheadings with their corresponding explanation:

subheading	explanation
Your responsibilities	financial information
Who we're looking for	contact information
About the job package	information about the employer
About your new office	description of the ideal candidate
How to apply	description of duties

Now go back to task **2b** on p. 194.

B5 Look them in the eye – the job interview   p. 196

2 Pieces of advice
Watch the video. With your partner, list and rank the given dos and don'ts of job interviews.
Five of the following aspects are dealt with in the video:
1 conversation openers
2 dress code
3 first impressions
4 hairstyle
5 no-go questions
6 professional documents
7 punctuality
8 selling yourself and your strengths
Which pieces of advice do you consider most important?

Now go back to task **3** on p. 196.

217

Support Pages

Language Practice

Focus on Grammar

LP 1 Simple present and present progressive 218
LP 2 Simple present and future tense. 219
LP 3 Simple present and present perfect 220
LP 4 Present perfect and simple past 221
LP 5 Infinitive or gerund after certain verbs. 222

LP 6 Infinitive or gerund after certain nouns 223
LP 7 The passive 224
LP 8 Conditional sentences 225
LP 9 Articles, quantifiers and countability. 226
LP 10 Using adjectives and adverbs . 227

Focus on Style

LP 11 Using the right register 228
LP 12 Avoiding German-sounding sentence patterns 228

LP 13 Emphasis. 229
LP 14 Linking words and phrases. . . 231
LP 15 Connecting your thoughts (sentence structure). 233

Focus on Vocabulary

LP 16 Avoiding Germanisms 234
LP 17 Spelling. 235
LP 18 Writing about texts 235
LP 19 Collocations 236
LP 20 Word formation 238

Focus on Grammar

▶ LP 1 Simple and progressive verb forms

a **BASIC** Choose the right form of the verb for each of the sentences below (make sure you choose the correct tense).
  1 A man came running out of the bank and (*jump*) into the waiting car.
  2 Sorry, I can't talk now – I (*make*) dinner for the family.
  3 Smoking (*cause*) over 600,000 deaths in the EU every year.
  4 It was a cold evening, and a light drizzle (*fall*). When no one (*come*) to unlock the gates the crowd (*get*) restless.
  5 The housing prices in London (*always be*) high, but at present they (*skyrocket*).
  6 The last time I talked to her, she (*look*) for a new job.

Most English verbs can be used in all tenses in both the simple and the progressive form:
Jasmin practises *the piano three hours a day. She*'s practising *now for her concert on Saturday.*

Simple form	Progressive form
• For states[1]: Our house *needs* repainting. • For actions that follow a plan or physical law: *Our plane* leaves *at 8:05 am. Water* boils *at 100 °C.* • Actions in a series (narration) • Verbs that describe what the author of a text does: *The author* criticizes *the government's lack of initiative.*	• For actions that are taking place at the present moment or were taking place at a certain point in time in the past: *I've* been waiting *here all morning! When the police arrived, two men* were loading *boxes into a van.* • For trends and developments: *It's* becoming *more and more difficult to find a permanent job. It's* getting *dark – let's go home.* • For descriptions of circumstances (weather, clothing etc.): *A cold wind* was blowing. *She* was wearing *a red woollen sweater over a plaid skirt.*

---

[1]**state** *Zustand*

218

Language Practice

LP 2 • Focus on Grammar

Verbs that describe a state (i.e. not an activity) are called **state verbs**. Normally, they can only be used in the simple form:
I *heard* a voice. Someone *needed* help. I *wanted* to help them, but I didn't *know* how.
A few state verbs can also be used in the progressive form, but with a different meaning. Compare the sentences in the table below and explain the difference in meaning:

Simple form	Progressive form
What do you *think* of his decision?	What *are* you *thinking* about?
You *look* upset – what's the matter?	Why *are* you *looking* at me like that?
For her, success is all that *counts*.	We*'re counting* on you to help us.
How *do* you *feel* about same-sex marriage?	He stayed at home because he *was*n't *feeling* well.
Everybody *has* a bad day now and then.	We *were having* lunch when my phone rang.

b Choose the right form of the verb for each of the sentences below:
1 I (*think*) you should go to her and tell her how you (*feel*) about what happened.
2 Lydia (*love*) going to parties, but she never (*feel*) like organizing one herself.
3 While I (*look*) at the photos on our website I (*have*) a great idea for our next campaign.
4 Everyone (*need*) the feeling that their life (*count*) for something.
5 The last time I (*see*) Bruce and Charlene they (*have*) a big argument about something .
6 When I visited Bob in hospital, I (*think*) he (*look*) awful, but he said that he (*feel*) better.

▮ TROUBLE SPOT
With **everybody/everyone**, the plural form of the possessive pronoun is commonly used.

Special uses: the progressive form used for emphasis
- Some speakers use the progressive form of state verbs, especially in the present perfect, to underline their message: 'New York? I've been wanting to go there for ages!' / 'I've been meaning to write to you since Christmas!'
- In some situations, the progressive form of the verb *be* is used to refer to behaviour that is temporary and (perhaps) not genuine: *Why are you being so stubborn? – Ignore him; he's just being a trouble-maker again.*
- The slogan of an American fast-food chain (*I'm loving it!*) belongs to the same category: using the progressive form of the state verb *love* has the effect of underlining the message and makes the slogan more memorable.

▶ LP 2 Present or future tense?

a BASIC Spot and correct the mistakes in the sentences below:
1 I don't know how he reacts when we tell him the truth.
6 'I need a can opener for this.' – 'No problem, I go look for one.'
3 Is it true that Kai goes abroad next year?
4 The weather forecast says there are scattered showers throughout the afternoon.
5 I'm sure my parents don't let me go to the rock festival.
6 The German students will wait at Stansted until their bus will come to collect them.

Language Practice
219

LP Focus on Grammar • LP 3

> Generally speaking, English – like German – uses the **present tense to talk about the present** and the **future tense to talk about the future**. However, there are a few exceptions to keep in mind:
> - In English, when offering to do something, the **will-future** is used (whereas the present tense would be used in German): *Hast du Durst? Ich hole uns etwas zu trinken. / Are you thirsty? I'll fetch us something to drink.*
> - In German, it is possible to talk about the future in the present tense: *Wir fahren morgen an die See.* You can do this in English too, but only with the **present progressive** when you talk about plans for the future: *We're leaving for the coast tomorrow.* A sentence like *Morgen regnet es wieder* can only be expressed in the *will*-future: *It will rain again tomorrow.*
> - **The future tense is not used** after *if, when, unless, until, as soon as* etc., even when you are referring to the future: *Phone me as soon as you arrive. – You won't get tickets unless you book in advance.*

b Use the key words and phrases to make complete sentences. All verbs are in the present or the future:
1 There's someone at the door. You / please / go / see who it is?
2 The PM says / he / attend to the problem / as soon as / government report / published.
3 In the course of the week / temperatures / drop slightly.
4 By the time / we / arrive at the airport / it / be / too late.
5 The people next door / have / their house repainted / next month.
6 The assistant director says / he / talk to the staff / before / situation / escalate any further.

▶ LP 3 Simple present and present perfect

a BASIC Decide which of the following sentences are correct. Correct the faulty ones:
1 I have wanted to meet her for as long as I can remember.
2 For the past three years, John is saving his money for a trip to New Zealand.
3 The author and her family live in London since 2006.
4 Four hundred years after his death, Shakespeare has continued to fascinate audiences around the world.
5 We are waiting for this bus for the last half an hour – I don't think it's coming.
6 Leonie has been an avid reader ever since she taught herself to read at the age of five.

> The **present perfect** is used in English for actions and states that began in the past, but are still going on or hold true. German uses the present tense in such cases.
>
> | German | English |
> | --- | --- |
> | Hunneman *leitet* die Organisation seit 2008. | Hunneman *has led* the organization since 2008. |
> | Rowling *arbeitet* seit drei Jahren an einem neuen Roman. | Rowling *has been working* on a new novel for three years. |
>
> The **present perfect** is closely connected with the present time. For that reason, English speakers often choose verbs in the present perfect where a German might use a different verb in the present.

LP4 · Focus on Grammar   **LP**

German	English
Kennst du den Roman Doktor Faustus?	*Have you ever read* Doktor Faustus?
Ich kenne Bratislava nicht.	*I've never been to Bratislava.*
Weißt du, ob Justin heute da ist?	*Have you seen Justin this morning?*
Wissen die Praktikanten schon Bescheid?	*Have the interns been informed yet?*

b Translate the following sentences into idiomatic English. Use the verb in brackets in the present perfect.
1 Kennst du den Film *Casablanca*? (see)
2 Kennst du Paris? (be)
3 Kennt ihr schon das neue türkische Restaurant am Zimmerplatz? (check out)
4 Ich bin noch nie Ski gelaufen. (try)
5 Weißt du über das Treffen heute Nachmittag Bescheid? (hear)
6 Kennst du dich mit 3D-Druckern aus? (use)

▶ LP4 Present perfect and simple past

a BASIC Complete the sentences with the correct form of the verb (present perfect or simple past).
1 When … you last … Thomas? (see)
2 The centre … opened in 2004. (be)
3 Until today, no one … a cure for cancer. (discover)
4 Sarah … me the revised version of the text just five minutes ago. (hand)
5 We're still friends, although I … her since we graduated. (not see)
6 I … the book when it first came out, but I … it. (read; not like)
7 Julia and Tobias … at a youth camp in Ireland in 2012. They … in contact ever since. (meet; keep)
8 My brother … to New Zealand yesterday, but we … from him yet. (fly; not hear)

Present perfect (This tense refers to a time that has not yet ended.)	Simple past (This tense refers to a time that is over.)
Use this tense • to present results: *Engineers at the Wyss Institute have developed a new kind of biodegradable plastic.* • to talk about states that have existed since some time in the past: *How long have you lived in Germany?* • to talk about actions in the past without saying when they happened: *She's been there before.* • to talk about actions that have happened more than once (or never): *I've seen that film at least five times. I've never been to Denmark.*	Use this tense when talking about events that happened in the past: *When I was a student, I lived in Exeter.*
Examples of signal words and phrases: • *already, ever, never, yet, often* • time phrases with *since* and *for* (*since 2013, for ten years*)	Examples of signal words and phrases: • *before, yesterday* • time phrases of the past (*ten minutes ago, last June, in 2010*) • *When …?*

■ TROUBLE SPOT

Signal words of the past can **never** be used together with the **present perfect**. Sentences such as ~~When have you last talked to him?~~ and ~~I have seen her just a few minutes ago~~ are always wrong!

Language Practice   221

Focus on Grammar • LP 5

b Choose the correct form of the verbs in brackets in the following text. You may use the present, the simple past or the present perfect:

Almost everyone (hear) of Stephen King, the best-selling author of dozens of horror stories. King (be) born in 1947 in Maine, USA, where many of his stories (be) also set. After graduating from the University of Maine in 1970, King (find) a teaching position at Hampden Academy. His first novel, Carrie, (be) published by Doubleday in 1973 and (bring) King national attention as well as financial independence. In the summer of 1999, King (be) walking down a road when he (be) hit by a car and badly injured. He (survive), but since his accident, he (write) much less. His son Joseph Hillstrom King, who (use) the pen name Joe Hill, (write) three novels and numerous stories, all of which (belong) to the genre fantasy/horror. Similar to his more famous father, Hill (win) numerous writing awards.

World-famous author, Stephen King

▶ LP 5 Infinitive or gerund after certain verbs

a BASIC Choose the correct form of the verb complement (infinitive or gerund) in the following sentences:
1 You can leave as soon as you have finished (clean up).
2 Many people dislike (be told) what to do.
3 How long have you wanted (go) there?
4 I don't mind (get) my hands dirty.
5 As she had never intended (take) the job, Sandy was surprised (receive) an offer.
6 She hoped (get) a better offer from a firm in Shanghai.

Infinitive or gerund?	Verbs	Example
verb + **infinitive**	most verbs that can take a complement	I *want to go* to Hawaii. I *wish to speak* to your boss. I'm *planning to study* physics.
verb + **gerund**	admit, avoid, consider, deny, dislike, enjoy, finish, give up, imagine, include, involve, justify, keep, mention, mind, miss, practice, risk, suggest	I *dislike waiting* for the bus. I *miss going* to school. ■ TIP To avoid mistakes, try learning these verbs by heart and then use the infinitive with the rest.
verb + **gerund or infinitive** (same meaning)	love, like, hate, prefer, begin, start, continue	I *love to play* badminton. / I *love playing* badminton.

A small number of verbs have **different meanings** when they are used with an infinitive or a gerund. Compare the sentences in the table below. What does the verb mean in each case?

Verb	Used with a gerund	Used with an infinitive
stop	Stop *shouting* like that!	Let's *stop to have* a break.
remember	I don't *remember seeing* him at the meeting.	Did you *remember to lock* the door?
forget	I'll never *forget seeing* London for the first time.	I *forgot to buy* a litre of milk – sorry!
mean	Sustainability *means not using* more than we produce.	I didn't *mean to make* her upset.
try	If you have the hiccups – *try holding* your breath.	We *tried to make* him change his mind, but he wouldn't listen.

Language Practice

LP 6 • Focus on Grammar

b Decide between a gerund or an infinitive in the following sentences:
1. For Melissa, the job in Los Angeles was a dream come true, but it meant (leave) her family and friends behind.
2. If we don't stop (dump) waste into the world's oceans, it may soon be too late.
3. Suzie mentioned (go) on a date but avoided (tell) us with whom.
4. I tried (reach) you by mobile, but I only got your mailbox.
5. John stopped (read) the newspaper and missed the train.
6. Anthony considered (run) the red light but then imagined (cause) an accident.
7. Students often say that they forgot (do) their homework, but no one really believes them.

▶ LP 6 Infinitive or gerund after certain nouns

a **BASIC** Spot the mistakes in the following sentences and correct them. Careful: not all sentences are wrong.
1. I don't know why she entered the competition – she doesn't have a chance of winning.
2. I'm afraid we don't have time of discussing the matter any longer.
3. Mark Zuckerberg wasn't the first person who had the idea to create a social networking site.
4. Our plan of camping in the wild turned out to be completely unrealistic.
5. Rosa Parks was one of the first African-Americans who had the courage of speaking out against racism.
6. After their traumatic experience, the victims had the need of talking to someone who could help them.
7. Students often face the problem to find affordable accommodations.
8. The stipend helped Jens of going to New York for a year.

In German, you can add information to any noun using an infinitive phrase: *der Wunsch, reich und berühmt zu sein*.
In English, generally an **infinitive** is used, a **gerund with *of***, or a ***that*-clause**:
the right *to state* your opinion
the dream *of becoming* a star
the fact *that* she could speak five languages.
However, these complements cannot be used interchangeably:

Infinitive or gerund?	Nouns	Example
noun + infinitive	right, wish, desire, longing, will, courage, strength, decision, time, need, ability	the right to bear arms, time to say good-bye, the will to live
noun + *of* + gerund	most other nouns	the risk of getting lost, the fear of being left behind
special cases	• chance, opportunity, plan: Either the infinitive or *of* + gerund can be used. • a/any chance: *of* + gerund is used more often. • the chance: The infinitive is used more often.	This is my chance to earn lots of money. / This is my chance of earning lots of money. Any chance of seeing him again? The chance to win this game is pretty slim.

Language Practice

LP Focus on Grammar • LP 7

There are a few **more special cases** worth remembering:

- The word *reason* can be used either with an infinitive or with *for* + gerund. When *reason* is followed by *for* + a person, an infinitive must be used: *There's no reason for us to give up without a fight.*
- The word *attempt* can be followed either by an infinitive or by *at* + gerund: *The government's attempt at covering up/to cover up the matter only made things worse.*
- The expression *(to) have trouble/difficulty* is used with a gerund without any preposition: *I had trouble starting the motor. Difficulty* can also be followed by *in* + gerund: *We had difficulty* (not: ~~difficulties~~) *in persuading her to come to the meeting.* Careful: In other contexts *difficulty* is treated like a normal noun (*of* + gerund): *the difficulty of living with a permanent disability*.

b Put the verb in brackets into the correct form; in some cases there is more than one correct solution:
1. All our attempts (reach) an agreement have failed.
2. The dream (find) a better life was reason enough for millions of immigrants (leave) their homeland.
3. The producer had trouble (find) a child star who could both act and dance.
4. Steven spent his first weeks in Kerala learning (cope) with the difficulties (live and work) in India.
5. I would be interested in hearing your reasons (reject) the proposal.
6. You can't imagine the difficulty we had (locate) a garage in Sofia that could repair our car.

▶ LP 7 The passive

a BASIC Make complete sentences in the passive using the key words:
1. Fitzgerald's classic novel, *The Great Gatsby*/first publish/1925
2. To date[1]/it/adapt for the screen/six times
3. The most recent version/released/2013
4. It/be/the first screen adaptation/that/film *(v)*/in 3D format
5. The title role/play/Leonardo DiCaprio
6. The film/criticize/some critics/as a costume spectacle
7. Most of the scenes/shoot/in Australia,/where huge sets/build/for the film

Rules for using the passive	Examples
The passive in English is formed using the verb *(to) be* and the **past participle**.	*Tchaikovsky's ballet Swan Lake was first performed in 1877.*
Generally, the passive is used when the person who does an action is unknown or unimportant.	*Three paintings were stolen from the museum last weekend.*
If the person or force that does something (the 'agent') is named in the sentence, it is introduced using the preposition **by**.	*The tower was damaged by lightning in 1988.*
Verbs that use a preposition keep the preposition in the passive.	*discriminate against sb. → African-Americans have often been discriminated against, not only in the past.*
If the so-called **personal passive** can be formed, it is usually first choice.	*We were given our ID cards at the main desk.* (The 'normal' passive would sound awkward here: *Our ID cards were given to us at the main desk.*)
Passive forms of the **infinitive** and the **gerund** can also be formed.	*(to) love → (to) be loved* *loving → being loved*

[1] **to date** *(adv)* bisher, bis jetzt

Language Practice

b Use an infinitive or a gerund in the passive to rewrite the underlined parts of the following sentences. You may have to change the word order. Avoid using a by-agent.
1 After the flood they had to rebuild most of the houses in the village. *(After the flood most of the houses in the village had to …)*
2 Teenagers hate it when adults treat them like children.
3 Even in his darkest moments, Colin never gave up the hope that he would be rescued.
4 It was her fear that people would laugh at her that held her back.
5 She told her doctor that she wanted him to tell her the truth.
6 No one likes the feeling that someone is discriminating against them.

> **Special uses: the *get*-passive**
>
> In colloquial English, many speakers form the passive using **get** instead of **be**. Common phrases are *get hurt, get killed, get lost, get caught*.
> The *get*-passive is also used to emphasize the difference between an action and a state:
> We soon got lost in a maze of tiny alleyways that all looked the same.
> I couldn't spot a single familiar landmark and finally had to admit that I was lost.

▶ LP8 Conditional sentences

a BASIC Complete the following sentences with the correct form of the verb in brackets:
1 If I discover a cancer cure, I (become) famous.
2 If I discovered a cancer cure, I (become) famous.
3 If I had discovered a cancer cure ten years ago, I (be) famous.
4 If someone (be) famous, everyone recognizes them on the street.
5 If Romeo (not crash) the Capulets' party, he might never have met Juliet.
6 If the sea level (rise) one meter, hundreds of coastal cities would be in danger.

A variety of conditional sentences are possible in English. Their use depends on the situation.	
An imagined condition in the **past** with an imagined consequence in the **past**.	If Sheila had taken part in the competition, she might have won a prize.
An imagined condition in the **past** with an imagined consequence in the **present**.	If you hadn't wasted all your money, you could afford to go with us to Greece.
An imagined condition in the **present** with an imagined consequence.	If Sarah worked harder, she would get better marks.
A possible condition in the **present** with a possible consequence.	If you have trouble with the new software, Kevin can / will help you.
A condition that can happen at any time and its consequence.	If the polar ice caps melt, the sea level rises / will rise.

Focus on Grammar • LP 9

b The text below presents some facts concerning the settlement of North America and its consequences. Draw conclusions from the facts using conditional sentences.
Example: *If European settlers had not come to America, herds of buffalo might still roam the Great Plains.*

When the first European settlers arrived at the shores of the New World, there were about three million Native Americans living in North America. Having no natural immunity to European diseases, thousands of natives fell ill and died. As they moved farther west, the white settlers pushed the natives off their land, at the same time decimating[1] the large herds of buffalo that roamed[2] the Great Plains. The Native Americans, whose way of life depended on the buffalo, could no longer exist. Ancient grasslands disappeared as farms were followed by railroads, towns, highways and factories, further restricting the freedom of movement of the native tribes. An ecological balance between man and nature that had existed for thousands of years was destroyed within a few decades.

▶ LP 9 Articles, quantifiers and countability

a BASIC Translate the nouns and noun phrases in brackets, deciding whether you need a singular or a plural and whether or not the definite article is necessary.
1 *(Die menschliche Gesellschaft)* hasn't made *(viele Fortschritte)* in dealing with the forces of *(das Böse)*.
2 We found *(einige interessante Informationen)* on the internet concerning *(die Kunst)* of the Aborigines.
3 *(Die Wissenschaft)* can provide us with *(Erkenntnisse)*, but it can't give us any *(Ratschläge)* on how to use it.
4 Despite all the *(Forschungen)* on cancer, there has been relatively *(wenig Fortschritte)*.
5 Although she grew up in L.A., her *(Kenntnisse)* of *(die Natur)* and *(die Umwelt)* is really impressive.

> Find more information on articles, quantifiers and countability here:
> **Webcode** context-00

b The table below shows which social networking site five young people regularly use:

	Sandy	Carol	Andrew	James	Marvin
Spacebook	X	X	X	X	X
Lightnigram	X		X	X	X
Chatter	X	X	X		
Mumblr			X		X
OurSpace					

1 Make four statements about the group. Example: *A few of them use Mumblr.*
2 Make two statements about Sandy and Carol: what have they got in common?

---

[1] **decimate sth.** kill large numbers of sth.   [2] **roam** walk around with no fixed goal

Language Practice

LP 10 • Focus on Grammar

▶ LP 10 Using adjectives and adverbs

a BASIC Put the words in brackets in the right form (adjective or adverb):
1. In science-fiction films, robots (traditional) appear in the role of (soulless) killing machines.
2. The engineers who develop robots for new applications (passionate) believe that they will make our lives (happy and safe).
3. For example, they will free us from (boring) tasks like cleaning the house or mowing the lawn.
4. Most of the (heavy) work in farming is already done (automatic) by machine.
5. (Remarkable) progress has been made in developing robots for a (large) number of everyday uses.
6. Ideas that sounded (impossible) only ten years ago are (rapid) becoming reality.
7. Perhaps someday we will be (complete) dependent on (intelligent) machines for almost everything.

Adjectives

Adjectives are used to modify (i.e. describe) a noun. They can be used directly before the noun (*a short holiday, a famous tourist spot*) or they are used after certain verbs:

Verbs of being, seeming, becoming etc.	Why *are* you sad? She *seemed* unhappy. Don't *get* nervous. Injustice always *makes* me angry.
Verbs that describe sense impressions	He *looks* nervous. That *sounds* wonderful. The soup *smells* great and it *tastes* great too. The stone *felt* cold to the touch.

Adverbs

Adverbs of manner are made from adjectives by adding *-ly*. (Exceptions: *fast, hard, early* and *late* are used as both adjectives and adverbs.)
Adverbs modify verbs, adjectives, or other adverbs:

Adverb modifies **verb**.	She got up *quickly* and ran to the window.
Adverb modifies **adjective**.	The team has been *incredibly* successful this season.
Adverb modifies **adverb**.	The experts worked *extremely* cautiously to defuse the bomb.

Certain adverbs can also be used to modify a whole sentence. Such adverbs are known as **sentence adverbs**. They always stand at the beginning of the sentence and are often separated by a comma from the rest of the sentence.

Adverb modifies **sentence**.	*Fortunately*, none of the passengers were seriously injured.

Other common sentence adverbs: *actually, admittedly, apparently, consequently, eventually, evidently, hopefully, incidentally, luckily, obviously, presumably, surprisingly, ultimately, understandably*.

b Use a sentence adverb instead of the underlined words in each of the sentences below:
1. More and more cars hit the road every year. <u>As a result</u>, the number of traffic jams also increases.
2. <u>A surprising fact is that</u> the interest in car ownership is declining.
3. <u>It seems that</u> many young urbanites regard a car as an unnecessary expense.
4. <u>It is easy to understand that</u> the interest in car ownership is lowest where cheap, reliable public transportation is available.
5. <u>In the course of time</u> cars may disappear altogether from our city streets.
6. <u>I hope that</u> this development will mean cleaner air in cities that presently have a huge smog problem.

Language Practice

LP Focus on Style • LP 11–LP 12

Focus on Style

▶ LP 11 Using the right register

a **BASIC** In the following excerpt from a student's film summary, the teacher has underlined some expressions in red to indicate that they are inappropriate. Rewrite the text, correcting the stylistic problems.

The film Outsourced *is about this guy named Todd Anderson. He works for an American firm that has outsourced its call centre to India to save money. Todd gets sent there to bring the Indian workers up to American standards. When he gets there, he's totally lost, cause he doesn't know the first thing about India. He tries to get the Indians to act like Americans, but it doesn't work out. He only starts getting somewhere when he begins listening to the Indians and taking them seriously.*

Like other languages, English has different registers for different situations:

Register	Typical situations	Typical features
Informal	Everyday communication between friends, spoken English	Short or incomplete sentences, short forms (*they've, gotta*), phrasal verbs, colloquial expressions (*make it big, chill out* etc.)
Neutral	Articles and essays on subjects of general interest	Mix of short and more complex sentences, no short forms, words of the general vocabulary
Formal	Official documents and speeches, business letters	Complex sentences, specialized or technical words

When writing essays for school, use the neutral register. Some teachers allow you to use short forms of negations in your writing (*don't, can't* etc.); ask if you aren't sure.

b After finishing school in Germany, you apply to a College of Arts in the United States. One day you receive the following letter:

> On behalf of the Admissions Committee I am pleased to inform you that you have been offered a place in the incoming freshman class. Your application convinced us that you have the talent and motivation required for academic success. Furthermore, after careful review of your family's financial situation, we have decided to award you a full scholarship, comprising all tuition fees as well as room and board for the duration of your studies.
> All our students are guaranteed on-campus accommodation in our newly-renovated dormitories (dual occupancy). Furthermore, the College provides a comprehensive 24/7 meal service. Should you decide to accept our offer, please reply by June 10th.

Look up the words and expressions you don't understand; most of them belong to the vocabulary of formal correspondence. Then write an email to your former host family in the US, telling them about the letter and its contents and asking about points that are unclear to you. Use a *neutral or moderately informal* style.

▶ LP 12 Avoiding German-sounding sentence patterns

a **BASIC** Find the mistakes in the following sentences and correct them.
1 If you ask me, Roland paid for his new smartphone far too much.
2 In 2010 was the number of severe storms higher than ever before.
3 Many teenagers use every day the internet to communicate with friends.

228

Language Practice

LP 13 • Focus on Style

4 I download always the latest version of the program.
5 The author writes that America ignores all too often the rest of the world.
6 She points out in her latest book the decline of America's influence in the world.
7 This last point illustrates the author with an anecdote.
8 The summer months can be in some parts of Germany quite cool.

You already know that in some ways German and English sentences are formed differently. Here are some points to observe when you are writing English:

German	English
Dependent infinitives and participles are placed at the end of the sentence *(Satzklammer)*: *Er kann* hervorragend *Klavier spielen.* *Er hat* neulich in der Aula *ein Konzert gegeben.*	A 'cluster' instead of a 'bracket' is used, i.e. closely connected words (subject, verb, object) stay together: *He can play the piano* marvelously. *Recently* he gave a concert *in the school hall.*
The subject moves to third position if there is an adverbial phrase at the beginning of the sentence: *Im November 1989 / wurden / die Übergänge zwischen Ost- und Westberlin / überraschend freigegeben.*	The subject always comes before the verb; in other words, the word order (S–V) stays the same when an adverbial phrase is put at the beginning of the sentence: *In November 1989 /* the checkpoints between East and West Berlin */ were unexpectedly opened.*
Verb and object are often separated: *Thomas und Harald* spielen *jeden Mittwoch Tennis.*	Verb and object **must** stay together: *Thomas and Harald* play tennis *every Wednesday.*
Even if there is no two-part verb, Germans tend to form a 'bracket sentence': *Dies ist* in einigen Fällen *ein Problem.* In English the sentence would sound strange: *This is in some cases a problem.*	**TIP** Begin your sentences with an adverbial phrase. This helps you to avoid the monotony of sentences that all begin with the subject: *Friedman is an optimist in this respect.* → *In this respect, Friedman is an optimist.*

b Rearrange sentences in the following text to make it more idiomatic:

Thomas L. Friedman and Michael Mandelbaum collaborated on the book *That Used to Be Us*, which in 2011 was published. The authors point out using numerous examples how the US in global competition has fallen behind. America has lost sight according to the authors of its traditional strengths and values. The authors make in the second half of the book a number of suggestions as to what should be done. Some of these suggestions sounded to a few of the book's critics quite unrealistic. The book was in spite of its gloomy message an instant bestseller.

▶ LP 13 Placing emphasis on key points 🎧 CD3 07

a **BASIC** Listen to three short conversations, then match them to the following techniques:
1 The important words in the sentence are stressed, i.e. spoken louder than the others.
2 The emphatic do-form of the verb is used.
3 The important word is made the subject of the reply.

Listen to the audio file on the CD or download it here:
 Webcode context-00

LP Focus on Style • LP 13

Some of the techniques for emphasis that are used when speaking can also be used in written English; others sound rather formal in spoken English and are mainly used in writing:

Speaking/ Writing	Technique	Example
Speaking	Stressing the important words in the sentence, i.e. speaking them louder than the others	–
Speaking and writing	Using the emphatic *do*-form of the verb	I *do* think that's the wrong decision.
	Making the important word the subject of the reply	*Running* is the sport I love most.
Speaking (esp. in formal contexts) and writing	Special use of *very*	*Very* is used in English to modify words like *first* and *last:* In *the very first* scene of the film… • At *the very last* moment … It can also be used where in German you would use *gerade* or *genau* to emphasize something: *Gerade* die Anonymität des Internets … • *The very* anonymity of the internet …
	especially, in particular	Careful: Unlike *besonders*, you hardly ever find them at the beginning of a sentence: *Sitting still for 45 minutes can be a challenge, especially for young children.*
	Other expressions	German compound nouns like *Hauptgrund* or *Hauptfaktor* can be translated with *the main* reason, *the most important* factor etc. To emphasize that you are naming the most important item in a list of facts or arguments, use *above all* or *most importantly* to introduce your sentence.

b Now decide how you could reply emphatically to the following questions using one of the techniques in the table:
1 Do you like Indian cuisine? (You like some dishes, but not the really spicy ones.)
2 What would you like – apple juice or cola? (You choose.)
3 Didn't you read the novel over the weekend? (You didn't finish, but you read the first half.)
4 You're from Hamburg, right? (You went to school there, but you were born in Kiel.)

c Translate these sentences into English:
1 Die Hauptursache von Hass ist Angst.
2 Besonders in den Entwicklungsländern haben viele Menschen keinen Zugang zu sauberem Wasser.
3 Wir erreichten unser Flugzeug in allerletzter Minute.
4 Vor allem gibt es eine wachsende Kluft *(a widening gap)* zwischen den armen und den reichen Ländern.
5 Schon im ersten Satz macht der Autor seine Meinung deutlich.
6 Die Hauptsache ist wohl die, dass es genug qualifizierte Arbeitskräfte *(workers)* gibt.

Language Practice

LP 14 • Focus on Style   LP

In written English, there are ways of structuring a sentence so as to emphasize a certain word or words:

Technique	Example	Comment
Using a subordinate clause that points to the most important idea in the sentence	Ralph Nader first criticized the US automobile industry. → *It was* Ralph Nader *who* first criticized the US automobile industry. Society needs people who put the common good above personal gain. → *What society needs is* people who put the common good above personal gain.	Pay attention to the forms of *be* used in the examples; why are they both in the singular?
Using a negation (*never, nowhere, not once* etc.) or *only* + time phrase (e.g. *only later*) at the beginning of the sentence. The verb is put in the question form (inversion).	*Never before have young people had* so many opportunities. *Only then did she realize* her mistake.	This structure is common in political speeches.
Using contrast	It was greed and arrogance, *not simply bad timing*, that led to the collapse of the bank. *Unlike earlier SNS*, Facebook appealed to users of all age groups. *Compared with the US*, China lacks a culture of creative entrepreneurship.	

d Rewrite the sentences to make them more emphatic, using the techniques from the table above.
1 Shared values hold a society together.
2 China's economy is growing rapidly; that of the EU isn't.
3 It has never before been so easy to communicate with people around the globe.
4 Western countries need a vision that includes the rest of the world.
5 Not lack of ambition, but fear of failure holds most people back.

▶ LP 14 Linking words and phrases

a BASIC Complete the following text with suitable linking words or phrases from the choices below.

at the same time · for example · for one thing · furthermore · moreover · on the other hand · for instance

Are Americans environmentally friendly? There is no simple answer to this question. In a recent survey, … (1), 65% of American adults agreed that 'preserving the environment is very important.' … (2), 22% of consumers who remodeled their homes in the last 12 months said they had used environmentally friendly products for their renovation. … (3), data from the last five years indicate that consumers are now less willing to pay more or give up convenience for green products. … (4), the percentage of U.S. adults who agreed with the statement 'I am willing to give up convenience in return for a product that is environmentally safe' has declined 16% in the past five years, from 56% in 2007 to 47% in 2011.

… (5), there is definitely a trend among younger Americans toward more environmental awareness. … (6), consumers aged 18–24 are the only adult age group whose willingness to give up convenience or pay more for green products has held steady over the past five years. … (7), 53% of consumers aged 18–24 recycle products and 4% participated in environmental groups or causes in the past 12 months.

Statistics from: Bart King, 'American Environmentally Friendly Buying Habits', 6 April 2012

Language Practice   231

LP Focus on Style • LP 14

Linking words and phrases are the signposts of written and spoken communication; they help readers and listeners find their way through texts. Choosing the right phrases also helps you as a writer to think critically about the relationship between your sentences. The table below shows you a selection of useful phrases and their functions.

Use	Linking word or phrase
Stating your opinion	In my opinion … • To my mind … • I think/feel/believe that …
Listing facts, arguments, etc.	First of all … • Firstly … • For one thing, … Secondly … • Furthermore … • What is more, … • Besides … • In addition … • Moreover … Finally … • Above all … • Most importantly …
Giving an example	for example … • for instance … • such as …
Emphasizing	In fact, … • As a matter of fact, … • Actually, …
Contrasting	On the one hand … On the other hand … • However … • … though … • Nonetheless … • Whereas … • Although … • In spite of …
Conceding a point	Of course … • Naturally … • Admittedly …
Referring to a point in time or a development	At the/that time … • In those days … • Eventually … • In the course of … • In the long run … • Meanwhile … • At the same time … • As a result …
Coming to a conclusion	All in all … • In the final analysis … • In conclusion … • Ultimately … • For the reasons mentioned above … • To sum up … • To conclude … • I would like to conclude by saying …

b In the following text, linking words and phrases have been left out. Decide where such 'signposts' are missing and choose appropriate ones from the table above. Then write an improved version of the text.

Google wants to change the world – again

Google revolutionized the way we use the Web in the 1990s with a new kind of search engine. Now it wants to change the way we navigate physical space. The California firm has developed a small car that drives itself. The car is equipped with GPS and a host of sensors that collect information about the surroundings as it moves. There is a steering wheel and a brake (for emergencies), but the car is programmed to work without a human driver.

Google is not interested in going into the car business. The real purpose is to change how we think about mobility. Why should you buy a car if you can get one whenever you need or want it? You want to go downtown, you flip open your smartphone and call for an autonomous taxi. The vehicle drops you off at your destination, then goes on to its next job.

There would be less need for huge parking lots and parking garages. There would be fewer emissions as people waste less time cruising around looking for a parking space. People who are unable to drive (because of age, disability, or because they are drunk) could still get from one place to another. Self-driving cars would be a new form of public transportation. The way cities are designed would change.

There are still problems to be solved. Who is responsible when an autonomous vehicle is involved in an accident? Will people overcome their fear of losing control over their cars? What about the transition period when human and non-human drivers share the same roads? It is only a question of time until these issues have been settled. The future is coming, and Google wants to get there first.

232

Language Practice

LP 15 • Focus on Style   LP

▶ LP 15 Connecting your thoughts (sentence structure)

a **BASIC** Your partner has given you this text to proofread. Rewrite it to improve the style without leaving out any information.

Frank McCourt was born in Brooklyn, New York in 1930, which was the first year of the Great Depression. Both of his parents were immigrants from Ireland. They had come to America like millions of other Irish men and women who were looking for a better life. But they didn't find a better life, they only found poverty and misery. The McCourts, who were disappointed with life in America, decided to move back to Ireland. But their new life in Limerick, which was the hometown of Frank's mother, was no better than their life in Brooklyn. Young Frank had to leave school to support his family. He did odd jobs to earn a few pounds. After he had saved enough money for a ticket to New York, he left Ireland for good and didn't even tell his family.

Texts that contain unnecessary words or that connect ideas too loosely don't read well. A few simple techniques can help you make your sentences more compact and connected:

Loose connection		Stronger connection
Relative clause: *Frank McCourt was born in Brooklyn, New York in 1930, which was the first year of the Great Depression.*	→	**Apposition:** *Frank McCourt was born in Brooklyn, New York in 1930, the first year of the Great Depression.*
Relative clause: *They had come to America like millions of other Irish men and women who were looking for a better life.*	→	**Participle construction:** *They had come to America like millions of other Irish men and women looking for a better life.*
Compound sentence: *But they didn't find a better life, they only found poverty and misery.* *After he had saved enough money for a ticket to New York, he left Ireland for good and didn't even tell his family.*	→	**Gerund construction:** *But instead of finding a better life, they only found poverty and misery.* *After saving enough money for a ticket to New York, he left Ireland for good without even telling his family.*

Participle phrases can also be used instead of adverbial clauses with a variety of meanings:

Example	Function of participle construction
Arriving in New York, he looked for a cheap room.	Time (simultaneous action)
Having served in the Army during the Korean War, Frank was offered the chance to go to college.	Time (antecedent action)
Wanting to improve his status, he got a degree in English from NYU.	Reason
McCourt taught in New York schools for thirty years, never forgetting the bitter poverty he had experienced in Ireland.	Accompanying circumstance

b Rewrite the final paragraph of the text on Frank McCourt, using participle phrases in suitable places to improve the style.

After he had retired from teaching, McCourt began writing his memoires. They appeared in fictionalized form in 1996 as Angela's Ashes. The novel was a worldwide success and also won its author a Pulitzer Prize. McCourt looks back on his childhood in Limerick with irony and wit, and he describes how hard life was for poor Irish families in the 1930s and 40s. McCourt was amused at the unexpected success of his book and said that it was the first time in history that a man had become rich by writing about being poor.

Language Practice

Focus on Vocabulary

▶ LP 16 Avoiding Germanisms

a **BASIC** Each of the following sentences contains a 'typically German' mistake in red. Copy the sentences and correct the mistakes:
1 The plot of the film is *typical for* romantic comedies.
2 Jackie stepped into the corridor to *phone with* her lawyer.
3 Young people often use the internet to watch videos or *hear music*.
4 Music critics *wondered* when the single 'Thrift Shop' by a little-known rapper duo stormed the US charts in 2013.
5 We can *meet us* later in the city centre.
6 Some schools have introduced programmes to prevent *cybermobbing*.

German and English have much in common. This is often a help, but sometimes it is a source of confusion. The table below lists some common pitfalls:

	source of confusion	examples
a	similar word, different meaning	aktuell ≠ actual; eventuell ≠ eventual; Meinung ≠ meaning; spenden ≠ spend; sich wundern ≠ wonder
b	similar expression, different preposition	married **to** sb. = verheiratet **mit** jdm.; contact **with** sb. = Kontakt **zu** jdm.; example **of** sth. = Beispiel **für** etwas; typical of sb. = typisch **für** jdn.; do sth. **about** sth. = etwas **gegen** etwas tun
c	word-for-word translation of German phrase	~~hold~~/make a speech; ~~with 29 years~~/at the age of 29; on the one ~~side~~/hand; ~~make~~/take a photo; ~~hear~~/listen to music
d	verb used with/without a preposition	phone sb. = mit jdm. telefonieren; surf the internet = im Internet surfen; discuss sth. = über etwas diskutieren; comment on sth: = etwas kommentieren; discriminate against sb. = jdn. diskriminieren
e	Denglish used instead of English	~~beamer~~ (projector); ~~mobbing~~ (bullying); ~~handy~~ (mobile/cellphone); ~~boxes~~ (loudspeakers)
f	reflexive in German, non-reflexive in English	meet = sich treffen; identify with sb. = sich mit jdm. identifizieren; concentrate on sth. = sich auf etwas konzentrieren; feel = sich fühlen

b For each of the following sentences, decide which word is missing (if any). If you aren't sure, the letter in brackets will tell you where to look in the table.
1 People write letters to the editor when they want to express their ... (a)
2 The press secretary refused to comment ... the minister's decision. (d)
3 In a speech that he ... on March 4, Obama called for a new initiative on gun control. (c)
4 Jared is the only character in the novel that readers could possibly identify ... with. (f)
5 Some teens spend far too much time surfing ... the internet. (d)
6 The author names three examples ... the abuse of power by the present government. (b)
7 It's high time for the town council to do something ... this problem. (b)
8 To show the DVD in our classroom, we need a ... and a pair of ... as well as a laptop. (e)

LP 17–LP 18 • Focus on Vocabulary

▶ LP 17 Spelling

a BASIC Copy the words below, adding the missing letters. Careful: sometimes no letters are missing!

1 int■rested	5 mis■understanding	9 standar■	13 wel■fare
2 nec■essary	6 d■scribe	10 politic■an	14 consc■ous
3 happ■ly	7 public■ly	11 av■rage	15 desp■rate■
4 chara■ter	8 refer■ing	12 assist■nt	16 non-viol■nce

> Unfortunately, there are very few rules for English spelling. The best strategy is to keep track of the words that you frequently misspell and practice writing them, for example before exams.

b The following text is a student's essay on a British novel. There are ten spelling mistakes. Correct them:

Never Let Me Go by Kazuo Ishiguro is one of the best novels I have ever read. The autor tells the story from the point of view of Cathy, a young women, who reflects on her live as a student at a boarding school called Hailsham, and later as a so-called 'carer'. At first the reader thinks this is just an other story about adolesence, but as the novel progresses, we slowly realize that there is something special about the young people at Hailsham: as human as they appear to the reader, they are really clones who must donate their organs to others when they have reached maturity. Although they seem to know this, they don't really understand their situation, and each of them clings to the hope that somehow they will be allowd to live a bit longer then the others. The novel has also been adapted for the screen, and although I usualy avoid films based on books I love, I have to admit that this one is outstanding and succedes brillantly in capturing the spirit of the novel.

▶ LP 18 Writing about texts

There are many special expressions that you need when you write essays in German. The same is true of English. Knowing these phrases makes it easier for you to express yourself clearly.

a BASIC The table below contains German and English phrases for text analysis. Both lists are in alphabetical order. Copy the table, matching the German phrases and their English equivalents:

German	English
1 angesichts …	a according to …
2 auf den ersten Blick	b as a rule
3 bei näherer Betrachtung	c as for … / as far as … is concerned
4 in Bezug auf …	d at first sight
5 dabei (d.h., während man etwas tut)	e focus on …
6 im Allgemeinen	f in connection with …
7 im Gegensatz zu …	g in contrast to …

German	English
8 im Großen und Ganzen	h in general
9 im Zusammenhang mit …	i in the process
10 in der Regel	j in view of …
11 laut …	k on closer examination
12 seitens …	l on the part of …
13 was … betrifft	m on the whole
13 … auf den Punkt bringen	n put … in a nutshell
15 … in den Mittelpunkt stellen	o with regard to …

235

Language Practice

Focus on Vocabulary • LP 19

b Translate the following sentences into English with the help of your table:
1. Auf den ersten Blick hält man den Autor für einen Befürworter[1] der amerikanischen Umweltpolitik[2].
2. Bei näherer Betrachtung erkennt der Leser, dass er viele Dinge in den USA kritisch betrachtet.
3. Der Autor stellt die Auswirkungen der globalen Erwärmung in den Mittelpunkt.
4. Der Autor schildert die Folgen des Fracking in den USA; dabei macht er deutlich, dass er diese Technik ablehnt.
5. Angesichts der Umweltbelastung[3] kann der Leser ihm nur zustimmen.
6. Im Gegensatz zu den Amerikanern, die Fracking im Großen und Ganzen akzeptieren, sind die Deutschen skeptisch eingestellt[4].
7. Im letzten Absatz bringt der Autor das ganze Dilemma auf den Punkt.

▶ LP 19 Collocations

Verbs and nouns

a BASIC Choose the right verb for each of the sentences below:
1. Young people today sometimes find it hard to get/make a living in a tight job market.
2. Sam's teachers urged him to give/pay more attention to his school work.
3. The girls apologized to their victim, saying that they hadn't meant to do/make any harm.
4. The journalist calls/attracts attention to the problems in the region.
5. We think our school should make/set a good example by banning plastic tableware from the canteen.
6. The storm made/did considerable damage on its way northward.

> In English as well as in German, certain nouns are used together with certain verbs, e.g. you can only *take* (not ~~make~~) a *photo* in English. These 'natural pairs' are called collocations. Knowing the most common ones will help you avoid mistakes. The table below contains a selection of verb-noun collocations:

call attention (to sth.)	do damage	meet expectations	set an example
change your mind	exert influence (on sb.)	pay attention (to sb.)	take measures
commit a crime	make a living	put pressure on sb.	take offence (at sth.)
do justice to sth.	make history	put sth. to a vote	take a photo (of sb./sth.)
do good/harm	make an impression	reach an agreement	tell the truth/a lie

b Complete the following sentences with the missing verb. All collocations are from the table above:
1. Did the hotel … your expectations?
2. The only way we'll ever … an agreement is to … the matter to a vote.
3. Yesterday, history was … as government officials and rebel leaders met for direct talks.
4. As a member of the Board of Overseers she still … considerable influence on University policy.
5. It is important to … a good impression when you go for a job interview.
6. To my mind the film doesn't … justice to the novel.
7. The management … pressure on the workers to accept a pay cut.
8. The police agreed that further measures should be … to stop young people from … crimes.

---

[1] **Befürworter** supporter   [2] **Umweltpolitik** environment policy   [3] **Umweltbelastung** negative environmental impact
[4] **skeptisch eingestellt** sceptical

Language Practice

LP 19 • Focus on Vocabulary

LP

Adjectives and nouns

c BASIC The grey boxes on the right contain adjectives and nouns that form collocations. Form matching pairs and use them to complete the sentences:

1 Let's step outside and get some … …
2 The firm finally agreed to the protesters' demands to avoid further … …
3 The Declaration of Independence names 'life, liberty and the pursuit of happiness' as basic … …
4 Listen, everybody! I just had a … …
5 The hurricane caused … … all along the coast.
6 African Americans have fought a long battle for … …
7 I can't believe how … Tamira's … are.
8 Don't make jokes about veggie burgers – Katrina has very … … about animal rights.
9 This boarding school has very … …, and all students are expected to obey them.
10 I wasn't surprised when Steve was chosen for the scholarship – I've always had a … … of his character.

bright	*air*
equal	*damage*
fresh	*feelings*
heavy	*idea*
high	*opinion*
human	*parents*
negative	*publicity*
strict (2x)	*rights (2x)*
strong	*rules*

> Some adjectives 'belong together' with certain nouns, forming a new 'compound noun': *a human being, fair play, real life*. Others are frequently used together and form a collocation (*hard work, poor health*). Knowing common adjective-noun collocations will help you avoid mistakes and express yourself more idiomatically.

d What adjective(s) could you use to describe each of the following nouns? Write down your ideas first, then check them with the help of a monolingual dictionary (look at the usage examples):

1 burden	3 example	5 rise	7 topic	9 price
2 conscience	4 gesture	6 treatment	8 argument	10 working conditions

e Use five of your collocations in sentences that illustrate their meaning, e.g. *In Germany, fracking is a very controversial topic*.

Prepositions

f BASIC Choose the correct preposition for each of the numbered gaps in the following sentences:

I agree (1) the author that it is high time to do something (2) the problem of toxic waste. We can't just turn our backs (3) the problem or wait (4) industry to take the initiative. Everyone who is worried (5) the future of life (6) this planet should get involved (7) a campaign (8) toxic waste. Photos (9) young children playing on heaps of toxic rubbish in India or other countries can easily be found (10) the internet or (11) newspapers and magazines. No one can look (12) such photos without feeling their own responsibility (13) the present situation.

> Many common expressions in English include a preposition. You can't learn them all, but the more you know, the fewer mistakes you will make. If you aren't certain which preposition to use with a certain word, look at the example sentences under the corresponding headword in a monolingual dictionary.

g Use a dictionary to find out which preposition(s) can be used with each of the following words:

1 a lack … something	6 appeal … something	11 remind someone … something
2 a novel written … someone	7 be critical … something	12 struggle … a goal
3 accuse someone … something	8 blame someone … something	13 sympathize … someone
4 allude … something	9 contribute … something	14 take a look … something
5 an attempt … something	10 good … sth.	15 thank someone … something

Language Practice

237

LP Focus on Vocabulary · LP 20

▶ LP 20 Word formation

Prefixes

a **BASIC** In the table below, match the prefixes to the correct meanings.

meaning	prefix(es)
1 against sth.	a multi-
2 for sth., in favour of sth.	b pseudo-
3 having two (sides, aspects etc.)	c re-
4 having only one	d pre-
5 having or connected with several	e anti- counter- neo-
6 not	
7 no longer	f semi-
8 done badly or wrongly	g ex-
9 one of two	h pro-

meaning	prefix(es)
10 new	i non- dis-
11 happening before sth.	j mono-
12 happening after sth.	k co-
13 again, for the second time	l bi-
14 not really	m post-
15 referring to or done by yourself	n ultra-
16 only half, not completely	o mis-
17 extremely	p self-

Adding a prefix to an existing word changes the meaning without influencing the grammatical class: *un + able → unable*. Knowing the meaning of prefixes can help you to understand words you have never seen before.
Some of the prefixes (especially anti-, non-, self-, neo- and pseudo-) are often separated from their root word with a hyphen: anti-aircraft, neo-Colonial etc.). But as there are no fixed rules for English spelling, it is best to check your dictionary to be sure.

b Use a prefix from the list above to create an expression that matches each of the following definitions.
Example: strong belief in your own abilities: *self-confidence*

1 a film that presents war in a negative light
2 a measure that produces the opposite of the intended effect
3 a former husband
4 one of the two captains of a team
5 a theory that pretends to be scientific but isn't
6 discover sth. for the second time, e.g. in later life
7 a person who is not a resident of the country they are staying in
8 interpret sth. the wrong way
9 an organization that operates in several countries
10 a worker who has some qualifications but fewer than a skilled worker
11 Germany after the war
12 having two poles

Suffixes

a **BASIC** Copy the table below and sort the words on the right into groups. Underline the suffixes.

nouns	verbs	adjectives

apparition · certify · complicity · egalitarian · enactment · furious · hypothesize · identical · laudable · marital · notification · obligatory · supportive

238 **Language Practice**

LP 20 • Focus on Vocabulary

Like German, English can form a new word by adding a suffix to an existing root: *present* + *-able* → *presentable*. Since the suffix determines whether the word is a noun, verb or adjective, recognizing common suffixes can help you figure out the meanings of unfamiliar words. You probably haven't seen any of the words in the box above before, but the suffixes give you information about what they mean.

b Drawing on your knowledge of English as well as other languages, make an intelligent guess as to the meaning of each word. When you have finished, check your answers using a dictionary.

Word families

a BASIC The table below contains words related to each other. Copy the table and fill in the blanks, using a dictionary if necessary. Make sure you know the meanings of all the words:

verb	noun	adjective	noun
act	(1)	active	activity
create	creation	(2)	creativity
depend (on)	(3)	dependent/dependable	dependability
rely (on)	reliance	reliable	(4)
select	selection	(5)	selectivity
compare	comparison	(6)	comparability
tolerate	(7)	tolerable	tolerability
adapt (to)	adaptation	adaptable	(8)
criticize	(9)	critical	…
destroy	(10)	destructive	destructiveness

b Use words from the table to rewrite the underlined parts of the following sentences. You may have to change the word order or add words in some cases:

Example: Meteorologists underestimated <u>how destructive Hurricane Ivor would be</u>.
→ Meteorologists underestimated the destructiveness of Hurricane Ivor.

1 We've had enough of speech-making; now is the time <u>to act</u>.
2 The author claims that classical music and popular music <u>can't be compared</u>.
3 All children <u>have a natural creativity</u>.
4 Gerald quit his job in India because <u>he could not tolerate</u> his working conditions.
5 Our firm expects all employees <u>to be reliable</u>.
6 <u>The fact that our country is dependent</u> on foreign oil and gas is a serious issue.
7 While doing her gap year in Uganda, Shirin demonstrated <u>how well she can adapt</u>.
8 The so-called Ivy League universities in the US are said to <u>select their students very carefully</u>.

Princeton, an Ivy League university

Everyday English

EE 1 Eating in and out .... 240 Fact File: Eating out – American style .... 240 EE 2 Planning a trip using the internet 241	EE 3 Dealing with medical emergencies .... 242 Fact File: Getting medical assistance 242	EE 4 Making phone calls .... 243 EE 5 Watch your valuables! 244

▶ EE 1 Eating in and out

Eating customs often vary from culture to culture and knowing a few basics can come in handy while abroad.

a TABLE TALK In what situation might someone use each of the following expressions?
1 Thanks, I'm fine.
2 Just help yourself.
3 It's delicious, but I'm full.
4 Could you pass the … please?
5 This has been a wonderful meal!
6 Could I have some more, please?

You can also find your role cards here:
 Webcode context-00

b ROLE-PLAY Use the phrases from part **a** and the role cards your teacher gives you to act out a short dialogue.

■ FACT FILE

Eating out: American style

In sit-down restaurants in the United States where you are served at your table, there are a few customs that you should be aware of that are different from those in Europe:
- 'Please wait to be seated', is posted near the entrance in many restaurants. You are expected to wait before seating yourself (even if the restaurant is completely empty!). Someone from the staff (a host or hostess) will probably ask how many are in your 'party' (ex: 'Just the two of you?' or 'How many are in your group?'), and either take you to a table or ask for your name so that they can call you when your table is ready.
- 'Designing your own meal' with your choice of meat and vegetable from the menu is not uncommon in the USA. A typical dish could be, for example, a sirloin steak with a choice of vegetable or side-salad and potatoes cooked in a specific way. Examine the menu and make your selection so that you are ready to order when the server arrives.
- 'Would you like a refill?' is a typical phrase in American restaurants. Most restaurants offer free refills of at least coffee and soft drinks. The server exchanges your empty glass for a full one or refills your glass at your table. Tap water (usually with ice cubes) is provided for free.
- A 'service charge' is usually not included on the bill. Servers are not well paid in most regions of the USA and a tip of 15–20% is expected. You can either leave a cash tip on the table or, if paying with a credit card, there will be a place on the bill where you can add a tip to the total.

In groups of 4–5, write and act out a short theatrical scene that takes place in an American restaurant. Use the information above and the vocabulary below to help you.

■ TIP

Soft drinks are called different things in different parts of the USA. As a general rule:
On the East and West Coasts: **soda**
In the Midwest: **pop**
In the South: **coke**
(even for soft drinks that are not Coca Cola)

■ TROUBLE SPOT
Ger. *Menü* ≠ Eng. **menu**

■ TROUBLE SPOT
entrée (BE) ≠ *entrée* (AE)

Some useful terms			
main dish entrée (AE)	*Hauptgericht*	menu	*Speisekarte*
entrée, starter (BE) appetizer (AE)	*Vorspeise*	four-course dinner / meal	*Vier-Gang-Menü*
side dish, side order	*Beilage*	tip	*Trinkgeld*
dessert sweet (BE), afters (BE, *infml*)	*Nachspeise*	VAT (BE) sales tax (AE)	*Mehrwertsteuer*
bill, check (AE) cheque (BE)	*Rechnung*	tap water	*Leitungswasser*

Skills File

EE 2 • Everyday English

▶ EE 2 Planning a trip using the internet

The internet is a handy tool for making travel plans. You can book travel arrangements and hotel accommodations, find out information about museums and other places of interest, order food and make restaurant reservations, as well as even reserve concert, theatre or movie tickets.
Imagine your class is planning a week-long trip to London. You will be in the city from Monday to Friday. Form three groups (A, B, C). Each group has its own planning task.

Group A: Getting around in London
Explore the options for public transport during your stay. London offers a variety of tickets with different prices and conditions. It might be helpful to know how many students there are in your class and their ages.
- Split your group into 3–4 smaller groups. Each of the mini-groups explores one option and presents it to the rest of the class.
- Consult relevant websites to find out what options are available, what conditions are attached to their use, and how much they would cost. Calculate the total cost for the group.

Find links to helpful websites here:
Webcode context-00

Group B: A day trip to Greenwich
While in London, your class wants to take a day trip to Greenwich. How will you get there? The closest station to your hotel is Bayswater Tube Station.
- Consider all possibilities (train/underground, boat, foot tunnel under the Thames, Docklands Light Railway, etc.)
- Divide your group into 3 mini-groups. Each mini-group puts together a different suggestion for travelling to and from Greenwich. Take into account what points of interest different travel options might offer along the way.
- What is the total price for the group (assuming that the group can travel the Tube at no extra cost)?

Find links to websites of interest here:
Webcode context-00

Group C: The Royal Museums Greenwich
The Royal Museums Greenwich (RMG) is made up of a complex of buildings and sites of historical, architectural and scientific interest.
- What does the RMG consist of? Use the internet to explore the various possibilities.
- Divide your group into 3 mini-groups. Each mini-group puts together a different suggestion for a visit to the RMG.
- What can you see and do? When and where? How much does it cost for your group?
- Are there adequate food options available there for a group of your size?

Find links to help start your search here:
Webcode context-00

Some useful terms			
peak (hours etc.)	Spitzenzeiten	fare	Fahrpreis
entry (to a building etc.)	Zutritt	swipe card	Magnetstreifenkarte
opening hours	Öffnungszeiten	vending machine	(Verkaufs-)Automat
admission (fee)	Eintritt(spreis)	destination	(Reise-)Ziel
exhibition	Ausstellung	venue	(Veranstaltungs-)Ort
surcharge	Aufschlag	closure	Schließzeit
concession/discount	Ermäßigung	pay-as-you-go credit	Prepaid-Guthaben

▬ FACT FILE
Greenwich ['grenɪtʃ], a district of South East London, is on 0° Longitude (Prime or Greenwich Meridian) and sets the global time standard (Greenwich Mean Time).

Skills File
241

EE Everyday English • EE 3

▶ **EE 3 Dealing with medical emergencies**   CD3 08

A medical emergency can happen anywhere. The cause can be an accident or a sudden illness. Before you go abroad, make sure you have health insurance coverage[1] for your country of destination. Travel medical insurance[2] is inexpensive and covers all medical expenses during a brief foreign stay.

FACT FILE

Getting medical assistance
In the event of an emergency, call 999 (UK), 911 (USA) or 000 (Australia). From mobile phones, the number 112 will also connect you with the emergency services in many countries.
Hospital: If you or someone else needs medical help, consult a physician/doctor or go to the outpatient clinic[3] of the nearest hospital, where you can be treated without being admitted to the hospital[4].
Pharmacy: In the UK and the US, shops that sell medicine are called pharmacies, drugstores (US) or chemist's (UK). They offer a wider range of products than a German *Apotheke*, including cosmetics, health and beauty products, and sometimes travel essentials.
Prescriptions: Medicine that has been prescribed by a doctor is dispensed at the pharmacy counter within the shop. In the US, you are given the exact dosage prescribed by the doctor. If, for example, your prescription says three capsules daily for five days, you will be given 15 capsules in a small bottle, not the original package.

TROUBLE SPOT
ärztliches Rezept = **prescription**
Kochrezept = **recipe** ['resəpi]

A group of students in the eighth class at your school are about to go on their first exchange to the UK. Prepare an informative and funny two-minute talk for them in English on medical assistance abroad.

a In the event that you need medical help, it is important that you understand the doctor's questions and can give precise answers. Test your knowledge by matching the English words to their German equivalents.

1	abdomen	11	have a temperature	a	allergisch	k	Schnittwunde
2	allergic	12	headache	b	Bauch, Unterleib	l	Schürfwunde
3	bowel movement	13	nausea [nɔːziə]	c	Durchfall	m	Schwindel
4	bruise [bruːz]	14	numb	d	Fieber haben	n	sich übergeben
5	congested	15	scrape	e	Halsschmerzen	o	Stuhlgang
6	constipated	16	shiver	f	Husten	p	taub
7	cough [kɒf]	17	sore throat	g	Impfung	q	Übelkeit
8	cut	18	stomach ache [eɪk]	h	Kopfschmerzen	r	verschnupft
9	diarrhoea [daɪəriə]	19	vaccination	i	Magenschmerzen	s	verstopft
10	dizziness	20	vomit	j	Prellung	t	zittern

b Sabine is staying with her host family in the USA. She isn't feeling well and her host parents take her to the doctor. Listen to the dialogue and answer the questions.
  1 How does Sabine describe her symptoms?
  2 What information does Dr Felter want from her?
  3 What does Dr Felter give her?

Listen to the audio file on the CD or download it here:
 Webcode context-00

c ROLE-PLAY **Partner A** is cycling near Bristol with his or her British host-brother, Toby. All of a sudden, Toby hits a hole in the road and falls off his bike. He is badly hurt. Phone for help! **Partner B** will be the person taking calls for emergency services in the Bristol area. Your teacher will give you role cards.

You can also find your role cards here:
 Webcode context-00

---
[1] **health insurance coverage** *Krankenversicherungsschutz*   [2] **travel medical insurance** *Auslandskrankenversicherung*
[3] **outpatient clinic** *Ambulanz*   [4] **admit to the hospital** *stationär aufnehmen*

EE 4 • Everyday English

▶ EE 4 Making phone calls

Talking on the telephone has become less common in the age of text messages, but there are still situations in which it is unavoidable. The box below lists example phrases that can be used when talking on the phone.

a Match the phrases from the box below to the following typical situations:
1. You phone a number and say who you are.
2. You explain why you are calling.
3. You answer the phone.
4. You are not the intended recipient of the call.
5. You ask for clarification.
6. You want to end the conversation and hang up.

a	Hello. My name is Lisa Weber. I'm calling from Cologne in Germany.	k	I think you've dialed the wrong number.
b	The reason I'm calling is …	l	I'm calling about the advert you posted …
c	I'm sorry, I didn't catch that. Could you repeat your name please?	m	Thank you for returning my call / Thanks for getting back to me. *(infml)*
d	May I ask why you are calling?	n	Good afternoon. Caroline Schlegel speaking.
e	Can I take a message?	o	Could you spell that, please?
f	It was nice talking with you.	p	I have a problem, could you connect me with Customer Services, please?
g	Good morning. This is Max Kunze in Dresden, Germany.	q	Robert Peters here. What can I do for you?
h	I'm afraid she isn't here. Would you like her to call you back?	r	Sorry, the line is busy. Would you like to speak to someone else?
i	I'd like to speak to …	s	Mr Adams tried to reach me while I was out. I'm returning his call.
j	May I ask who's calling, please?	t	Thank you for your call.

b ROLE-PLAY Work together with a partner. Use the information on the role cards your teacher gives you to carry out a conversation on the phone.

Some useful terms	
line	Leitung
engaged (BE), busy (AE)	besetzt
dial a number	eine Nummer wählen
answer the phone	einen Anruf entgegennehmen
return sb.'s call, get back to sb.	jem. zurückrufen
hold	in der Leitung bleiben
put sb. through (to sb.)	jem. (zu jem.) durchstellen
hang up	auflegen

You can also find your role cards here:
 Webcode context-00

Everyday English
243

Everyday English • EE 5

▶ EE 5 Watch your valuables!

When staying abroad, whether on holiday or as part of an exchange programme, you will need money. There are different ways of taking money abroad.

a Match the lettered boxes to their corresponding method of taking or accessing money abroad.

Money Management Methods:
1 a bank card / debit card (AE)
2 a credit card
3 traveller's cheques
4 cash

A
- must be exchanged for local currency
- no way of preventing a thief from using it

B
- equivalent to the German 'ec-Karte'
- can be used to withdraw cash at an ATM[5] (cash machine or 'hole in the wall' in the UK) or to pay for goods and services in many countries as long as it has the Maestro symbol

C
- can be used to pay bills in many hotels and restaurants without a PIN
- can sometimes be used with the PIN to withdraw cash from an ATM
- common brands accepted worldwide are: Visa, MasterCard and American Express.

D
- must be bought before you leave home
- can be cashed in any bank during opening hours

[5] **ATM** *Geldautomat*

Plastic money is very practical, but use caution:
- Before you travel, check whether your bank at home has a partnership with a bank where you're staying abroad. It might be cheaper for you to use that bank to withdraw cash.
- In many countries, ATMs are not inside banks, but on the walls outside. For safety reasons, try to use an ATM in a well-lit area or inside the bank building.
- Make sure nobody can see the number keys while you are entering your PIN.
- Be aware that there will probably be a fee every time you withdraw cash from a foreign ATM.

If your card is lost or stolen, take immediate action:
- Make sure you know how to reach your bank and/or credit card company in case you need to block or cancel your card. (The phone number can change depending on where you are traveling.)
- Phone and have the card blocked as soon as you realize your card is lost or stolen.
- Report the theft to the local police.

b ROLE-PLAY Oh, no! You have been robbed! Report the theft to the local police. Use role cards from your teacher and the vocabulary in the box below for your dialogue.

You can also find your role cards here:
 Webcode context-00

Some useful terms			
wallet	Portemonnaie	bank card, debit card	ec-Karte
purse	Geldbörse	have your card blocked / canceled	deine Karte sperren lassen
cash	Bargeld	suspicious [sə'spɪʃəs] behavior / persons	auffälliges Verhalten / Personen
pickpocket	Taschendieb	report a crime etc. (to the police)	eine Straftat usw. anzeigen

Communicating across Cultures

CC 1 Cultural awareness 245
CC 2 The language of politeness . . . 246
CC 3 Polite behaviour 247
CC 4 Meeting and greeting 247
CC 5 Making small talk 248
CC 6 Talking about sensitive issues . 248
      Fact File: Political correctness . 249
CC 7 Making polite complaints 249

▶ CC 1 Cultural awareness

Like a fish out of water: A fish doesn't know what water is – until the water suddenly isn't there anymore. Likewise, we often take the culture we grow up with for granted – customs, body language, how people interact in everyday situations – and don't really notice it while it surrounds us. As a result, experiencing different cultures can open our eyes to aspects of our own culture as well as give us insight into ways other people behave.

a Put yourself in each of the following situations and choose the reaction that comes the closest to your own.
   1 A crowded cafeteria at lunchtime. You have been waiting patiently for the last ten minutes. Someone comes into the room, spots a gap near the front of the queue and jumps in.
     a You look away and say nothing.
     b You grumble to your neighbor, 'So selfish!'
     c You shout out loud, 'Hey you! Go to the back of the queue!'
   2 While waiting at the bus stop, you see an exchange student who is in one of your courses. He or she comes over to chat and stops about thirty centimetres in front of you (try it out with a partner, using a ruler to measure the distance between the tips of your noses).
     a You take a step backward.
     b You turn a bit to the side to avoid facing the other student directly.
     c You stand your ground and look the other person directly in the eye.
   3 You get a note from a guidance counselor asking you to come to her office after school. When you arrive, the door is half open; the counselor is working at her desk.
     a You walk in, say hello and sit down opposite her.
     b You stand in the doorway and say, 'You wanted to see me.'
     c You knock lightly on the door and say, 'Excuse me, may I interrupt you?'

b In groups of not more than three, compare your reactions to the situations in exercise **a** and your reasons for choosing them. Discuss the following points:
   • How do you feel about (not) playing by the rules?
   • How close is too close – when do you feel that someone is invading your personal space?
   • What does eye contact signify?
   • What does an open (or closed) door mean?
Compare your views and decide which forms of behaviour you think are typical in your society.

Communicating across Cultures

CC2 The language of politeness

a People don't always say what they really mean; sometimes they even say the opposite:

To a certain degree, understatement and exaggeration are part of national culture. Americans tend to be highly enthusiastic ('Fantastic!' – 'I'd love to!' – 'I'm dying to meet him!'), whereas the British are more reserved in their way of expressing themselves ('I'm afraid we've got a bit of a problem.'). These are, of course, just generalizations, as each person has their own style.

In conversations, always try to be friendly and polite, but remember that polite phrases cannot always be taken literally. The list on the left in the table below shows some polite phrases you might hear, especially in the UK. First, decide what you think they mean, then choose the 'translation' from the list on the right.

1 That's not bad.	a I'm just being polite.
2 I wouldn't mind.	b I'm very annoyed.
3 Very original work.	c I expect you to read it.
4 You must come over for dinner.	d I'd love to.
5 I was a bit disappointed that …	e That's really good.
6 You might want to have a look at it.	f I expect you to apologize.
7 I'm sure it was my mistake.	g Hopeless stuff.

b The table below contains polite phrases that can be used in everyday situations. Match them, then use one or two of the matching pairs to write a short dialogue (with a partner, if you prefer):

1 Would you mind if I borrowed one of these? I can't find mine.	a Great idea! I'd love to!
2 Sorry, I didn't know …	b Sure, come in and have a seat.
3 Thanks a lot!	c Certainly. Here you are.
4 Is it all right with you if I …?	d I'll have to think about that.
5 Could I bother you for a minute?	e Sure, help yourself.
6 Would it be possible for me to …?	f That's all right. Don't worry about it.
7 We were wondering if you would be interested in …	g You're very welcome.
8 Could I get a …, please?	h Of course. Feel free.

CC 3–CC 4 • Communicating across Cultures

► CC 3 Polite behaviour

Leon is an exchange student in the USA. Read the following descriptions of everyday situations and decide whether he breaks any rules of polite behaviour. Then discuss your reactions in a group. Have you experienced similar situations? Why do you feel that certain behaviour is polite or impolite?

> *Compare your views with additional comments here:*
> 🖐 **Webcode** context-00

1 Leon meets his host parents and host brother, Matt, for the first time. He offers them his hand in greeting.
2 Leon calls his host parents 'Frank' and 'Brenda'.
3 At his American home, Leon always keeps his bedroom door shut.
4 Leon and Matt are watching TV when Matt's grandparents enter the room. Leon stays seated.
5 It's dinner time and Leon is very hungry. He starts eating as soon as he has something on his plate.
6 Leon can't follow the conversation at the dinner table, so he starts playing games on his smartphone.

► CC 4 Meeting and greeting

a The phrases below can be used in different social situations: when you meet someone for the first time, when you meet a friend on the street, or when you want to end a conversation. Copy the table below and put the phrases from the list in the correct column (some can be used more than once).

1 Fine thanks. And you?
2 Hi, how's it going? (infml)
3 Hi, nice to meet you. (infml)
4 How are things going? (infml)
5 How do you do? (fml)
6 Sorry, I've got to run. (infml)
7 I'd like you to meet XY.

8 It's been wonderful talking to you.
9 Not too bad. What about you? (infml)
10 (I'm very) Pleased to meet you.
11 Thanks, and the same to you!
12 See you later. (infml)
13 Bye now. Take care! (infml)
14 Have a good time!

Meeting someone for the first time	Meeting someone you know	Saying goodbye

b Select an appropriate response from your table for each of the following situations:

1 You work for an organization that employs mostly young people. Your supervisor brings a new colleague over to meet you and says: 'Hi Rebecca, this is James, our new trainee.' You say:
2 You see a co-worker in the hallway. She says: 'Hi, how are things going?' You say:
3 Going back to your office, you see your supervisor talking to an older woman. He calls you over and says: 'Rebecca, I'd like you to meet our regional coordinator, Deirdre O'Connor.' You say:
4 After Ms O'Connor has asked you a couple of questions about your job, you want to end the conversation and go back to work. You say:
5 You drive a friend to the train station. As he gets out of the car, he says: 'See you later!' You say:
6 You're a bit late for work when you run into an old friend. When she starts telling you all about her new boyfriend, you make it clear that you're in a hurry and say:
7 On the last day of work before the holidays, a co-worker waves to you as you are leaving and calls out: 'Have a good break!' You say:

> ■ TIP
> • 'How do you do?' isn't really a question; it is just a very formal way of saying 'Nice to meet you'.
> • When someone asks 'How are you?', they usually don't want a medical update. Just say 'Fine, thanks' or 'Not too bad, thanks'.

Communicating across Cultures • CC 5–CC 6

▶ CC 5 Making small talk 🎧 CD3 09

Small talk is an art. That means that some people are, by nature, better at it than others. However, everybody can work on their skills and practice developing them.

a Listen to two short conversations and describe the differences between them. Why is one more successful than the other?

Listen to the audio file on the CD or download it here:
Webcode context-00

b The list below contains tips for making small talk. In each tip, one or more phrases is missing. Complete the tips with phrases from the box on the right:
1 Stand roughly at arm's length from your partner and … while you are talking.
2 Choose a topic that involves something you and your partner … (e.g., social or regional background, personal experiences, present situation, the weather, etc.).
3 Don't ask any questions that you wouldn't …
4 Avoid … ('Do you like sport?'); use … instead ('What's your favourite sport'?).
5 Give your partner the opportunity to talk about him- or herself before you make a comment or …
6 Encourage your partner to … by interjecting remarks such as 'That's really interesting!' or 'Wow! That must have been awesome!'.
7 Pay attention to the silences; they may be a sign that your conversation is …
8 Phrases like 'It's been great talking to you' or 'We'll have to continue this conversation some other time' can help you to … elegantly.

a	change the subject
b	keep talking
c	have in common
d	end the conversation
e	coming to a natural end
f	open questions
g	look them in the eye
h	want to answer
i	'yes-or-no' questions

c **ROLE-PLAY** You meet someone new at a youth hostel in Germany. Use the role cards your teacher gives you to guide your conversation with a partner.

You can also find your role cards here:
Webcode context-00

d Choose a new partner and practice making small talk without the help of role cards. Try to keep your conversation going for at least two minutes.

▶ CC 6 Talking about sensitive issues 🎧 CD3 10

Which topics are considered sensitive and which are absolutely taboo varies from culture to culture. A good indicator is humour: which topics do people make jokes about? Which do they seem to avoid? (Watching comedy shows on TV can tell you a lot about social norms.)

a Imagine you are going to the USA for a year. Rank the 10 topics below on a scale from 1 (harmless) to 10 (taboo) as discussion topics. Compare lists with your partner or in a group and discuss your reasons.

food preferences • sports • patriotism • gun control • religion and church-going • parents' jobs • politics • race relations • career goals • America's role in the world

b Leon, a German exchange student, is asked by his social studies teacher about his impressions of life in the USA. Listen to two different versions of the story and make notes on the differences. How is the tone of the conversation affected by the way Leon responds?

Listen to the audio file on the CD or download it here:
Webcode context-00

CC7 • Communicating across Cultures

FACT FILE

Political correctness
In the mid-20th century in the USA, political correctness became an important topic when minority groups criticized how people spoke about them as a form of discrimination. Other groups soon followed suit.

Racial minorities: During the Civil Rights Movement, African-Americans rejected names such as 'negro' or 'colored' that identified them on the basis of skin colour. They preferred the term 'African-American', which was similar to traditional terms such as 'Irish-American' or 'Italian-American'. (Note: Today, it is also acceptable to use the adjective 'black'.) American Indians often want to be called 'Native Americans' or 'First Nations Peoples', and the indigenous peoples of Canada and Alaska prefer to be called 'Inuit' or 'Alaska Natives' instead of 'Eskimos'.

Gender: There are various job titles in English that refer only to the male (or, less often, to the female) gender: postman (AE: mailman), salesman, actress, stewardess, etc. Such terms have generally been replaced by gender-neutral ones: 'the chair' (instead of 'chairman/chairwoman'), postal carrier (AE: mail carrier), salesperson, flight attendant, etc.

Health: Certain terms used to refer to health issues are sometimes regarded as discriminatory, as they can suggest that there is something inherently wrong with people. People who are physically handicapped should be referred to as 'physically disabled' and mentally challenged people have 'special needs', 'learning disabilities' or are 'intellectually impaired'. Other politically correct terms would be, for example, 'vision impaired' for the blind or 'hearing impaired' for the deaf.

Think of other politically correct terms that are used in German. Can you find the English equivalents?

▶ CC7 Making polite complaints CD3 11, 12 and 13

Travelling abroad is always complicated, and mix-ups and misunderstandings can easily happen. The important thing is to stay calm and, if necessary, get competent help as quickly as possible.

a Michaela Börner from Düsseldorf is spending a year abroad in North Carolina. When she arrives at the airport in Charlotte, her host family is waiting for her. Listen to the dialogue. What phrases do they use to greet each other? What questions have to be resolved before they can communicate easily?

b At the baggage claim, Michaela and her host family wait for Michaela's suitcase. Listen to the sound file and identify the English words for the following terms:

1 Förderband   2 Gepäckstück   3 Haupthalle   4 Schalter   5 zurückbekommen

*Listen to the audio files on the CD or download the audio files that correspond to exercises **a**, **b** and **c** here:*
Webcode context-00

c Michaela and her host family go to the baggage services office. Listen to the sound file. Write down the English equivalents of the following expressions:

1 Kann ich Ihnen behilflich sein?
2 Darf ich bitte …?
3 Ist das so richtig?
4 Ihr Ärger ist verständlich.
5 Sie dürfen sich jederzeit an uns wenden.
6 Wäre es vielleicht möglich, dass unser Gast …
7 Sie waren sehr hilfreich.
8 Gern geschehen.

d When you encounter a situation for the first time, you may be confronted with vocabulary you haven't heard before. Here is a short list of words that Michaela had trouble understanding. Just as Amanda would have tried to help Michaela, try explaining in English what the following terms mean.

1 baggage receipt   2 written confirmation   3 toll-free number   4 reimbursement

e ROLE-PLAY Waiting at the airport baggage claim, you see your suitcase coming down the belt. Read the role card your teacher gives you and act out the scene with your partner.

You can also find your role cards here:
 Webcode context-00

Skills File

Language and study skills
SF 1 Dealing with unknown words **P** 250
SF 2 Learning new words 251
SF 3 Using a dictionary **P** 252
SF 4 Using a grammar book **P** 253
SF 5 Doing research **P** 253
SF 6 Doing project work 254
SF 7 Making visual aids **P** 255
SF 8 Structuring ideas 256
SF 9 Paraphrasing **P** 256
SF 10 Working with closed test formats 257

Text skills
SF 11 Analysing pictures **P** 258
SF 12 Analysing charts and graphs **P** 259
SF 13 Analysing cartoons **P** 261
SF 14 Reading strategies **P** 263

P A task allows you to practise the skill.

SF 15 Marking up a text / Making and taking notes 264
SF 16 Identifying text types (non-fiction) 265
SF 17 Analysing stylistic devices . . . 266
SF 18 Analysing non-fiction 268
SF 19 Analysing narrative prose. . . . 269
SF 20 Analysing drama 271
SF 21 Analysing poetry 273

Listening and viewing skills
SF 22 Listening 275
SF 23 Analysing a film 276

Speaking skills (monologues and dialogues)
SF 24 Giving a presentation 278
SF 25 Giving a speech **P** 280
SF 26 Taking part in an interview **P** . 282
SF 27 Having a discussion 282
SF 28 Having a debate 284

Writing skills
SF 29 Writing a formal letter or email 286
SF 30 Writing an application **P** 287
SF 31 Writing a summary **P** 289
SF 32 Writing a review **P** 290
SF 33 Writing a report **P** 293
SF 34 Argumentative writing. 294
SF 35 Writing a character profile . . . 296
SF 36 Writing a text analysis **P** 298
SF 37 Doing a creative writing task . 299
SF 38 Writing a well-structured text 300
SF 39 Quoting a text **P** 301
SF 40 Proofreading **P** 303

Mediation skills
SF 41 Mediation of written and oral texts **P** 304

Download the suggested answers to the Skills File PRACTICE tasks here:
 Webcode context-00

Language and study skills

▶ SF 1 Dealing with unknown words

READING, LISTENING AND MEDIATING ENGLISH INTO GERMAN
When you read or listen to texts, you usually won't understand every single word. Luckily, in many cases, you won't need to because you can understand texts without knowing each individual word. However, if the meaning of a word is essential to a sentence, there are some techniques that can help you work it out.

Look at the highlighted words in the text on the left and, on the right, read what strategies to use to work out their meaning.

In order to remain competitive, the industrial nations have to raise their productivity, encourage innovation and lower their production costs.

To reduce costs and to maximize profits, multinational companies often relocate facilities to other countries (= outsourcing) to profit from lower wages they pay their workers and from less restrictive laws. The problem is that it diminishes work prospects for workers here.

- *competitive:* think of words from the same word family (*competition / (to) compete / competitor*)
- *encourage:* identify parts of the word that you know (*courage* → *give someone courage*)
- *maximize:* think of similar words in other languages (German *maximieren*) but watch out for false friends (*prospects* = Aussichten, not: Prospekte)
- *multinational:* identify suffixes or prefixes (*multi* = many → *multinational* = belonging to many nations)
- *wages:* use the context of the word ('pay their workers')

250
Skills File

SF 2 • Language and study skills

SF

> **PRACTICE**
>
> Using different strategies, try to infer the meaning of the underlined words:
>
> One of the Queen's <u>recurrent</u> royal responsibilities was to open Parliament, an <u>obligation</u> she had never <u>previously</u> found particularly <u>burdensome</u> and actually rather enjoyed: to be driven down the Mall on a bright autumn morning even after fifty years was something of a treat. But not any more.
>
> From: Alan Bennet, *The Uncommon Reader*, 2008 (cf. *Context* p. 96)

SPEAKING, WRITING AND MEDIATING GERMAN INTO ENGLISH

When you want to express a certain concept in English when talking, writing or mediating and you don't know the word, you can paraphrase it. (▶ SF 9: Paraphrasing)

▶ SF 2 Learning new words

Learning vocabulary is a lifelong activity – even in your own language you never stop learning new words. There are different methods for expanding your vocabulary. Try out a variety of methods until you find the one that works best for you.

Step 1: Identify words that could be useful to you. These might be:
- words that are related to the topic you are dealing with (e.g. Shakespeare's dramas)
- words that help you talk or write about texts or topics in class
- words that go together with other words (collocations) or that belong to a word family that you already know
- words that belong to a neutral *register (words that are either very formal or very informal can only be used in limited situations).

Step 2: Arrange your words in a suitable form. This could be a mind map or a list – or you might want to use index cards. Indicate the meaning of your words by:
- giving synonyms (e.g. *dogma* = *belief / principle*)
- giving antonyms (e.g. *upheaval* ≠ *stability*)
- making sketches/drawings
- giving examples (e.g. the arts = *art, music, literature etc.*)
- giving the German equivalent (e.g. *achievement* = *Errungenschaft*).

If possible, write down words in contexts or collocations; this will help you to use them in a sentence (e.g. *be torn between, remember sb. for sth.*).

> The Elizabethan Age is often remembered as a Golden Age for its many achievements in the arts. However, England was struggling for peace and stability at home – religious, social, political and economic developments challenged society.
>
> People were torn between a traditional world view and a more modern one; they generally accepted the Earth as the centre of the cosmos and the Church as the centre of life on Earth, but were keen to discover new truths beyond the old dogmas. Shakespeare's drama reflects this upheaval.

Step 3: Use your new vocabulary as soon and as often as possible, e.g. include it in a short text, prepare a one-minute speech, study your index cards etc.

Step 4: Revise your vocabulary regularly; first in short intervals, then in longer ones.

> **TIP**
>
> Be active when learning new words: do not just write them down, say them out loud as well. Sometimes movements, e.g. walking around while learning or giving them a rhythm or tune, can also be helpful.

Skills File

SF Language and study skills • SF 3

▶ SF 3 Using a dictionary

There are both mono- and bilingual dictionaries. Both serve different purposes and they complement each other. They can be digital or print.

USING A BILINGUAL DICTIONARY

Here you can look up translations of words. For example if you do not know the English word for *Ruf* you can look it up in the German-English section or type it into your digital dictionary.

- The running heads at the top of each page help you find the right page quickly (top left-hand corner: first entry on page, top right-hand corner: last entry at bottom of page).
- In the example on the right, *Ruf* is the head-word: the different translations are listed, numbers or letters in boxes indicate the different meanings.
- The notes in *italics* help you to find the particular meaning you are looking for.
- Examples and collocations are found below the headword.

> **Ruf**
> **1** *auch übertragen* call /kɔːl/; *lauter* shout /ʃaʊt/: *der Ruf nach schärferen Gesetzen* the **call for** tougher laws
> **2** ≈ *Ansehen* reputation /ˌrepjuˈteɪʃn/

From: Schulwörterbuch English G 21

> ■ TIP
>
> - To find the pronunciation of an English word, check the English-German section of your dictionary or listen to the soundfile in a digital dictionary.
> - In the English-German section you will also find references to irregular verb forms, irregular plural forms, etc.
> - Always read the additional information next to your headword (above: in *italics*). This will prevent you from using the wrong translation.

USING A MONOLINGUAL DICTIONARY

Sometimes a monolingual dictionary can prove more helpful than a bilingual dictionary because it doesn't only give equivalents of words in another language, but definitions and example sentences. In this way, an English-English dictionary will help you to find the words that fit best to express exactly what you want to say. If you don't understand an English word of Latin or Greek origin, a monolingual dictionary will usually be more helpful than a bilingual one because the bilingual one will often give you a translation that is similar to the English word, e.g. *cosmopolitan* = *Kosmopolit*.

- In order to choose the right meaning from those given, always read the whole entry.
- The information on usage and style helps you to avoid using the wrong *register.
- Looking at the examples of common collocations and idioms can help you avoid false friends.
- Many dictionaries provide more specific information on typical error areas.

> **grim** /grɪm/ *adj.* (**grim·mer**, **grim·mest**) **1** looking or sounding very serious: *a **grim face/look/smile*** ◊ *She looked grim.* ◊ *with a look of **grim determination** on his face* ◊ ***grim-faced** policemen* **2** unpleasant and depressing: *grim news* ◊ *We face the grim prospect of still higher unemployment.* ◊ *The outlook is pretty grim.* ◊ *Things are **looking grim** for workers in the building industry.* **3** (of a place or building) not attractive; depressing: *The house looked grim and dreary in the rain.* ◊ *the grim walls of the prison* **4** [not before noun] (*BrE, informal*) ill/sick: *I feel grim this morning.* **5** [not usually before noun] (*BrE, informal*) of very low quality: *Their performance was fairly grim, I'm afraid!* ▶ **grim·ly** *adv.*: *'It won't be easy,' he said grimly.* ◊ *grimly determined* **grim·ness** *noun* [U]

From: Oxford Advanced Learner's Dictionary

PRACTICE

Translate the following sentences:
1 *Genetisch veränderte Lebensmittel haben in vielen europäischen Ländern einen eher schlechten Ruf.*
2 *Es gibt auch noch den Ruf nach mehr Beschränkungen für den freien Markt.*
3 *Sein Rufen schien niemand zu bemerken.*

252
Skills File

SF4–SF5 • Language and study skills — SF

▶ SF4 Using a grammar book

A grammar book is useful for correcting mistakes and improving your grammar. You should consult it when you come across a grammar problem while writing a text (e.g. if you are not sure whether or not to use a gerund) or when you realize that you keep making mistakes in certain fields of grammar. To identify these areas, analyse the feedback you receive from your teacher on your tests or homework.

Step 1: Find your grammatical problem area (e.g. word order or tenses) in the contents page or in the index pages at the back of the book. Read the relevant entry (both rules and examples).

Step 2: In order to avoid mistakes in the future, use your grammar book in different ways, e.g.:
- Copy problematic grammar rules onto index cards and use them to revise your grammar points. (Use the same colours for similar aspects or leave space on the cards for examples you add later etc.)
- Create a poster with your own typical grammar traps.
- Look for the grammar point in question in texts you are working with or in your own texts.
- Do some exercises on the topic.
- Say the rule and some example sentences out loud, perhaps using your grammar card.

PRACTICE

In your latest test the sentences on the right have been marked as wrong. Say what grammar topic you will look up in your grammar book, then correct the mistakes.

1 *They never went to England before.*
2 *They have known each other since six years.*
3 *If they would be older, they would do it.*
4 *Alicia feels not comfortable.*
5 *She asked me if I am happy.*
6 *They were all the time there.*

▶ SF5 Doing research

For projects, presentations or other school work you usually have to research individual aspects and find specific information. For this you can use the internet, but also other sources of information. Here are some ways to make your research more effective.

THE PREPARATION STAGE

Step 1: Clarify what your topic is, then brainstorm it. Decide what information you need so that you can structure your research accordingly.

Step 2: Plan your research:
- Decide which sources are helpful for your research: the internet, textbooks, encyclopaedias, newspapers or magazines, experts or contemporary witnesses?
- Concentrate on English language sources. Using German information and translating it into English will take a long time and often leads to unidiomatic English.
- Make a list of keywords that you want to check.

THE RESEARCH STAGE

Step 1: Check your sources: Older publications may contain outdated information; information published by individuals, interest groups or companies may be biased (i.e. have a tendency to be in favour of this group or company). Check for cross-references and do not just rely on one source.

Step 2: Make notes on the information you find. (▶ SF15: Marking up a text / Making and taking notes)
- Using index cards might make it easier to organize the information later.
- Copy the exact wording and note down the source (▶ SF39: Quoting a text), as it normally needs to be given in a bibliography (an alphabetical list of sources used) at the end of your presentation or project work.

SF Language and study skills • SF6

TIP

When doing research on the internet, the following tips may help you to find useful information:

How can you determine whether a website provides reliable information?	Domain names ending with *.gov* or *.edu* indicate that the information is likely to be accurate, as it is usually an official website. Sites of scientific institutions are also usually reliable.
	Personal blogs or homepages often just give statements by individuals – they tend to be biased.
How can you limit the number of hits so that you will find useful information more quickly?	Brainstorm which keywords would most likely appear in the perfect article to answer your search question. Combine them to get the most exact results. Typing in 5–7 keywords is better than just two or three. The more specific the word(s), the better.
How can you find the original source of a quote?	Enter the full quote or parts of it, using quotation marks. This way you will only find websites with that exact quote. From these, you will normally be able to find the original source of a quote.

PRACTICE

'German vs. British political system – similarities and differences'. Use the internet and/or printed works to find out about the German political system and compare it to your findings from Chapter 5, p. 98.

▶ SF6 Doing project work

A project is a complex task usually done in a group, involving several hours of work and often resulting in a written or oral product, e.g. a wall display or a presentation. Project work typically proceeds along the following stages:

Step 1: Plan your work:
- Agree on a topic or look closely at the topic assigned to you.
- Decide what has to be done and how to present your results (e.g. a display, a presentation, a web page, a class magazine).
- Discuss how everybody can contribute best to the project and assign the tasks accordingly.
- Agree on a schedule, including regular group meetings at which all group members give status reports, present their results so far and discuss problems.

Step 2: Research your topic. (▶ SF5: Doing research)

Step 3: Organize your findings (▶ SF8: Structuring ideas) and start preparing your final result, i.e. your presentation (▶ SF24: Giving a presentation) and/or any kind of written material (e.g. a wall display, a written text to be handed in, your web page etc. (▶ SF7: Making visual aids). Bear in mind any specifications you were given by your teacher (e.g. length of presentation or text etc.).

Step 4: Check your written and visual material. Is it well organized and clear? Is the English correct? (▶ SF40: Proofreading) Give your product to someone else in your group to check it again.

Step 5: Present your results. (▶ SF24: Giving a presentation)

Step 6: After your presentation, assess your work. With your group, discuss what went well and what you could do better next time or ask your audience or teacher for feedback.

Skills File

SF 7 • Language and study skills

▶ SF 7 Making visual aids

Visual aids can have three purposes:
- *to help you get a clearer picture of the content of a text*
- *to structure information before writing a text* (▶ SF 8: Structuring ideas)
- *to present information to accompany a presentation* (▶ SF 24: Giving a presentation).

Some typical examples of visual aids are
- *timelines: order of events, dates*
- *flow charts: cause and effect*
- *pie charts: percentages, amounts* (▶ SF 12: Analysing charts and graphs)
- *clusters/mindmaps: structured ideas.*

The following instructions explain how to make a flow chart after reading a text:

Step 1: Read the text and highlight the most important information. (▶ SF 15: Marking up a text / Making and taking notes)

The reduction of oxygen-giving forests, especially the tropical rainforests, is one component of the climate change that scientists have been observing over the past few decades. This global warming appears to be causing the polar ice caps to melt, which could lead to the flooding of many coastal regions. At the same time as we rob the earth of its natural resources, we pollute the air and water with the waste products of those resources. Some of the emissions our technology produces are to blame for the greenhouse effect, which further contributes to the global warming phenomenon.

Step 2: Work out how the different aspects are connected.
- *reduction of forests: leads to climate change / global warming*
- *climate change / global warming: leads to melting of the polar ice caps*
- *melting of the polar ice caps: can cause floods*
- *pollution of air and water through waste: emissions cause greenhouse effect*

Step 3: Show the connection with arrows or other symbols.

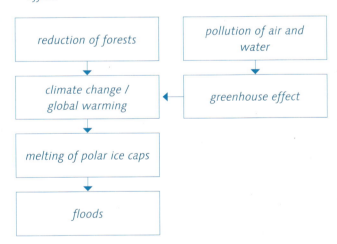

■ **TIP**

Use single terms or short phrases if possible; otherwise your chart will look too full and be visually confusing.

PRACTICE

Have a look at the second paragraph of the Fact File on p. 101. Make a visual aid to present the information in a suitable way.

Skills File

SF Language and study skills • SF8–SF9

▶ SF8 Structuring ideas

Structuring ideas is an important step after collecting information and before preparing a text (which may be written or spoken). Arranging your arguments in a logical order is a prerequisite to an effective text. (▶ SF38: Writing a well-structured text)

Step 1: When you have collected your ideas, decide on an order in which to present them:
Most texts you produce will follow the general structure **1. Introduction** → **2. Main part / Body** → **3. Conclusion**. Decide on the order in which to present your ideas in the main part. Often the text-type you are being asked to produce will demand a specific structure (▶ SF16: Identifying text types). For example, if you are asked to discuss a statement you will proba-bly divide up your ideas into pro- and con-arguments (▶ SF34: Argumentative writing). Other possibilities are a chronological order or *problem* → *cause* → *solution*. It may be helpful to use a flow-chart (▶ SF7: Making visual aids) at this stage.

> **OUTLINE**
> **1. Introduction**
> **2. Main part / Body**
>   I. Main idea 1
>   A. Important fact
>   1. Supporting fact
>   2. Supporting fact
>   a. Example or detail
>   b. Example or detail
>   B. Important fact
>   …
>   II. Main idea 2
>   …
> **3. Conclusion**

Step 2: Make an **outline** of your text (cf. the box on the right).
All 'main ideas' are of equal importance, as are the 'important facts', etc.

Step 3: Add the ideas you have collected to your outline. Use keywords.

Step 4: Before you start producing the final text or notes, review your outline. Make sure you have found the most appropriate place for each piece of information. (▶ SF38: Writing a well-structured text)

▶ SF9 Paraphrasing

Paraphrasing is useful when you don't know the exact word or phrase in a conversation, when writing a text or mediating into English. There are different techniques for paraphrasing:

Paraphrasing technique	Example
Antonym Antonyms denote the opposite of the original word.	*Reichtum:* 'the opposite of poverty'
Comparison Comparisons help you illustrate what you mean by creating images.	*Handschuh:* 'It's like a hat for your hand.'
Definition or explanation (often using relative clauses) With definitions or explanations, relative clauses help you add detail to general terms (e.g. 'a person', 'a machine').	*Freiwillige/r:* 'a person who offers to do some-thing but doesn't ask for money in return' *Navigationsgerät:* 'a machine that tells you how to get to your destination; often in a car'

PRACTICE

Paraphrase the German words and phrases using the strategies in brackets:

Krankenschwester (definition/explanation) *Dach* (comparison)

unangenehm (antonym) *langweilig* (antonym)

Herbergsvater (definition/explanation) *Garage* (comparison)

Skills File

SF 10 • Language and study skills   SF

► SF 10 Working with closed test formats

Both in lessons and in written examinations closed test formats are used to develop and test your reading and listening skills. To succeed in these test formats, it is essential to know them well and to be aware of useful strategies.

There are different types of closed test formats:

- **multiple choice task:**

  Choose the sentences that correspond with how you understand the poem.
  A The speaker is saying that his poetry is an essential part of his life.
  B The speaker is saying that rhythm is all that matters.

- **matching task:**

  Match the following sentences and phrases with the stages of a formal conversation in the box below.
  Bye. – It's very convenient for me to meet you here. – I absolutely hate that kind of job. – I actually think I am quite good at working in a team as …

  - Introducing yourself
  - Getting into the conversation
  - Showing interest in the other person …

- **true/false statements:**

  Listen to the first interview again. Are the sentences below true or false? Correct the false answers.
  1 The first interviewee understands why some people would like to have an elected president instead of a monarch.
  2 The Queen is his favourite member of the royal family.

- **note-taking:**

  Listen to the statements again, this time taking notes. Point out positive and negative aspects of living in each of the places.

- **gapped text / sentence or table completion:**

  Complete the following statements about the history of tea.
  1 The British made their first cup of tea sometime in the middle of the … century.
  2 In the 19th century, tea became popular among … people.

Step 1: Preparing for the test

- Read the instructions carefully and work out exactly what information you have to look for. It might be useful to underline keywords in the task.
- Anticipate what you might read or hear: Try to imagine the situation and guess what might happen. (► SF 22: Listening)

Step 2: Doing the test

- Don't panic if you don't understand every word you hear or read. The context or your background knowledge will help you to understand the text. (► SF 1: Dealing with unknown words)
- Focus on the information that is necessary to complete your task. (► SF 14: Reading strategies; ► SF 15: Marking up a text / Making and taking notes)
- In listening tasks, you are normally allowed to listen to a recording twice. Try to complete as much as possible during or immediately after the first listening and use the second listening to concentrate on the missing information or to correct what you have already done. (► SF 22: Listening)
- Keep an eye on the time when working on reading tasks. First work on the questions you are sure about, then go back to the questions you struggle with. Tasks that require you to read for gist only allow you a short time to skim the texts. (► SF 14: Reading strategies)
- Never leave an item unanswered. If you do not know the answer, make a sensible guess – you have a 25% chance of getting the right answer in a multiple choice item with four options!
- Don't waste time thinking about spelling: Spelling is usually not marked as long as the meaning of the answer is clear.
- After you have completed the test check your answers and use left-over time for corrections.

257
Skills File

SF Text skills • SF 11

Text skills

▶ SF 11 Analysing pictures

There are different types of pictures: photos, posters, paintings, drawings, or sketches. Often they are combined with written text, either as a title or a caption.

John Gast, *American Progress*, 1872

Step 1: Basic information

- State your first impression of the picture.
- Read the title or caption and identify the general topic.
- Check when (and where) the picture was created or published.

- *title: 'American Progress'*
- *general topic: American settlers moving west / conquering the continent*
- *artist, date: John Gast, 1872*

> ■ LANGUAGE HELP
> - This picture/painting/photo/poster/drawing/sketch … shows/provides proof of/gives information on/introduces the topic of/conveys the impression that/depicts/portrays/illustrates/is about/ …
> - In the picture, … can be seen.

Step 2: Description

Choose one of these approaches:

- Start with the main subject, i.e. a dominant object, describe it in detail, then describe the background (useful for a picture with one dominant image).
  OR
- Start at the left of the picture and work across to the right or vice versa (useful for pictures with a lot of activity).
  OR
- Start at the top of the picture and work down to the bottom or vice versa (useful for pictures where the interest tails off towards the top or bottom).

- *dominant figure in the middle of the painting: woman, made to appear like a goddess or angel, holding a book in her left hand, moving towards the left of the picture, …*
- *painting shows landscape with a lot of detail*
- *right-hand side: bright, especially at the top; background: ships and railway lines*
- *in the bottom right-hand corner: farmers and a horse-drawn coach*
- *left-hand side: considerably darker / more threatening: clouds, ragged mountains, wild landscape*
- *bottom-left corner: Native Americans*
- *…*

Skills File

SF 12 • Text skills

Step 3: Analysis and interpretation
Draw conclusions about what the picture is meant to convey, whether it does this effectively and how it achieves its effect. You can look at …
- the technique, colours
- the effect on the viewer
- who is addressed and why
- the artist's/photographer's intention/message.

- right half of the painting (i.e. east) represents the American east (where the first settlers landed and lived); left half of the painting represents the 'wild west'
- colours and light: the east appears warm/bright; the west seems to be threatening and dark ('wild' west)
- all objects/people (trains, coaches, people, dominant figure) move from right to left → westward movement of American settlers → picture illustrates the idea of 'Manifest Destiny', which was …
- dominant figure: could represent culture, learning and progress (cf. the title); her angelic impression underlines the importance and positive connotation the artist places on those aspects

LANGUAGE HELP
- The artist's/photographer's use of … creates …/ conveys the impression of …
- By … the picture effectively illustrates …
- The dominance of …/ The way the light/shadow … directs the viewer's attention to …
- As the foreground/ background is …, the impression given is that …
- … is a symbol of …/… helps to create an atmosphere of/ which …
- This has the effect that …

Step 4: Evaluation
Evaluate the picture by analysing how or how well it achieves an effect and by describing its effect on you.

- painting clearly/effectively illustrates the idea that American people were chosen by God to conquer the American continent

PRACTICE
Analyse one of the pictures on p. 114.

▶ SF 12 Analysing charts and graphs

Charts and graphs present complex information visually. There are different types, e.g. pie charts, bar charts, line graphs or tables.

pie chart ('Tortendiagramm')

bar chart ('Säulendiagramm')

line graph ('Kurvendiagramm')

table ('Tabelle')

Skills File

SF Text skills • SF 12

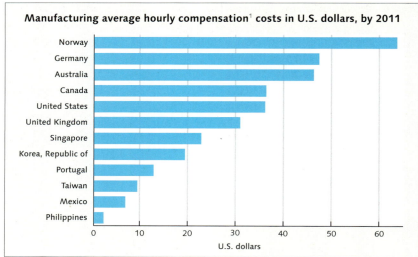

From: the website of the U.S. Department of Labor

When analysing charts and graphs like the one on the right, follow these three steps:

Step 1: Identify the type of chart or graph you are dealing with. Analyse the source:
- Is the source reliable?
- Is the data up to date?

- *bar chart*
- *source: U.S. Dept. of Labor: reliable*
- *data from 2011: not exactly up to date*

Step 2: Describe the graph/chart:
- What is it about and what information does it give?

- Does it show a development or does it compare different items at one point in time?
- Does it use absolute figures or percentages?

- *shows the differences in the hourly wage of workers in manufacturing in different countries in 2011*
- *gives the hourly compensation in $ (absolute numbers)*
- *compares data from 2011*
- *at the top of the ranking: countries with the highest hourly compensation (Norway: first, Philippines: last)*
- *countries at the bottom: hourly compensation is less than a sixth of the countries at the top*

■ **LANGUAGE HELP**

- The bar chart / pie chart / line graph / table … shows the different / compares the size/number of … / deals with / is about … / contrasts … with …
- It shows … in contrast to…
- It is taken from / It contains data from … / It was published in …

Bar chart:
- The bars are arranged horizontally/vertically.
- There are big/vast/surprising differences between …
- At the top/bottom of the ranking comes…
- … is first/last in rank
- … has the largest / second largest …

Pie chart:
- The chart is divided into … segments, which show/ represent …
- The smallest/biggest segment / The segments representing … and … constitute the majority … / A huge majority/minority is …

Line graph:
- The graph shows the relationship between … and …
- … is twice/three times as high as … / … There are more than / nearly twice as many … as there are …
- increase/decrease / reach a high point / rise/fall/ drop/ grow steadily

---

[1]**compensation** wage

260

Skills File

Step 3: Draw conclusions from the chart/graph.

- *vast differences in the hourly wage → huge differences in the production costs of the goods → outsourcing of time-consuming jobs to countries with a lower hourly wage*

PRACTICE

Look at the table on the right and decide whether the figures would best be shown in a pie chart, a bar chart or a line graph and why. Use a computer to design the chart.

The world's most livable cities		
Rank	**City**	**Score (out of 100)**
1	Melbourne/Australia	97,5
2	Vienna/Austria	97,4
3	Vancouver/Canada	97,3
4	Toronto/Canada	97,2
5/6	Calgary/Canada Adelaide/Australia	96,6
7	Sydney/Australia	96,1
8	Helsinki/Finland	96,0
9	Perth/Australia	95,9
10	Auckland/New Zealand	95,7

From: *The Telegraph*, 6 August 2014

▶ SF 13 Analysing cartoons

The following steps will help you to describe and analyse a cartoon systematically.

Step 1: Basic information

- What is your first impression of the cartoon?

  first impression: humorous, eye-catching, cartoon exaggerates a common school situation to illustrate a serious topic
- What is the cartoon about?
- What is its topic?

  topic: genetic engineering and its uncontrollable consequences
- (Where/when was it published?)

Step 2: Description

- Describe the cartoon systematically.
  - *classroom with students who all have brought colourful fantasy animals/monsters with them*
  - *in the background: blackboard with writing 'Genetic Engineering 101' (= name of the class); in front of the class: teacher looking angry*
  - *one student: putting up his hand, looking at his dinosaur-like animal*
  - *caption: the teacher's words*
- What people, events or trends does the cartoon refer to? Mention any labels, speech bubbles or captions. (▶ SF 11: Analysing pictures)

'Okay – is there anybody ELSE whose homework ate their dog?'

SF Text skills • SF 13

> **LANGUAGE HELP**
> - In the centre/foreground/background/At the top/bottom of …
> - On the left/right side of the cartoon …
> - Underneath there is … The caption reads …

Step 3: Analysis

The following questions may help you when analysing a cartoon:
- Are the figures or issues presented in a positive or negative light? How is this impression achieved?
- Does the cartoon make use of *symbols or *irony? Explain their use.
- Does the cartoon depict well-known persons? Who are they and what is their role in connection with the topic of the cartoon?
- What point is the cartoonist trying to make? What means are used to get the message across?
  - *cartoonist reverses a common classroom cliché: a common excuse for students who don't have their homework is that their dog ate their homework; here, the homework (i.e. the genetically engineered animal) has eaten the dog*
  - *illustrations of the fantasy animals: exaggerated, eye-catching, funny shapes and colours*
  - *cartoon = criticism of uncontrollability of genetic engineering; even experts (here: the teacher) are unable to control the risks*

> **LANGUAGE HELP**
> - The cartoon may be meant to show …/ It is very eye-catching because of its use of …/ It speaks to the observer directly by …
> - The layout/use of colour/… is criticizing/ making fun of …
> - The cartoon conveys its message through …/ brings its message across by …

Step 4: Evaluation

Is think the cartoon effective or not? Give reasons, using your background knowledge about the topic.

*The cartoon criticizes the dangers of scientific research and genetic engineering effectively. To get its message across, it uses a funny twist by turning a well-known *cliché upside-down. By choosing a seemingly harmless setting to illustrate the devastating consequences of genetic engineering, the cartoonist criticizes it in a forceful way.*

'I'd like to change my major from electrical engineering to English or something.'

> **PRACTICE**
> Describe and analyse the cartoon on the left.

262 Skills File

SF 14 • Text skills

▶ SF 14 Reading strategies

When working with longer texts, there are different ways of reading. Which strategy you need to apply depends on what you want to do with your text: look for the main ideas or specific information, read for pleasure or analyse it. You also need to have a strategy to deal with unknown words (▶ SF 1: Dealing with unknown words).

SKIMMING
Skimming (or reading for gist) means going through a text quickly to identify its main ideas. This technique is helpful when there is lots of material to be taken in and only a limited amount of time, e.g. when you are doing research on a certain subject and you have to find out which texts could be relevant for your topic.

Step 1: Look at illustrations, pictures, keywords, headings or subheadings to get an idea of the content of the given text.

Step 2: Don't read every sentence. Let your eyes run over the whole text and look for words or phrases that contain useful information.

Step 3: Read the first and the last sentence of each paragraph – one of them usually states the main idea of that paragraph and the very last sentence of the text often contains a summary.

Step 4: Summarize the text. If you are able to do this without a problem, your skimming was probably successful.

SCANNING
Scanning means looking out for for specific information. You can use this technique when you want to find answers to a particular question or to compare particular aspects in different texts.

Step 1: Think of keywords or phrases that might be useful to search for when looking for the information you need.

Step 2: Move your eyes quickly down the page. Stop when you find a keyword or phrase and read the part where you found it. Then continue scanning the text.

EXTENSIVE READING
Extensive reading means reading for pleasure, e.g. when reading a novel. You read at your own speed and concentrate on what's happening (the events of the plot) without looking up unknown words.

CLOSE READING
Close reading is necessary when analysing a text (▶ SF 17–21). You will need to understand not only what is being said in the text, but also how it is being said. To do that, you will have to read the text more than once and make sure you understand every word.

> **PRACTICE**
> 1. Skim the text 'Young, educated – and leaving the country' (p. 162) and note down what the text is about in a few words.
> 2. Scan the third paragraph of 'India then and now' (p. 114) for facts and figures showing which challenges India has to face.

Skills File

SF Text skills • SF 15

▶ SF 15 Marking up a text / Making and taking notes

When working with photocopied texts or printouts, you can mark up important information so that you can find it more easily when you are working with the text again, e.g. when you are writing about it or preparing for a test.

> ■ TIP
>
> When working with a borrowed book, put a transparency on the page and mark important information on it.

MARKING UP A TEXT

Step 1: As you read the text, bear in mind what information you are looking for. You may want to read the task/ question again.

Step 2: When you find the relevant information in your text, mark it by underlining, highlighting or circling the relevant words or passages. Only mark keywords.

> ■ TIP
>
> 1. Use different colours for different tasks.
>
> 2. Also mark words which show that a different opinion or a contrast is being introduced to help you understand the logical structure of the text.

Step 3: Finally, add headings or keywords in the margin or summarize passages with short phrases or sentences.

Tasks:
a Point out what recruiters do and how they work.
b Collect tips on how to write a CV to arouse a recruiter's interest.

How to please recruiters
Clare Whitmell

A recruiter can be your short cut into a new job. With a good understanding of industry trends – and insider knowledge of that particular employer's preferences and needs – a recruiter will be briefed to find exactly the right candidate with a specific set of skills, experience and qualities. To even be considered for the role, you need to make sure that your CV hits the right notes with them.

Recruiters can be generalists working in a number of sectors or headhunters specialising in one, but there are a few pet hates they all share. Avoid these and you'll be giving yourself a better chance of getting into the yes pile each time. [...]

Zena Everett, director and career coach at Second Careers and career guru at Mumsnet, has researched how headhunters, recruiters, employers and HR professionals screen CVs. She found that they all – without exception – looked first at the most recent work experience and job title. These must be relevant for the CV to get a second look in a competitive job market.

For recruiters to put you forward to an employer, they need to see that your background matches the role. A simple way to ensure that you're giving your CV the best possible chance is to search the job description for key criteria, then make sure you include relevant details on your CV that show you're a good match.

From: the website of *The Guardian*, 8 April 2014

recruiters' knowledge

recruiters' tasks

recruiters' areas of work

Show that your most recent work experience is relevant for the job.

Show that you fulfil the most important criteria for the new job.

MAKING AND TAKING NOTES

In cases where you cannot mark up a text (either because you are not working with your own book or because you are listening to an audio file), you can first *take notes* (i.e. extract important information from the text), then *make notes* (i.e. organize your ideas). Making notes will also help you structure your own ideas, e.g. after brainstorming or when preparing for a speaking task (▶ SF 8: Structuring ideas; ▶ SF 24–28).

264 Skills File

SF 16 · Text skills   **SF**

▶ SF 16 Identifying text types (non-fiction)

In class you often have to analyse texts. The first step of the analysis is to identify the text type you are dealing with.

Texts can be classified into two main categories:

Fictional texts (i.e. literary texts, *Dichtung*, ▶ SF 19–21)	Non-fictional texts (i.e. *Sachtexte*, ▶ SF 18)
• The text describes a world that was created in the mind of its *author. • Its *setting, *characters and events may or may not seem realistic.	• The text talks about the real world. • It was written to convey information, convince the reader or criticize something.

Knowing what type of non-fictional text you're dealing with and what characteristic features this text type has will help you to anticipate what kind of information might be given and how it might be presented. Follow these steps:

Step 1: Skim the text (▶ SF 14: Reading strategies) and try to get a general idea of its content:
- Sum up in one or two sentences what the text is about.
- If possible, find out when and where it was published (newspaper, book, journal, internet).

Step 2: Examine the text more closely. Look at:
- its content and purpose: Is the text meant to inform, persuade, entertain, …?
- its *style and *tone: Is the language formal or informal, simple or complex?

Step 3: Identify the text type. The following table will help you.

Non-fictional texts	
Text type and examples	**Contents and purpose**
Expository texts: *feature story, *news story, summary, etc.	• contain comprehensive and detailed information • are intended to be objective and factual • give no personal opinion • describe a situation, scientific findings, historic occurrences
Descriptive texts: travel book, biography, etc.	• describe actual places, objects, events or people based on the writer's observations and impressions • are intended to create a vivid picture in the reader's mind • tend to give a lot of detail
Argumentative texts: *editorial, *column, *letter to the editor, *review, *speech, *comment, etc.	• discuss problems and controversial ideas • evaluate a topic by giving reasons and stating the pros and cons of an issue • show a clear line of argument • tend to use expert opinions, statistics, quotations and technical/scientific language • aim to convince the reader
Persuasive texts: *speech, advertisement, etc.	• use stylistic devices • often use imperatives as an appeal to do something specific • try to persuade or convince the reader/listener
Instructive texts: manual, brochure, etc.	• are intended to instruct the readers, tell them what to do or how to do it • use imperatives and passive constructions (▶ LP 7: The passive)

265

Skills File

SF Text skills • SF 17

▶ SF 17 Analysing stylistic devices

When you listen to or read texts, you will normally notice that they have some kind of effect on you – you might strongly agree or disagree or you might feel amused, entertained, informed or perhaps irritated. This effect is created through the way the text is written, and especially by the *stylistic devices used. So when analysing texts, you should try to find out how certain effects are created. Stylistic devices may relate to sound (e.g. *alliteration), structure (e.g. *repetition, *parallelism) or meaning (e.g. *imagery).

Step 1: When reading the text pay attention to the effects that certain passages have on you.

Step 2: Study the passages in question to find the stylistic devices that create these effects. In the table below there are some examples.

Step 3: Consider why these effects may have been intended in this context. (▶ SF 36: Writing a text analysis)

> **■ TIP**
>
> If you cannot pinpoint any specific effects while listening or reading, you can try it the other way round: Study the text for the most common stylistic devices (cf. the table below) and see if you can find a reason why the author may have used them.

Example	Effect	Stylistic device
'The most restless, the most adventurous, the most innovative, the most industrious of people [...].' From: William J. Clinton, 'The changing face of America', 13 June 1998; cf. *Context* p. 144, ll. 14ff.	• reader/listener may feel overwhelmed, impressed by positive qualities	• *enumeration of superlatives
'What do the changes mean? They can either strengthen and unite us, or they can weaken and divide us.' From: William J. Clinton, 'The changing face of America', 13 June 1998; cf. *Context* p. 144, ll. 27ff.	• reader/listener may feel drawn into the argumentation by being asked a direct question • reader/listener feels a little under pressure, even manipulated to answer the question in a specific way	• *rhetorical question • *contrast of two possible answers: one with strongly positive, the other with strongly negative *connotations
'With a growing UK Muslim population currently standing at 2.7 million (Census 2011) with a £20.5 billion a year spending power and expected to rise to 5.5 million people by 2030 (Pew Report, *The Future of the Global Muslim Population* 2011) access to delicious halal food in the UK is becoming increasingly important.' From: the website of Halal Focus; cf. *Context* p. 106, ll. 15ff.	• reader may feel convinced by factual information/objective numbers	• statistical data • reliable sources (Pew Report)
'Many Indians despair over the divisiveness[1] of caste and would prefer to wish it away. However, the hold of the Indian way of life is also a bulwark[2] against the onslaught[3] of the global culture.' From: Gurcharan Das, *India Unbound*, 2001; cf. *Context* p. 117, ll. 14ff.	• reader may have difficulty understanding individual words, may find this irritating	• *register, sophisticated/academic choice of words ('divisiveness', 'hold', 'bulwark', 'onslaught')

---

[1] **divisiveness** force that splits people into different groups   [2] **bulwark** (*fml*) thing that protects sth.   [3] **onslaught** strong attack

266

Skills File

SF 17 • Text skills

From the beginning of a job advert for a park ranger: 'Yes, you read right. As our ex-island caretaker is regretfully handing over the keys to his island hacienda[4] we're looking for someone to take his place.' *From: the website of the Queensland tourism board, 5 March 2013; cf. Context p. 193, ll. 1ff.*	• reader may feel directly addressed and involved, connected to the writer	• direct address of reader without introduction • imitation of spoken language, of personal interaction • use of personal pronouns ('we', 'you')
'For me, school had been a Darwinian exercise. A daily gauntlet[5] of ridicule, abuse, and isolation.' *From: Ernest Cline, Ready Player One, 2012; cf. Context p. 16, ll. 21ff.*	• reader will be able to picture the situation very clearly	• *images/*metaphors ('Darwinian exercise', 'gauntlet of ridicule') • incomplete sentence
'War is as old as Europe. Our continent bears the scars of spears and swords, canons and guns, trenches[6] and tanks[7], and more.' *From: Herman Van Rompuy, 'From war to peace', 10 December 2012; cf. Context p. 160*	• reader gets a lively idea of the wounds inflicted on Europe through war • list of nouns draws reader's attention to the numerous weapons which caused the injuries	• *personification of an object ('continent bears the scars') • alliterations ('spears and swords', 'trenches and tanks')
'I fear the day technology will surpass our human interaction. The world will have a generation of idiots.' (Albert Einstein)	• reader may be taken aback by this provocative statement • the reader's interest will be aroused	• *exaggeration (to stress a point)
'... we're talking the ultimate reality TV, where the public can monitor [...] prisoners' whole lives on death row[8]. They can [...] make up their own minds about a convict's worthiness for punishment. Then each week, viewers across the globe can cast a vote to decide which prisoner is executed next. It's humanity in action – the next logical step toward true democracy.' *From: DBC Pierre, Vernon God Little, 2003; cf. Context p. 27, ll. 9ff.*	• reader will be irritated/shocked by the description of the game show as 'humanity in action' • text evokes indignation	• *irony: author uses the term 'humanity in action' to denote the exact opposite: a truly inhumane TV show

---

When analysing the effects created by a text, make sure you also pay attention to its *tone (i.e. the way a writer treats his/her topic). The tone may be formal, intimate, playful, ironic, humorous, etc.)

■ LANGUAGE HELP

The author	uses employs makes use of	a metaphor a simile enumeration irony personification	to illustrate … to show … to emphasize … to underline … to draw the reader's attention to …

---

[4] **hacienda** large farm   [5] **gauntlet** fight with a lot of people attacking you   [6] **trench** *Schützengraben*
[7] **tank** *Panzer*   [8] **death row** cells for prisoners who are waiting to be executed

Skills File

SF Text skills • SF 18

▶ SF 18 Analysing non-fiction

When analysing a non-fictional text you have to say more than just what it is about. You have to find out what type of text it is, for example a *feature story, an *editorial or a *comment (▶ SF 16: Identifying text types). By looking at how its content, its structure and its language interact you can find out what its function and its message might be.

Here is an excerpt from a newspaper article written by a young British woman. Analyse the way she presents her own experiences as a non-white woman in Great Britain.

Step 1: Read the text and decide what type of text it is. Collect extracts that help you analyse the text, e.g. its line of argument, *stylistic devices, choice of words etc. (cf. the highlighted passages). (▶ SF 17: Analysing stylistic devices)

> ... It's not that I'm embarrassed about my ethnic background. I don't think about it much, though it's good for jokes ('I'm half Iranian, half American – so basically, I hate myself'). But some people seem to want me to think about it. 'Why don't you visit Bombay?' they enthuse. 'You'd love it.' They may be right, but have yet to explain to me why I'd love it more than Tokyo, or Guatemala, or any of the other places I haven't yet been. It's an odd misconception that you should somehow feel connected to a far-flung country because your ancestors lived there centuries ago, even if your entire life has been spent morris dancing[1] in Loughborough. 5 10

From: Ariane Sherine, 'It may not be racist, but …', the website of *The Guardian*, 3 March 2010

Step 2: Organize your findings. Make sure all examples e.g. for stylistic devices go together.

- *line of argument: does not think much about her background (l. 1), people seem to think she ought to care about it (ll. 3–4), she thinks her parents' country of origin is just as relevant for her as any other country (ll. 5–7)*
- **humour: joke (ll. 2–3), compares her parents' country of origin with other countries she does not know (ll. 5–7)*
- *choice of words: 'odd misconception' (l. 7), 'far-flung country' (l. 8), 'ancestors' (l. 9), 'morris dancing' (l. 10): humorous*
- **stylistic devices: *exaggeration 'centuries ago' (l. 9), quotations (ll. 4–5)*

Step 3: Analyse the effect that is created by the stylistic devices that you have identified.

- **humour, choice of words: give the text a light-hearted tone*
- *quotations: help the reader imagine the specific situation, make the text more lively*
- **exaggeration: shows how absurd she finds other people's ideas*
- *light-hearted tone: she's not seriously offended*

Step 4: Examine the connection between the effect identified in **Step 3** and the author's line of argument.

- *readers ought to realize how ridiculous it is to keep identifying the descendants of immigrants with their parents' country of origin, to not accept them as fellow-citizens*
- *no acid criticism, no fierce accusation of racism, but a fairly lighthearted account of people's everyday misconceptions*

---

[1] **morris dance** *(v)* do a traditional English dance

268 Skills File

SF 19 • Text skills SF

TIP	LANGUAGE HELP
When working on **Step 1** do not only follow the chronology of the text and wait until something catches your eye. Make sure you examine the text systematically by checking its use of stylistic devices, its choice of words etc.	• The author uses vivid/colloquial/objective/emotive … language. • The sentences are long-winded/paratactical/simple/complex/ … • The author's tone is friendly/humorous/critical/optimistic/sarcastic … • His/her choice of words underlines … • The stylistic devices used support/emphasize/underline … • The reader can easily picture the situation/follow her/his train of thought/line of argument …

▶ SF 19 Analysing narrative prose

When you have to analyse a *short story, a *novel or any other *narrative text you are usually asked to pay attention to one or two specific aspects. The most common aspects for a text analysis are:

Aspect	Example
Character constellations or relationships (▶SF 35: Writing a character profile) • Who is in the story? • What relationships do the *characters have to each other? Are they dependent on each other/equals etc.? • Do they belong to similar/different groups (social/ethnic etc.)? • Do they serve as foils for each other, i.e. do they contrast with another character to highlight particular qualities of the other character? • How does the author characterize them, *directly or *indirectly? • Are the characters *round or *flat?	High-school student Mitch is a reporter for the school magazine and on his way to his first interview with his former PE-teacher McNulty: I parked my mom's Ford Focus by the gym, eased out of the front seat, and looked around. When I spotted McNulty loading tackling sleds[1] into a school van, I tensed. To him, I'd always be a fat loser and nothing more. But a reporter has to have the courage to approach people, ask them questions […]. From: Carl Deuker, *Payback Time*, 2010; cf. *Context* p. 190, ll. 1ff. • *reporter and coach share a history* • *reporter feels inferior; tries to overcome his fear* • *…*
The *narrator or the narrative perspective • Who is telling the story and to whom? Is it a *first-person narrator, a *third-person narrator or an *omniscient narrator? • How much does the narrator know or not know? What are the limiting factors? Does the narrator have a *limited or an *unlimited point of view?	Some nights I lie next to Tony, here in America where I live like a worm avoiding the sunlight, and I wonder if he knows. And is it only because it was his brother that he does not sense that another man's body has come between us. From: Shauna Singh Baldwin, *English Lessons*, 1996; cf. *Context* p. 128, ll. 46ff. • *first person narrator (*protagonist), probably female, might be an immigrant* • *tells the reader a secret that apparently the husband does not know; but since the narrator cannot know the husband's thoughts, neither he/she nor the reader know for sure* • *…*

[1] **tackling sled** *Angriffsschlitten (schweres Trainingsgerät im American Football)*

Skills File

269

Text skills • SF 19

The *plot

- How are the events connected by cause and effect to form a plot?
- How does the author attract or keep the reader's attention by creating *tension or *suspense?
- Is there a *climax and/or a *turning point?
- Does the story have an ending or a conclusion? Or is there an *open ending/a *denouement?

Dan, a high-school student whose parents have recently lost their jobs, is approached by another student, who tries to recruit him for a protest march:

> I felt myself tense. All my friends, plus a couple of kids at the sign-up table, were watching and listening. 'Why do you ask?' 'Seems like a good time,' he said. Had he heard that we'd lost our home? Did he think that would make me more sympathetic to his cause? 'Why's that?' I gave him a hard look.

From: Todd Strasser, *No Place*, 2014; cf. *Context* p. 150, ll. 4ff.

- *tension between characters is building up
- *suspense: reader does not know if the secret is going to be discovered
- …

The *setting and the *atmosphere

- Where and when does the action take place?
- Are there any people? How do they react to the setting?
- How does the setting influence the atmosphere? (E.g. sunny spring days usually create an optimistic atmosphere, a crowded place may create a tense or exciting atmosphere etc.)
- Are you told directly or do you have to draw your own conclusions?

Her Majesty the Queen is on her way to open Parliament:

> One of the Queen's recurrent royal responsibilities was to open Parliament, an obligation she had never previously found particularly burdensome[1] and actually rather enjoyed: to be driven down the Mall[2] on a bright autumn morning even after fifty years was something of a treat.

From: Alan Bennett, *The Uncommon Reader*, 2008; cf. *Context* p. 96, ll. 1ff.

- autumn, sunny
- the Queen: about to do a job she enjoys
- positive atmosphere (to be concluded from the setting)
- …

LANGUAGE HELP

- The relationship between the characters is strongly influenced by … Their power struggle reveals itself when … Their lack of communication shows …
- X's behaviour when … reveals that …
- The description underlines/emphasizes …/conveys the impression that …
- The image suggests …
- By using words like … the author stresses …

- The overall effect is … It can be portrayed as …
- The perspective is biased/one-sided …
- As the first-person narrator has a limited perspective, the reader must … The author chose an omniscient narrator because …
- The story has an open ending, so …
- In the end the conflict is solved when …

---

[1] **burdensome** implying hard work   [2] **the Mall** road leading to Buckingham Palace

Skills File

SF 20 • Text skills

▶ SF 20 Analysing drama

A *drama or *play is a script in which a *playwright presents what *characters say and what they do. A drama is written to be performed on stage, so when you read a play, you will enjoy it more if you imagine what it would look and sound like on stage.

When analysing drama, typical aspects to look at are:

Aspect	Examples and explanations
Structure - Is the play divided up into *acts and *scenes or is there a different structure? - What function do these divisions have in the play? - Do they correspond to action, time, place or a combination of these?	- Shakespeare's plays used to be performed without intermissions – *rhyming couplets would indicate the end of one scene. Nowadays his plays are conventionally edited to have four or five acts and scene divisions, which usually mark a change in the set of characters on stage. - Most modern plays have two or three acts. Some (e.g. *Artefacts*, cf. pp. 102f.) have no act division at all and are meant to be performed without a break. Still, *Artefacts* is divided into three parts, which are set in the two different countries. *Clybourne Park* (cf. pp. 141f.) has two acts, separated by a time gap of 50 years.
The construction of action - Does the script contain *stage directions? If so, what information do they provide? - How does the **action** unfold through the **dialogue**? - Are there *monologues? What function do they have? - What kind of **language** is used?	- In *Clybourne Park* (cf. pp. 141f.) there are some stage directions. They describe how actors should speak certain lines or move (e.g. 'chuckles with amazement, shakes his head', p. 142, ll. 109f.), but there are very few descriptions of settings or actions except at the beginnings of each of the two acts. - Dramatic dialogue has to be very carefully constructed (and yet sound realistic) so that it never gets boring and gives enough clues about what is actually happening. - Monologues usually serve to show a character's thoughts to the audience, but not to the other characters, i.e. they are not part of the interaction. Shakespeare often made use of them to give the audience more insight into a character's mind. - In the extract from *Macbeth* (cf. pp. 76f.) Lady Macbeth uses aggressive language, calling her husband a coward when he hesitates to commit the murder as planned. His question 'If we should fail?' shows his hesitation, whereas her answer 'We fail!' shows her determination to succeed (cf. p. 76, ll. 36f.). This interchange actually drives the action forward because it serves to persuade Macbeth to act as planned. - In *Artefacts*, Kelly's informal language (cf. pp. 102f.) serves to characterize her as a modern British teenager and makes the dialogue more realistic, e.g. 'Yeah, all right then, tell me what I think.' (ll. 69)

Skills File

SF Text skills • SF 20

Characters
(▶ SF 35: Writing a character profile)
- Who are the *characters?
- What information do we get about them and what issues do they have to deal with in the play?
- Do they develop over the course of the play?
- Do they stand for a particular idea or are they part of the play's message?

- Normally it's not the playwright who tells us directly about the characters, but as in real life we get an idea of them through the way they act or talk about themselves, their lives or about others. *Monologues in particular can give the audience an insight into a character's motivations, feelings or problems.
- Macbeth (cf. pp. 76f.) develops from a man reluctant to kill into a ruthless murderer. In *Artefacts* (cf. pp. 102f.) Kelly first refuses to go to Iraq, but later we see that she has actually gone there.
- In *Clybourne Park* (cf. pp. 141f.), the members of the white community who oppose black neighbours represent racist ideas. Lady Macbeth (cf. pp. 76f.) represents ruthless ambition as she is even willing to commit murder to achieve the ultimate success she wants.

Audience
- What does the audience know or see that the characters don't know or see?
- What is left to the audience's imagination?

- In Shakespeare's *Romeo and Juliet*, Romeo has heard that Juliet is dead and kills himself. The audience however knows that she only looks dead – an example of *dramatic irony.
- Sometimes characters speak of actions that do not actually happen on stage, even though they are important for the plot.

■ LANGUAGE HELP
- The play is divided into … acts and … scenes / The development of the action corresponds with the play's division into acts/scenes …
- The overall theme of the play is …
- In the play the conflicts develop between …
- The audience is drawn into the plot by … / The action is supposed to please/shock/enrage/fascinate the audience …
- The … act ends in a cliffhanger / In the end the conflict is solved …

- The stage directions draw a concise picture of the scenery / There are almost no stage directions, so … / The play works with almost no props / a bare stage …
- Even though X appears as a friendly character at first, he later shows … / … stands for / represents …
- The social differences between the characters can be seen in the language they use … / The characters speak in *blank verse …

The Globe Theatre, London

■ TIP
play = Theaterstück
drama = Drama (i.e. text form), e.g. modern drama or Elizabethan drama (i.e. the plays produced during the time when Queen Elizabeth I reigned)
playwright, dramatist = Stückeschreiber/in, Dramatiker/in
character = Figur
actor, actress = Schauspieler/in

SF 21 • Text skills

▶ SF 21 Analysing poetry

When you are asked to analyse a poem, you should not only look at its poetic features such as its form, its *rhythm or its language, you must also look at its content and link this to the poem's form. Only then will you be able to fully understand what the poem conveys.

Here is a poem by Gavin Ewart, followed by a step-by-step guide.

Ending Gavin Ewart

The love we thought would never stop
now cools like a congealing[1] chop[2].
The kisses that were hot as curry
are bird-pecks[3] taken in a hurry.
The hands that held electric charges   5
now lie inert[4] as four moored barges[5].
The feet that ran to meet a date
are running slow and running late.
The eyes that shone and seldom shut
are victims of a power cut.   10
The parts that then transmitted joy
are now reserved and cold and coy[6].
Romance, expected once to stay,
has left a note saying gone away.

From: the website of the Poetry Archive

Step 1: Read the poem two or three times, then summarize it in one or two sentences. Consider	• two people in a relationship that has lasted for some time
• the poem's title, *setting and *theme	• title: ending of a relationship
• the *speaker and the addressee	• couple: one person is speaker, one is addressee
• the link between the title and the poem's content.	• contrast: what the relationship was like before and what it is like now
Step 2: Look at the poem's structure (*stanzas, *rhythm, *rhyme scheme, *metre). (It may help to read the poem out loud to get a feeling for the way it sounds.)	
• Is it built regularly or are there interruptions in the rhythm or rhyme scheme?	• seven couplets
• Is there a *refrain?	• each couplet rhymes (aa, bb, cc, etc.) → regular pattern, conventional
• Is it a *sonnet?	• regular metre, regular rhyme scheme

---

[1] **congeal** (here) become unpleasantly dry   [2] **chop** thick slice of meat with a bone attached to it   [3] **peck** quick kiss / bird's bite
[4] **inert** unable to move   [5] **moored barge** (here) small boat that has been fixed to land   [6] **coy** not willing to give away much about yourself

SF Text skills • SF 21

Step 3: Examine the poem's language more closely. Look for
- *imagery, e.g. *simile, *metaphor, *analogy, *personification
- sound effects, e.g. *alliteration, *assonance, *onomatopoeia
- *contrasts, *repetitions and specific sentence structures (simple/complex sentence, *enjambement)
- mythological/literary/social/historical references
- *symbols.

Step 4: Describe the poem's effect and analyse how it is achieved by connecting your findings on its form to its content.

- *contrast between past and present, e.g. 'love that never ends' (l. 1) ↔ 'congealing chop' (l. 2)*
- *changes are conveyed through descriptions of body parts: hand (l. 5), feet (l. 7), eyes (l. 9), parts (l. 11)*
- *vivid images for love in the past, e.g. 'hot curry' (l. 3), 'electric charges' (l. 5)*
- *images of disconnectedness/cold/passiveness of love today, e.g. 'lie inert as four moored barges' (l. 6), 'power cut' (l. 10)*
- *personification: 'romance' (l. 13)*
- *short and simple sentences*
- *down-to-earth metaphors*
- *clear and regular structure → monotony, conventionality*
- *clear and precise images → easy to understand, common problem*
- *→ lack of drama*
- *…*

■ **LANGUAGE HELP**

- The poem by … deals with / is about … In the poem … describes / reflects on … The poet addresses the topic of …
- The title reminds the reader of … / refers to …
- The poem is made up of … / consists of … verses / stanzas.
- The rhyme scheme is … / There is no consistent rhyme scheme. The word … rhymes with … The use of … creates a certain rhythm.
- Line … runs into line …, which emphasizes …

- The poet employs specific images, such as metaphors or similes, in order to …
- The diction/register is simple/colloquial/formal, which intensifies the feeling of …
- The most prominent stylistic device used in the poem is …, which serves to …
- All in all, … The overall effect is … The poem aims to show/illustrate/convey/express the idea that … The overall message of the poem is …

274 Skills File

SF 22 • Listening and viewing skills

Listening and viewing skills

▶ SF 22 Listening

When you have to deal with a listening task at school, you are normally first given time to read the questions you will have to answer. These questions may be closed such as multiple choice (▶ SF 10: Working with closed test formats) but they can also be more open. After reading the tasks you are usually allowed to listen to the audio file twice.

> **TIP**
>
> In contrast to listening at school, you will not normally have the opportunity to listen to something twice in real life situations, e.g. to a train announcement. You then need to be able to identify relevant information right away – or you may ask people for clarification who have listened to the same thing. In a conversation, you may ask the speaker to repeat what they have said.

LISTENING FOR GIST

Listening for gist is what you do to find out what the main topic of a spoken text is, e.g. when you want to see if an audio file is relevant for you.

Step 1: Before listening for gist, collect information on the following if possible:
- the text type (e.g. newscast, lecture, panel discussion, interview) and its addressee
- the situation and *setting
- the number of speakers and their role in the audio file. For example, will there be conflicting points of view?
- the topic dealt with in the audio file and what points of view or concepts you are likely to encounter.

Step 2: When listening for gist,
- do not try to understand every detail that is said
- watch out for 'signpost expressions' that show somebody's train of thought, e.g. *the biggest issue is …, the most important argument is, on the one hand …* etc.
- listen carefully to a speaker's intonation; it may help you identify their attitudes or intentions.

Step 3: Summarize the text so as to prove that you can identify its topic.

LISTENING FOR DETAIL

You listen for detail if you need specific information, e.g. tips given for a specific problem.

Step 1: Before listening for detail,
- remember what you know about the text (its speaker, addressee, situation, setting and/or topic) and try to anticipate what might be said in the text
- collect keywords that are relevant to your question, e.g. names, dates or numbers
- prepare your notepad so that you can take notes quickly. (▶ SF 15: Marking up a text / Making and taking notes)

Step 2: When listening for detail,
- watch out for the keywords you collected
- take notes, using abbreviations and symbols.

Skills File

SF   Listening and viewing skills • SF 23

▶ SF 23 Analysing a film

*Watching a film can make you laugh or cry, feel angry or scared. Those reactions are not only caused by the story the film tells but also by the way it tells its story. Just like written texts can provoke a reaction in their readers through the choice of words and *stylistic devices, films can achieve a certain response in the viewer through, for example, their camera work, editing and sound.*

BEFORE VIEWING

Step 1: Find out what kind of film you are going to watch and try to get an idea of what to expect by looking at available information on the film (e.g. film posters, reviews, DVD covers, magazine information). What genre does it belong to (feature film, documentary, video clip, commercial etc.)?

WHILE VIEWING

Step 1: Watch one or more scenes and make notes on how the characters act, what the *setting is like or what information is presented. You may also add some observations on cinematic devices such as camera angle, sound and light. A **viewing log** can help you structure your notes. Here is one example for the first scene of *Never Let Me Go* (you may choose other categories to serve your own purposes):

Scene	What?	Where?	Who?	Camera	Sound	Light	Effect
1	a patient (Tommy) is being prepared for a surgery	hospital: operating room	carer (Kathy) and patient	close-up of Kathy, over-the-shoulder shot towards Tommy → Kathy's point of view	only voice-over of Kathy, no other sound	operating room is illuminated, no additional light	very emotional
…	…	…	…	…	…	…	…

Step 2: Watch the specific scenes once more and have a closer look at the cinematic devices used and the effect they achieve. Add your observations to your viewing log. The table below may help you.

Camera angle/movement or sound	Example	Possible effect
The camera seems to be looking through the eyes of the character or is looking directly over his or her shoulder (**over-the-shoulder shot**). One character's face is shown in **close-up** (cf. the picture on the right), while the other characters are presented through **long** or **medium shots**.		The character's emotions are revealed and you identify with that character.
A character is shown through a **low-angle shot**.		The character appears bigger. He or she seems to be dominant, i.e. to have power over the other characters in this scene.

276 Skills File

SF 23 • Listening and viewing skills

A character is shown through a **high-angle shot**.		The character appears smaller. He or she seems to be inferior, i.e. to have less power than the other characters in this scene.
Two or more characters are shown through **eye-level shots**.		The characters appear to be on the same level.
The scene is rather dark. People and objects cannot be clearly distinguished. The **soundtrack** is eery or moves towards a *climax.		The viewer may feel tense or scared.
There are short **shots** and lots of **cuts**. *Flashbacks (showing past events) or **flash-forwards** (showing future events) are used.		The *action is fast-paced and exciting.
The camera takes a steady position.		The action appears slower.
The music is uplifting, pleasant or catchy.		The viewer feels relaxed and in a good mood.

■ LANGUAGE HELP

- The film is about … / shows … / tells the story of …
- The music intensifies/fades as … / creates/builds tension/suspense/joy/…
- The actor's body language and facial expressions add to the feeling of …
- In this scene the music and lyrics / the props support the plot / underline the feeling of …

- The soundtrack/lighting/editing establishes/re-inforces the mood of the scene.
- The camera movement creates a feeling of …
- The camerawork/soundtrack helps to … / under-lines/emphasizes …
- The close-ups reveal his/her emotional state.
- The props in her room characterize her as a … person.

DVD **PRACTICE**

You are going to watch an extract from *The Hunger Games*, a 2012 science fiction film. It depicts a dysto-pian state in which every year a group of teenagers, the 'tributes', are forced to take part in a televised event and fight each other to the death until only the victor remains alive. In the extract you are going to watch the protagonist Katniss is being chased by other tributes.

1. Watch the extract and use a viewing log to structure your observations. Work with a partner to complete your notes.

2. The extract is full of contrasts: the wild forest vs. the television headquarters, Katniss on her own vs. the group of other tributes, the wild chase vs. a moment of rest when the other tributes let Katniss be for some time. Choose one of the contrasts, watch the extract again and examine the cinematic devices used to create this contrast.

SF Speaking skills (monologues and dialogues) • SF 24

Speaking skills (monologues and dialogues)

▶ SF 24 Giving a presentation

Informing an audience about a topic is an important skill to master and one that will be useful not only in school (classroom presentations etc.) but also in later life (university/work etc.). To give a successful presentation the following steps may be a helpful guide.

PLANNING A PRESENTATION

Step 1: Find out about the general framework for your talk, e.g.
- its topic
- the time limit for your presentation
- your audience and their background knowledge of the topic
- the kind of equipment available (smartboard, blackboard, flip chart, digital/video projector, laptop).

Step 2: Research your subject and make notes in English. (▶ SF 15: Marking up a text / Making and taking notes)
- If you are working in a team, decide who is going to work on which aspect.
- Use different sources so that you cover all relevant aspects and your information is reliable. (▶ SF 5: Doing research).

PREPARING A PRESENTATION

Step 1: Decide what information you need and work out a structure for it. (▶ SF 8: Structuring ideas)

Step 2: Think of ways to make your talk interesting and easy to understand for your audience:
- Plan the beginning of your presentation carefully: refer to interesting or funny facts or give anecdotes which lead to the topic of your presentation.
- Remember the KISS-rule: **K**eep **i**t **s**hort and **s**imple!
- Keep your audience's attention by naming interesting or funny details or examples.
- Check whether there are words or phrases that need to be explained to the audience so that they can follow your presentation.
- If suitable, prepare charts, visuals, diagrams etc. to present facts and figures visually. (▶ SF 7: Making visual aids)

Step 3: Prepare a handout or poster or use a presentation programme to accompany your presentation:
- Design them in a way that helps your audience to follow your presentation (cf. the tips on the right).
- Proofread your material. (▶ SF 40: Proofreading)
- Before the actual presentation, make sure that any electronic media you want to use are working and that you can handle them.

■ TIP

When preparing a **poster** or **wall-display**:
- Give it a clear structure or line of thought that guides the reader through the various sections of the poster.
- Make it visually attractive and informative.
- Present complex information visually, e.g. through diagrams.
- Keep a good balance between visuals and written information.
- Make sure that the writing can be read from the back of the room.
- Use bullet-points, short sentences or keywords and try to avoid any redundancies.
- Indicate the sources you used.

When preparing a **handout**:
- Decide if you want to distribute it before the presentation so that it helps your audience to follow your talk (in that case it might make sense to leave room for notes) or if you want to hand it out after the presentation to remind your audience of the main points (in that case tell them that a handout will be distributed at the end).
- Give it a clear structure.
- Present the most important information, key quotations, diagrams and/or charts on it.
- Use bullet-points, short sentences or keywords and try to avoid any redundancies.
- Indicate the sources you used.

---

278 Skills File

SF 24 • Speaking skills (monologues and dialogues)

Step 4: If you are giving your presentation in a team
- decide who is going to present which parts
- check that the different parts add up to a coherent presentation
- make sure that everybody takes part in the presentation.

Step 5: Prepare notes that will guide you through your presentation and help you to speak freely without reading from the page. (▶ SF 15: Marking up a text / Making and taking notes)

> **TIP**
> Write keywords or notes on index cards, number the cards and use only them during your presentation.

Step 6: Practise your presentation:
- Look up the pronunciation of difficult words in a dictionary.
- Practise your presentation in front of friends or a mirror or record it, e.g. using a smartphone. If you are doing a team presentation, practise as a team.
- Make sure you don't exceed your time limit.

DOING A PRESENTATION

Step 1: Give your presentation:
- Wait until the audience are quiet, then greet them and give an overview of your presentation.

> **LANGUAGE HELP**
> 'Hello everybody. My talk today is going to be on … First I will give you a general idea of … After that I will tell you more about … At the end of the talk I will explain why … and give you some examples.'

- Speak clearly, loudly and not too fast. Make suitable pauses.
- Speak freely and don't read out complete sentences.
- Avoid extremely long sentences and too many figures or new words. Remember that your audience can only listen to your presentation once.
- Refer to your poster, wall-display or handout if appropriate, but don't read it out word for word.
- Try to maintain eye-contact with your classmates.
- If you use new or difficult words, help your audience by writing them on the board and explaining them.

> **TROUBLE SPOT**
> **word by word** = one word at a time, one word after the other
> **word for word** = in exactly the same words

Step 2: Round off your presentation by
- summarizing the most important aspects
- thanking your audience for their attention
- asking them if they have any questions.

> **LANGUAGE HELP**
> 'So, as I have pointed out, … It is important to keep in mind that … That was my presentation on … Thank you for listening. I hope you enjoyed my/our presentation. Do you have any questions?'

Skills File

SF
Speaking skills (monologues and dialogues) • SF 25

► SF 25 Giving a speech

When you give a speech you want to reach your audience and persuade them of your point of view on a topic. In order to achieve this goal, you need two things: firstly, a well-structured text with carefully chosen words and *stylistic means and secondly, an effective way of delivering it.

PLANNING A SPEECH

Step 1: Find out about the general framework for your speech, e.g.
- its topic
- the time available

- the purpose of your speech: do you want it to inspire people / lead to a specific action / …?
- your audience and their background knowledge / attitudes.

- *task: convince your student body council that your school should become more environmentally friendly*
- *purpose: lead to action*

- *audience: some students have talked about it in class; some might be tackling the issue already*

Step 2: Brainstorm and/or research your topic: collect any ideas, stories or arguments that fit your topic and form your own opinion on it. Make notes (► SF 15: Marking up a text / Making and taking notes).

- *things you can do every day, e.g. separate rubbish, turn off lights, don't use paper cups for your coffee, …*
- *may be inconvenient at first, but will become normal*

PREPARING A SPEECH

Step 1: From your ideas choose essential points that are relevant to your topic and the message you wish to get across to your audience. Make notes and organize them
- by structuring them into introduction/ body/conclusion (► SF 8: Structuring ideas)
- by choosing the best two to five ideas for the body of your speech and putting them in a suitable order (► SF 8: Structuring ideas).

- *introduction: watching* The Day after Tomorrow *made me depressed – how can I make a change?*
- *body: little things done by normal people can make a change; it's no use blaming politicians for not acting; …*
- *conclusion: be the change!*

Step 2: Unless you are a highly experienced speaker, write out your complete speech:
- Choose the correct *register for your specific audience, e.g. scientific, colloquial, … (► LP 11: Using the right register)

- Use your own experience.

- Use clear and short sentences. Make logical connections clear by using linking words (► SF 38: Writing a well-structured text).

- *register: colloquial, e.g. 'Look at this school. We are a huge number of people. Think about the mountain of rubbish we produce every day. Is it really necessary?'*

- *personal experience: 'We throw away a lot of different things at school: paper, Kleenex, sweet wrappers, broken pens.'*
- *short sentences: 'So, take a stand. Ask the school for separate bins for paper, plastic and other rubbish.'*

280
Skills File

SF 25 • Speaking skills (monologues and dialogues)

- Be persuasive: use *stylistic devices to convince your audience, e.g. *contrasts, *rhetorical questions, *enumerations, *alliterations, direct address of audience …

contrast: 'A small act – like closing the window before you leave – can have a big effect.'

Step 3: Write introduction and conclusion:
- Write a conclusion: sum up the main points, give a final effective example supporting your message, further food for thought or an appeal for action.
- When you have prepared most of your speech, think of a good introduction, e.g. a true story, a quotation, a rhetorical question, an interesting statistic, a joke.

conclusion: 'You could argue that some students might not be interested in environmentally friendly behaviour and I have to agree. That is why I need your support. Set an example. Do the right thing. Help our school become active in our fight for a healthier planet.'

introduction: 'Last Saturday I watched the film *The Day after Tomorrow* and felt really depressed. I don't want my world to be flooded or frozen over. I want to be able to live in a beautiful, clean world. So if I want that, what can I do to make a change?'

Step 4: Prepare the presentation of your speech:
- Print out your speech in a format that is easy to read out from (fonts and margins not too small). If you know your speech by heart write keywords or notes on index cards.
- Mark passages and words that you want to emphasize.

Step 5: Practise your speech by reading or saying it out loud (check the pronunciation of difficult words if necessary). Even if you read it, try to make it sound as if you were delivering it freely. Practise it in front of friends or a mirror or record it, e.g. using a smartphone. Make sure you don't exceed your time limit.

> **TIP**
> Write keywords or notes on index cards, number the cards and use only them during your presentation.

GIVING A SPEECH

Giving a speech is not like reading something out (even if you have written it down). Try to speak as freely as possible and maintain the attention of your audience.

- Wait until the audience are quiet, then greet them and state your topic.
- Speak clearly, loudly and not too fast. Pause in suitable places.
- Use facial expressions and gestures to emphasize important points.
- Try to maintain eye-contact with your listeners.
- Thank your audience for their attention.

> **PRACTICE**
> Your school is planning to introduce bilingual classes for History and Biology. The lessons are to be held in English from Year 8 on. Decide on your position, then write and practise a speech. Present it to your classmates.

Skills File

SF Speaking skills (monologues and dialogues) • SF 26–SF 27

▶ SF 26 Taking part in an interview

In lesson situations but also when applying for a job you may be asked to take part in interviews, either asking or answering questions. It is essential to prepare for an interview and to follow some general guidelines.

PREPARING FOR AN INTERVIEW

- On the basis of your role card or the task given prepare questions you are going to ask (as interviewer) or think of possible answers to questions you might be asked (as interviewee).
- For **job interviews,** you need to be prepared to say why you might be suitable for the offered position. Do research on the company you are applying for and prepare some questions you might want to ask. It might be useful to rehearse a job interview with a friend or parent.

MASTERING THE INTERVIEW

- Speak loud enough and clearly. Be aware of your non-verbal communication: Try to maintain eye-contact with the interviewer/interviewee and smile when saying hello at the beginning or thanking your interviewer/interviewee at the end. (▶ CC 4: Meeting and greeting)
- As an **interviewer**: Start off by using your prepared questions, but be flexible – phrase new questions if some interesting aspect is touched on or rephrase a question if you feel that it was not answered fully.
- As an **interviewee**: Take your time to think about your answers rather than blurting out a reply that does not show you in a good light. Do not simply answer questions with *yes* or *no*, but use your answers to show your qualifications or to express your thoughts. If you have not understood a question fully, ask the interviewer to clarify it.

■ LANGUAGE HELP

Interviewer
- Nice to meet you. / Thank you for coming.
- To start off, would you like to say something about …? / First, let me ask you … / My next question would be … / If you think so, then why didn't you … / Let's get back to my original question …
- You just said …, how does that relate to …?
- Thank you very much for taking part in this interview.

Interviewee
- Nice to meet you too. / Thank you for inviting me today. / I am fine, thank you.
- I am not sure I have understood your question correctly. / Sorry, could you rephrase that?/ I'm glad you asked that question because … / … is very important to me, as … / A good example of the aspect you mention is … / Let me explain that in some more detail.
- Thank you for the chance to speak to you.

PRACTICE

You want to find out your fellow students' priorities for their future lives – earning a lot of money or following their dreams? Choose someone from your class and prepare and conduct an interview with them.

▶ SF 27 Having a discussion

In a (classroom) discussion you exchange ideas and opinions with others. Discussions may be spontaneous or they may be more formal, e.g. in panel discussions or debates (▶ SF 28: Having a debate). If possible, you should prepare for the discussion so that you have your arguments and useful words and phrases ready.

THE PREPARATION STAGE

Step 1: Research the topic and make notes (▶ SF 5: Doing research, ▶ SF 15: Marking up a text / Making and taking notes). Form an opinion on it and note down arguments. In a role-play you may have to take a position which is not really your own, so make sure that your arguments are in line with *your role*. Think of counter-arguments and of ways to reject them.

282 **Skills File**

SF 27 • Speaking skills (monologues and dialogues)   SF

Step 2: Structure your notes (▶ SF 8: Structuring ideas) and arrange them in a way that helps you to have the relevant facts ready during the discussion.

Step 3: Prepare an initial statement on the topic; this will ease your way into the discussion. If you are assigned a specific role, be prepared to introduce yourself.

THE DISCUSSION STAGE

Step 1: State your point of view on the topic, e.g. give your prepared statement.

Step 2: Listen to what others say and refer back to their statements, e.g. by saying which of their arguments do not convince you and why. You might also counter an argument by asking a provocative question. Remember to bring in the facts you collected to support your view.

■ LANGUAGE HELP

Stating your opinion	Agreeing	Disagreeing
• In my opinion/view … • As far as I'm concerned … • Well, I'd say … • It's a fact that … • The way I see it, … • Personally, I think … • If you ask me … • It seems to me that … • I think/feel/reckon/believe … • First of all … / To start with I'd like to point out that … • There can be no doubt that … • Nobody will deny that … • I'm absolutely convinced that …	• I quite agree. • I couldn't agree with you more. • Quite!/Exactly!/Precisely! • Certainly!/Definitely! • You're quite right. • I agree entirely/completely. • That's just how I see it/feel about it. • You've got a good point there. • That's exactly how I see it. • Yes, indeed.	**Polite disagreement:** • I'm afraid I don't quite agree there. • I'm not so sure, really. • Do you really think so? • Well, that's one way of looking at it, but … • I'm not convinced that … • Well, I have my doubts about that. **Strong disagreement:** • I doubt that very much. • That doesn't convince me at all. • I don't agree with you at all. • I disagree entirely. • It's not as simple as that.

Asking for clarification	Signalling that you would like to say something	Adding a point
• I'm sorry, but I don't understand/know what you mean by … • Could you give an example/explain that, please? • Can you prove that?/I would be very interested in some data/examples that prove your statement.	• May I interrupt?/Excuse me, I would like to add to that. • An important aspect is missing here, namely … • That illustrates perfectly what … • Can I just say/explain that …? • I would just like to jump in here, to clarify that … • I hope you don't mind me interrupting, but it is important to stress …	• Another thing is … • What's more, … • On top of that, … • We must also consider … • I would like to add to that … • Have you ever considered/thought about …

Buying time	
• Well, that is an interesting point./I see what you mean. • I think the question we were discussing was …	• You have given your opinion, however … • Why don't we see what X has to say about that?

Step 3: At the end of the discussion, summarize your point of view or your main arguments.

■ LANGUAGE HELP

• I have shown that …/It has become clear that …
• Let me just state again that it is vital to …/The most important argument is …/At the end of the day you can't deny that …

• If we don't … then…/In spite of everything we have heard from the other side …

283

Skills File

Speaking skills (monologues and dialogues) • SF 28

Step 4 *(optional)*: If a chairperson has moderated the discussion, he/she may summarize the main line of the discussion and round it off.

> **LANGUAGE HELP**
> - We have seen/heard that … / The majority on the panel/in the audience thinks that … / Some are in favour of …, others against it, but in general you can say that …
> - The general trend seems to be … / On the one hand, … On the other hand, …
> - All in all this discussion has shown …

▶ SF 28 Having a debate

A debate is a formal discussion of a 'motion' (proposal) that ends in a vote. Similar to a discussion, the aim of a debate is to present arguments as convincingly as possible, so participants need well-prepared arguments as well as rhetorical skills. There is often a particular set of rules for the debate, which participants have to agree on before holding the debate. The following steps outline how you could go about holding a formal debate.

Step 1: Organizing a debate

The 'motion' (i.e. a controversial topic) is the starting point for a debate. Often it is provided by the teacher, but in other cases, your class may be asked to suggest a number of motions and then agree on one of them. The motion is then phrased in a formalized way:

- 'This house proposes that *(… students should be allowed to use smart phones during lessons)*.'
- 'This house would *(… abolish the death penalty world-wide)*.'
- 'This house believes that *(… minimum wages are a threat to the German economy)*.'

The class is then divided into two groups, one for and one against the motion.
Usually a chairperson and a timekeeper are chosen and a time-limit for each speaker is specified (often 3–6 minutes per speaker).

Step 2: Preparing the debate

- In your group (either for or against the motion) research the topic, collect and note down arguments for your side. Your personal opinion on the motion is not relevant here – you must argue for your team. List and rank the arguments that you have for your team in order of importance.
- Write your arguments on index-cards so that you have them ready during the debate.
- Think of arguments for the opposing view and ways to reject them.
- Choose speakers for your side. The other students are the audience, called the 'floor'.

Step 3: Holding the debate

A debate follows a clear structure. The 'chair' will make sure that the rules are followed and that time-limits are respected.

A debate in the House of Hommons

SF 28 • Speaking skills (monologues and dialogues)   **SF**

Team in favour of the motion

FIRST PROPOSAL: The first speaker proposes the motion (= argues in favour of the motion) and gives some main arguments.

> **LANGUAGE HELP**
> - This house firmly believes that …
> - Not only is … but also …

SECOND PROPOSAL: The second speaker of the affirmative team presents further arguments in favour of the motion. He/she also responds to the aspects mentioned by the first speaker of the opposing team, outlining where the positions conflict.

> **LANGUAGE HELP**
> - The opposing team has tried to create the impression that …
> - However, we can prove that …
> - It is therefore evident that …

Team opposing the motion

FIRST OPPOSITION: The first speaker of this team opposes the motion (= argues against the motion).

> **LANGUAGE HELP**
> - We strongly advise against following the proposed motion because …
> - The most obvious reason for this is that …

SECOND OPPOSITION: The second speaker of the opposing team presents further arguments against the motion and/or restates the position of his/her team. The main task here is to defeat the arguments presented by the team in favour of the motion.

> **LANGUAGE HELP**
> - Again it needs to be stated that by following the arguments of the team in favour of the motion, …
> - … would lead to / cause …

A short recess may be taken here to prepare for the following 'rebuttals'.

FIRST REBUTTAL: The team against the motion defends their arguments and tries to rebut the arguments of the affirmative team.

SECOND REBUTTAL: The affirmative team supports their point of view and tries to rebut the arguments of the opposing team.

THIRD REBUTTAL: The opposing team give their closing statements.

FOURTH REBUTTAL: The affirmative team give their closing statements.

Rules for the debate:
- Speakers may not interrupt each other at any point.
- Speakers must wait their turn.
- The time-limits as given by the chair must be respected.
- Speakers must remain polite and respectful of the other team.
- Statements must be backed up by giving examples or proof, by referring to research, experience etc.

Step 4: Concluding the debate
- The 'floor' (i.e. the audience) may ask questions and/or present their ideas on the topic.
- The 'house' (i.e. everyone present) may take a vote on the motion by a show of hands, not based on what they personally agree or disagree with, but on who made the better case by presenting the best arguments and speaking most convincingly.
- Members of the two debating teams may get some feedback from their classmates.

Skills File

SF

Writing skills • SF 29

Writing skills

▶ SF 29 Writing a formal letter or email

When applying for a place at university, asking for information from a company or organization, etc., your email or letter should follow certain formal rules.

Buechelstrasse 52
53157 Bonn
Germany

Write your address (without your name) in the top right corner of your **letter**. Don't use typical German letters like *ä, ö, ü* or *ß*.

Ref. Nr.: 315/14
Joanne Sutton
14 Springfield Place
Chelmsford
CM2 7ZA
United Kingdom

Write the address of the person or company you are writing to on the left. If you have a reference number, write it above the recipient's address.

3 February 2015

Write the date on the right.

Show what the letter is about in a heading.

Application for an internship

Start your letter with *Dear Madam or Sir* if you don't know the recipient's name, otherwise write *Dear Mr/Mrs/Ms ...* In BE, there is usually no comma after the greeting; in AE a colon after the greeting is used in formal letters.

Dear Mrs Sutton

I am writing to apply for an internship at the National Gallery. I will be finishing school in July 2014, with A-levels in English, Art, History and Maths. As I have always had a particular interest in art and history, I would like to get a deeper insight into work in this field before I start my university course in art history at the University of Cologne in October 2014. As your website specifies that short-term internships are possible, I would be delighted to be given a chance to work at the National Gallery.

Always start with a capital letter (e.g. *With great interest, I read ...*).

State the reason you are writing in the opening paragraph.

I enclose a copy of my CV, which shows that I have some experience of running educational classes and as a tour guide at our local museum in Bonn. I have also had the opportunity to take part in several art classes. As I speak English and German, I would also be able to deal with international visitors.

Add more detailed information in the following paragraphs e.g. about reasons for applying, qualifications, why you are the right person for the position etc.).

I would welcome the opportunity of enhancing my experience. As I am reliable, willing to learn and enthusiastic, I would certainly be a helpful addition to the team at the National Gallery.

Use long forms (*I am / We are/I would*) rather than short forms (*I'm / We're/I'd*) and abbreviations.

Thank you for considering my application for the internship. I look forward to hearing from you soon.

If you are asking for information or a favour, thank the recipient in advance.

Yours sincerely,

Finish your letter with *Yours faithfully* if you don't know the recipient's name, otherwise write *Yours sincerely* (AE: *Sincerely, Sincerely yours* or *Yours truly*).

Lea Sindern
Lea Sindern

Type your name at the end of the letter, leaving space for a handwritten signature.

286

Skills File

SF 30 • Writing skills

When writing a **formal email**
- you don't need to include the recipient's address or the date in the body of your email, as they appear automatically in the header
- open and close your mail the same way you would when writing a formal letter
- do not use emoticons, smileys, etc.
- type your name and contact details at the bottom.

A **letter to the editor** follows most of the conventions of a formal letter or email. Note the following, however:
- Nowadays, letters to the editor are very often sent by email. Watch out for contact information on the magazine's or paper's website.
- Your letter should be brief.
- Start like this: *Sir or Madam* (i.e. leave out *Dear*).
- Omit the closing remarks (*Yours faithfully/sincerely*).
- Don't forget to give your name, address and phone number.

▶ SF 30 Writing an application

If you want to apply for a holiday job or a position in a company (e.g. an internship), you should send them a cover letter and a CV (curriculum vitae).

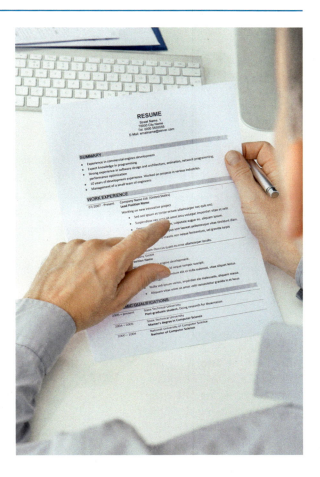

THE COVER LETTER
The cover letter for an application (cf. p. 286) follows the rules of a formal letter (▶ SF 29). Since you are presenting yourself, it is important to avoid mistakes and to use formal language (▶ LP 11: Using the right register). State in what ways you are suited for the position you are applying for. Show that you have collected information about the company you are writing to and that you have a real interest in the position advertised. Mention what documents you are enclosing. At the end of the letter, express hope for a reply or an invitation to an interview.

THE CV (*AE*: résumé ['rezəmeɪ])
Your CV (cf. p. 288) gives information about you, about your education, qualifications, etc. to the person you are applying to. A CV should be clear and effective – remember the KISS rule ('Keep it short and simple'). Use a clear and easy-to-read font, highlight particularly relevant information, and don't forget to check your CV for spelling mistakes.

SF Writing skills • SF 30

CURRICULUM VITAE
Lukas Meister

Rheinuferstrasse 2, 53158 Bonn, Germany
Telephone: +49(0)201 000 8177 Mobile: +49 178 000 4235
Email: Lukasmeister@mail.de

Give your personal details: name, contact details, nationality, etc.

Personal statement

I have always enjoyed working with visual media, i.e. films, photographs, etc. and with computers. Being creative, I enjoy developing ideas to solve problems.
English is my favourite subject at school and I expect to improve my language skills further and to become a more independent person by spending time in the UK.

Add a personal statement explaining why you are suitable for the specific place or job.

Education

2008–date	Secondary School: Alfred-Krupp-Schule, Essen
2004–2008	Primary/Elementary School Gartenstrasse, Essen

Show the stages of your education so far (schools, exams, etc.).

Qualifications/skills

IT skills	Excellent knowledge of MS Word, PowerPoint, Excel, web design, photoshop
Language skills	German native speaker; good written and spoken English, basic French
Technology	Winner of the gold medal 2014 for 'school inventors' in the 'Junior Ingenieur Akademie' (school engineering course)

List your qualifications and present your key skills, especially those the employer is looking for.

Work experience

May 2014	Placement: two weeks at local IT company, organized by my school

Give information on any work experience.

Hobbies and interests

Member of school drama club, member of school computer club, member of after-school basketball club. I enjoy listening to and playing music and making films.

Write something about your hobbies or interests.

References

Available on request

Note down that references are available on request.

PRACTICE

Read the job advert on the right. Then write an application, consisting of a cover letter and your curriculum vitae, for the position of management assistant. (You may also make up a person applying for the job.)

SELLIT

International advertising company based in Nottingham, UK, is looking for a Management Assistant (entry level) for office-based work.
Requirements:
- degree in International Management
- good IT-skills
- fluent English (spoken and written)
- long-term availability.

CONTACT:
Sellit
Peter Miller
pmiller@sellit.co.uk
12 Springfield Road
Nottingham
NG1 5ZA
Great Britain

SF31 • Writing skills SF

► SF31 Writing a summary

When you work with written or spoken texts, you are often asked to summarize the text or certain aspects of it. To do this, you need a proper overview of the text, its content and its message. Then you have to decide what to include in your summary and what to leave out. The following steps and rules can guide you.

PLANNING YOUR SUMMARY

Step 1: Listen to or read the text carefully. Either make notes or mark the most important words and phrases (► SF15: Marking up a text / Making and taking notes). Find out which text type you are dealing with (► SF16: Identifying text types).

Step 2: Listen to or read the text again and try to answer the '5 Ws' (Who? What? Where? When? Why? Perhaps also *What is the consequence?*). To get a better understanding of the text, you may also want to use the reading strategies explained in ► SF14: Reading strategies.

Step 3: Decide which passages of the text (marked green in the example below, cf. *Context* pp. 172ff.) contain essential information that needs to be part of your summary and which passages can be left out. Take your time to check which parts of the text contain examples, numbers, comparisons, quotes, *imagery, direct speech, etc. – these parts do not belong in a summary.

Linguistic diplomacy: the Eurovision Song Contest *R.L.G.*

Where?/What? Last Saturday saw Denmark win the Eurovision Song Contest, the country's third win in the contest's history. A prototypically apple-cheeked[1] blonde took the trophy for her
Who? country, but she did so with the rather un-Danish name of Emmelie de Forest and the
What? equally un-Danish title, 'Only Teardrops'.

The contest has always been about more than music. Every year comes a slew[2] of artic-   5
What/Why? les about the political nature of the voting. Countries that share ethnic or political friend-
(Examples) ships routinely give each other high marks: Greece and Cyprus typically give each other the maximum of 12 points while stiffing[3] Turkey with *nul points*[4], for example. Estonia and Latvia this year gave Russia 12 points, no doubt because those countries' large Russian populations voted for their neighbour.   10

What? Language, of course, plays a role in this as well. 'Ethnicity'[5] in Europe is often linguistic: an ethnic Russian is not apparent on the streets of Riga until he opens his mouth.
Why? Linguistic neighbours will tend to be generous to one another. Finland and Estonia are
(Examples/ friendly not only because they are nearby but because their Finno-Ugric languages resem-
numbers) ble each other, while being utterly unrelated to their neigbours'. (Hungarian is also   15
Finno-Ugric.) Each country can give 12 points to only one other country, and this year Denmark and Sweden gave their 12's to Norway, Norway its 12 to Sweden, as befits[6] the Scandinavian language continuum.

But the Scandinavians share something else besides apple-cheeked blondes and North
What? Germanic languages: their tendency to sing in English. In that, they are like most coun-   20
tries nowadays. But some interesting variation clouds the picture.

From: the website of The Economist, 20 May 2013

---

[1] **apple-cheeked** having cheeks (= *Wangen*) the colour of apples   [2] **slew** (*ifml*) large number
[3] **stiff sb. with sth.** (*here*) reject / mildly insult sb.   [4] **nul points** [nyl pwɛ] (*French*) nil (= no) points
[5] **ethnicity** fact of belonging to a particular race   [6] **befit sb.** (*fml*) be suitable for sb.

289
Skills File

SF Writing skills • SF 32

WRITING YOUR SUMMARY

Step 1: Write your summary in your own words.

1 Write an introductory phrase, mentioning the essential aspects, such as the title, *author, topic, main message and source of the text. (► LP 18: Writing about texts)

> **LANGUAGE HELP**
> - The story/text is about …
> - The text deals with …
> - In the text the reader gets to know …
> - The topic of the text is …
> - The article shows …

2 Use the present tense (► LP 3: Simple present and present perfect). Don't copy the original text – use your own words. Use linking words to connect your ideas (► SF 38: Writing a well-structured text).

3 Round off your text by restating the main message or *action.

Step 2: Check your summary. Does it contain the most important facts and ideas from the original text? Have you left out examples, unnecessary details, etc.? Have you checked the spelling, punctuation, tenses, etc.? (► SF 40: Proofreading, ► LP 12: Spelling)

The article 'Linguistic diplomacy: the Eurovision Song Contest', written by an author abbreviated as R.L.G. and published in The Economist *on 20 May 2013, investigates the languages of songs entered for the Eurovision Song Contest and points out that English has had a leading role over the years.*

In the article, the author takes Denmark's win of the last ESC as a starting point to look into different influencing factors of the voting.
After mentioning political reasons, i.e. neighbouring or politically close countries, the writer moves on to the main topic: the chosen languages of the songs being entered. Countries seem to give more points to songs from countries sharing the same language. Using the starting point of Denmark's win again, the writer focuses on the dominance of English …

All in all, the text focuses on … and invites the reader to make up their mind whether …

> **PRACTICE**
>
> Summarize the extract from Alan Bennet's *The Uncommon Reader* (pp. 96f.) in no more than 200 words.

► SF 32 Writing a review

When writing a review, you provide information on a book, play or film you have read or watched, as well as expressing your opinion about it. Reviews are meant to either recommend the work in question or to discourage people from reading or seeing it.

PREPARING YOUR REVIEW

Step 1: Read the book or watch the film/play you want to write about, making notes of interesting, very good or very bad aspects. It may be useful to consider typical elements of the text-type in question (► SF 16: Identifying text types).

Step 2: Add to your notes, writing down important information about the book or the film. Structure your ideas (► SF 8). The grid on the next page will help you to identify the relevant aspects, but you could also use a mindmap to structure your ideas.

290
Skills File

SF 32 • Writing skills

Header		
Title	*2012*	
Running time	*157 minutes*	
Your rating	**** (out of five) (= okay)*	
Year	*2009*	
Director's name	*Roland Emmerich*	
Introduction Basic information: type of movie/book, characters	- *disaster film / science fiction action film* - *science fiction writer Jackson Curtis tries to rescue his two children and his ex-wife from a geological and meteorological super-disaster*	
Main part Short summary of the plot (Be careful: perhaps your readers don't want to be told the ending before they have read the book or watched the film themselves.) Cast/characters	- *2009: scientist discovers that the temperature of the Earth is rising unexpectedly; international leaders plan to save a certain number of people on Arks* - *2012: Jackson Curtis (John Cusack), a divorced writer of science fiction, takes children Noah (Liam James) and Lily (Morgan Lily) camping in Yellowstone National Park, hears fears about the end of the world by Charlie Frost (Woody Harrelson)* - *they return home; earthquakes are everywhere; Jackson rents plane for his children and ex-wife; they leave LA before California is destroyed* - *family tries to get to the Arks; the President of the US dies in a tsunami* - *Jackson and his family reach the Arks and manage to get on board*	
Comments Your opinion, e.g. on *plot, *actors, *characters, *dialogues, special effects, the 'message', etc.	- *great special effects in the depiction of the catastrophe, impressive when famous buildings collapse* - *dramatic music/great sound* - *the film is fun to watch if you like action films* - *John Cusack convincing as Jackson Curtis: not the typical action hero, but likeable and a bit quirky – good contrast to the action scenes* *BUT:* - *parts of the film are not logical, i.e. characters use mobile phones while the earth is exploding around them* - *film has some quite scary parts* - *film is far too long* - *all in all, film seems to be a bit far-fetched*	
Conclusion Summary of your opinion, recommendation/target group	- *quite good science fiction disaster film with great action scenes* - *too long and partly exaggerated* - *only suitable for lovers of action/disaster movies – don't expect too much!*	

Scenes from the film 2012

SF Writing skills • SF 32

WRITING YOUR REVIEW

• Start with a catchy title and a **header** which contains basic facts. • Use the present tense. • Avoid imprecise words like *good, really bad* etc. • Start with an **introductory paragraph** with basic information.	*A film review:* **2012:** *not quite the perfect disaster* *2009 running time: 157 minutes rating: *** (okay)* *The science fiction disaster film 2012, directed by Roland Emmerich, is an action-packed and generally enjoyable film, which has some riveting images and lots of gripping scenes, but which is also rather far-fetched in many places …*
• In the **main part** first give a short summary of the plot without giving away the end of the film/book.	*After a scientist …* *After having obtained a map from Charlie, who dies while reporting about the events, the family tries to get to the Arks, …*
• Then **comment** on the positive or negative aspects of the book/film/play.	*The special effects in 2012 are definitely worth seeing: images of the earth being destroyed are powerful and often scary. The special effects are sometimes truly breath-taking …* *… all this is underlined by a dramatic score. So for all lovers of action films, 2012 definitely is fun to watch. It even has some good acting: John Cusack shines in his role as …*
• Finish your review by **summarizing** the main aspects and by giving a **recommendation** whether the book/film is worth watching/reading. • Use linking words to connect your ideas. (▶ SF 38: Writing a well-structured text; ▶ LP 12: Linking words and phrases; ▶ LP 15: Connecting your thoughts)	*But is the film a real masterpiece? Unfortunately not. It is irritating for the viewers that …* *… And last but not least, the film might be considered just a bit too scary for the faint-hearted!* *All in all, it might have been a good idea to tone the film down a little.* *So here is my final verdict. Is 2012 a perfect film or is it a disaster? It is neither one nor the other but it is a perfect disaster film, and lovers of action films and disaster are going to get their money's worth – and perhaps even more than they bargained for. However, if you are looking for a scientifically correct, logical plot and deeper insights into life, I recommend finding a different film for your Saturday night.*
• Proofread your text. (▶ SF 40: Proofreading; ▶ LP 17: Spelling)	

PRACTICE

Choose a film that you enjoyed watching in the past six months. Write a short review, focusing on the film's strengths and – if you found any – weaknesses and recommending it to your classmates.

292 **Skills File**

SF 33 • Writing skills

▶ SF 33 Writing a report

Reports offer factual information about a recent event. The information is given in a chronological order and the language used is objective and formal.

The following instructions guide you through the steps of writing a report. Your task is to write a report on the stolen toasters, based on the drama extract on the right.

Steps	Example
Step 1: Gather as much information about the event as possible. Try to answer the '5 Ws' (who? where? what? when? why? and if possible: what are the consequences?). If your report is based on a fictitious event (e.g. from a novel or play) you might need to add missing details such as last names, place names or dates.	(The play is set in a Los Angeles suburb.) *Very early morning, between night and day*, no crickets, coyotes yapping feverishly in distance before light comes up. A small fire blazes up in the dark from alcove¹ area, sound of LEE smashing typewriter with a golf club, lights coming up, LEE seen smashing typewriter methodically then dropping pages of his script into a burning bowl set on the floor of alcove, flames leap up. AUSTIN has a whole bunch of stolen toasters lined up on the sink counter along with LEE's stolen TV. The toasters are of a wide variety of models, mostly chrome, AUSTIN goes up and down the line of toasters, breathing on them and polishing them with a dish towel. Both men are drunk, empty whiskey bottles and beer cans litter floor of kitchen, they share a half-empty bottle on one of the chairs in the alcove, LEE keeps periodically taking deliberate ax-chops² at the typewriter, using a nine-iron³ as AUSTIN speaks, all of their mother's house plants are dead and drooping. AUSTIN *[Polishing toasters]* There's gonna' be a general lack of toast in the neighborhood this morning. Many, many unhappy, bewildered breakfast faces. I guess it's best not to even think of the victims. Not to even entertain it. Is that the right psychology? LEE *[Pause]* What? AUSTIN Is that the correct criminal psychology? Not to think of the victims? LEE What victims? *[He takes another swipe at typewriter with nine-iron, adds pages to the fire.]* AUSTIN The victims of crime. Of breaking and entering. I mean is it a prerequisite⁴ for a criminal not to have a conscience? LEE Ask a criminal. *[Pause. LEE stares at AUSTIN.]* What're you gonna' do with all those toasters? That's the dumbest thing I ever saw in my life. AUSTIN I've got hundreds of dollars' worth of household appliances⁵ here. You may not realize that. LEE Yeah, and how many hundreds of dollars did you walk right past? AUSTIN It was toasters you challenged⁶ me to. Only toasters. I ignored every other temptation. LEE I never challenged you! That's no challenge. Anybody can steal a toaster. *[He smashes typewriter again]* From: Sam Shephard, *True West*, 1981

¹**alcove** part of a room where the wall goes further back to make an extra little space
²**take ax-chops** hit hard as if cutting wood with an ax
³**nine-iron** kind of golf club
⁴**prerequisite** necessary precondition
⁵**household applicances** machine that is designed to do a particular thing in the home
⁶**challenge sb. to sth.** invite sb. to do sth.

Skills File
293

Writing skills • SF 34

| Step 2: | Put the information in chronological order. If necessary, add further details. | • *a new case of breaking and entering*
• *last night*
• *suburb of L.A.*
• *stolen: toasters worth hundreds of dollars*
• *...* |

Step 3: Write your report:
- Use the simple past. (▶ LP 4: Present perfect and simple past)
- Start off with a summarizing sentence.
- If you write a longer report, divide it into paragraphs. (▶ SF 38: Writing a well-structured text)
- Use linking words to connect your ideas. (▶ SF 38: Writing a well-structured text)
- Make your report sound formal and matter-of-fact by using objective language and the passive voice where possible. (▶ LP 7: The passive; ▶ LP 11: Using the right register)
- Don't state personal thoughts, feelings or opinions. Try to focus on the facts, even if you use quotes from witnesses.

Step 4: Proofread yout text. (▶ SF 40; ▶ LP 17: Spelling)

■ LANGUAGE HELP
- On ... a ... occurred ... It is believed that ...
- The police confirmed that .... People are concerned about ... It is assumed that ... Sources revealed that ... was last seen ... Witnesses claim ... Under mysterious circumstances ... has disappeared.
- Latest events have shown ... Motives are as yet unclear.

> **PRACTICE**
>
> Look at the examples given for **Step 2**. Add further details from the text or invent them. Then put them in a suitable order and write your report.

▶ SF 34 Argumentative writing

When writing an argumentative text, you have to structure your text clearly and argue in a logical manner.

THE PLANNING STAGE
The starting point for an argumentative text can be a statement, a text you have read or a thesis you have been given, for example:
- 'For learners of English at German schools, Shakespeare's plays are incomprehensible, outdated and simply irrelevant. Therefore, his plays ought to be deleted from the curriculum of English classes.' Discuss.

Step 1: Brainstorm your topic and make notes.

Step 2: Collect pro and con arguments.

> In a written **discussion** (*Operator: discuss*) you give arguments for and against something and come to a justified conclusion. In a **comment** (*Operator: comment on/write a comment*) you want to convince the reader of your own opinion on an issue. You have to give arguments to support it and may even introduce counter-arguments which you refute to make your own arguments even stronger.

Pro: *Shakespeare's plays ought to be deleted from the curriculum of English classes.*	**Con:** *Shakespeare's plays should not be deleted from the curriculum of English classes.*
• *Students struggle with the language and ideas of the Elizabethan Age and therefore don't enjoy studying Shakespeare's works.* • *Students would benefit more from reading about events, characters and stories that are relevant to their own daily lives.* • *...*	• *Shakespeare's works are a vital part of English culture – learning about him and his works is part of general knowledge.* • *The topics and conflicts dealt with in Shakespeare's works are universal and can easily be transferred to a modern world (cf. the numerous modern versions of his plays).* • *...*

294

Skills File

SF 34 • Writing skills SF

Step 3: Arrange your arguments in a logical way, following either of these two patterns:

Pattern A	Pattern B
Present the arguments for and against in separate paragraphs:	Answer each argument immediately with its counter-argument:
1. Introduction	1. Introduction
2. Arguments pro	2. Argument 1 ► counter-argument 1
3. Arguments con	3. Argument 2 ► counter-argument 2
4. Conclusion	4. Argument 3 ► counter-argument 3
	5. Conclusion

It is usually a good idea to finish with the argument that supports your position most strongly because this is the one the reader will remember most. Sometimes, however, it may be helpful not to postpone your strongest argument until the very end, because you want to catch the reader's attention.

- ▪ *my position: con, i.e. Shakespeare's works should not be deleted from the curriculum*
- ▪ *line of argument: pattern B (argument → counter-argument)*
- ▪ *argument 1: Most students find Shakespeare's texts difficult to read.*
  → counter-argument 1: Shakespeare's texts are a vital part of English culture and are often referred to in everyday speech, so understanding them will eventually help students in everyday situations.
- ▪ *argument 2: Shakespeare's texts are set in a remote past, so students can't profit from them in their everyday lives. → counter-argument 2: Once students have understood a text from Shakespeare's plays, they will realize that the themes dealt with depict universal conflicts which can easily be transferred to modern life.*
- ▪ *…*

THE WRITING STAGE

Step 1: Write your introduction. Refer to the topic. In a comment, you can give your point of view here.

Young people today are confronted with a world that is becoming more and more complex and which offers new technology, new information and new forms of literature. Classic literature, notably the plays by William Shakespeare, no longer seem to be relevant to some people today. So they claim that Shakespeare's plays ought to be taken off the curriculum for English classes.

Step 2: Present your line of argument, following either pattern A or B (see above). Use linking words (► SF 38: Writing a well-structured text; ► LP 14: Using linking words and phrases; ► LP 15: Connecting your thoughts)

Many students claim that reading Shakespeare's plays is a challenge and not worth the effort: they argue that not only his language but also the ideas from his times are incomprehensible to young people in the 21st century.
However, Shakespeare's plays are a vital part of English culture – quotations from his plays have found their way into everyday English, into sayings and proverbs. Knowing about Shakespeare's works provides an important background for understanding the heritage of modern language and modern texts.
When I was first made to read Romeo and Juliet in school, I also struggled with Shakespeare's language and ideas and initially only saw the story in its historic context. But once I had fully understood …

> ███ TIP
>
> Your arguments will appear more convincing if you
> 1. quote authorities, experts or statistics; present facts
> 2. refer to your personal experience whenever possible

Skills File

SF · Writing skills · SF 35

Step 3: Write a conclusion. Round off your text by stating your thesis once again, but do not give new information and do not use the same phrases that you used in the introduction.

In conclusion, it seems clear that taking Shakespeare's plays off the curriculum for English classes would mean that students would be denied the chance of getting to know …

Those precious works of English literature should therefore remain a compulsory part of the curriculum for English classes.

Step 4: Proofread yout text. (▶ SF 40)

▶ SF 35 Writing a character profile

*Characters in fictional texts are presented through descriptions by the *narrator or other characters (*direct characterization) and through their appearance, language, attitude, behaviour, relationships to other characters and their thoughts and actions (*indirect characterization).

> ■ **TIP**
>
> When writing a character profile, do not describe *what* the character does, but explain *why* he/she says or does what he/she does.

Read the excerpt from the *novel *Payback Time* on pp. 190f. and describe Coach McNulty's character.

Step 1: Collect relevant passages in the text and make notes on

- general information we get about the character (outward appearance, social background, etc.)

- what the narrator or other characters say about the character you are dealing with

- what the character says about him-/herself

- what the character says and does.

- 'He took a seat behind a neatly organized desk.' (l. 9)

- (Mitch:) 'To him I'd always be a big fat loser and nothing more.' (l. 3)

- 'But McNulty's eyes were scary. I squirmed[1] as he stared at me, feeling like a snot-nosed preschooler who'd been caught marking a wall with crayons[2].' (l. 44)

- 'I do not intend to spend my life coaching high school.' (l. 57)

- ' "What's funny?" McNulty said, his blue-gray eyes glittering like shiny stones.' (l. 18)

- ' "No, no, no," McNulty said, pointing the pencil at me again. 'No questions – not today, not ever.' (l. 34)

- 'You write down or tape what I tell you. When I'm done, jazz it up[3] whatever you want, but never make me, my coaches, or my players look bad. Understand?' (l. 35)

- ' "Understood?" he said again, a threat in his voice.' (l. 46)

- 'Every sports story needs pictures. Either you've got to take them yourself, or you've got to get a photographer. Didn't you know that?' (l. 63)

---

[1] **squirm** *sich winden*   [2] **crayon** *Buntstift*   [3] **jazz sth. up** *(infml)* make sth. more interesting or attractive

296

Skills File

SF 35 • Writing skills | SF

Step 2: From your notes draw conclusions about the character.
Always note down examples from the text to give evidence on what you have concluded.

- *according to Mitch: judges people by their outward appearance and athletic ability, not their character → superficial, biased*
- *neatly organized desk → disciplined, conscientious*
- *controls what is being done and said → hungry for power superior, patronizing*
- *uses intimidation to achieve his aims → ruthless, cold*
- *makes others feel stupid → patronizing, condescending*

■ LANGUAGE HELP

- X appears to be … is portrayed as … This behaviour shows/ indicates … Evidence for this can be found in lines … The way she/he talks implies that …
- Her/his dress sense shows … This proves that … X is a person who can be considered courageous/optimistic/trustworthy/unreliable/disloyal/etc. …

Step 3: Write up your text.
- Structure your text (▶ SF 8) into
  – introduction (should include names, general information, the role the character plays in the story, etc.)

  – main part (should include details about the character, e.g. character traits, ambitions, aims, problems, inner conflicts, etc.)

  – conclusion (should summarize why the character acts/ reacts she way he/she does).

- Use the present tense. (▶ LP 3: Simple present and present perfect)

- Use linking words to connect your ideas. (▶ SF 38: Writing a well-structured text; ▶ LP 14: Linking words and phrases)

- Support your findings using quotes from the text. (▶ SF 39: Quoting a text)

Step 4: Proofread yout text. (▶ SF 40; ▶ LP 17: Spelling)

- *Coach Mc Nulty is a PE teacher and high school football coach who considers himself destined for greater things and therefore openly displays his superiority and power.*
- *…*

- *Mc Nulty is very ambitious and does not 'intend to spend [his] life coaching high school football' (l. x).*
- *To make sure he can achieve that goal he is willing to use threats ('Understood?', l. x)*
- *He is very condescending towards the reporter.*
- *…*

- *In summary, one can say that Coach Mc Nulty's ruthless ambition, his condescension and his patronizing manner reveal him to be an unfeeling, cold-hearted character and not a stereotypical friendly high school coach and teacher.*

Skills File

SF Writing skills • SF 36

▶ SF 36 Writing a text analysis

*Text analyses can be done with different types of texts, *fictional or *non-fictional texts. The aspects you analyse may differ from text type to text type (see the entries in the Skills File to find out which information is relevant for each text type, ▶ SF 18–21), but the process of analysing texts is usually the same for all of them.*

PREPARING YOUR TEXT ANALYSIS

Step 1: Read the task carefully to make sure you know exactly what you are asked to do (cf. 'Verbs for tasks', pp. 340f.). Sometimes you will be given a specific aspect to analyse, sometimes you will be free to select aspects yourself. The following are some suggestions for questions you might ask yourself:
- Which *stylistic devices are used? To what effect? (▶ SF 17: Analysing stylistic devices)
- Which noteworthy words and phrases are used? To what effect?
- How does the structure of the text add to its general meaning/*line of argument?
- How is the reader influenced by the text? To what effect?
- What information is being withheld? Why/To what effect?
- In what way does this text differ from other texts of the same type? (▶ SF 16: Identifying text types)
- …

Step 2: Read the text carefully and make sure you understand it properly. Use a dictionary where necessary (▶ SF 3). Make notes on features or aspects of the text that strike you as relevant to your analysis (▶ SF 15: Marking up a text/Making and taking notes). Remember to note down references from the text that support your analysis (▶ SF 39: Quoting a text).

Step 3: Structure your ideas (▶ SF 8). Do not follow the text chronologically, but structure your ideas according to the different aspects you are analysing.

WRITING YOUR TEXT ANALYSIS

Step 1: Write an introductory sentence in which you give the source and author of the text, the topic and a first general idea to answer your question. Write only one short paragraph, e.g.
In his speech given at Portland State University on 13 June 1998, President Bill Clinton focuses his speech around the topic of ethnic diversity in the US and stresses its positive aspects and the opportunities it offers, using various stylistic devices to bring his message home. (Cf. pp. 144f.)
Use the present tense. (▶ LP 18: Writing about texts)

Step 2: Write the main part of your text:
- Present your findings to support the central idea you stated in the introduction.
- Use different paragraphs for different ideas and introduce these paragraphs with topic sentences to guide the reader. Use linking words. (▶ SF 38: Writing a well-structured text)
- Remember to provide evidence from the text, i.e. to use quotations. (▶ SF 38: Quoting a text)

Step 3: Write a short conclusion:
- Refer to your introduction and write a concluding sentence in which you restate your first general idea or your main findings.
- Do NOT add new aspects at this point!
- Do NOT give your personal opinion or an evaluation!

Step 4: Proofread yout text. (▶ SF 40; ▶ LP 17: Spelling)

PRACTICE

Read the text 'Linguistic diplomacy: the Eurovision Song Contest' (pp. 172f.). Write an outline (▶ SF 8) for the following task: 'Analyse the different means the author of this article uses to get the reader's attention.'

298

Skills File

SF 37 • Writing skills | SF

▶ SF 37 Doing a creative writing task

Most creative writing tasks ask you to create a text using an existing piece of writing as a starting point.

NON-FICTIONAL TEXTS
Your creative task may take a *non-fictional text (such as a *speech or newspaper *article) as a starting point. In this case you usually have to assume a certain perspective and evaluate a situation through the eyes of a fictitious *character. You might, for example, be asked to read an article on a climate conference and then write an article from the perspective of a reporter who attended the conference. (▶ SF 18: Analysing non-fiction, ▶ SF 34: Argumentative writing).

FICTIONAL TEXTS
When dealing with *fictional texts a common creative task might be to write an ending to a story or to rewrite the story from a *character's point of view, i.e. to change perspective.

Continuation of a story
Step 1: Brainstorm ideas. Look at the *setting, events, dates, characters and their relationships in the original text and watch out for hints as to how the story might continue.

Step 2: Compare your ideas to the original text to make sure they don't contradict the reality depicted in the story.

Step 3: Identify the *narrative perspective of the original text (e.g. *first-person or *third-person narrator) and consider what limitations that specific perspective might have or not have.

Step 4: Write your continuation. Try to imitate the style and language used in the original.

Change of perspective
A change of perspective means that you take over the role of one of the characters in the story from whose perspective the story is *not* told. You retell its events from your point of view e.g. in a diary entry, a letter or an interior monologue.

Step 1: Brainstorm ideas. Pay attention to the relationships your character is involved in and to specific features such as his/her social status, age, special character traits etc.

Step 2: Ask yourself what your character might think and feel in a specific situation and also what your character knows and doesn't know.

Step 3: Write your text in a way that is appropriate to your character. Age, social status and other features usually determine how you speak or write.

Step 4: Pay attention to the *text type you're using. For example if you write a letter, you must address the addressee and sign it; if you write a dialogue, you should use typical elements of spoken language; if you write a diary entry you should focus on thoughts and feelings.

TIP

- Do not stray too far from the original text because your text may become illogical or far-fetched.
- Do not invent things that contradict the events of the original story.

299

Skills File

SF | Writing skills • SF38

▶ SF38 Writing a well-structured text

A well-structured text makes it easy for your reader to follow your line of thought and to understand your text. The structure you use will depend on the kind of text you are writing. For instance, if you are telling a story or writing a report (▶ SF33: Writing a report), you might want to relate the events in a chronological order. However, there are some rules which apply to all kinds of texts.

Step 1: Collect ideas. Make an outline for your text and structure your ideas accordingly. (▶ SF8: Structuring ideas)

Step 2: Write your text:
- Begin a new paragraph for each new event, point, argument or idea.
- Structure your text visually, for example by leaving spaces between your paragraphs.
- Make the first sentence in each paragraph a **topic sentence**, i.e. a sentence that states what the paragraph will be about.
- Use **linking words** to make the connections between individual ideas clear (▶ LP14: Linking words and phrases; ▶ LP15: Connecting your thoughts).

Step 3: Proofread your text. (▶ SF40: Proofreading; ▶ LP17: Spelling)

■ LANGUAGE HELP

Linking words

Enumeration/ Structure	first, second, third; firstly, secondly, …; to begin/start with …, in the first place …; next, then; finally, last (but not least), lastly, to conclude
Addition	furthermore, moreover, in addition (to that), above all, what is more …
Comparison	equally, likewise, similarly, in the same way …
Summary/Conclusion	then, all in all, to conclude, to sum up, in summary/conclusion …
Exemplification	namely, for instance/for example (e.g.), that is to say …
Reasoning	that is why … because …, one reason for this is that …
Result	consequently, as a consequence, therefore, thus, after all, as a result, this leads to/ results in …
Reformulation	or rather, to put it another way, in other words …
Alternatively	on the one hand … on the other hand …, either … or, neither … nor …
Contrast	on the contrary, in contrast to, opposite to, unlike …
Concession	however, nevertheless, still, though, in spite of that, despite that, …

Skills File

SF 39 • Writing skills   **SF**

▶ SF 39 Quoting a text

Quoting is used when you want to support your own statements (e.g. in an analysis) by giving evidence from other texts or the text you are working on. You can either paraphrase (i.e. use your own words to express ideas from a text, ▶ SF 9) or you can quote (i.e. use the exact words of the text).

Here are some rules for quoting properly:
- Repeat exactly what the author wrote – this also refers to spelling, punctuation etc.
- Use quotation marks to show where the quote begins and ends: A quote must be clearly indicated as someone else's thoughts to avoid the impression of plagiarism. Remember that in English, quotation marks start and end above the line ('…').
- Always give the exact **source** of your quotation: line or verse numbers and – when dealing with longer texts – page numbers). If you are quoting from more than one text, indicate author and year of publication. Remember the correct **abbreviations**: *p./l.* is used for one page/line (e.g. 'p. 4'); *pp/ll.* for more than one page/line (e.g. 'pp. 11–14'). *f./ff.* after the number of a page/line means 'and the following page(s)/ line(s)'.
- Especially when working on projects you may have to quote from more than one text. In this case you need to indicate in a **bibliography** which texts you have used. For each text, provide the author, title, place and date of publication, publisher or URL.

Strategy	Example
Quoting a word or phrase If you want to refer to individual words from the text (e.g. in an analysis or when you want to focus on the exact wording of the text), you can incorporate words/phrases into your own sentence. Be careful: Work the quotations into your sentences as smoothly as possible so that they fit syntactically.	• *In the prologue to* Romeo and Juliet, *the unhappy ending of the play is already foreshadowed by the phrase 'starcrossed lovers' (Prologue, v. 6).* • *In her text 'Better than its reputation' Anne Applebaum starts off with her impression 'that the American dream is looking rather tarnished' (p. 153, l. 8), especially when compared to East Asia, which she describes as 'the new land of opportunity' (p. 153, l. 11).*
Quoting a complete sentence If you want to quote complete sentences make sure that you explain them, refer to or comment on them, so as to avoid isolated or disconnected quotations. Using quotes without further comment may give the impression that you have no ideas of your own! Use a colon (:) to separate the quotation from your introductory phrase or sentence.	*Americans and Europeans feel that their wealth and power oblige them to get involved: 'Americans, like Europeans, have long believed that strength and wealth entail responsibility' (p. 153, ll. 36–37).*
Quoting from poems or plays in verse With texts written in verse, indicate the end of lines by a slash (/). When quoting from plays, provide the act, scene and verse, i.e. II/2/6 = act II, scene 2, verse 6.	*In Aoife Mannix's poem 'Keeping the accent' the speaker experiences that her accent, which used to be a reason for others laughing at her, is now seen as something positive: 'Then he tells me my accent is so cute, / he is going to give me one of the drinks for free' (p. 171, ll. 5f.).*

..........▶

301

Skills File

SF Writing skills • SF 39

Deleting from or adding to a quote	'*But these differing responses [...] also signify a different set of attitudes to power [...]: Americans, like Europeans, have long believed that strength and wealth entail responsibility*'. (p. 153, ll. 35f.)
If you want to leave out part of a quote indicate this by using square brackets [...]. If you need to add to a quote, for example to make it fit into your sentence syntactically or logically, indicate this by adding words in square brackets, too. Make sure that you don't change the meaning of the quote and that it is still syntactically correct.	
Quoting from a text that uses quotation marks	*In Genesis, the first book of the Bible, it says: 'And God said, "Let there be light" and there was light'* (Genesis 1.6).
When quoting a passage that contains direct speech and therefore already includes quotation marks, use two different kinds of quotation marks, i.e. '...' and "...".	

■ TIP

Check your assignment before using quotes – when answering comprehension questions, you are often asked to express ideas from the text in your own words and are therefore not supposed to quote.

PRACTICE

In the following extract from an essay on the development of the political and economic system of the United States, certain passages have been underlined. Quote them to complete the sentences given below the text. Add line references.

Political and Economic Freedom   *Milton and Rose Friedman*

Ever since the first settlement of Europeans in the New World – at Jamestown in 1607 and at Plymouth in 1620 – America has been a magnet for people <u>seeking adventure, fleeing from a tyranny, or simply trying to make a better life for themselves and their children</u>.

<u>An initial trickle</u>[1] swelled after the American Revolution and the establishment of the United States of America and became <u>a flood</u> in the nineteenth century, when millions of people streamed across the Atlantic, and a smaller number across the Pacific, driven by misery and tyranny, and attracted by the promise of freedom and affluence[2].   5

When they arrived, they did not find streets paved with gold; they did not find an easy life. <u>They did find freedom and an opportunity to make the most of their talents</u>. Through hard work, ingenuity[3], thrift[4], and luck, most of them succeeded in realizing enough of their hopes and   10
dreams to encourage friends and relatives to join them.

From: *Free to Choose*, New York 1980

1 The text states that the people who came to the US did this for a variety of reasons, as there were people …

2 The text describes the rising number of immigrants as … after the American Revolution and as … during the nineteenth century.

3 Even though the immigrants couldn't expect to become rich without effort, they did get the chance to fulfil their dreams if they were willing and able to work hard: …

---

[1] **trickle** small flow (usu. of liquid)   [2] **affluence** wealth   [3] **ingenuity** ability to find solutions to problems
[4] **thrift** careful spending of money

302   Skills File

SF 40 • Writing skills — SF

▶ SF 40 Proofreading

Whenever you write a text, it is important to check the correctness and the style of the English you have used. Ideally ask someone else to read it through. Others will often see more because they are not as involved with the text as you are. If possible, read your text out loud. This will help you spot if you have accidently left out any words.

Step 1: Checking structure
- Check that you have included an introduction and a conclusion. (▶ SF 8: Structuring ideas)
- Check that you have followed all the rules for a sensible text structure, e.g. topic sentences, paragraphs, etc. (▶ SF 38: Writing a well-structured text)
- Make sure that your paragraphs include more than one sentence but still focus on one basic thought, argument or idea.

Step 2: Checking style
- Look at your sentences. If your text consists of lots of unconnected main clauses only, then add linking words to express logical connections between your ideas and thus make your text more readable. (▶ SF 38: Writing a well-structured text)
- Make sure you used the right collocations. (▶ LP 19: Collocations) If in doubt, look them up in a dictionary. (▶ SF 3: Using a dictionary)
- Check for repetitions. Substitute words you have used repeatedly with synonyms.

- *He is a very conscientious person. He goes to work even when he feels sick. People know that when he is not at work, something serious must have happened.* →
  He is a very conscientious person who goes to work even when he feels sick. That is why people know that when he is not at work, something serious must have happened.
- *Social networks can hurt people's privacy.* →
  Social networks can violate people's privacy.

- *Not everybody can achieve the American Dream but there are some people who work hard and achieve it in the end.* →
  Not everybody can achieve the American Dream but there are some people who work hard and reach it in the end.

Step 3: Checking correctness
- Keep a checklist of mistakes you have regularly made in the past, e.g. correct tenses in the *if*-clause, the use of adverbs, etc. Look specifically for these mistakes when reading your text.
- Check spelling and punctuation. (▶ LP 17: Spelling) If possible take advantage of your computer's spell-checker, but always double-check its suggestions rather than accepting them blindly.

- **She is terrible upset about her husband's death.* →
  She is terribly upset about her husband's death.

> **TIP**
>
> Try to think in English when you write because otherwise phrases or sentence patterns sometimes sound more German than English.

303

Skills File

SF | Mediation skills • SF 41

PRACTICE

The following is the beginning of a student's text analysis. It includes nine mistakes (both grammatical and stylistic errors). Find all the mistakes and correct them.

In the short story 'No speak English' from Sandra Cisnero the main character which is called Mamacita, is a beautiful woman. Actually she never leave her apartment, instead the narrator basically speculates about why she behaves in this way. He only knows that she is married and has one kid and he only knows that she speaks only eight words of English. The narrator thinks that she doesn't like English. She always listens to the Spanish radio shows. The husband wants that she integrates into US-American society but she misses her real home, Mexico, too much.

Mediation skills

► SF 41 Mediation of written and oral texts

Not everybody speaks and understands both German and English. So you may sometimes find yourself in a situation where you have to help people understand each other – where you have to mediate between speakers of German and English or where you have to explain what is written in texts in the other language.

Your English-speaking e-pal is leaving school next year but is finding it difficult to decide on his career plans. You have just read the article below and want to send him an email giving some useful advice on how to proceed.

Hilfen bei der Berufswahl

Wenn die Berufswahl für Jugendliche ansteht, dann tun sich viele häufig schwer. Sie wissen nicht so recht, ob sie lieber studieren sollen oder erst einmal einen Beruf erlernen möchten. Weiter lernen oder gleich Geld verdienen? Ein Studium nach der Ausbildung beginnen und damit weiter auf Unterstützung angewiesen sein? Oder in einem handwerklichen Beruf Karriere machen? Alles scheint offen und alles möglich. […]

Was soll man nun aber tun, wenn man als Jugendlicher eine Ausbildung finden möchte? Erst einmal sollte für die Berufswahl des Jugendlichen klar sein, welche Interessen er hat. Dafür gibt es im Internet oder auch bei der Bundesagentur für Arbeit verschiedene Tests. Soll lieber mit Menschen oder Tieren, mit Maschinen und Geräten gearbeitet werden? Sind die eigenen Fähigkeiten eher theoretischer Natur oder besteht eine Veranlagung zum praktischen Basteln? Gibt es aus der Schule Neigungen, die sich beruflich nutzen lassen? […] Wichtig ist, dass mit der Suche nach einem Ausbildungsplatz für den Jugendlichen zeitig begonnen wird, denn häufig endet die Einstellung der neuen Azubis schon im Jahr vor dem Abschluss in der Schule. Auch für einen Studienplatz sollte sich der Schüler rechtzeitig bewerben, vor allem wenn es sich um einen Studienplatz handelt, der an einen Numerus Clausus gebunden ist, oder um einen, für den es nur eine begrenzte Zahl an freien Plätzen gibt.

From: the website of *Deine Stärken*

304

Skills File

SF 41 • Mediation skills — SF

How to proceed	Example
Step 1: Select the relevant information from the text, bearing in mind what specific information your partner needs. Remember: the mediated text will usually be much shorter than the original because you select only the information you need.	• *first find out what you enjoy doing* • *get some help from online-tests or the 'Bundes-agentur für Arbeit'* • *start early*
Step 2: Analyse the communicative situation: • Who are you talking or writing to? What is the appropriate *style and *register? (▶ LP 11: Using the right register) • What text type are you expected to produce (an informal letter or email, an article for a school magazine? (▶ SF 29: Writing a formal letter or email; ▶ SF 33: Writing a report) • Will you be speaking or writing? (Speaking allows you to use gestures and other non-verbal means of communication.)	• *Your friend needs to know the basic steps he can take to decide on his career.* • *a friend → informal language* (If you were e.g. giving a speech at a symposium on young people's career choices you would use a formal style.) • *an email* • *written text*
Step 3: Structure the relevant information, then phrase it in the target language. (▶ LP 12: Avoiding German-sounding sentence-patterns) Watch out for aspects that are specific to one culture and explain them in more detail. (▶ LP 12: Avoiding Germanisms) If you don't know words in the other language, paraphrase them. (▶ SF 9: Paraphrasing)	*The article I have read gives you some advice:* • *The first step is to find out what you enjoy and what you are good at. You can use online-tests or you can get help at the Job Centre.* • *It's important to start early – here in Germany you have to apply well before for trainee programmes or places at university.* • *'Bundesagentur für Arbeit': Job Centre / a state institution that helps people find jobs*

PRACTICE

A 'Career's night' is being held at your school for your entire year group. You are asked to give a short talk in German about what careers young people tend to choose and why. Using the text 'Teenagers' career aspirations' (p. 185), prepare a script for your speech (▶ S 25 Giving a speech).

Exam Practice

EP 1 How to do exams in general **P** 306
EP 2 Working with texts **P** 307
   EP 2.1 Aspect I: comprehension 308
   EP 2.2 Aspect II: analysis/interpretation 308
   EP 2.3 Aspect III: beyond the text 309

P A task allows you to practise this skill.

EP 3 Mediation **P** 315
EP 4 Listening and viewing **P** 316
EP 5 Speaking 318
EP 6 Closed test formats 321

Download the suggested answers to the PRACTICE tasks here:
 Webcode context-00

▶ EP 1 How to do exams in general

You are likely to come across many different tests and exams for English at school, for your *Abitur* or after school. Before sitting an exam, you should therefore familiarize yourself with its specific format. However, there are certain general tips that might help you to be successful. In this *Exam Practice* you will find guidance for both written and oral test formats.

BEFORE THE EXAM
Start early and organize your work.

Collecting information
- Make sure you know how to use aids that are allowed in the exam, e.g. dictionaries. (▶ SF 3: Using a dictionary; ▶ SF 4: Using a grammar book)
- Find out details of the exam situation. Who will be present? Where will it take place? How long will you have? (Especially for oral exams:) Will you be given preparation time? (▶ EP 5)
- Try to get hold of old test papers to see what they require.
- Make sure you understand what the different tasks require from you (cf. 'Language for tasks', p. 340).
- Learn about the evaluation criteria of the exam – this will help you to focus on the relevant aspects (e.g. how important is grammatical correctness in closed test formats? ▶ SF 10: Working with closed test formats; ▶ EP 6).

Practising
- Go over old tests or homework tasks to identify your problem areas and learn from your mistakes.
- Don't practise what you already know but focus on your weak areas. (▶ LP 1–29)
- Practise the specific type of exam you will be sitting. If you have to pass an oral exam, practise with a partner. If you have to write an essay, write essays or different parts of an essay.

IN THE EXAM
- Be on time for the exam.
- Read the instructions of the test carefully, they provide crucial information. Make sure you understand what you are supposed to do – it may help to highlight the instructions.
- If you are allowed to choose between different tasks, read all alternatives before deciding which one you want to do.
- If you notice that you are becoming nervous, take a quick break before continuing.
- Use your time efficiently, e.g. leave enough time for checking your work.

Exam Practice

EP 2 | **EP**

PRACTICE

A teacher has added this comment to a student's essay:

The argumentation of your essay is convincing. You might put forward some more arguments though and back up all your findings with passages from the text. The overall structure of your essay is well-chosen, but try to connect the paragraphs more effectively. Linking words and special phrases may help you to do so. Your style of writing is your strength: You write fluently and right to the point. You have expanded your vocabulary successfully and most passages are idiomatic. There are hardly any mistakes, but you should revise conditional sentences.

1 Look at the following list of criteria and say whether the student's essay fulfilled them very well or just satisfactorily or whether it needs improvement in that area.

Criteria		
Content: quality	Content: quantity	Structure
Use of quotes	Linking words	Useful phrases for interpretation
Vocabulary: general flexibility	Ability of expression	Grammar

2 Look at the sections Skills File (pp. 250–305) and Language Practice (pp. 218–239) and identify relevant sections that could help the student to improve his/her weak areas.

3 Now collect your own 3–5 weak areas and identify the relevant sections in Skills File and/or Language Practice. Develop an action plan to work on your weak areas.

▶ EP 2 Working with texts

In most of your exams you will be faced with one or more texts, which you have to respond to (▶ SF 11–13, ▶ SF 16–21). These may include:

- *fictional texts (e.g. *short stories, *poems; extracts from *novels, *dramas or film scripts)
- *non-fictional texts (e.g. *articles, *speeches)
- visuals (e.g. *cartoons, pictures, films, advertisements, leaflets).

You may be given a single written text or a written text combined with another text or a visual. You will be expected to work on different tasks. For instance, you may be asked to analyse a short story or to mediate a newspaper article. In order to be successful you will need to apply different skills, e.g.:

- skimming, scanning (▶ F 14: Reading strategies)
- underlining or highlighting important sections (▶ SF 15: Marking up texts / Making and taking notes)
- making notes in the margin (▶ SF 15: Marking up texts / Making and taking notes)
- making notes on a separate piece of paper, e.g. mind maps, outlines, drawings (▶ SF 7: Making visual aids; ▶ SF 8: Structuring ideas)
- writing a well-structured text (▶ SF 38).

In general, when dealing with a text you will be asked to consider the following three aspects:

Aspect I	Aspect II	Aspect III
comprehension (focus on content) ▶ EP 2.1	analysis/interpretation (focus on form and function) ▶ EP 2.2	composition (focus on evaluation and re-creation) ▶ EP 2.3

In an exam, you may be given tasks that clearly relate to one of these three aspects, or there might be complex tasks that combine two or all three of the aspects.

Exam Practice 307

EP 2.1–2.2

► EP 2.1 Aspect I: comprehension

This type of task focuses on the content of a text and is intended to check whether you have understood the information. Comprehension tasks can be quite open, i.e. they require you to write a free text, as in summary writing (► SF 31) or answering comprehension questions. They can also occur in the form of closed test formats, e.g. multiple choice or true/false exercises (► SF 10: Working with closed test formats; ► EP 6).

TYPICAL INSTRUCTIONS FOR ASPECT I (OPEN TASKS)

Here are some instructions that are frequently used for aspect I. To see the complete list of instructions, have a look at pp. 340–341 ('Verbs for tasks').

Instruction	Example	What you are expected to do	Tips
outline ['– –] *umreißen, skizzieren*	**Outline** the writer's views on …	*Give the main features, structure or general principles of a topic, omitting minor details.*	Structure your answer using main and subordinate points.
state *darlegen*	**State** the author's opinion on the main character's decision.	*Specify something clearly.*	Be precise and brief.
summarize (*also:* **give/write a summary of; sum up**) *zusammenfassen*	**Summarize** the incident in the church in no more than four sentences.	*Give a concise account of the main points of something.*	Be concise; leave out details and examples.

To practise this aspect, have a look at **Practice I** (p. 312) or **Practice II** (p. 313).

► EP 2.2 Aspect II: analysis/interpretation

In this part of the exam, you 'read between the lines' of a text. You might examine why an author gives the text a certain form, why he/she characterizes the figures in a drama in a certain way etc. To do exactly what you are asked to do, make sure you understand the instructions (cf. 'Verbs for tasks', p. 340). Also, provide a suitable structure for your findings (► SF 8: Structuring ideas).

TYPICAL INSTRUCTIONS FOR ASPECT II

Here are some instructions that are frequently used for aspect II. To see the complete list of instructions, have a look at pp. 340–341 ('Verbs for tasks').

Instruction	Example	What you are expected to do	Tips
analyse (BE), **analyze** (AE) ['ænəlaɪz]/ **examine** [ɪg'zæmɪn] *analysieren, untersuchen*	**Analyse** the main elements of the poster. **Examine** the writer's attitude towards the protagonist.	*Describe and explain certain aspects and/or features of the text in detail.*	Do not just list e.g. stylistic devices the author uses, but always connect them to the effect they are used to create.
explain *erklären*	**Explain** the main character's reaction to her mother in the first scene.	*Describe and define in detail.*	Do not just describe something, but give reasons why it is the way it is.

Exam Practice

Authors always write their texts to achieve an effect – they may want to persuade or inform the readers, they may try to arouse compassion or contempt for a character in their story etc. When analysing a text, you need to examine which means the author has used to create a specific effect (▸ SF 17: Analysing stylistic devices; ▸ SF 18: Analysing non-fiction; ▸ SF 19–21: Analysing fiction). The table below gives some examples.

Category	Some typical means	Possible effects
Techniques of persuasion	quote from or use statistics from reliable sources and experts	creates credibility
	example from everyday life	makes an argument more comprehensible and concrete
	direct address of reader	makes the reader sympathize with a concept or adopt the writer's view
Use of language	use of *images (e.g. *metaphor, *symbol, *simile, *personification)	helps to evoke a graphic, vivid picture in the reader's mind
	use of *stylistic devices such as *anaphora, *alliteration or *repetition	stresses a certain aspect
	use of *irony, *sarcasm	creates humour, emphasizes a point or message
	use of technical jargon	creates credibility, makes the writer appear more expert
Narrative techniques	use of a *first-person narrator	helps the reader to identify with the narrator, to understand his or her attitude

To practise this aspect, have a look at **Practice I** (p. 312) or **Practice II** (p. 313).

▸ EP 2.3 Aspect III: beyond the text

Part III of the exam requires you to produce a written text. It may be based on a text or on visuals (e.g. cartoons or photos) or it may take just a topic as a starting point. It may be called *comment, composition, creative writing* or *writing*.

In some exams you will be asked to write a certain type of text. The task may also give you aspects that need to be (or may be) taken into consideration. The following table gives you an idea about the most common text types, their purpose, content/structure and specific language.

Text type	Purpose	Content/Structure	Language
*Feature article	• inform sb. • entertain sb. • provide background information	• catchy headline • first paragraph must arouse reader's interest (example, anecdote) • use of anecdotes, examples, quotes • personal angle	• less formal language, some slang may be used
*Report (▸ SF 33: Writing a report)	• inform sb. • provide background information • influence sb.	• catchy headline • clear paragraphs • from general aspects to detail	• less formal language, some slang may be used

Exam Practice 309

EP 2.3

*Comment (▶ SF34: Argumentative writing)	• pass judgment on an issue • express and support your opinion	• introduction: outline of topic and attitude • body: arguments for personal position, refutation of counter-arguments • conclusion: summary of personal position • use of examples to illustrate arguments	• formal/neutral language
Argumentative essay Discussion (▶ SF34: Argumentative writing)	• weigh up both sides of an issue remaining fairly neutral	• introduction: outline of topic • body: pros and cons of the issue • conclusion: summary of arguments, statement of personal opinion • use of examples to illustrate arguments	• formal/neutral language
(Written) Interview (▶ SF37: Doing a creative writing task)	• present a topic/a person's views • portray a celebrity	• introduction: basic facts on interviewee • official welcome of interviewee • body: interviewee's answers to questions (which should be polite, may be provocative) • concluding statement or question; words of goodbye and expression of gratitude	• imitation of spoken language • polite language
Letter (e.g. letter to the editor, cover letter for an application, personal letter) **Email** (▶ SF34: Writing a formal letter or email)	• various, e.g. apply for a job, tell reader about a topic, express your opinion	• content varies according to addressee and purpose • structural elements: letterhead, greeting, body, signature	• varies according to addressee and purpose
Review (▶ SF32: Writing a review)	• describe something you have read or experienced (book, film, etc.) and express your opinion on it • make recommendations	• introduction – body (brief summary, evaluation) – conclusion	• varies according to type of magazine or newspaper • use of words that describe the film/book etc. and your opinion in a differentiated way (adjectives, adverbs; words with positive or negative connotations)

310

Exam Practice

Speech script (▶ SF25: Giving a speech)	• various, e.g. move/convince/inform/entertain sb.	• introduction: welcome audience; outline topic and intention of speech • body: well-structured arguments backed up with evidence/examples • conclusion: summary, appeal to listeners, expression of gratitude	• varies according to context, i.e. audience, speaker, occasion • stylistic devices

Your task may also be creative writing (▶ SF37: Doing a creative writing task), i.e. you may be asked to add something to an already existing text (mostly fictional) or to change it. You might change the *point of view of a text, add an ending to a story (or write a different one), add a part to the text or fill a gap in it (e.g. an *interior monologue). Remember that your writing must match the language style of the original.

You may also come across 'free' creative writing tasks. They are not based on or linked to a certain text but require you to apply your knowledge and skills – as for example when writing a poem on a given topic.

TYPICAL INSTRUCTIONS FOR ASPECT III

If you are not given a certain text type to write, you may find one of the tasks listed in the table below. See pp.340–341 for a complete list of instructions ('Verbs for tasks').

Instruction	Example	What you are expected to do	Tips
comment on ['kɒment] *kommentieren, Stellung nehmen zu*	**Comment on** the speaker's belief that …	*State clearly your opinions on the topic in question and support your views with evidence.*	State your opinion on the topic clearly and support it with convincing arguments.
discuss *diskutieren, erörtern*	**Discuss** how education influences attitudes towards immigration.	*Investigate or examine by argument; give reasons for and against.*	Structure your ideas clearly. Weigh up both sides of an issue and support your final position with arguments.
justify *begründen, rechtfertigen*	**Justify** your answer.	*Show adequate grounds for decisions or conclusions.*	If possible and suitable, use statistics or research results as support.

In all your writing tasks make sure to apply general writing skills such as structuring a text or linking ideas (▶ SF8: Structuring ideas; ▶ SF38: Writing a well-structured text).

To practise aspect III, have a look at **Practice I** (p.312) or **Practice II** (p.313).

EP | EP 2.3

Working with a non-fictional text: aspects I, II and III

PRACTICE I

A great honour *Ewen MacAskill*

NSA whistleblower Edward Snowden said he was humbled and honoured after Glasgow University students voted overwhelmingly for him to serve as their rector for the next three years. In a statement to the Guardian, Snowden described it as bold and historic decision in support of academic freedom. 'In a world where so many of our developing thoughts and queries and plans must be entrusted to the open internet, mass surveillance is not simply a matter of privacy, but of academic freedom and human liberty,' Snowden said. The vote is purely symbolic as Snowden is unlikely to be in a position to become a working rector, able to represent students at meetings of the university's administrators. He is wanted by the US for leaking tens of thousands of documents to journalists and has been granted temporary asylum in Russia. The result of the online election was announced to candidates and their supporters shortly after polls closed at 5pm on Tuesday. Snowden was nominated by a group of students at the university who said they had received his approval through his lawyer. He defeated the former champion cyclist Graeme Obree, the author Alan Bissett and the Rev Kelvin Holdsworth, who also stood for the post. Chris Cassells, Snowden's spokesman for the rectorial election campaign, said: 'We are delighted to see Edward Snowden elected as the new rector of the University of Glasgow. We have a proud and virtuous tradition of making significant statements through our rectors and today we have once more championed this idea by proving to the world that we are not apathetic to important issues such as democratic rights.' [...] Charles Kennedy, the outgoing rector and former Lib Dem leader, said: 'It has been a pleasure and a privilege to serve the students of the University of Glasgow for the past six years. The post of rector is an important one, and I would like to wish my successor all the very best for his term of office.'

Snowden, in his statement, said: 'I am humbled by and grateful to the students of Glasgow University for this historic statement in defence of our shared values. We are reminded by this bold decision that the foundation of all learning is daring: the courage to investigate, to experiment, to inquire.' He added: 'If we do not contest the violation of the fundamental right of free people to be left unmolested in their thoughts, associations, and communications – to be free from suspicion without cause – we will have lost the foundation of our thinking society. The defence of this fundamental freedom is the challenge of our generation, a work that requires constructing new controls and protections to limit the extraordinary powers of states over the domain of human communication. This election shows that the students of Glasgow University intend to lead the way, and it is my great honour to serve as their rector.'

1 **whistleblower** *Enthüller*
2 **rector** *(BE)* head of a university or college
3 **bold** *(here)* brave
7 **leak sth.** *(here)* reveal sth.
11 **Rev Kelvin Holdsworth** clergyman of the Scottish Episcopal Church in Glasgow
16 **Lib Dem** (= The Liberal Democrats) a socially liberal political party in the United Kingdom
20 **humble sb.** *jdn. mit Demut erfüllen*
23 **daring** ready to do dangerous or unusual things, brave
25 **unmolested** not disturbed by anybody

From: the website of *The Guardian*, 18 February 2014

1 Possible task for aspect I
Summarize the article in your own words. (▸ SF 31: Writing a summary)

> **TIP**
> Since you may not underline or mark texts in this book, make notes on the relevant information before starting to write. (▸ SF 15: Marking up a text / Making and taking notes)

2 Possible task for aspect II
Examine the way in which MacAskill tries to convince his readers. Focus on his line of argument, techniques of persuasion and use of language. (▸ SF 18: Analysing non-fiction)

> **TIP**
> Reread EE 2.2, then collect ideas and structure them before starting to write. (▸ SF 8: Structuring ideas)

Exam Practice

EP 2.3

3 Possible tasks for aspect III

Before working on the tasks your might want to do some research on the controversy around Edward Snowden.

a Some people have called Snowden a traitor because he leaked confidential information from the NSA. Discuss this view. ▶ LANGUAGE HELP (▶ SF 34: Argumentative writing)

b Write an interview with an American politician who considers Snowden a hero who opened the world's eyes to mass surveillance. ▶ LANGUAGE HELP (▶ SF 37: Doing a creative writing task)

c Imagine you are a student at Glasgow University before Snowden's election as rector. You have been asked to give a speech in front of undecided fellow students convincing them (not) to vote for him. Write a speech.
▶ LANGUAGE HELP (▶ SF 25: Giving a speech)

> **LANGUAGE HELP**
> - endanger national security
> - destabilize international relationships
> - commit a crime
> - cause unpredictable political turmoil
> - be on an ego-trip
> - brave hero
> - support freedom of speech
> - fundamental democratic right
> - trigger a much needed debate
> - defense of democratic values
> - principles of the American Dream
> - international peacekeeping

Working with a fictional text: aspects I, II and III   **PRACTICE II**

In the novel The Uncommon Reader Queen Elizabeth II discovers a travelling library outside of Buckingham Palace. She starts to borrow books regularly and slowly, her character begins to change. In this excerpt she is talking to her equerry after performing a ceremony.

The monarch's truly human side   Alan Bennett

'Less spontaneous this morning, ma'am,' one of the bolder equerries ventured to say.

'Was I?' said the Queen, who would once have been most put out at even this mildest of criticisms, though these days it scarcely impinged. 'I think I know
5 why it is. You see, Gerald, as they kneel one looks down on the tops of people's heads a good deal and from that perspective even the most unsympathetic personality seems touching: the beginnings of a bald patch, the hair growing over the collar. One's feelings are almost maternal.'

The equerry, with whom she'd never shared such confidences before and
10 who ought to have been flattered, simply felt awkward and embarrassed. This was a truly human side to the monarch of which he'd never been previously aware and which (unlike its counterfeit versions) he did not altogether welcome. And whereas the Queen herself thought that such feelings probably arose out of her reading books, the young man felt it might be that she was
15 beginning to show her age. Thus it was that the dawn of sensibility was mistaken for the onset of senility.

Immune to embarrassment herself, as she was to any that she might cause, the Queen would once not have noticed the young man's confusion. But observing it now she resolved in the future to share her thoughts less promis-
20 cuously, which was a pity in a way as it was what many in the nation longed for. Instead she determined to restrict her confidences to her notebooks, where they could do no harm.

The Queen had never been demonstrative; it was not in her upbringing; but more and more these days, particularly in the period following Princess Diana's
25 death, she was being required to go public about feelings she would have

equerry [–'– –] male officer who acts as an assistant to the royal family
1 **venture to do sth.** wagen etwas zu tun
4 **scarcely** almost not
   impinge have a noticeable effect
7 **bald patch** area on top of the head without hair
8 **collar** Kragen
   maternal mütterlich
10 **be flattered** sich geschmeichelt fühlen
   awkward embarrassing, uncomfortable
12 **counterfeit** fake
14 **arise out of sth.** happen as a result of sth.
15 **dawn of sensibility** Anflug von Empfindsamkeit
16 **onset** beginning
19 **promiscuously** (here) with lots of people
22 **harm** damage, injury
23 **be demonstrative** show your feelings in public
   upbringing education
24 **Princess Diana** (1961–1997) first wife of the Queen's son Charles

EP 2.3

and it was only now that she understood that her predicament was not unique and that she shared it, among others, with Cordelia. She wrote in her notebook: 'Though I do not always understand Shakespeare, Cordelia's "I cannot heave my heart into my mouth" is a sentiment I can readily endorse. Her predicament is mine.'

26 **predicament** situation where it is hard to know what to do
27 **Cordelia** character from William Shakespeare's drama *King Lear*
29 **endorse sth.** say publicly that you support sth.

30

From: *The Uncommon Reader*, 2007

1 Possible task for aspect I
Briefly describe the situation as well as the monarch's and Gerald's attitudes and feelings.

2 Possible task for aspect II
Explain how the Queen's behaviour and her explanation for it differ from the equerry's view. Examine how the author employs *narrative perspective to show both sides. (▶ SF 19: Analysing narrative prose)

Step 1: Put a transparency over the text and mark relevant passages revealing information on
   1 the Queen's behaviour and how she explains it
   2 the equerry's observations and how he explains them.

Step 2: Add your observations to the structure below to create an outline (▶ SF 8: Structuring ideas). Don't forget to use quotes and to indicate the lines. (▶ SF 39: Quoting a text)

Paragraph 1: narrative perspective
   …
Paragraph 2: the Queen's behaviour and her self-image
   2.1. Her behaviour
   …
   2.2. How she explains it
   …
Paragraph 3: the equerry's view
   3.1. The equerry's observations
   …
   3.2. How he explains them
   …

Step 3: Add suitable notes for introduction and conclusion, then write a coherent text. (▶ SF 38: Writing a well-structured text)

Introduction
   • an 'uncommon' picture of the British monarch
   • Queen's new hobby → effect on her behaviour → effect on her subjects / the equerry
Conclusion
   • omniscient third-person-narrator → two perspectives (Queen, equerry)
   …

3 Possible tasks for aspect III
   a Discuss whether the British monarch is supposed to 'go public about feelings' (l. 24) considering his/her duties and function. (▶ SF 34: Argumentative writing)
   b The Queen takes Cordelia's utterance as a starting point for her notebook entry (l. 28). Finish her entry reflecting on her latest experience and self-image. (▶ SF 37: Doing a creative writing task)

EP3 EP

EP3

► EP3 Mediation

Mediating basically means to summarize information (from a written or oral text) in another language. (► SF40: Mediation of written and oral texts). Your task is normally embedded in some kind of context, so you have to consider the situation and your relationship to the addressee to find out what information to select from the original text and in what form to put it. *Form* here can refer to a specific *text type but also to a suitable *register.

To get the maximum number of points in your exam, it is helpful to know which criteria your teacher will apply when assessing your exam:

- content: selection of relevant aspects for the situation given (answers given to all the addressee's questions, but no superfluous information)
- form: choice of suitable text type and ability to apply its rules
- appropriateness of *style and *register for the given situation
- powers of expression: ability to deal with unknown words / technical terms or culture-specific concepts; lexical and syntactical flexibility etc.
- grammar: amount and types of mistakes.

> **■ TIP**
>
> Be aware of (cultural) misunderstandings, German idioms and false friends. (► CC 1–7) Do not translate word for word because cultural peculiarities often do not have a translation. Paraphrase. (► SF9: Paraphrasing)

PRACTICE

Your British friend is coming to visit you. She has heard that a new Primark shop has just opened in your town and cannot wait to go there during her stay with you. You come across the article below.

Erschütternder Hilferuf in Kleid von Primark eingenäht

In westlichen Kleiderläden verführen bunte, billige Klamotten zum Kauf. Die Arbeitsbedingungen der Näherinnen in den indischen Textilfabriken sind dabei meist ganz weit weg. Nicht so für eine britische Primark-Kundin: Denn jemand hatte eine Botschaft in ihr Kleid genäht. Die britische Primark-Kundin Rebecca Gallagher hat überraschend erfahren, unter welchen Bedingungen ihr Kleid offenbar hergestellt wurde,
5 berichtet die „South Wales Evening Post online". Sie habe in ihrem zwölf Euro teuren Sommerkleid von Primark ein Etikett mit einer Nachricht gefunden. „Forced to work for exhausting hours", zu Deutsch etwa „gezwungen, stundenlang bis zur Erschöpfung zu arbeiten", sei handschriftlich auf dem Etikett gestanden, das jemand mit der Hand zwischen die anderen genäht hatte. Es sei ihr aufgefallen, als sie nach der Waschanleitung geschaut habe, erzählte die 25-Jährige der Zeitung. Daraufhin habe sie gelobt, das Kleid nie wieder
10 anzuziehen. Sie fühle sich schuldig und habe Angst, dass eine übermüdete Arbeiterin sich dafür in einem Sweatshop irgendwo in einem fernen Land quälen musste. „Um ehrlich zu sein, habe ich noch nie darüber nachgedacht, wie die Kleider hergestellt werden", sagte sie. „Aber das hat mich jetzt zum Nachdenken darüber gemacht, woher wir unsere billigen Klamotten bekommen." Ein Primark-Sprecher sagte der Zeitung, ihm seien keine weiteren Vorfälle dieser Art bekannt. Trotzdem bat er um Rückgabe: „Wir wären der Kundin
15 dankbar, wenn sie das Kleid an uns übergeben würde, damit wir untersuchen können, wie das Schildchen an das Kleid gelangte und ob dieser Sache weiter nachgegangen werden muss."

Vor mehr als einem Jahr stürzte das Rana Plaza in Bangladesch ein. Beim schwersten Unglück in der Textilindustrie starben mehr als 1130 Menschen, mehr als 2500 wurden teils schwer verletzt. Die Arbeitsbedingungen der Näherinnen, die dort zu Dumpinglöhnen Hosen, T-Shirts und Kleider für westliche Kunden
20 herstellen, gerieten in die Kritik. Zu den Unternehmen, die in einer der Fabriken in dem Gebäude produzieren ließen, gehörte auch das irische Unternehmen Primark.

From: the website of *Focus*, 25 June 2014

315

Exam Practice

EP4

1 Possible mediation task

After reading the article, you are no longer sure about buying clothes that are connected to sweatshops. Write an email to your friend (in English) in which you express your concerns.

Step 1: Look at the following pieces of information from the text and say whether you would include them in your email or not.

1. A British customer found a message sewn into her Primark dress saying 'forced to work for exhausting hours'.
2. The customer is 25-year-old Rebecca Gallagher.
3. She found the message when looking for the washing instructions.
4. The shopper feels guilty because of the exploitation of workers in clothes factories.
5. Primark asked the young woman to return the dress to find out how the label got there.
6. In 2013, more than 1130 people were killed when a factory which produced clothes for western companies collapsed in Bangladesh.

Step 2: Collect more information from the text that you consider relevant for your email, then structure your ideas. (▶ SF8: Structuring ideas)

Step 3: Read the following model answer, which is not at all perfect. Say what might be improved.

> Hi there,
>
> I have a serious problem. Primark forces children to produce cheap clothes. I read that in an article in some newspaper. A woman discovered a label sewn in her Primark dress saying 'forced to work for exhausting hours.' She only paid €12 for the dress. There was also an accident in one of those sweatshops abroad. It's horrible, isn't it? I suggest we don't go there.
>
> Hope to hear from you soon!

Step 4: Write your email, bearing in mind the following points:

- Form: email (fairly informal)
- Addressee: a friend from the UK you do not know that well (→ don't be too informal!)
- Situation: Your friend wants to go to the new Primark shop, but you would like to dissuade her.
  - Don't get right to the point: make polite small talk first, maybe tell her how happy you are about the visit.
  - Try to voice your doubts about the idea without offending your friend. You might suggest some kind of compromise.

▶ EP4 Listening and viewing

Your exam task may be based on a short audio (e.g. an interview, a speech) or video (e.g. an interview, a documentary, an extract from a film) of about four minutes.

To prepare for this exam, use every opportunity you get to listen to spoken English. For instance, listen to BBC radio or watch your favourite British or American TV show on DVD or online in English. Start with English subtitles and switch them off when you feel ready. If possible, listen to a wide variety of speakers (different accents, different speeds, various topics).

In listening tasks, you will often only be asked to answer questions on aspect I, i.e. text comprehension (▶ EE2.1), and they are often closed test formats such as multiple choice (▶ SF10: Working with closed test formats; ▶ SF22: Listening). Viewing tasks, but also some listening tasks, go beyond simple understanding and require you to analyse the film clip or audio, so make sure you are familiar with aspects to examine. (▶ SF23: Analysing a film)

316

Exam Practice

EP 4 EP

There is usually a standard exam procedure when it comes to listening or viewing:

Step 1: You get some time to read the instructions and further information and vocabulary, if provided. The questions will normally come in the same order as the information in the recording.

Step 2: First listening/viewing: You are allowed to write while listening/viewing, so start working on your tasks right away. Try to complete as much as possible.

Step 3: Time to work on the tasks. Fill in missing information and/or read through the tasks again. Mark things you are not sure about and any gaps that are still there.

Step 4: Second listening/viewing: Try to fill any gaps that might be left and check the answers you've already noted down.

Step 5: Time to complete your tasks and check your answers.

In a viewing activity your teacher might show you the video a third time.

■ TIP

Before listening/viewing:
- Read the instructions carefully and ensure you know what you have to focus on.
- Try to make predictions about the audio/video and the answers to the questions.

While listening/viewing:
- Read all answers, even if you are sure that you have found the correct one. The differences between the right and the wrong answers are often subtle or tricky.
- If you need to take notes, only jot down keywords or short phrases.
- If your task requires you to write a text, try to note down particular phrases from the audio/video and use them as quotes in your text.

After viewing/listening:
- Don't leave an item unanswered. If you don't know the answer, make an educated guess – you still stand a good chance of getting the credit for it (e.g. 25% in a multiple choice item with four options!)
- If you are asked to write a text, …
  - don't forget to use all the background information from the instructions.
  - back up your findings with concrete evidence, i.e. refer to relevant phrases or expressions used by a speaker/actor or describe special (cinematic) moments.

Listening (► SF 22: Listening)   PRACTICE

Former First Lady Hillary Rodham Clinton was US Secretary of State from 2008 to 2012. You are going to listen to an extract from an interview with her broadcast on BBC 4 on 3 July 2014, in which she speaks about the challenges as a female Secretary of State and women's issues in general.

🎧 **CD3** 14

perseverance *Beharrlichkeit*
hostility *Feindseligkeit*
private capacity private life
inconsequential unimportant
break through the highest glass ceiling
die letzte Hürde nehmen
renowned famous
assertive *durchsetzungsfähig*

1 Choose the correct answers. Sometimes more than one answer is correct.

  a On women as US Secretary of State:

    1 When Clinton came to office, three women had done the job of US Secretary of State before.

    2 Having a female Secretary of State has changed the way people perceive women considerably.

    3 In countries like the UK, a female US Secretary of State is nothing special.

    4 Hillary Clinton never got used to being the only woman in the room on meetings in some foreign countries.

                                             ·········►

317

Exam Practice **EP**

EP EP5

    b To Clinton, making women and girls an important element of US foreign states policy is …
       1 a necessity
       2 a luxury
       3 both a luxury and a necessity
       4 neither a luxury nor a necessity.
    c During her fight for women's rights she was often faced with …
       1 hostility
       2 interest
       3 people rolling their eyes at her
       4 people who considered this topic an unimportant hobby horse of hers.

2 List three brutal actions that girls are confronted with in a lot of countries according to Clinton.
3 List two fields of life in which women still face challenges in Western civilization.
4 List two ways in which women break the law in Saudi Arabia.
5 How does Clinton decide if and how to speak out in cases where women are treated badly?

Viewing (▶SF23: Analysing a film)

> **PRACTICE**

Margaret Thatcher was the first and only female British Prime Minister (1979–1990). Her nickname 'the Iron Lady' was coined because of her tough opposition towards the Soviet Union and socialism as such in the Cold War era. The scene from the film *The Iron Lady* (2011) that you are going to watch shows her with the members of her Cabinet discussing a new tax.

▶ DVD

council estate *(here)*
(oft sehr armer) Wohnort
resent sth. (strongly) dislike sth.
slacker *(ifml) Faulenzer/in*
sovereignty *Souveränität*
concession *Zugeständnis*
beret type of French hat

1 Possible task for aspect I
Briefly sum up the content of the scene.

2 Possible tasks for aspect II
    a Examine Margaret Thatcher's character as presented in this scene. Focus on her attitudes and her behaviour towards the members of the Cabinet present. (▶ SF35: Writing a character profile)
    b Analyse the cinematic devices employed to create this picture of Thatcher. (▶ SF23: Analysing a film)

3 Possible tasks for aspect III
    a Assess Margaret Thatcher's leadership qualities as shown in this scene.
    b After the meeting, two Cabinet members talk about the incident, commenting on Thatcher's leadership qualities. Write their dialogue.

▶ EP5 Speaking

Many exams nowadays are exclusively communication exams or they may include a part in which you have to prove your communicative capacity. Preparing for and successfully passing a speaking exam is different from a written exam because you need to use different skills and strategies (▶ SF24–S28).

Usually, oral exams consist of two parts which are thematically linked, a monologue and a dialogue:

Monologue	Dialogue
In this part, you are asked to give a presentation based on e.g. a diagram, statistics, picture, cartoon, quote or short text.	In the second part, you are asked to interact with a partner or a group of students in a role-play or a discussion. It may be based on the material you have worked on for the monologue. Your fellow students have probably dealt with similar material.

318 Exam Practice

EP 5 | EP

To prepare for your exam, ask your teacher about the specific conditions of your exam, e.g.
- What kind of prompts can you expect (i.e. cartoons, pictures, quotes, etc.)?
- Will you be given time to prepare only the monologue or both parts?
- If there is preparation time for the dialogue, will it be at the very beginning or shortly before the dialogue?
- How long will the preparation time be?
- How long will both parts of the exam be?
- How many people will take part in the dialogue?
- Will the participants in the dialogue be other students or teachers?

To get the maximum number of points in your exam, it is helpful to know which criteria you teacher will apply when assessing your exam:
- communicative strategies (structure, eye contact, interaction with partners etc.)
- pronunciation (clarity, fluency, intonation, accuracy)
- powers of expression (choice of words, ability to deal with unknown words/technical terms, flexibility etc.)
- grammar: amount and types of mistakes
- content: quality and meaningfulness of statements/arguments etc.

■ TIP

Before the exam:
- Practise monologues by describing a picture to a fellow student. (▶ SF 24: Giving a presentation)
- Learn phrases which you can use during presentations, speeches or discussions (cf. the table on p. 320).
- Study your classroom material and look for controversial issues which could be discussed, then collect arguments for and against them.
- Watch (current) political debates online to get an idea of the culture of reflection and debate.

In the exam:
- If there is a preparation time, use it to arrange your material so that you can use it effectively. Structure your ideas clearly. Use clear handwriting. Use abbreviations, keywords etc. (▶ SF 7: Making visual aids)
- You may have to adopt a role or defend a position which you don't like. Try to disregard your personal opinion, stick to the facts and give evidence if possible.
- In the dialogue part, take your time to react but do not hesitate too long. (▶ SF 27: Having a discussion)
- Ask for clarification of crucial points. Be provocative and polite at the same time; avoid attacks or insults.
- Don't be too emotional.
- Use appropriate body language and facial expressions.
- Choose the right moment to sum up your points and introduce a new aspect.

Exam Practice

Stages of conversation

Every communicative situation consists of different stages. If you know about these stages and useful expressions to use, you can keep a conversation going and make it successful:

Stage of conversation	Explanation	Phrases
starting a conversation	You either introduce the situation or explain the topic.	Well, our topic seems to be very controversial … Why don't we … first? Recently, I heard that somebody …
expressing one's opinion	You elaborate the arguments concerning the topic.	I'm convinced that … It seems to me that … To me …
involving a partner	You invite a partner who so far hasn't contributed much to the conversation.	What do you think about …? Is there anything you'd like to add? How about you? Would you agree with that?
contradicting	You politely express that you have an opposing opinion.	That's not the way I see it. That is true to a certain extent but …
interrupting	You try to find your way into the conversation without cutting the other person short.	Sorry to interrupt you but … May I interrupt you for a moment, please?
asking for clarification	You are not sure that you have understood your partner correctly.	Excuse me, I didn't quite catch your point about … Do you mean …? Sorry, could you say that again, please?
gaining time to think	You need time to think or work on your own argumentation.	Well, that's a good point, but I think … Well, now, let me see … It's difficult to say exactly, but … If I understood the question correctly, … I don't know whether this is what you meant, but …
summing up	You bring the conversation to an end, e.g. by mentioning the most important aspects or giving a view into the future or establishing a compromise.	So, to sum up … In brief … To cut a long story short …

EP 5

PRACTICE

1 Monologue: Preparing and giving a presentation (▶ SF 24: Giving a presentation)
   a Work with a partner. Each of you choose one of the cartoons below, then prepare a presentation in which you comment on it.
   b Partner A presents his/her cartoon first, then you swap roles.

'Congratulations, it's a Versace!'

2 Dialogue: Discussing a topic (▶ SF 27: Having a discussion)
You are going to have a discussion on the benefits and dangers of scientific progress.
   a Work with a partner. Read the role cards below, then decide who is going to take which role.

Partner A	Partner B
Your little brother had leukemia and the doctors were able to treat it with a bone marrow transplant[1]. You are glad about scientific progress and the possibility that it might one day help to prevent leukemia.	You suffer from strong allergic reactions to certain foods and you suspect it's because you might have eaten genetically modified soy[2]. You are afraid of fast progress in science because you fear that its side effects cause more harm than good.

[1] **bone marrow transplant** *Rückenmarksspende*   [2] **soy** *Soja*

   b Collect arguments for your position. Also collect counter-arguments and think of possible ways to refute them. You might tackle the following issues: pre-implantation genetic diagnosis, designer babies, genetically modified food, genetic engineering in health care, stem cell research etc.
   c Discuss the topic for about 10–15 minutes. Begin by introducing yourself and your general standpoint. You can take your cartoon as a starting point for the debate.

Exam Practice

▶ EP6 Closed test formats

In many exams in and after school there are special forms of tests that are called 'closed test formats' (▶ SF10: Working with closed test formats).

They include:
- multiple choice tests with one or more correct answer/s
- true/false/not in the text
- sentence completion by gap-filling
- multiple matching: matching questions, statements or headings to different texts or sections of a text
- gapped text/sequencing: locating and replacing missing segments of a text
- note-taking: writing down a limited number of aspects you find in a text for every key point mentioned on a worksheet.

Closed test formats tend to occur mostly in listening and reading comprehension tasks (▶ EP2.1, EP4). In language tests such as TOEFL, Cambridge Certificate, TELC etc. they may also be used for grammar or vocabulary.

To be successful in a closed test format, the following skills may be helpful:
- strategies of dealing with unknown words (▶ SF1: Dealing with unknown words)
- the ability to identify different *text types and to know what to expect from them. For example, if you follow a discussion, you can expect the speakers to have different opinions on a topic.
- knowledge about typical text structures and the use of linking words, which may indicate e.g. a contrast, an addition, a conclusion (▶ SF8: Structuring ideas; ▶ SF38: Writing a well-structured text).

If you are taking part in a test for a language certificate such as TOEFL etc., you should try to get information from this organization. Look for sample questions to get a better idea of what to expect in the exam. Since some of these tests are computer-based, you should get some computer practice in how to handle them.

▪ TIP

- Read the instructions carefully and ensure you know what you have to focus on.
- Try to make predictions about the listening/reading text and about the answers to the questions.
- Read all answers, even if you are sure that you have found the correct one. The differences between the right and the wrong answers are often subtle or tricky.
- Fill in answers to questions that you are sure about straight away. If you are unsure, leave the item aside and come back to it later.
- Don't skip questions you cannot answer. Make educated guesses – you still stand a good chance of getting the credit for a question (e.g. 25% in a multiple choice item with four options!)
- There will be no deduction of credits for wrong grammar or spelling (as long as your answers are comprehensible) and no extra credits for power of expression, so don't spend much time on checking them.
- You will not be given any points for answers in German, so stick to English in all cases.

Glossary

*An asterisk indicates that the term has its own entry in the Glossary. For an alphabetical list of terms see p. 339. Words in the Glossary which are in blue print are also to be found in the list.

Literary texts

▶ Fiction

A fictional text is an imaginative work in which an author ['ɔːθə] creates his or her own world and/or presents an invented story. The reader is expected to accept this world or story as existing or true (this is called suspension of disbelief). Fiction can take different forms. The main types are *narrative prose (e.g. *novels, *short stories) and *drama.
Fiction usually comprises a variety of elements, such as *characters, *action and plot, *setting and *atmosphere. The *mode [məʊd] of presentation (scenic or panoramic) and the *point of view adopted (first-person or third-person, limited or unlimited, reliable or unreliable *narrator) play a central role in how the reader reacts to the story.
A literary text is often structured and held together by a specific theme or a so-called motif [məʊˈtiːf], which may be a recurring image or a specific phrase or sentence.

▶ Narrative prose

A narrative ['nærətɪv] prose text is a *fictional text which is told by a narrator (cf. *narration) and is written in prose [prəʊz], i.e. writing that is formed by sentences in a continuous flow and is broken up only by paragraphs (cf. verse [vɜːs], which is used in poetry and refers to a single line of a poem, or a stanza ['stænzə].) Typical examples of narrative prose are *novels and *short stories. Fiction can further be subdivided by aspects of content (e.g. *coming-of-age stories and *fables).

novel ['nɒvl] *Roman* ■ TROUBLE SPOT **novel** = *Roman* Not: ~~Novelle~~	A novel is a long and complex fictional narrative text often divided into chapters. The storyline and structure of a novel are normally more complicated than those of shorter fictional works and, accordingly, there may be greater variety and a more detailed development of *characters ['kærəktəz] and *setting (i.e. the time and the place). In every novel the author must decide from which *point of view the story will be told. In some cases there is more than one narrator (cf. *narration). No other art form can recreate life on the same scale as the novel with its almost unlimited possibilities.
short story [ˌʃɔːt ˈstɔːri] *Kurzgeschichte*	There is no generally accepted definition of the short story that clearly separates it from other narrative texts like the *novel. However, there are some elements that can be regarded as characteristic. Most short stories can be read at one sitting and concentrate on one *character, situation, dilemma or problem. In a short story the characters, the situation, etc. are not fully developed (unlike in a novel); the focus is on one single aspect which undergoes a change in the course of the story. There are different types of short stories, e.g. the *coming-of-age story or the 'slice of life' story (which shows just one particular aspect of everyday life).
microfiction, flash fiction *Kürzestgeschichte*	Microfiction (or flash fiction) is an extremely short fictional text. It refers to a new literary genre [ʒɒ̃rə, ˈʒɒnrə] that originates from the *short story. Although there is no general agreement regarding its length, microfiction is much shorter than a short story and usually does not exceed one thousand words.

323

Glossary

fable *Fabel*	A fable is a short narrative text in which animals represent human types or act like human beings. Fables are usually didactic since they intend to teach a moral lesson, make a satirical comment ['kɒmɛnt] or illustrate some general truth. A moral may be understood from the text or there may be a moral (epilogue ['epɪlɒg]) at the end, which in modern fables is often ironic (cf. *irony).
coming-of-age story *Entwicklungsroman,* *Initiationsgeschichte*	A coming-of-age story is a *short story or *novel in which the process of growing up is portrayed. Usually the protagonist (cf. *character) is a child or an adolescent who undergoes an experience which changes his/her outlook on life and marks an important stage in his/her development towards maturity and adulthood. The coming-of-age story is sometimes referred to as the 'story of initiation'.
frame story *Rahmenhandlung*	A frame story is a *novel or *short story which contains one or more quite independent stories within it. The main story provides the frame for the other stories. Often the main story consists of a *character in one *setting recounting another story in another setting.

► Poetry

A poem is a piece of creative writing structured by lines and rhythm ['rɪðəm] (the arrangement of stressed and unstressed syllables in a line). The lines of a poem are often arranged into groups called stanzas. Phrases or lines repeated at intervals throughout a poem form the refrain [rɪ'freɪn]. To emphasize the structure and to create certain effects, traditional poets frequently make use of *rhyme. Modern poetry often uses free verse [friː vɜːs], which makes little use of rhyme. The poetry comes from *repetition, *imagery and the arrangement of words and stresses in the poem. Poems are often lyrical ['lɪrɪkl] (i.e. they express personal thoughts and feelings), but they can also be narrative (i.e. they tell a story).
The speaker is the voice in which a poem is spoken, especially when the personal pronoun *I* is used. This speaker is not always identical with the voice of the poet.

sonnet ['sɒnɪt] *Sonett*	A sonnet is a special form of a poem that consists of 14 lines. Sonnets became popular in England in the 17th century and were mostly used for love poetry, but later they came to embrace a wide number of themes. There are various types of sonnets with different structures and forms. Shakespeare's sonnets comprised three quatrains ['kwɒtreɪns] (i.e. four lines with a shared rhyme scheme) and a couplet ['kʌplət] (i.e. two successive lines which rhyme). The couplet has a rhyme scheme that differs from the rest of the sonnet and it is used to sum up the theme [θiːm] or thought. The couplet is usually accompanied by the volta ['vɒltə], i.e. the turning point in a sonnet, which can be identified by words like *but*, *yet* or *and yet*. *Example:* William Shakespeare, 'Sonnet 116'; cf. *Context* p. 85)
shape poem, **concrete poem** *konkrete Poesie*	A shape poem (also called a concrete ['kɒnkriːt] poem) is a poem in which the printed words form a shape or picture. The shape usually reflects the theme or contents of the poem.
rhyme [raɪm] *Reim*	Rhyme is the similarity of sounds between certain words (especially stressed syllables), usually at the end of lines. When identifying the rhyme scheme ['raɪm skiːm] (i.e. which words at the end of the lines rhyme), it is usual to use small letters to indicate that words share a rhyme. If the words *abide, thee, wide* and *see* occur respectively at the end of four successive lines, the rhyme scheme is written as **a b a b** (this pattern is called alternate [ɔːl'tɜːnət] rhyme). If '*abide, thee, wide* and *see* occur respectively at the end of four successive lines, the rhyme scheme is written **a a b b** (this pattern is called rhyming couplets). Other letters are then used for other rhymes.

Glossary

metre [ˈmiːtə] *Metrum, Versmaß*	Metre is the regular rhythm of the words in a poem. Traditionally, this is achieved by the arrangement of stressed and unstressed syllables in the line of a poem. The most common metre in English is the iambic pentameter [aɪˈæmbɪk penˈtæmɪtə], which consists of a line of five feet (each foot consists of an unstressed syllable followed by a stressed syllable).	*Example:* O **no**! It **is** an **ev**-er *fix*-ed **mark** From: William Shakespeare, 'Sonnet 116'; cf. *Context* p. 83 The syllables **in bold** are stressed.

▶ Drama

A drama or play is written to be performed by actors or actresses in a theatre, in a film, or on TV or on the radio. The author of a play is called a playwright [ˈpleɪraɪt] or dramatist [ˈdræmətɪst] while a scriptwriter creates scripts for films and television. Plays are usually divided into several acts (in classical drama, there were usually five acts, but modern plays normally consist of three and sometimes of only one act). An act may be subdivided into scenes.

A scene [siːn] is a smaller unit of action in which there is no change of place or break in time. The actors take on roles of *characters, perform the *action and express themselves in the form of dialogues, monologues or soliloquies. While a dialogue [ˈdaɪəlɒg] involves at least two actors engaged in a conversation, the monologue [ˈmɒnəlɒg] is a lengthy speech by just one character in the company of others. The soliloquy [səˈlɪləkwi] differs from the monologue as it is spoken by one person who is alone on stage. It can give the audience more knowledge of events or individuals than the other characters and actions can take on different meanings for the audience than for the other characters of the play (this literary device is called dramatic irony). The actors' way of speaking, their appearance and their movements, as well as the *setting, the arrangement of props, the sound and lighting, etc. are often given in the stage directions – this helps an acting company perform a play.

tragedy [ˈtrædʒədi] *Tragödie, Trauerspiel*	A tragedy is a type of *drama in which the protagonist (cf. *character) passes through a series of misfortunes towards his or her downfall. Usually the downfall is brought about partly by the protagonist's own fault, e.g. through too much pride, weakness, uncertainty, etc. *Example:* William Shakespeare, *Macbeth*; cf. *Context* pp. 76f.
comedy [ˈkɒmədi] *Komödie, Lustspiel*	A comedy is a type of *drama which deals with a light topic or a more serious one in an amusing way. A comedy always has a happy ending. *Example:* William Shakespeare, *The Taming of the Shrew*; cf. *Context* pp. 82f.
feature film *Spielfilm*	A feature film is a full-length film that has a story and *characters, who are played by actors. A feature film is based on a film script, which the director then turns into a film. Important elements in a film are the dialogue, the use of camera techniques and the acting.
tv/radio series [ˈsɪəriːz] *Fernseh-/Radioserie*	A series is a regular programme on TV or radio about the lives and problems of a character or, more usually, a group of *characters. A series may centre on a couple or family life or a leading character's career, and some involve magic and/or fantasy. Each programme is self-contained, i.e. it deals with a particular issue or storyline which is concluded at the end of the programme. The lives of the characters evolve slowly over the course of a series. *Example:* *Downton Abbey*, 2010; cf. *Context* p. 111

Glossary

sitcom *Sitcom*	A sitcom (= situation comedy) is a comic *TV/radio series which usually centres around a *character or group of characters, who are often stereotypes as they do not evolve over the series. It may be filmed in front of a live audience or have canned laughter added to make the audience aware of or to reinforce the funny lines.
soap (opera) 'Seifenoper'	A soap (= soap opera) is a regular TV or radio programme about the everyday lives of a group of people. The storyline of a soap, unlike that of a normal *TV/radio series, develops from programme to programme and may often end with a cliff-hanger ['klɪfhæŋə] (an exciting situation that makes you want to know what will happen next) to encourage the audience to tune in to the next episode.

▶ Narrator

The narrator [nə'reɪtə] is the voice or *character who tells the story and is part of the fictional world created by the author. There are three types of narrator:

first-person narrator	The narrator is a character in the story and refers to him- or herself as *I*. The reader must take care when reading the text, as only one person's point of view is given.	*Example:* I'd attended school in the real world up until the sixth grade. It hadn't been a very pleasant experience. From: Ernest Cline, *Ready Player One*, 2012; cf. *Context* p. 16
third-person narrator	The narrator is not a character in the story and refers to the characters as *he*, *she* or *they* or by their names. *Example:* It was with some relief that she got back into the coach and reached behind the cushion for her book. It was not there. Steadfastly waving as they rumbled along, she surreptitiously felt behind the other cushions. From: Alan Bennett, *The Uncommon Reader*, 2008, cf. *Context* pp. 96ff., ll. 34–36 In this example, the narrator is a third-person narrator as he is not part of the fictional world and refers to the protagonist by using the personal pronoun *she* (= the Queen). This excerpt is, however, told from the Queen's point of view (i.e. there is a *limited point of view) as the readers experience the story from her perspective. They are informed about her feelings and are also puzzled about the disappearance of her book.	
omniscient narrator [ɒm'nɪsɪənt]	The narrator has an *unlimited point of view, i.e. he or she can move freely in place and time and enter the minds of the characters at will.	

▶ Point of view

The point of view is the perspective from which characters, events, etc. are presented in a fictional story. This has an important effect on the reader: for example, we tend to respond more sympathetically to a character whose mind we enter, as we experience for ourselves what the character goes through. A fictional work can have several points of view (depending on the *narrator):

Glossary

limited point of view	A first-person *narrator can have a limited point of view; a *character in fictional work does not know everything that occurs, therefore he or she imposes his or her understanding and interpretation on the action.
	A third-person *narrator can have a limited point of view; the *narrator looks at the events and characters from the perspective of one of the characters or from the outside (as an observer narrator) and so does not have access to the thoughts and feelings of all the characters.
unlimited point of view	A third-person narrator can have an unlimited point of view; the narrator can move freely in place and time and enter the minds of the *characters at will (here we speak of an omniscient [ɒmˈnɪsɪənt] narrator).

Often, the point of view changes to make for more interesting reading. A reader must ask him- or herself how reliable a narrator is. Often one cannot take everything in a fictional work at face value:

reliable narrator [rɪˈlaɪəbl]	The reader may take everything the narrator tells at face value.
unreliable narrator [ˌʌnrɪˈlaɪəbl]	The reader must find out just how much of what the narrator says can be accepted. First-person narrators are usually unreliable as they give only one perspective on the action and the characters.

▶ Mode of presentation

The way a writer narrates events is known as mode of presentation. There are two modes of presentation, and usually a combination of both is used in a narrative text:

scenic presentation	If the author shows an event in detail as it occurs, using dialogue, depicting thoughts and emotions, describing a scene, etc., he or she uses scenic presentation (also known as showing). *Example:*

> When they arrived at the palace she had a word with Grant, the young footman in charge, who said that while ma'am had been in the Lords the sniffer dogs had been round and security had confiscated the book. He thought it had probably been exploded.
>   'Exploded?' said the Queen. 'But it was Anita Brookner.'
> The young man, who seemed remarkably undeferential, said security may have thought it was a device.
>   The Queen said: 'Yes. That is exactly what it is. A book is a device to ignite the imagination.'
>
> From: Alan Bennett, *The Uncommon Reader*, 2008; cf. *Context* pp. 98ff., ll. 42–50

interior monologue [ɪnˈtɪərɪə ˈmɒnəlɒg]	This is a particular kind of *scenic presentation in which the author depicts the thoughts and feelings passing through a character's mind. Often an interior monologue does not follow a chronological [ˌkrɒnəˈlɒdʒɪkl] order, since when people think, their thoughts jump from one subject to another. Interior monologues are normally narrated in the present tense. However, it is more common to find reported thought, in which the thoughts are presented as reported speech (i.e. in the past tense).

327

Glossary

panoramic presentation	If the author tells the story as a condensed series of events, summarizing in a few sentences what happens over a longer period of time (e.g. an hour, a week, months), he or she uses panoramic presentation (also known as 'telling'). *Example:*
	For me, school had been a Darwinian exercise. A daily gauntlet of ridicule, abuse, and isolation. By the time I entered sixth grade, I was beginning to wonder if I'd be able to maintain my sanity until graduation, still six long years away.
	From: Ernest Cline, *Ready Player One*, 2012; cf. *Context* p. 16, ll. 21–23

▶ Characters

Characters are the people in a fictional text. They are usually presented through their actions, speech and thoughts as well as by description. The main character in a story is called the protagonist [prə'tægənɪst]. There are generally speaking two types of characters in fictional works:

round character	A round character may be similar to real individuals and have several traits and behave in a way that is life-like. A round character usually changes in the course of a story. The main character in a story, the protagonist, is almost always a round character.
flat character	A flat character has only a limited number of traits or represents only a single quality. A crude representation of a character which is meant to be laughed at is called a caricature.

> ■ TROUBLE SPOT
>
> When talking about the characters in a fictional text, do not use the words *people* or *person*.

▶ Characterization

Characterization [ˌkærəktəraɪ'zeɪʃn] is the way in which the author presents his or her characters. We usually distinguish between two kinds of characterization, which are often combined by authors in their presentation of the characters.

direct [də'rekt, dɪ'-, daɪ'-] or **explicit** characterization	The reader is told about a character's personality directly by a) the narrator, b) another character or c) by the character him- or herself.	*Example:* 'But McNulty's eyes were scary.' From: Carl Deuker, *Payback Time*, 2010; cf. p. 190
indirect [ˌɪndə'rekt, ˌɪndaɪ'rekt] or **implicit** characterization	The reader is expected to draw conclusions about a character by studying his or her behaviour, opinions, choice of words and/or way of talking. *Example:*	
	I cleared my throat. 'How about we get started? I've got some questions. First –''No, no, no,' McNulty said, pointing the pencil at me again. 'No questions – not today, not ever. This job takes forever and pays peanuts. Here's how it works. You write down or tape what I tell you. When I'm done, jazz it up whatever you want, but never make me, my coaches, or my players look bad. Understand?'	
	From: Carl Deuker, *Payback Time*, 2010; cf. p. 190	

Glossary

> **TROUBLE SPOT**
>
> An author *characterizes* somebody, i.e. invents the traits of a character. A reader *describes the character* of somebody when talking about his or her traits.

> **LANGUAGE HELP**
>
> - main/central/major character/figure
> - minor/secondary character/figure
> - hero/heroine

► Action

Action ['ækʃn] is everything that happens in a fictional story. Action may be on two levels:

external action [ɪkˈstɜːnl]	The author describes what the *characters do and the events that take place. *Example:* [...] she got back into the coach and reached behind the cushion for her book. It was not there. Steadfastly waving as they rumbled along, she surreptitiously felt behind the other cushions. From: Alan Bennett, *The Uncommon Reader*, 2008; cf. *Context* pp. 96ff.
internal action	The author describes what is going on in the minds of the characters, i.e. the reader is shown the thoughts of the characters. *Example:* She was dreading the two hours the whole thing was due to take, though fortunately they were in the coach, not the open carriage, so she could take along her book. From: Alan Bennett, *The Uncommon Reader*, 2008; cf. *Context*

► Plot

Plot [plɒt] refers to the structure of events in a fictional story. The story is usually told through cause and effect. The English novelist E.M. Forster described plot in these terms: '"The king died and then the queen died" is a story. "The king died and then the queen died of grief", is a plot.' (*Aspects of the Novel*, 1927). The plot usually develops in a number of stages:

1. **exposition** [ˌekspəˈzɪʃn]	The *characters, theme, *setting, etc. are introduced.
2. **rising action**	A conflict [ˈkɒnflɪkt] is developed.
3. **climax** [ˈklaɪmæks]	The conflict reaches its highest point.
4. **turning point**	There is a change in the conflict or *suspense.
5. **falling action**	The suspense is reduced.
6. **denouement** [deɪˈnuːmɒ̄] (also known as the **solution** [səˈluːʃn]	Some resolution of the conflict is achieved.
which may also be: **surprise ending**	The reader's expectations concerning the course of the story are not fulfilled but instead an unexpected solution of the conflict is presented.
or instead: **open ending**	The conflict is not fully resolved and the reader is left wondering what might happen next.

A plot will have some element of suspense and tension. In order to create suspense or to make a story more exciting, authors also make use of flashbacks and foreshadowing:

329

Glossary

suspense [səˈspens] *Spannung*	Suspense is created when the reader does not know the outcome of a conflict (the struggle or opposition between different forces, characters, etc.) or of the action.
tension [ˈtenʃn] *(An)spannung*	Tension is the emotional reaction to the conflict, which rouses the attention of the reader and makes him or her curious about the further development of the plot; this is usually achieved by the expectations concerning the outcome of the conflict.
flashback [ˈflæʃbæk] *Rückblende*	Authors do not always tell their stories strictly chronologically [ˌkrɒnɒlədʒɪkli]. In some stories the authors make use of flashbacks, i.e. the *narrator goes back into the past to describe a scene that has relevance to the plot.
foreshadowing [fɔːˈʃædəʊɪŋ] *Vorwegnahme*	Foreshadowing (also called anticipation) is the technique of hinting at later events in a fictional text so that the reader or audience is prepared for them or can anticipate them. *Example:* In William Shakespeare's *Macbeth*, the three witches allow the audience to believe that Macbeth will become king.

■ TROUBLE SPOT

happy ending
Not = ~~happy end~~

■ LANGUAGE HELP

- open/surprise/unexpected/happy/sad/tragic ending
- centre around sth.
- a conflict between … and …

► Atmosphere

Atmosphere [ˈætməsfɪə] is the feeling or mood created by an author in his or her work. The *setting, use of language and *characterization all contribute to the atmosphere of a work.
Example:

> One of the Queen's recurrent royal responsibilities was to open Parliament, an obligation she had never previously found particularly burdensome and actually rather enjoyed: to be driven down the Mall on a bright autumn morning even after fifty years was something of a treat.

From: Alan Bennett, *The Uncommon Reader*, 2008; cf. *Context* pp. 96ff., ll. 1–4

Here the description of the Queen's drive down the Mall together with the bright autumn morning creates a positive atmosphere.

► Setting

Setting is the time and place in which a literary work takes place. The setting can have symbolic overtones; it may serve to reveal something about the characters and also contribute to the *atmosphere of the story.
Example: The extract quoted above from the novel *The Uncommon Reader* by Alan Bennett (cf. *Context* p. 98, ll. 1–4) is set in contemporary Britain on a sunny autumn morning. The season contributes to the positive and light-hearted atmosphere of the story.

Glossary

Non-fictional texts

▶ Non-fiction

A non-fictional text [ˌnɒn-ˈfɪkʃənl tekst] (e.g. *news stories, *advertisements, *speeches, *letters, etc.) normally refers to the real world whereas a *literary text creates its own fictional world. Non-fictional texts may serve a variety of practical purposes, e.g. to inform, persuade, express personal opinions, criticize, etc. There is a variety of non-fictional text types:

news story *Zeitungsbericht*	The terms news story, news item and news report can be used interchangeably to refer to reports of recent events of general interest that appear in newspapers, on television or on the radio. News items can be of any length. In theory, news stories are meant to be objective and unbiased presentations of the facts, providing answers to the five w's, i.e. the questions *who?, what?, when?, where?* and *why?*. In practice, totally impartial reporting is impossible. The choice of words, the *style and *tone, the choice of detail and examples, the emphasis [ˈemfəsɪs] given to certain aspects of the story, the position of the article in the paper and on the page, the headline and layout all contribute to influence the reader. There are two common formulas used in news stories: a) The pyramid, in which the most important item or element in the story is reported first and then the rest of the information is offered in descending order of importance. b) The Wall Street Journal formula, in which the news story starts with a particular (usually personal) example to attract the reader's attention before the topic is discussed. It differs from a feature story in that the latter puts more emphasis on the personal account in order to illustrate a topic, while the former uses the personal account merely to attract the attention of the reader. *Example:* 'It's OK to like the Germans'; cf. *Context* p. 110
biography [baɪˈɒɡrəfi] *Biografie*	A biography is a book or text written by one person about the life of another person. If the person writes his or her own life story, this is referred to as an autobiography [ˌɔːtəbaɪˈɒɡrəfi]. Usually the biography belongs to the genre of non-fiction as it portrays the life of a person that really exists/existed. However, there are also fictional biographies, where the author invents a character and his life story (e.g. *Robinson Crusoe*).
feature story *Zeitungsreportage*	A feature story deals with a topic by concentrating on a particular person or on particular people. It often takes an individual case as its starting point to discuss the different aspects of the topic on a personal level and leaves the reader to draw more general conclusions from this individual case. The writer of a feature story makes use of direct quotes from the people involved in the story and relies on first-hand reporting, i.e. the journalist writes mostly about things and people he or she has actually encountered. A feature story often opens with the description of an event or a person in order to attract the reader's attention. *Example:* 'Eastern Europeans in the UK'; cf. *Context* p. 107

Glossary

editorial [ˌedɪˈtɔːriəl] *Leitartikel*	An editorial (in British English also known as a *leading article* or *leader*) an article that expresses the opinion of the newspaper's editor or editorial team about an item of news or a political or social issue, etc. In American usage an editorial can also be a comment [ˈkɒment] on radio or television that expresses the opinion of the station or network. Unlike *columns, editorials are not supposed to be personal and do not appear with a byline, i.e. with a line that gives the writer's name.
column [ˈkɒləm] *Kolumne*	a) *Column* is the term used for any of the vertical sections into which the printed page of a newspaper is divided. b) *Column* is the term used for a regular item in a newspaper or magazine which either deals with a particular subject (e.g. gardening, gossip, financial, agony column) or is written by a particular writer (called a columnist). Columnists often write highly personal essays on topics of their choosing. Unlike *editorials, columns appear with a byline, i.e. with a line that gives the writer's name.
speech *Rede, Ansprache*	A speech is an address delivered to an audience. A speaker may try to establish contact with his or her listeners in various ways: by flattering them, addressing them directly (direct address) or using the first-person plural (e.g. *we*, *our*) to involve them in what he or she is saying. A speaker may appeal to shared experiences and values, e.g. by quoting from or alluding to sources such as the Bible or history. A speaker often uses *stylistic devices to heighten the impact of what he or she is saying. Contrast [ˈkɒntrɑːst] may be used to highlight differences between the speaker and his or her opponents. *Repetition and *alliteration often help the audience follow the speech and remember key ideas and phrases. *Example:* '9/11 – A game changer'; cf. *Context* pp. 24f.
essay *Essay*	An essay is a text form in which the writer expresses his or her personal views on some topic. Essays can vary widely in length, subject matter and *tone, some being serious and others light-hearted and entertaining.
letter *Brief*	There are many types of letters. They can be personal or business-oriented, depending on the relationship between the sender and receiver, the occasion and the purpose of the letter. Letters are a very flexible text form and comprise thank-you notes, emails, covering letters (in American English, *cover letters*), letters of complaint, *letters to the editor, etc. The beginnings and endings of letters follow certain conventions. Usually, letters consist of the following parts: **1** the address of the sender (and in the case of a business letter, the address of the recipient), **2** the date, **3** the salutation (e.g. *Dear Mark*), **4** the body of the letter, i.e. the information the sender wants to convey, **5** a conventional phrase to close the letter (e.g. *Yours faithfully*, *Yours sincerely*, *Love*) and **6** the signature. *Example:* the letter from Chetan Bhagat to Gandhi; cf. *Context* pp. 123f.
letter to the editor *Leserbrief*	A letter to the editor is a letter in which a reader expresses his or her opinion concerning an article in a newspaper/magazine or a problem which is of public interest. The letter may criticize or support an article, or state a personal opinion concerning a topic which is being discussed in public or attract the attention of other readers to a topic that has been ignored or is worthy of attention.
blurb [blɜːb] *Umschlag-text, Klappentext*	A blurb is the short promotional text on the back cover of a book or a DVD case.
advertisement [ədˈvɜːtɪsmənt] *Werbung, Anzeige, Annonce*	An advertisement (informally also called an *advert* or *ad*) is a text which attempts to persuade people to do something (e.g. buy a particular product or contribute money to a cause). It normally consists of pictures and text (called *copy*) and is designed to catch the attention of the reader through its layout.

Glossary

Common elements of advertisements are *wordplay in the title or headings and *humour to win the sympathy of the reader. Advertisers often use the AIDA formula (**A**ttention, **I**nterest, **D**esire, **A**ction) in their advertisements.
Newspaper or magazine advertisements dealing with job offers, buying, selling or renting something, etc. are called *small* or *classified ads.* Advertisements on the radio or on television are known as *commercials*.
Example: 'The best job in the world is back!', cf. *Context* p. 193

blog [blɒg] *Blog*	A blog is a regularly updated website created by an individual or a small group. Usually, the chosen language is colloquial and informal.
cartoon *Karikatur, Cartoon*	A cartoon is an amusing drawing in a newspaper or magazine that deals with human nature or a current political or social issue. Complex issues are reduced to memorable pictures. Cartoons often include captions or speech bubbles. Techniques employed by cartoonists include caricature ['kærɪkətʃʊə], *exaggeration, *wordplay and the use of *symbols. Cartoons usually presuppose that the reader has background knowledge of the political, social and cultural issues being dealt with, which often makes them difficult for the non-native reader to understand. *Example:* 'Being five. A boy and his blog'; cf. *Context* p. 10

Style and Language

▶ Style

Style [staɪl] is the way in which a text is written. In order to examine the style of a text it is necessary to examine aspects such as the *register, the *diction and the *tone of the text, as well as the grammar and the sentence structures used in the text.

tone *Ton(fall)*	Tone [təʊn] is the way in which a writer treats his or her topic, thereby reflecting his or her emotional attitude towards that topic and also towards the reader. The tone can be formal, intimate, solemn, playful, serious, ironic (cf. *irony), humorous (cf. *humour), angry, etc.
humour ['hjuːmə] *Humor*	Humour is based on the human ability to see and laugh at the strangeness of a *character, an action or comment, etc. because it is unexpected or unsuitable in a particular situation. At one end of the spectrum, humour is gentle, understanding and tolerant and makes the reader smile at human weaknesses; at the other end, it is divisive, bitter or sarcastic, evoking contempt and moral indignation at human vices and corruption. Not all forms of humour will be appreciated by every segment of society since humour relies on shared cultural values. *Example:* [The Queen] got quite good at reading and waving, the trick being to keep the book below the level of the window and to keep focused on it and not on the crowds. From: Alan Bennett, *The Uncommon Reader,* 2008; cf. *Context* pp. 96ff., ll. 1–9 Here the Queen's well-known behaviour of waving at the crowd is ridiculed by the fact that she is reading a book at the same time.

Glossary

diction *Diktion, Ausdruck,* *Wortwahl*	Diction is the words a writer chooses for his or her text. Diction is very important as words influence the reader or listener. In many argumentative texts, for example, the writer will use words that have a positive connotation [ˌkɒnəˈteɪʃn] (i.e. the associations a word has beyond its literal or dictionary meaning) to support his or her arguments or words with negative connotations to attack those he or she opposes. The choice of words often reveals the writer's attitudes. A writer can also use emotive language (i.e. words and expressions with particular connotations that appeal to the reader's or listener's emotions) and so influence him or her to react in a particular way. When the writer makes use of the literal and limited meaning of a word, regardless of the ideas and emotions it might connote, this is called denotation [ˌdiːnəʊˈteɪʃn].
register [ˈredʒɪstə] *Sprachebene,* *Stilebene*	Register is the level of language (the choice of words, grammar, etc.) used in a particular situation. The register in a text may be formal, neutral or informal.

Formal style consists of difficult vocabulary, often of Latin origin, and complex sentence structure; it is usually only used for serious purposes, e.g. essays or academic publications, or in official situations, and would not be appropriate in normal everyday conversation.
Example:

> A new widely-debated approach is gene pharming. Pharma crops are genetically modified plants like maize that produce much-needed medicines.

From: 'Science – motor of progress?', cf. Context, p. 32, ll. 22–29

The writer uses difficult words and grammar so that the reader must examine the sentence closely to understand what the writer is saying.

Neutral style falls between formal and informal style and is the style generally used by educated people; it is used in feature stories, news stories, etc.
Example:

> [P]eople's 'likes' and 'dislikes' are carefully stored, along with a great number of other details gathered about the users, to be exploited by businesses or political organizations.

From: 'Living interactive lives', cf. Context, p. 12, ll. 6–9

The writer uses straightforward sentence structures and words that are formal (e.g. *exploited*) and informal (e.g. *dislikes*).

Informal style is characterized by fairly simple, often elliptical sentences, short forms (e.g. *can't*, *you'll*), phrasal verbs an colloquial words, often of Germanic origin; it is used between friends or in a relaxed or informal situation.
Example:

> That waitress sized us up in two seconds. We're black, and 'black people don't tip' so she wasn't gonna waste her time; someone like that, nothing you can do to change their mind.

From: Crash, 2004

The short forms like *we're*, *wasn't*, the use of simple words like *do*, *go* and phrases like *to size sb. up* any *gonna* indicate that the characters are using informal style. Informal style may include the use of slang and/or taboo words:

Glossary

	Slang is very informal language, mainly used in dialogue between people of the same age or from a similar background, etc. Taboo [təˈbuː] words are generally considered obscene, vulgar or shocking and are used only if the writer is trying to make a particular point or shock his or her reader.
layout *Layout, Aufbau*	The way elements are arranged on a printed page is known as the layout. The layout includes elements such as the type and size of letters, the use of **bold** or *italic* typeface, underlining, headings and sub-headings, bullets (= dots or other symbols used at the beginning of a text passage), the size and number of columns, the length of paragraphs, the use of insets, the colour and the placement of illustrations. The layout determines whether a text attracts the attention of the reader and is pleasant to read, and it helps writers to structure their texts and to emphasize certain words, phrases or passages. The layout is particularly important when considering newspaper articles, *advertisements and brochures.
thesis [ˈθiːsɪs] *These*	An idea or a view that an author of an argumentative text presents and discusses in a formal way.
antithesis [ænˈtɪθəsɪs] *Antithese*	An antithesis is an idea that is the opposite of an idea (thesis) already put forward by a writer. Often the writer will put forward the antithesis in order to stress his own thesis.

▶ Stylistic Devices

Stylistic devices [staɪˈlɪstɪk dɪˈvaɪsɪs] (also called *rhetorical devices* [rɪˈtɒrɪkl dɪˈvaɪsɪs]) are methods and techniques used to produce a particular effect. Stylistic devices may e.g. relate to sound (e.g. *alliteration), structure (e.g. *repetition, *parallelism) or *imagery.

> **LANGUAGE HELP**
>
> *The author uses alliteration/contrast/exaggeration/repetition …* (uncountable nouns)
> *In line 5 there is a metaphor/allusion/symbol/rhetorical question/pun* (countable nouns)

Imagery

metaphor [ˈmetəfə, ˈmetəfɔː] *Metapher*	A metaphor is a comparison between two things which are basically quite unlike one another without using the words *as* or *like* (cf. *simile).	*Example:* There's daggers in men's smiles. From: William Shakespeare, *Macbeth*
personification [pəˌsɒnɪfɪˈkeɪʃn] *Personifikation*	Personification is the technique of representing animals or objects as if they were human beings or possessed human qualities. *Example:* Love's not Time's fool, though rosy lips and cheeks. Within his bending sickle's compass come: / Love alters not with his brief hours and weeks, / But bears it out even to the edge of doom. From: William Shakespeare, 'Sonnet 116', cf. *Context*, p. 85 Here, both love and time are personified. Love in particular is described as a person with the appearance of 'rosy lips and cheeks'.	

335

Glossary

simile ['sɪməli] *Vergleich*	Like a metaphor, a simile is a type of comparison. But while *metaphors say that something *is* something else, a simile says that something *is like* something else and uses the words *like* or *as* to draw the comparison.	*Example:* My mistress eyes are nothing like the sun. From: William Shakespeare, 'Sonnet 18'
symbol ['sɪmbl] *Symbol* ■ TROUBLE SPOT **symbol of sth.** Not: ~~symbol for sth.~~	A symbol is a thing, word or phrase signifying something concrete that stands not only for itself but also for a certain abstract idea. As in the case of a metaphor or a simile the meaning of a symbol goes beyond the literal. *Example:* A red rose is often a symbol of love.	

Sound

alliteration [ə,lɪtə'reɪʃn] *Alliteration*	Alliteration is the repetition of a sound, normally a consonant, at the beginning of neighbouring words or of stressed syllables within such words, to produce a usually rhythmic, but sometimes also comic effect. *Example:* Around the rugged rock the ragged rascal ran.	
assonance ['æsənəns] *Assonanz*	Assonance is the repetition of the same or similar vowel sounds within stressed syllables of neighbouring words.	*Example:* Beside the lake, beneath the trees, Fluttering and dancing in the breeze. From: William Wordsworth, 'I wandered lonely as a cloud'
onomatopoeia [,ɒnə,mætə'piːə] *Lautmalerei*	Omatopoeia is the use of a word which imitates the sounds it refers to, e.g. *buzz* or *hum*. In a group of words or a phrase it may evoke a particular feeling, mood, sound or movement.	*Example:* Only the stuttering rifles' rapid rattle. From: Wilfred Owen, 'Anthem for doomed youth' The repetition of 't's and 'r's sounds like the shooting of rifles which the words describe.

Structure

accumulation [ə,kjuːmjə'leɪʃn] *Akkumulation,* *Ansammlung*	Accumulation is a listing of words and expressions with similar meaning. Thus, the words are emphasized or become more descriptive. *Example:* Then shall our names / Familiar in his mouth as household words / Harry the King, Bedford and Exeter / Warwick and Talbot, Salisbury and Gloucester, Be in their flowing cups freshly remembered. From: William Shakespeare, *Henry V* This excerpt displays an accumulation of several addresses for 'King Harry'.

Glossary

analogy [əˈnælədʒi] *Analogie*	Analogy is the comparison of two things which are similar in several aspects. By comparing an object, situation or person to something familiar, the explanation becomes easier to understand. *Example:* What's in a name? That which we call a rose. / By any other word would smell as sweet. / So Romeo would, were he not Romeo called. From: William Shakespeare, *Romeo and Juliet* Juliet states that just like a rose that will always keep its sweet smell whichever name it is called, Romeo will stay the same even if he changes his name.

anaphora [əˈnæfərə] Anapher	Anaphora is a form of parallelism which repeats the same word or group of words at the beginning of successive clauses.	*Example:* I open the door. Come in, I say. Come in and eat with us. From: Imtiaz Dharker, 'The right word', cf. *Context* p. 89, ll. 30–32
enjambement [ɪnˈdʒæmbmənt] *Enjambement*	Enjambement describes incomplete syntax at the end of the line where the meaning runs over to the next line without any punctuation at the end. An enjambement is also called *run-on-line*.	*Example:* The child steps in And carefully, at my door, Takes off his shoes. From: Imtiaz Dharker, 'The right word', cf. *Context* p. 89, ll. 32–35
enumeration *Aufzählung*	Enumeration is the listing of words, phrases or ideas. In instructive or argumentative texts the list of enumerated elements can be given numbers or dashes so the reader can see each new element clearly.	*Example:* [G]o, my son, multiply, divide, conquer. From: Philip Levine, 'Corporate Head'; cf. *Context* p. 189
parallelism [ˈpærəlelɪzəm] *Parallelismus*	Parallelism is the deliberate repetition of similar or identical words, phrases, sentence constructions, etc. in the same or neighbouring sentences. Parallelism draws the attention of the reader to certain ideas that the writer may consider important. It may be used to show that the elements are of similar importance, or it may be used in a climactic sequence, with the most important element listed at the end.	*Example:* Which alters when it alteration finds, Or bends with the remover to remove. From: William Shakespeare, 'Sonnet 116', cf. *Context* p. 85

repetition *Wiederholung*	Repetition is the deliberate use of a word or phrase more than once in a sentence or a text to create a sense of pattern or form, or to emphasize certain elements for the reader or listener.

Glossary

Miscellaneous

allusion [ə'luːʒn] *Allusion, Anspielung*	Allusion is the direct or indirect reference to something or somebody the reader or listener is supposed to recognize and respond to. An allusion may be to a work of literature, a historical event, a religious text like the Bible, etc. *Example:* 'This place is like the garden of Eden'. This allusion refers to the 'garden of God', i.e. paradise, which appears in the Bible, in the book of Genesis.
cliché ['kliːʃeɪ]	A cliché denotes the fact that an expression has been overused to the extent that the original meaning has been lost. It may also refer to predictable events or actions.
exaggeration [ɪg,zædʒə'reɪʃn] *Übertreibung*	Exaggeration is the use of a strong overstatement. It may be used to create either a serious or comic effect. A single phrase containing an exaggeration is called hyperbole [hʌɪ'pəːbəli]. (cf. also *understatement)	*Example:* I fear the day technology will surpass our human interaction. The world will have a generation of idiots. *(Albert Einstein)*
irony ['aɪrəni] *Ironie*	Irony is the term used when a person makes fun of somebody or something without openly doing so. A person using irony may use certain words and actually mean the opposite of what those words normally mean. Also, a person may appear to support someone or something while at the same time making it clear (e.g. by his or her tone of voice or through his or her choice of words) that he or she is actually criticizing or revealing the contradictions in the other person's behaviour. A text which uses irony to ridicule or make fun of an institution, person, set of beliefs, etc. is called a satire ['sætaɪə].
juxtaposition [,dʒʌkstəpə'zɪʃn] *Gegenüberstellung*	A very strong contrast ['kɒntrɑːst] of opposing ideas, arguments, views, mostly introduced by words like *but*, *however* or *nevertheless*.
rhetorical question *rhetorische Frage*	A rhetorical question is a question to which the answer seems obvious and is therefore not necessary. Such question push the reader or listener to a certain conclusion. As such they are popular in political speeches, etc. when a person is trying to influence others.	*Example:* What do the changes mean? They can either strengthen and unite us, or they can weaken and divide us. From: Clinton, 'The changing face of America'; cf. *Context* p. 146 Here the rhetorical question is used to draw the reader/listener into the argument by posing a direct question. The reader/listener might feel a little under pressure, even manipulated to answer the question in a specific way.
understatement *Untertreibung*	Understatement is a statement in which the true magnitude of an idea, event or fact is minimized, so that something is deliberately presented as being much less important, valuable, etc. than it really is. Understatement is often used for ironic effect, e.g. saying 'It is a bit cold today', when the temperature is 10 degrees below freezing. (cf. also *exaggeration)

Glossary

wordplay or **pun** [pʌn] *Wortspiel*	Wordplay (also called pun) is the use of a word which may be understood in two different ways or which may be put into a different context ['kɒntɛkst] to alter the meaning. *Example:* The magician got so mad that he pulled his hair out. Here, the word *hair* alludes to *hare* (= *Hase*), an animal commonly associated with magicians.

Alphabetical list of words in the Glossary

Words in **bold** print have their own entries in the Glossary.

accumulation 336
act 325
action 329
actor/actress 325
ad 332
advert 332
advertisement 332
alliteration 336
allusion 337
alternate rhyme 324
analogy 336
anaphora 337
anticipation 330
antithesis 335
article 331, 332
assonance 336
atmosphere 330
author 326
autobiography 331
biography 331
blog 333
blurb 332
byline 332
caricature 333
cartoon 333
character 328
characterization 328
classified ads 332
cliché 337
cliffhanger 326
climax 329
column 332
comedy 325
coming-of-age story 324
comment 331
commercial 332
concrete poem 324
conflict 329
connotation 333
contrast 332
copy 332
couplet 324
denotation 333
denouement 329
dialogue 325
diction 333
direct address 332

direct characterization 328
drama, dramatic text 325
dramatic irony 325
dramatist 325
editorial 331
emphasis 331
enjambement 337
enumeration 337
epilogue 324
essay 332
exaggeration 338
explicit characterization 328
exposition 329
external action 329
fable 323
falling action 329
feature story 331
feature film 325
fictional text/fiction 323
first-person narrator 326
flashback 330
flash fiction 323
flat character 328
foreshadowing 330
formal style 334
frame story 324
free verse 324
genre 323
humour 333
hyperbole 338
iambic pentameter 325
implicit characterization 328
indirect characterization 328
informal style 334
internal action 329
interior monologue 327
image/imagery 335
irony 338
juxtaposition 338
layout 335
leader 331
leading article 331
letter 332
letter to the editor 332
limited point of view 327
line 324
lyrical (poem) 324

metaphor 335
metre 325
microfiction 323
mode of presentation 327
monologue 325
motif 323
narrative (prose) 323
narrator 326
neutral style 334
news item 331
news report 331
news story 331
non-fiction,
non-fictional text 331
novel 323
omniscient narrator 326
onomatopoeia 336
open ending 329
panoramic presentation 328
parallelism 337
personification 335
play 325
playwright 325
plot 329
poem/poetry 324
point of view 326
prose 323
protagonist 328
pun 338
quatrain 324
refrain 324
register 334
reliable narrator 327
repetition 337
reported thought 327
resolution 329
rhetorical device 335
rhetorical question 338
rhyme 324
rhyme scheme 324
rhyming couplet 324
rhythm 324
rising action 329
round character 329
satire 338
scene 325
scenic presentation 327

script 325
scriptwriter 325
setting 330
shape poem 324
short story 323
showing 327
simile 335
sitcom 326
slang 334
soap 326
soliloquy 325
solution 329
sonnet 324
speaker 324
speech 332
stage directions 325
stanza 324
style 332
stylistic devices 335
surprise ending 329
suspense 330
suspension of disbelief 323
symbol *(n)*, **symbolic** *(adj)* 336
taboo words 334
telling 328
tension 330
text type 331
theme 323
thesis 335
third-person narrator 326
tone 333
tragedy 324
turning point 328
tv/radio series 325
understatement 338
unlimited point of view 327
unreliable narrator 327
verse 323
volta 324
wordplay 338

339

Verbs for Tasks ('Operatoren')

Context uses the same special vocabulary ('Operatoren') for tasks that is used in standard tests, including the 'Abitur'. Be sure you understand what's required of you when you come across one of the verbs below.

'Anforderungsbereich I' COMPREHENSION
refers to text comprehension and definition.

'Anforderungsbereich II' ANALYSIS
focuses on text analysis and comparison, and stylistic devices.

'Anforderungsbereich III' BEYOND THE TEXT
concentrates on discussion, comment, evaluation and text production.

The instructions say	Example	What you are expected to do
'Anforderungsbereich I' COMPREHENSION		
describe (*also:* **give/write a description of**) *beschreiben*	**Describe** the writer's invention and what it is used for.	*Give a detailed account of something.*
outline ['– –] *umreißen, skizzieren*	**Outline** the writer's views on …	*Give the main features, structure or general principles of a topic, omitting minor details.*
state *darlegen*	**State** the author's opinion on the main character's decision.	*Specify something clearly.*
summarize (*also:* **give/write a summary of; sum up**) *zusammenfassen*	**Summarize** the incident in the church in no more than four sentences.	*Give a concise account of the main points of something.*
'Anforderungsbereich II' ANALYSIS		
analyse (*BE*), **analyze** (*AE*) ['ænəlaɪz] / **examine** [ɪgˈzæmɪn] *analysieren, untersuchen*	**Analyse** the main elements of the poster. **Examine** the writer's attitude towards the protagonist.	*Describe and explain certain aspects and/or features of the text in detail.*
explain *erklären*	**Explain** the main character's reaction to her mother in the first scene.	*Describe and define in detail.*
compare *vergleichen*	**Compare** how the characters are portrayed in the film and in the novel.	*Point out similarities and differences between two or more things.*
contrast [kənˈtrɑːst] *kontrastieren, gegenüberstellen*	**Contrast** the rights of African Americans in the 1960s and today.	*Emphasize the differences between two or more things.*

Verbs for Tasks (Operatoren)

The instructions say	Example	What you are expected to do
'Anforderungsbereich III' BEYOND THE TEXT		
comment on ['kɒment] *kommentieren, Stellung nehmen zu*	**Comment on** the speaker's belief that …	*State clearly your opinions on the topic in question and support your views with evidence.*
discuss *diskutieren, erörtern*	**Discuss** how education influences attitudes towards immigration.	*Investigate or examine by argument; give reasons for and against.*
assess [ə'ses] *auswerten, beurteilen, bewerten*	**Assess** the effectiveness of the government's approach to fighting poverty.	*Consider the points for and against something in a balanced way.*
evaluate [ɪ'væljueɪt] *einschätzen, bewerten*	**Evaluate** the author's view of the impact Obama's speech had on his audience.	*Form an opinion after carefully considering and presenting advantages and disadvantages.*
justify *begründen, rechtfertigen*	**Justify** your answer.	*Show adequate grounds for decisions or conclusions.*

Charts

The British System of Government

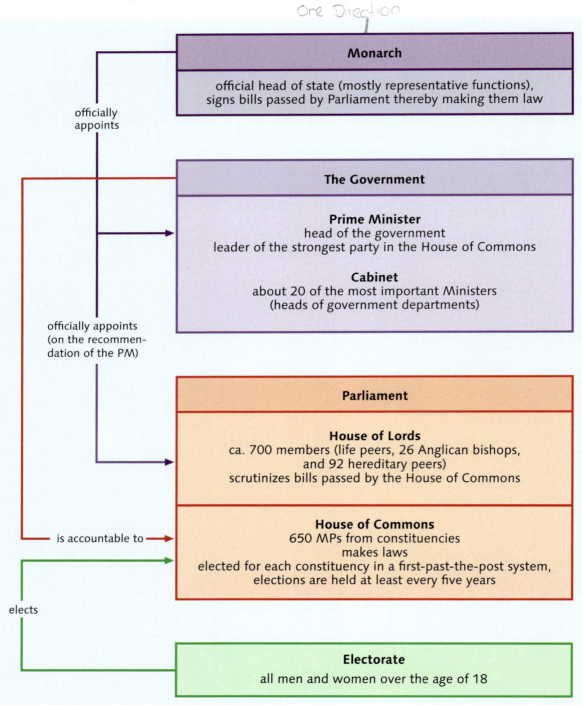

Charts

The American System of Government

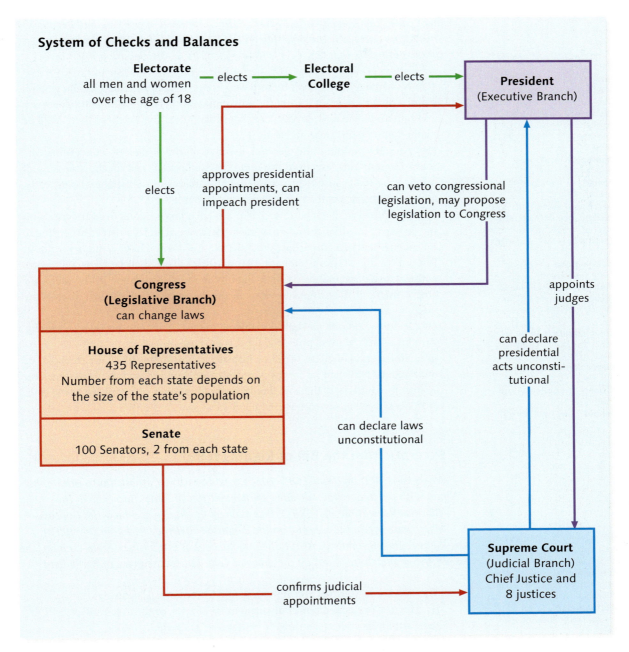

Historical Documents

Excerpts from the Magna Carta (1215)

Until King John (king from 1199–1216) was forced by his barons to sign a document called the Magna Carta ('great charter'), the will of the king had been law. The Magna Carta was the first step on the long road which led to the constitutional principle that the 'Law is King'. Six of its 63 articles are printed here.

(12) No scutage or aid shall be imposed in our kingdom, unless by the general council of our kingdom; except for ransoming our person, making our eldest son a knight and once for marrying our eldest daughter; and for these there shall be paid no more than a reasonable aid. [...]

(14) And for holding the general council of the kingdom concerning the assessment of aids, except in the three cases aforesaid, and for the assessing of scutage, we shall cause to be summoned the archbishops, bishops, abbots, earls, and greater barons of the realm, separately by our letters. [...]

(20) A freeman shall not be amerced for a small offence, except in accordance with the degree of the offence and for a grave offence he shall be amerced according to its gravity, without imperilling his status; and a merchant similarly without imperilling his stock-in-trade; and similarly a villain shall be amerced always without loss of wainage – if their liability is to us. And none of the aforesaid amercements shall be imposed except by the sworn evidence of worthy men of the neighbourhood.

(38) In future no official shall put anyone to trial merely on his own testimony, without reliable witness produced for this purpose.

(39) No freeman shall be taken or imprisoned, or deprived of his freehold, or outlawed, or banished, or in any way destroyed, nor will we take or order action against him, unless by the lawful judgment of his peers, or by the law of the land.

(40) We will sell to no man, we will not deny to any man, either justice or right.

Vocabulary (Magna Carta)

1 **scutage** ['skjuːtɪdʒ] (in feudal times) money paid by a knight instead of doing military service, or by a landowner instead of personal service
6 **aforesaid** [– '– –] mentioned before
7 **summon sb.** (*fml*) order sb. to come to you
9 **freeman** ['– –] (in feudal times) a citizen
amerce sb. make sb. pay a fine
in accordance with sb./sth. *in Übereinstimmung mit jdm./etwas*
11 **imperil sth.** [– '– –] endanger sth.
12 **stock-in-trade** goods kept on sale by a merchant
villain ['vɪlɪn] (*hier*) Leibeigene/r
13 **wainage** (*old use*) profit or produce from the cultivation of land
if their liability is to us if the offence they committed was against us
14 **sworn evidence** *Aussage unter Eid*
16 **official** (*n*) person in a position of authority
18 **freehold** ownership of land

Excerpts from the Bill of Rights (1689)

When James II (king from 1685–1688) tried to restore Catholicism to Britain, he met with resistance from all sides. Parliament forced James into exile in the 'Glorious Revolution' of 1688. Prince William of Orange and his wife, Princess Mary, were offered the throne on the condition that they accepted the 'Bill of Rights'. Thus Britain's constitutional monarchy was established. From then on, the British monarch ruled not by the grace of God, but by the grace of Parliament.

The said Lords Spiritual and Temporal, and Commons [...] do declare:

(1) That the pretended power of suspending of laws, or the execution of laws, by regal authority, without consent of Parliament, is illegal.

(2) That the pretended power of dispensing with laws or the execution by laws by regal authority as it has been assumed and exercised of late is illegal.

(4) That levying money for or to the use of the Crown by pretence of prerogative, without grant of Parliament, for longer time or in other manner than the same is or shall be granted, is illegal.

Vocabulary (Bill of Rights)

1 **said** (*adj; fml*) mentioned before
Lords Spiritual archbishops and bishops
Lords Temporal lords who are concerned with worldly affairs, rather than with spiritual things; together with the Lords Spiritual they constitute the House of Lords
Commons House of Commons consisting of representatives of counties and towns
5 **of late** in recent times
6 **by pretence of prerogative** by claiming that the king has the right to do sth.

Historical Documents

(5) That it is the right of the subject to petition the King, and all commitments and
prosecutions for such petitioning are illegal.

(6) That the raising or keeping a standing army within the kingdom in time of
peace, unless it be with the consent of Parliament, is against law.

(8) That elections of members of Parliament ought to be free.

(9) That the freedom of speech, and debates and proceedings in Parliament, ought
not to be impeached or questioned in any court or place out of Parliament.

(10) That excessive bail ought not to be required nor excessive fines imposed; nor
cruel and unusual punishment inflicted.

(13) And that for redress of all grievances, and for the amending, strengthening,
and preserving of the laws, Parliament ought to be held frequently.

9 **commitment** (old use) =
committal act of sending sb. to
prison
15 **impeach sth.** (here) prevent sth.
16 **bail** Kaution
impose a fine demand money
as punishment
18 **redress of grievances** (fml)
correction of sth. considered
unfair

Excerpts from the Declaration of Independence (1776)

*Unhappiness with British rule had been on the rise in the American colonies
during the 1760s. In 1775, open fighting broke out between British troops and
American colonists – the beginning of the Revolutionary War. When Congress
adopted the Declaration of Independence on 4 July, 1776, this ended more than a
century and a half of colonial dependency, even though the war was to go on until
1783.*

When in the Course of human events, it becomes necessary for one people to
dissolve the political bands which have connected them with another, and to
assume among the powers of the earth, the separate and equal station to which the
Laws of Nature and of Nature's God entitle them, a decent respect to the opinions
of mankind requires that they should declare the causes which impel them to the
separation.

We hold these truths to be self-evident, that all men are created equal, that they
are endowed by their Creator with certain unalienable Rights, that among these
are Life, Liberty and the pursuit of Happiness. That to secure these rights, Governments are instituted among Men, deriving their just powers from the consent of
the governed. That whenever any Form of Government becomes destructive of
these ends, it is the Right of the People to alter or to abolish it, and to institute new
Government, laying its foundation on such principles and organizing its powers
in such form, as to them shall seem most likely to effect their Safety and
Happiness.

3 **assume sth.** etwas übernehmen
station (old-fashioned or fml)
status
5 **impel sb. to sth.** force sb. to do
sth.
8 **endow sb. with sth.** (fml)
give sb. sth.
unalienable (old use)
= **inalienable** [ɪnˈeɪlɪənəbl] (fml)
that cannot be taken away
9 **pursuit of sth.** (fml) act of trying
to achieve sth.
10 **consent** [–'–] (n) agreement

The Bill of Rights (1791)

*At the time the Constitution of the USA was discussed and ratified, critics felt it
did not sufficiently protect individuals against abuse of their civil liberties and
rights by the federal government. Therefore, ten amendments to the Constitution
known as the Bill of Rights were proposed by Congress and passed in 1791.*

First Amendment Congress shall make no law respecting an establishment of
religion, or prohibiting the free exercise thereof; or abridging the freedom of
speech, or of the press; or the right of the people peaceably to assemble, and to
petition the government for a redress of grievances.

1 **respecting** concerning
2 **the free exercise thereof**
deren freie Ausübung
abridge sth. limit sth.
4 **redress of grievances** (fml)
correction of sth. considered
unfair

345

Historical Documents

6 infringe sth. *(fml) etwas verletzen*
8 but except
11 effects *(pl; fml)* personal property
seizure ['siːʒə] *Beschlagnahme*
12 warrant *Durchsuchungs- oder Haftbefehl*
13 affirmation *eidesstattliche Erklärung*
15 hold sb. to answer for sth. accuse sb. of sth. (in a court of law)
16 infamous ['ɪnfəməs] evil, shameful
presentment [– '– –] *formelle Anschuldigung*
indictment [ɪn'daɪtmənt] *Anklage*
grand jury *(AE)* panel of 12 or 23 citizens who investigate accusations and officially charge criminals to be tried before a jury if there is sufficient evidence
19 in jeopardy of life and limb ['dʒepədi] *in Gefahr für Leib und Leben*
21 due process of law proper legal procedures
26 ascertain sth. [ˌæsə'teɪn] *(fml)* determine sth.
28 obtain sb. *(hier) jdn. vorladen*
counsel lawyer giving legal advice
30 common law unwritten law based on custom, usage and former decisions of courts of law
31 trial by jury *Verfahren vor Geschworenen*
32 try sth. examine and decide sth. in a court of law
34 bail *Kaution*
37 construe sth. [– '–] interpret sth.
disparage a right [dɪs'pærɪdʒ] *ein Recht schmälern*

Second Amendment A well-regulated militia, being necessary to the security of a free state, the right of the people to keep and bear arms shall not be infringed.

Third Amendment No soldier shall, in time of peace be quartered in any house, without the consent of the owner, nor in time of war, but in a manner to be prescribed by law.

Fourth Amendment The right of the people to be secure in their persons, houses, papers, and effects, against unreasonable searches and seizures, shall not be violated, and no warrants shall issue, but upon probable cause, supported by oath or affirmation, and particularly describing the place to be searched, and the persons or things to be seized.

Fifth Amendment No person shall be held to answer for a capital, or otherwise infamous crime, unless on a presentment or indictment of a grand jury, except in cases arising in the land or naval forces, or in the militia, when in actual service in time of war or public danger; nor shall any person be subject for the same offense to be twice put in jeopardy of life or limb; nor shall be compelled in any criminal case to be a witness against himself, nor be deprived of life, liberty, or property, without due process of law; nor shall private property be taken for public use, without just compensation.

Sixth Amendment In all criminal prosecutions, the accused shall enjoy the right to a speedy and public trial, by an impartial jury of the state and district wherein the crime shall have been committed, which district shall have been previously ascertained by law, and to be informed of the nature and cause of the accusation; to be confronted with the witnesses against him; to have compulsory process for obtaining witnesses in his favor, and to have the assistance of counsel for his defence.

Seventh Amendment In suits at common law, where the value in controversy shall exceed twenty dollars, the right of trial by jury shall be preserved, and no fact tried by a jury, shall be otherwise re-examined in any court of the United States, than according to the rules of the common law.

Eighth Amendment Excessive bail shall not be required, nor excessive fines imposed, nor cruel and unusual punishments inflicted.

Ninth Amendment The enumeration in the Constitution, of certain rights, shall not be construed to deny or disparage others retained by the people.

Tenth Amendment The powers not delegated to the United States by the Constitution, nor prohibited by it to the states, are reserved to the states respectively, or to the people.

Preamble to the Charter of the United Nations (1945)

Drafted immediately after the Second World War, the Charter of the United Nations set out to formulate the aims of this new organization.

2 scourge [skɜːdʒ] *(fig)* person or thing that causes suffering
4 reaffirm sth. *etwas erneut bekräftigen*

WE, THE PEOPLES OF THE UNITED NATIONS, DETERMINED,

to save succeeding generations from the scourge of war, which twice in our lifetime has brought untold sorrow to mankind, and

to reaffirm faith in fundamental human rights, in the dignity and worth of the human person, in the equal rights of men and women and of nations large and small, and

Historical Documents

to establish conditions under which justice and respect for the obligations arising from treaties and other sources of international law can be maintained, and

to promote social progress and better standards of life in larger freedom,

10   AND FOR THESE ENDS

to practise tolerance and live together in peace with one another as good neighbours, and

to unite our strength to maintain international peace and security, and

to ensure, by the acceptance of principles and the institution of methods, that

15   armed force shall not be used, save in the common interest, and

to employ international machinery for the promotion of the economic and social advancement of all peoples,

HAVE RESOLVED TO COMBINE OUR EFFORTS TO ACCOMPLISH THIS AIM.

7 **obligation** *Verpflichtung*
10 **end** aim, purpose
14 **ensure sth.** *(BE)* = *(AE)* **insure sth.** guarantee sth.
18 **resolve** decide firmly

Preamble to the Universal Declaration of Human Rights (1948)

The Universal Declaration of Human Rights, which was adopted by the General Assembly of the United Nations on 10 December, 1948, outlines a basic view of human rights, but it is not a legally binding document.

Whereas recognition of the inherent dignity and of the equal and inalienable rights of all members of the human family is the foundation of freedom, justice and peace in the world,

Whereas disregard and contempt for human rights have resulted in barbarous

5   acts which have outraged the conscience of mankind, and the advent of a world in which human beings shall enjoy freedom of speech and belief and freedom from fear and want has been proclaimed as the highest aspiration of the common people,

Whereas it is essential, if man is not to be compelled to have recourse, as a last

10   resort, to rebellion against tyranny and oppression, that human rights should be protected by the rule of law,

Whereas it is essential to promote the development of friendly relations between nations,

Whereas the peoples of the United Nations have in the Charter reaffirmed their

15   faith in fundamental human rights, in the dignity and worth of the human person and in the equal rights of men and women and have determined to promote social progress and better standards of life in larger freedom,

Whereas Member States have pledged themselves to achieve, in co-operation with the United Nations, the promotion of universal respect for and observance of

20   human rights and fundamental freedoms,

Whereas a common understanding of these rights and freedoms is of the greatest importance for the full realization of this pledge,

Now, therefore, the GENERAL ASSEMBLY proclaims this UNIVERSAL DECLARATION OF HUMAN RIGHTS as a common standard of achievement for all

25   peoples and all nations, to the end that every individual and every organ of society, keeping this Declaration constantly in mind, shall strive by teaching and education to promote respect for these rights and freedoms and by progressive measures, national and international, to secure their universal and effective recognition

1 **whereas** because of the fact that
inalienable [in'eɪlɪənəbl] *(fml)* that cannot be taken away from you
4 **disregard** *(n) Missachtung*
contempt feeling that sb./sth. is without value and deserves no respect
5 **outrage sb.** make sb. very shocked and angry
advent of sth./sb. coming of sth./sb. (an important event, person, technology, etc.)
9 **compel sb. to do sth.** *(fml)* force sb. to do sth.
have recourse to sth. *Zuflucht zu etwas nehmen*
as a last resort *als letzten Ausweg*
14 **reaffirm sth.** *etwas erneut bekräftigen*
18 **pledge yourself to sth.** formally promise to do sth.

Historical Documents

30 jurisdiction *Zuständigkeit, Gerichtsbarkeit*

and observance, both among the peoples of Member States themselves and among the peoples of territories under their jurisdiction.

Preamble to the Treaty of Rome (1957)

The European Economic Community (EEC), the precursor to today's much larger European Union, was established on 27 March, 1957, when the six founding members – France, West Germany, Italy, Belgium, the Netherlands and Luxembourg – signed the Treaty of Rome, which is also called the Treaty Establishing the European Community.

5 determined [dɪ'tɜːmɪnd] *(adj)* having made a firm decision to do sth.

7 resolved *(adj) (fml)* having made a firm decision to do sth.

11 concerted [– '– –] *(adj)* *gemeinsam, gemeinschaftlich*

13 anxious to do sth. ['æŋkʃəs] wanting to do sth. very much

15 backwardness state of having made less progress than normal

17 abolition *Abschaffung*

21 pool sth. collect sth. (money, information, etc.) from different people or groups so that it can be used by all of them
resource supply of sth. that a country, an organization or a person has and can use, esp. to increase their wealth

His Majesty the King of the Belgians, The President of the Federal Republic of Germany, The President of the French Republic, The President of the Italian Republic, Her Royal Highness the Grand Duchess of Luxembourg, Her Majesty the Queen of the Netherlands,

DETERMINED to lay the foundations of an ever closer union among the peoples of Europe,

RESOLVED to ensure the economic and social progress of their countries by common action to eliminate the barriers which divide Europe,

AFFIRMING as the essential objective of their efforts the constant improvements of the living and working conditions of their peoples,

RECOGNIZING that the removal of existing obstacles calls for concerted action in order to guarantee steady expansion, balanced trade and fair competition,

ANXIOUS to strengthen the unity of their economies and to ensure their harmonious development by reducing the differences existing between the various regions and the backwardness of the less favoured regions,

DESIRING to contribute, by means of a common commercial policy, to the progressive abolition of restrictions on international trade,

INTENDING to confirm the solidarity which binds Europe and the overseas countries and desiring to ensure the development of their prosperity, in accordance with the principles of the Charter of the United Nations,

RESOLVED by thus pooling their resources to preserve and strengthen peace and liberty, and calling upon the other peoples of Europe who share their ideal to join in their efforts,

HAVE DECIDED to create a EUROPEAN COMMUNITY ...

Acknowledgements

Texts

pp. 14–15: Reprinted with permission – Torstar Syndication Services; **pp. 18–19:** © Misti Crane / The Columbus Dispatch; **pp. 22–23, p. 58 B:** Excerpt from "Greyhound Tragedy" from REVENGE OF THE LAWN by Richard Brautigan. Copyright © 1971 by Richard Brautigan. Reprinted by permission of Houghton Mifflin Harcourt Publishing Company. All rights reserved; **p. 26:** © Dilbahar Askari / fudder.de; **p. 27:** © 2011 by Tess Gallagher; **pp. 31–35:** Copyright © 2006 by Jordan Sonnenblick. All rights reserved. Published by Arrangement with SCHOLASTIC INC., 557 Broadway, New York, NY 10012 USA / This Book was negotiated through Literary Agency Thomas Schlück GmbH, 30827 Garbsen; **pp. 40–41:** © Gideon Spanier 2012 / London Evening Standard; **pp. 43–44:** © Martha Irvine / 2012 Associated Press, reproduced by permission of The YGS Group; **p. 46:** © Jimmy Smallwood / BBC News Magazine 2010; **pp. 49–50:** From: STRUCK BY LIGHTNING by Chris Colfer. Copyright © 2012 by Christopher Colfer. By permission of Little, Brown and Company. All rights reserved; **p. 52:** © Yuriko Wahl-Immel / DER STERN, 2013; **pp. 56–57, p. 58 A:** © Manasi Subramaniam; **p. 59:** THE CANAL PATH MURDERS / © Margaret Hodgson / Telegraph Media Group Limited, reprint in 'Best Practice', 2012; **pp. 64–65:** © Anette Dowideit, Steffen Fründt, Sebastian Jost, Christiane Kühl / Die WELT, 2009; **pp. 69–70:** © Cory Doctorow / craphound.com; **pp. 72–73:** © Kim Hampton; **p. 76:** © Sara D LaJeunesse / The Pennsylvania State University; **p. 80:** © Roger McGough; **p. 81:** "im rlly gd @ txting" copyright © 2013 Kenn Nesbitt. All Rights Reserved. Reprinted by permission of the author, poem 'Fog': © Carl Sandburg Family Trust, c/o: Adams Hendon Carson, Crow & Saenger; **p. 82:** poem 'Actor': © Tanmay Tiwary, poem 'Jealousy': from R. Ellison: And When You Are Young, repr. by the permission of the London Association for the Teaching of English / © Ruth Ellison; **p. 83:** © Taylor Mali, 2002; **p. 84:** © Richard Edwards, 1986; **p. 91:** Emma Brighton: Memories from Reutlingen / UK-German Connection http://www.ukgermanconnection.org/?location_id=3547&item=6056; **p. 97:** © Maia Srebernik / www.ukgermanconnection.org/education-edl; **pp. 100–101:** © Camp Counselors USA, Sausalito, CA / www.ccusa.com; **pp. 102–103:** © Lucy Harper, 2013; **pp. 108–111:** © Roger Hall, 1985; **pp. 118–119:** Bureau of Public Affairs, U.S. Department of State; **pp. 122–123:** from "Is It Time to Embrace the E-Book?", BBC Radio 4, 7 August 2008; **p. 128:** © Roger McGough; **p. 144:** © Gideon Spanier 2012 / London Evening Standard; **p. 146:** © Eurodesk Deutschland. **pp. 100–101:** © Camp Counselors USA, Sausalito, CA / www.ccusa.com; **pp. 102–103:** © Lucy Harper, 2013; **pp. 108–111:** © Roger Hall, 1985; **pp. 118–119:** Bureau of Public Affairs, U.S. Department of State; **pp. 122–123:** from "Is It Time to Embrace the E-Book?", BBC Radio 4, 7 August 2008; **p. 128:** © Roger McGough; **p. 144:** © Gideon Spanier 2012 / London Evening Standard; **p. 146:** © Eurodesk Deutschland **pp. 100–101:** © Camp Counselors USA, Sausalito, CA / www.ccusa.com; **pp. 102–103:** © Lucy Harper, 2013; **pp. 108–111:** © Roger Hall, 1985; **pp. 118–119:** Bureau of Public Affairs, U.S. Department of State; **pp. 122–123:** from "Is It Time to Embrace the E-Book?", BBC Radio 4, 7 August 2008; **p. 128:** © Roger McGough; **p. 144:** © Gideon Spanier 2012 / London Evening Standard; **p. 146:** © Eurodesk Deutschland **pp. 100–101:** © Camp Counselors USA, Sausalito, CA / www.ccusa.com; **pp. 102–103:** © Lucy Harper, 2013; **pp. 108–111:** © Roger Hall, 1985; **pp. 118–119:** Bureau of Public Affairs, U.S. Department of State; **pp. 122–123:** from "Is It Time to Embrace the E-Book?", BBC Radio 4, 7 August 2008; **p. 128:** © Roger McGough; **p. 144:** © Gideon Spanier 2012 / London Evening Standard; **p. 146:** © Eurodesk Deutschland **pp. 100–101:** © Camp Counselors USA, Sausalito, CA / www.ccusa.com; **pp. 102–103:** © Lucy Harper, 2013; **pp. 108–111:** © Roger Hall, 1985; **pp. 118–119:** Bureau of Public Affairs, U.S. Department of State; **pp. 122–123:** from "Is It Time to Embrace the E-Book?", BBC Radio 4, 7 August 2008; **p. 128:** © Roger McGough; **p. 144:** © Gideon Spanier 2012 / London Evening Standard; **p. 146:** © Eurodesk Deutschland **pp. 100–101:** © Camp Counselors USA, Sausalito, CA / www.ccusa.com; **pp. 102–103:** © Lucy Harper, 2013; **pp. 108–111:** © Roger Hall, 1985; **pp. 118–119:** Bureau of Public Affairs, U.S. Department of State; **pp. 122–123:** from

Acknowledgements

"Is It Time to Embrace the E-Book?", BBC Radio 4, 7 August 2008; **p. 128:** © Roger McGough; **p. 144:** © Gideon Spanier 2012 / London Evening Standard; **p. 146:** © Eurodesk Deutschland **pp. 100–101:** © Camp Counselors USA, Sausalito, CA / www.ccusa.com; **pp. 102–103:** © Lucy Harper, 2013; **pp. 108–111:** © Roger Hall, 1985; **pp. 118–119:** Bureau of Public Affairs, U.S. Department of State; **pp. 122–123:** from "Is It Time to Embrace the E-Book?", BBC Radio 4, 7 August 2008; **p. 128:** © Roger McGough; **p. 144:** © Gideon Spanier 2012 / London Evening Standard; **p. 146:** © Eurodesk Deutschland

Photos / Illustrations

p. 10: A: Stokkete / Shutterstock, B: Malivan_Iuliia / Shutterstock, C: Antonio Guillem / Shutterstock; **p. 11:** D: Andresr / Shutterstock, E: Syda Productions / Shutterstock, F: F1 Online / © Sandro Di Carlo Darsa / PhotoAlto, G: F1 Online / © Hero Fancy, H: Wallenrock / Shutterstock; **p. 12:** Sergey Nivens / Shutterstock; **p. 13:** © Chalkthoughts (Marc & Mike) / http://chalkthoughts.com; **p. 14:** Pavel Losevsky / ClipDealer; **p. 15:** Warren Goldswain / Shutterstock; **p. 16:** beermedia / Fotolia; **p. 17:** CREATISTA / Shutterstock; **p. 20:** © JERRY LAMPEN / EPA / picture-alliance / dpa; **p. 21:** kreizihorse / Fotolia; **p. 24:** fotomek / Fotolia; **p. 26:** JoshuaKahle / Fotolia; **p. 27:** Shebeko / Shutterstock; **p. 28:** avian / Fotolia; **p. 30:** Cornelsen Schulverlage (photo: © Dan Burn-Fort / Getty Images); **p. 36:** A: bloomua / Shutterstock, B: © Tomas Rodriguez / Corbis; **p. 37:** C: Goodluz / Shutterstock, D (boy): © Daniel Koebe / Corbis / Glow Images-Fancy, D (girl): Sylvie Bouchard / Shutterstock; **p. 38:** bloomua / Fotolia; **p. 40:** © 2012 David Horsey, Our Connected World. All rights reserved. Distributed by Tribune Media Services; **p. 42:** vege / Fotolia; **p. 43:** © Rob Cottingham / Noise to Signal; **p. 45:** giadophoto / Fotolia; **p. 46:** stop sign: Sarawut Padungkwan / Shutterstock, 'Add as Friend': Grounder / Shutterstock; **p. 49:** DFree / Shutterstock; **p. 53:** Juan Gaertner / Shutterstock; **p. 54:** Konstantin Chagin / Shutterstock; **p. 58:** Roland Beier, Berlin; **p. 59:** Tom Gauld: 'Really Short Story' (in: The Guardian, September 10, 2013) / © Guardian News & Media Ltd 2013; **p. 60:** laptop: artjazz / Shutterstock, screen (pixels): ansem / Shutterstock, globe: rtguest / Shutterstock, drop: Pixel Embargo / Shutterstock, skull symbol: Lightspring / Shutterstock; **p. 61:** A: M. George / Fotolia, B: Filipe Matos Frazao /

Shutterstock, C: picture-alliance / dpa, D: Jesse Kunerth / Shutterstock; **p. 62:** Tetra / GlowImages; **p. 64:** © JGI / Jamie Grill / Blend Images / Corbis; **pp. 64–65:** patch cord isolated: Bart_J / Shutterstock; **p. 65:** michaeljung / Shutterstock; **p. 66:** mobile phone: Nik Merkulov / Shutterstock, South Africa flag: Iakov Filimonov / Shutterstock, flags of Canada, Germany, Malaysia: Paul Stringer / Shutterstock, all other flags: Globe Turner / Shutterstock; **p. 67:** © Bas van Abel / Fairphone.com; **p. 68:** Paul Stringer / Shutterstock; **p. 69:** © Imaginechina / Corbis; **p. 72:** Cartoon 'Plastic Again (Albatross chick + mother)' / © John S. Pritchett; **p. 73:** junk raft: © Peter Bennett / mauritius images / Alamy, bag: Photographee.eu / Fotolia; **p. 75:** top: ROLEX DELA PENA / EPA / picture-alliance / dpa, bottom: drubig-photo / Shutterstock; **p. 76:** © NASA / Corbis; **p. 78:** Goodluz / Shutterstock; **p. 80:** © Peanuts Worldwide LLC / Distr. Universal Uclick / Distr. Bulls; **p. 86:** IR Stone / Shutterstock; **p. 87:** © Kaplan International Colleges – Sprachreisen weltweit; **p. 88:** top left: Sakuoka / Shutterstock, bottom right: olegtoka / Shutterstock; **p. 91:** Oskar Eyb / imageBroker / mauritius images; **p. 94:** © Helmut Meyer zur Capellen / Glow Images / ImageBroker (courtesy of Stowe School, Buckingham, UK); **p. 95:** © Jstone / Shutterstock; **p. 96:** © Europarat; **p. 97:** top: Iliveinoctober / Shutterstock, bottom: Thomas Amby / Shutterstock; **p. 98:** cartoon: © Mike Flanagan / www.CartoonStock.com, top right: Drazen / Shutterstock, bottom right: Vladimir Prusakov / Shutterstock; **p. 99:** © Camp Counselors USA, Sausalito, CA / www.ccusa.com; **p. 101:** photo: © Mark Peterson / Corbis, USA flag map: Thomas Pajot / Shutterstock; **p. 102:** left: Elena Elisseeva / Shutterstock, middle: Hurst Photo / Shutterstock, right: Richard Thornton / Shutterstock; **p. 103:** Big Cheese / vario images; **p. 104:** top: © Mike Baldwin / www.CartoonStock.com, bottom: © Rex May Baloo; **p. 105:** © Aaron Bacall / www.CartoonStock.com; **p. 106:** man with handycam: vadimmmus / Shutterstock, camera view finder: Dave Barnard / Shutterstock; **p. 108:** top: PHOTOAISA / INTERFOTO, bottom: Ferenc Szelepcsenyi / Shutterstock; **p. 112:** Trueffelpix / Fotolia; **p. 117:** © NASA / Corbis; **p. 121:** Roland Beier, Berlin; **p. 122:** top: Roland Beier, Berlin, middle: Heritage Images RM / GlowImages, bottom: © Markus Gann / ClipDealer; **p. 125:** © Kresten Forsman / www.CartoonStock.com; **p. 126:** © Mike Mosedale / www.CartoonStock.com; **p. 128:** top: Andrey Kuzmin / Fotolia, bottom: © Liam McArdle /

Acknowledgements

Photoshot; **p. 129:** © Clive Goddard / www. CartoonStock.com; **p. 130:** © Jose Luis Pelaez Inc / Blend Images / Corbis; **p. 134:** © Harry Margulies / www.CartoonStock.com; **p. 141:** © 20th Century Fox / Cinetext; **p. 142:** Tang Yan Song / Shutterstock; **p. 143:** left: Koall / Imago, right: Katja Hoffmann / Laif; **p. 145:** © Jose Luis Pelaez Inc / blend / vario images; **p. 146:** website design and logo: © Eurodesk Deutschland / www.rausvonzuhaus.de, photos: backdrop: yanlev / Fotolia, 'Programmarten': storm / Fotolia, 'Länderinfos': michaeljung / Fotolia, 'Lastminute': Alexander Raths / Fotolia, 'Forum': krimar / Fotolia; **p. 147:** kebox / ClipDealer; **p. 148:** F1 online; **p. 153:** © Amnesty International; **p. 154:** © Transfair e.V. (FairTrade Deutschland); **p. 155:** © Huw Aaron / www.CartoonStock.com; **p. 156:** © Rob Cottingham / Noise to Signal; **p. 160:** Adam Gregor / Fotolia; **p. 161:** Ivan Flammia / sdrummelo / toonpool.com; **pp. 165–168:** Roland Beier, Berlin; **p. 169:** top: Roland Beier, Berlin, bottom: United Archives / mauritius images; **p. 170:** Roland Beier, Berlin; **p. 172:** © ZUMA Press, Inc. / Alamy / mauritius images; **p. 174:** © 2011 Leigh Rubin; **p. 183:** top: Aleksandr Markin / Shutterstock, bottom: Andrey Burmakin / Shutterstock; **p. 186:** Oliver Le Moal / Shutterstock; **p. 189:** dollar chain: Scott Rothstein / Shutterstock, guitar: Artmim / Shutterstock, palm tree: Flux B / Shutterstock, rucksack: f9photos / Shutterstock; **p. 193:** flag USA: Globe Turner / Shutterstock, German flag: Paul Stringer / Shutterstock. **p. 102:** left: Elena Elisseeva / Shutterstock, middle: Hurst Photo / Shutterstock, right: Richard Thornton / Shutterstock; **p. 103:** Big Cheese / vario images; **p. 104:** top: © Mike Baldwin / : © Rex May Baloo / www.CartoonStock.com; **p. 105:** © Aaron Bacall / www.CartoonStock.com; **p. 106:** man with handycam: vadimmmus / Shutterstock, camera view finder: Dave Barnard / Shutterstock; **p. 108:** top: PHOTOAISA / INTERFOTO, bottom: Ferenc Szelepcsenyi / Shutterstock; **p. 112:** Trueffelpix / Fotolia; **p. 117:** © NASA / Corbis; **p. 121:** Roland Beier, Berlin; **p. 122:** top: Roland Beier, Berlin, middle: Heritage Images RM / GlowImages, bottom: © Markus Gann / ClipDealer; **p. 125:** © Kresten Forsman / www.CartoonStock.com; **p. 126:** © Mike Mosedale / www.CartoonStock.com; **p. 128:** top: Andrey Kuzmin / Fotolia, bottom: © Liam McArdle / Photoshot; **p. 129:** © Clive Goddard / www. CartoonStock.com; **p. 130:** © Jose Luis Pelaez Inc / Blend Images / Corbis; **p. 134:** © Harry Margulies /

www.CartoonStock.com; **p. 141:** © 20th Century Fox / Cinetext; **p. 142:** Tang Yan Song / Shutterstock; **p. 143:** left: Koall / Imago, right: Katja Hoffmann / Laif; **p. 145:** © Jose Luis Pelaez Inc / blend / vario images; **p. 146:** website design and logo: © Eurodesk Deutschland / www.rausvonzuhaus.de, photos: backdrop: yanlev / Fotolia, 'Programmarten': storm / Fotolia, 'Länderinfos': michaeljung / Fotolia, 'Lastminute': Alexander Raths / Fotolia, 'Forum': krimar / Fotolia; **p. 147:** kebox / ClipDealer; **p. 148:** F1 online; **p. 153:** © Amnesty International; **p. 154:** © Transfair e.V. (FairTrade Deutschland); **p. 155:** © Huw Aaron / www.CartoonStock.com; **p. 156:** © Rob Cottingham / Noise to Signal; **p. 160:** Adam Gregor / Fotolia; **p. 161:** Ivan Flammia / sdrummelo / toonpool.com; **pp. 165–168:** Roland Beier, Berlin; **p. 169:** top: Roland Beier, Berlin, bottom: United Archives / mauritius images; **p. 170:** Roland Beier, Berlin; **p. 172:** © ZUMA Press, Inc. / Alamy / mauritius images; **p. 174:** © 2011 Leigh Rubin; **p. 183:** top: Aleksandr Markin / Shutterstock, bottom: Andrey Burmakin / Shutterstock; **p. 186:** Oliver Le Moal / Shutterstock; **p. 189:** dollar chain: Scott Rothstein / Shutterstock, guitar: Artmim / Shutterstock, palm tree: Flux B / Shutterstock, rucksack: f9photos / Shutterstock; **p. 193:** flag USA: Globe Turner / Shutterstock, German flag: Paul Stringer / Shutterstock. **p. 102:** left: Elena Elisseeva / Shutterstock, middle: Hurst Photo / Shutterstock, right: Richard Thornton / Shutterstock; **p. 103:** Big Cheese / vario images; **p. 104:** top: © Mike Baldwin / www.CartoonStock.com, bottom: © Rex May Baloo / www.CartoonStock.com; **p. 105:** © Aaron Bacall / www.CartoonStock.com; **p. 106:** man with handycam: vadimmmus / Shutterstock, camera view finder: Dave Barnard / Shutterstock; **p. 108:** top: PHOTOAISA / INTERFOTO, bottom: Ferenc Szelepcsenyi / Shutterstock; **p. 112:** Trueffelpix / Fotolia; **p. 117:** © NASA / Corbis; **p. 121:** Roland Beier, Berlin; **p. 122:** top: Roland Beier, Berlin, middle: Heritage Images RM / GlowImages, bottom: © Markus Gann / ClipDealer; **p. 125:** © Kresten Forsman / www.CartoonStock.com; **p. 126:** © Mike Mosedale / www.CartoonStock.com; **p. 128:** top: Andrey Kuzmin / Fotolia, bottom: © Liam McArdle / Photoshot; **p. 129:** © Clive Goddard / www. CartoonStock.com; **p. 130:** © Jose Luis Pelaez Inc / Blend Images / Corbis; **p. 134:** © Harry Margulies / www.CartoonStock.com; **p. 141:** © 20th Century Fox / Cinetext; **p. 142:** Tang Yan Song / Shutterstock;

Acknowledgements

p. 143: left: Koall / Imago, right: Katja Hoffmann / Laif; p. 145: © Jose Luis Pelaez Inc / blend / vario images; p. 146: website design and logo: © Eurodesk Deutschland / www.rausvonzuhaus.de, photos: backdrop: yanlev / Fotolia, 'Programmarten': storm / Fotolia, 'Länderinfos': michaeljung / Fotolia, 'Lastminute': Alexander Raths / Fotolia, 'Forum': krimar / Fotolia; p. 147: kebox / ClipDealer; p. 148: F1 online; p. 153: © Amnesty International; p. 154: © Transfair e.V. (FairTrade Deutschland); p. 155: © Huw Aaron / www.CartoonStock.com; p. 156: © Rob Cottingham / Noise to Signal; p. 160: Adam Gregor / Fotolia; p. 161: Ivan Flammia / sdrummelo / toonpool.com; pp. 165–168: Roland Beier, Berlin; p. 169: top: Roland Beier, Berlin, bottom: United Archives / mauritius images; p. 170: Roland Beier, Berlin; p. 172: © ZUMA Press, Inc. / Alamy / mauritius images; p. 174: © 2011 Leigh Rubin; p. 183: top: Aleksandr Markin / Shutterstock, bottom: Andrey Burmakin / Shutterstock; p. 186: Oliver Le Moal / Shutterstock; p. 189: dollar chain: Scott Rothstein / Shutterstock, guitar: Artmim / Shutterstock, palm tree: Flux B / Shutterstock, rucksack: f9photos / Shutterstock; p. 193: flag USA: Globe Turner / Shutterstock, German flag: Paul Stringer / Shutterstock. p. 102: left: Elena Elisseeva / Shutterstock, middle: Hurst Photo / Shutterstock, right: Richard Thornton / Shutterstock; p. 103: Big Cheese / vario images; p. 104: top: © Mike Baldwin / www.CartoonStock.com, bottom: © Rex May Baloo / www.CartoonStock.com; p. 105: © Aaron Bacall / www.CartoonStock.com; p. 106: man with handycam: vadimmmus / Shutterstock, camera view finder: Dave Barnard / Shutterstock; p. 108: top: PHOTOAISA / INTERFOTO, bottom: Ferenc Szelepcsenyi / Shutterstock; p. 112: Trueffelpix / Fotolia; p. 117: © NASA / Corbis; p. 121: Roland Beier, Berlin; p. 122: top: Roland Beier, Berlin, middle: Heritage Images RM / GlowImages, bottom: © Markus Gann / ClipDealer; p. 125: © Kresten Forsman / www.CartoonStock.com; p. 126: © Mike Mosedale / www.CartoonStock.com; p. 128: top: Andrey Kuzmin / Fotolia, bottom: © Liam McArdle / Photoshot; p. 129: © Clive Goddard / www.CartoonStock.com; p. 130: © Jose Luis Pelaez Inc / Blend Images / Corbis; p. 134: © Harry Margulies / www.CartoonStock.com; p. 141: © 20th Century Fox / Cinetext; p. 142: Tang Yan Song / Shutterstock; p. 143: left: Koall / Imago, right: Katja Hoffmann / Laif; p. 145: © Jose Luis Pelaez Inc / blend / vario images; p. 146: website design and logo: © Eurodesk Deutschland / www.rausvonzuhaus.de, photos: backdrop: yanlev / Fotolia, 'Programmarten': storm / Fotolia, 'Länderinfos': michaeljung / Fotolia, 'Lastminute': Alexander Raths / Fotolia, 'Forum': krimar / Fotolia; p. 147: kebox / ClipDealer; p. 148: F1 online; p. 153: © Amnesty International; p. 154: © Transfair e.V. (FairTrade Deutschland); p. 155: © Huw Aaron / www.CartoonStock.com; p. 156: © Rob Cottingham / Noise to Signal; p. 160: Adam Gregor / Fotolia; p. 161: Ivan Flammia / sdrummelo / toonpool.com; pp. 165–168: Roland Beier, Berlin; p. 169: top: Roland Beier, Berlin, bottom: United Archives / mauritius images; p. 170: Roland Beier, Berlin; p. 172: © ZUMA Press, Inc. / Alamy / mauritius images; p. 174: © 2011 Leigh Rubin; p. 183: top: Aleksandr Markin / Shutterstock, bottom: Andrey Burmakin / Shutterstock; p. 186: Oliver Le Moal / Shutterstock; p. 189: dollar chain: Sconal; p. 154: © Transfair e.V. (FairTrade Deutschland); p. 155: © Huw Aaron / www.CartoonStock.com; p. 156: © Rob Cottingham / Noise to Signal; p. 160: Adam Gregor / Fotolia; p. 161: Ivan Flammia / sdrummelo / toonpool.com; pp. 165–168: Roland Beier, Berlin; p. 169: top: Rolanck, German flag: Paul Stringer / Shutterstock. p. 102: left: Elena Elisseeva / Shutterstock, middle: Hurst Photo / Shutterstock, right: Richard Thornton / Shutterstock; p. 103: Big Cheese / vario images; p. 104: top: © Mike Baldwin / www.CartoonStock.com, bottom: © Rex May Baloo / www.CartoonStock.com; p. 105: © Aaron Bacall / www.CartoonStock.com; p. 106: man with handycam: vadimmmus / Shutterstock, camera view finder: Dave Barnard / Shutterstock; p. 108: top: PHOTOAISA / INTERFOTO, bottom: Ferenc Szelepcsenyi / Shutterstock; p. 112: Trueffelpix / Fotolia; p. 117: © NASA / Corbis; p. 121: Roland Beier, Berlin; p. 122: top: Roland Beier, Berlin, middle: Heritage Images RM / GlowImages, bottom: © Markus Gann / ClipDealer; p. 125: © Kresten Forsman / www.CartoonStock.com; p. 126: © Mike Mosedale / www.CartoonStock.com; p. 128: top: Andrey Kuzmin / Fotolia, bottom: © Liam McArdle / Photoshot; p. 129: © Clive Goddard / www.CartoonStock.com; p. 103: Big Cheese / vario images; p. 104: top: © Mike Baldwin / www.CartoonStock.com, bottom: © Rex May Baloo / www.CartoonStock.com;

Cover: gary 718 / Shutterstock